# Emotional Labor in the 21<sup>st</sup> Century

# ORGANIZATION AND MANAGEMENT SERIES

*Series Editors*

Arthur P. Brief
*University of Utah*

Kimberly D. Elsbach
*University of California, Davis*

Michael Frese
*University of Lueneburg and National University of Singapore*

Ashforth (Au.): *Role Transitions in Organizational Life: An Identity-Based Perspective.*

Bartel/Blader/Wrzesniewski (Eds.): *Identity and the Modern Organization.*

Bartunek (Au): *Organizational and Educational Change: The Life and Role of a Change Agent Group.*

Beach (Ed.): *Image Theory: Theoretical and Empirical Foundations.*

Brett/Drasgow (Eds.): *The Psychology of Work: Theoretically Based Empirical Research.*

Brockner (Au): *A Contemporary Look at Organizational Justice: Multiplying Insult Times Injury.*

Chhokar/Brodbeck/House (Eds.): *Culture and Leadership Across the World: The GLOBE Book of In-Depth Studies of 25 Societies.*

Darley/Messick/Tyler (Eds.): *Social Influences on Ethical Behavior in Organizations.*

De Cremer/van Dick/Murnighan (Eds): *Social Psychology and Organizations.*

De Cremer/Tenbrunsel (Eds): *Behavioral Business Ethics: Shaping an Emerging Field.*

Denison (Ed.): *Managing Organizational Change in Transition Economies.*

Dutton/Ragins (Eds.): *Exploring Positive Relationships at Work: Building a Theoretical and Research Foundation.*

Elsbach (Au): *Organizational Perception Management.*

Earley/Gibson (Aus.): *Multinational Work Teams: A New Perspective.*

Fayard/Metiu (Aus): *The Power of Writing in Organizations: From Letters to Online Interactions.*

Garud/Karnoe (Eds.): *Path Dependence and Creation.*

Grandey/Diefendorff/Rupp (Eds.): *Emotional Labor in the 21st Century: Diverse Perspectives on Emotion Regulation at Work.*

Harris (Ed.): *Handbook of Research in International Human Resource Management.*

Jacoby (Au.): *Employing Bureaucracy: Managers, Unions, and the Transformation of Work in the 20th Century, Revised Edition.*

Kossek/Lambert (Eds.): *Work and Life Integration: Organizational, Cultural and Individual Perspectives.*

Kramer/Tenbrunsel/Bazerman (Eds): *Social Decision Making: Social Dilemmas, Social Values and Ethical Judgments.*

Lampel/Shamsie/Lant (Eds.): *The Business of Culture: Strategic Perspectives on Entertainment and Media.*

Lant/Shapira (Eds.): *Organizational Cognition: Computation and Interpretation.*

Lord/Brown (Aus.): *Leadership Processes and Follower Self-Identity.*

Margolis/Walsh (Aus.): *People and Profits? The Search Between a Company's Social and Financial Performance.*

Messick/Kramer (Eds.): *The Psychology of Leadership: Some New Approaches.*

Miceli/Dworkin/Near (Aus): *Whistle-blowing in Organizations.*

Nord/Connell (Aus): *Rethinking the Knowledge Controversy in Organization Studies: A Generative Uncertainty Perspective.*

Pearce (Au.): *Organization and Management in the Embrace of the Government.*

Peterson/Mannix (Eds.): *Leading and Managing People in the Dynamic Organization.*

Rafaeli/Pratt (Eds.): *Artifacts and Organizations: Beyond Mere Symbolism.*

Riggio/Murphy/Pirozzolo (Eds.): *Multiple Intelligences and Leadership.*

Roberts/ Dutton (Eds): *Exploring Positive Identities and Organizations: Building a Theoretical and Research Foundation.*

Schneider/Smith (Eds.): *Personality and Organizations.*

Smith (Ed.): *The People Make The Place: Dynamic Linkages Between Individuals and Organizations.*

Thompson/Choi (Eds.): *Creativity and Innovation in Organizational Teams.*

Thompson/Levine/Messick (Eds.): *Shared Cognition in Organizations: The Management of Knowledge.*

Zaccaro/Marks/DeChurch (Eds.): *Multiteam Systems: An Organization Form for Dynamic and Complex Environments*

# Emotional Labor
## in the 21st Century

Diverse Perspectives on
the Psychology of Emotion
Regulation at Work

Edited by

## Alicia A. Grandey,
## James M. Diefendorff, and
## Deborah E. Rupp

Routledge
Taylor & Francis Group
NEW YORK AND LONDON

First published 2013
by Routledge
711 Third Avenue, New York, NY 10017

Simultaneously published in the UK
by Routledge
27 Church Road, Hove, East Sussex BN3 2FA

*Routledge is an imprint of the Taylor & Francis Group, an informa business*

Library of Congress Cataloging in Publication Data
Emotional labor in the 21st century : diverse perspectives on the psychology of emotion regulation at work / [edited by] Alicia Grandey, James Diefendorff, Deborah E. Rupp.
    p. cm. — (Organization and management ; 48)
Includes bibliographical references and index.
1. Nonverbal communication in the workplace. 2. Employees—Attitudes. 3. Customer relations. 4. Interpersonal relations. 5. Psychology, Industrial. I. Grandey, Alicia. II. Diefendorff, James. III. Rupp, Deborah E., 1975-
HF5549.5.N64E46 2012
331.25'6—dc23                                    2012008813

ISBN: 978-1-84872-949-0 (hbk)
ISBN: 978-0-203-10085-1 (ebk)

Typeset in Berling
by Keystroke, Station Road, Codsall, Wolverhampton

Printed and bound in the United States of America
by Edwards Brothers, Inc.

# Contents

*List of Illustrations*                                              *x*

*Series Foreword*                                                    *xi*
ART BRIEF, KIM ELSBACH, AND MICHAEL FRESE

*Dedication*                                                        *xii*

*Foreword*                                                         *xiii*
ARLIE HOCHSCHILD

*About the Editors*                                                 *xvi*

*Contributors*                                                     *xviii*

*Acknowledgements*                                                  *xx*


PART I
Overview                                                             1

1 *Bringing Emotional Labor into Focus: A Review and*
*Integration of Three Research Lenses*                               3
ALICIA A. GRANDEY, JAMES M. DIEFENDORFF, AND
DEBORAH E. RUPP


PART II
Person Perspectives: Within, Between, Dyadic and
Group                                                               29

2 *Episodic Intrapersonal Emotion Regulation: Or,*
*Dealing with Life as it Happens*                                   31
DANIEL J. BEAL AND JOHN P. TROUGAKOS

3 *Motivation, Fit, Confidence, and Skills: How Do Individual Differences Influence Emotional Labor?*     57
JASON J. DAHLING AND HAZEL-ANNE M. JOHNSON

4 *The Social Effects of Emotion Regulation in Organizations*     79
STÉPHANE CÔTÉ, GERBEN A. VAN KLEEF, AND THOMAS SY

5 *Emotional Labor at the Unit-level*     101
KAREN NIVEN, PETER TOTTERDELL, DAVID HOLMAN, AND DAVID CAMERON

PART III
Occupational Perspectives: Customer Service, Call Centers, Caring Professionals     125

6 *The Customer Experience of Emotional Labor*     127
MARKUS GROTH, THORSTEN HENNIG-THURAU, AND KARYN WANG

7 *Call Centers: Emotional Labor Over the Phone*     153
DANIELLE VAN JAARSVELD AND WINIFRED R. POSTER

8 *Attending to Mind and Body: Engaging the Complexity of Emotion Practice Among Caring Professionals*     175
REBECCA J. ERICKSON AND CLARE L. STACEY

PART IV
Contextual Perspectives: Organization, Gender, Culture     197

9 *Emotional Labor: Organization-level Influences, Strategies, and Outcomes*     199
S. DOUGLAS PUGH, JAMES M. DIEFENDORFF, AND CHRISTINA M. MORAN

10 *Social and Cultural Influencers: Gender Effects on Emotional Labor at Work and at Home*     223
KATHRYN J. LIVELY

11 *A Cultural Perspective on Emotion Labor*                    **251**
BATJA MESQUITA AND ELLEN DELVAUX


PART V
Multi-Disciplinary Perspectives: Reflections and
Projections                                                    **273**

12 *Reflections and Projections from Pioneers in Emotions*
*Research*                                                     **275**

Emotional Labor: Looking Back Nearly 20 Years                  *276*
BLAKE E. ASHFORTH AND RONALD H. HUMPHREY

Emotional Labor Across Five Levels of Analysis: Past,
Present, Future                                                *282*
NEAL ASHKANASY AND CATHERINE DAUS

Conceptualizing Emotional Labor: An Emotion Regulation
Perspective                                                    *288*
JAMES GROSS

Reflecting on Emotional Labor as a Social Meme                 *294*
ANAT RAFAELI

Back to the Future                                             *300*
AMY S. WHARTON


Author Index                                                   **306**
Subject Index                                                  **319**

# List of Illustrations

## FIGURES

1.1 Growth of academic research with "emotional labor/labour" in the title or anywhere in article    4

2.1 Emotion regulation episodes during a day in the life of a hypothetical retail customer service employee    36

4.1 A Generic Model of the Social Effects of Emotion Regulation    80

5.1 Framework for Unit-level Emotional Labor (FUEL)    113

6.1 Conceptual Framework    129

12.1 A process model of emotion regulation that highlights five families of emotion regulation strategies (from Gross & Thompson, 2007).    290

## TABLES

1.1 Viewing Emotional Labor (EL) Through Three Focal Lenses    6

1.2 Emotional Labor or Not? Illustrating the Fuzzy Boundary with Examples    19

3.1 Overview of Theoretical Perspectives and Individual Differences in the Emotional Labor Literature    59

10.1 Changes in Evaluation-Potency-Activation (EPA) Profiles for Gendered Roles    240

# Series Foreword

Wow! Alicia Grandey, James Diefendorff, and Deborah Rupp have produced an important book on an important topic, emotional labor. They have assembled a stellar cast of contributors that collectively take stock of the work that has been built upon Arlie Hochschild's seminal 1983 book, *The Managed Heart: Commercialization of human feelings*. More than that, Grandey, Diefendorff, and Rupp's collection both deepens and broadens the study of emotional labor with its focus on individuals, occupations, organization, and culture, especially gender construals. For those of us interested in the life in work organizations, their book is required reading. Obviously, we couldn't be prouder for them to join our series.

Art Brief
Kim Elsbach
Michael Frese

# Dedication

AG: To Tim, for your constant co-parenting and support.

JMD: To Linda, Adam, and Jacob, for your love and support.

DER: To my family.

AG, JMD, and DER: To all those who manage emotions with others to perform their work – May this book increase the awareness of and respect for your labor.

# Foreword

As I sat five rows back in a Recurrent Training room at the Delta Airlines Stewardess Training Center in the early 1980s, listening to a pilot tell recruits to "smile like you really mean it," I remember noticing the young woman next to me jotting down the advice verbatim. I had been talking for months to flight attendants from various airlines – gathering interviews for the *Managed Heart* – so I had a sense of what feelings: anxiety, fear, ennui, resentment, as well as an eagerness to serve – might underlie that smile. It was that "pinch" between such feelings and the pilot's call for authenticity that led me to write down in my own notebook, "emotional labor." Never did I dream that some thirty years later, seated at my computer, exploring the internet, I would discover some 559,000 mentions of "emotional labor," or with the British spelling "emotional labour" and its unpaid form, "emotion work." Or that I would learn from the lucid introduction by Alicia, James, and Deborah (Grandey, Diefendorff, & Rupp, 2012, Chapter 1) of the 10,000 mentions of the term in academic articles, 506 of them with the term in the title. Nor did I imagine having the honor of writing a preface to this path-breaking state-of-the-art new book on emotional labor.

While I'm pleased that the term – and with the help of this book, the evolving concept of – emotional labor has sparked interest, the basic reason for such interest is the extraordinary rise in service work itself. Indeed, as a contributor to the American gross domestic product, the manufacturing sector has declined to 12 percent while the service sector has risen to 25 percent. Day care centers, nursing homes, hospitals, airports, stores, call centers, classrooms, social welfare offices, dental offices – in all these workplaces, gladly or reluctantly, brilliantly or poorly, employees do emotional labor.[1]

But how much of it do they do? And in what way? Some speak of "energizers."[2] The coordinator of hospital volunteers, for example, may elicit a cheerful sense of shared mission. Alternatively, executive leadership trainers and military trainers may energize recruits in the spirit of get-out-there-and-defeat-the-enemy. Others speak of "toxin handlers" – complaints clerks, bankruptcy court personnel, bank officials dealing with house foreclosure, divorce lawyers, meter maids, and company specialists who handle the firing of workers.[3] Their job is to deliver bad news, and often to receive the brunt of customer frustration, despair and rage. There are those who don't so much handle the bad news of others as face a real chance of experiencing pain or loss of their own: soldiers, fire fighters, high rise window-washers and aerial acrobats, for example.

And there are other examples too. The poor sales clerk working in an elite clothing boutique manages envy. The Wall Street stock trader manages panic. The judge, as legal researcher Terry Maroney shows, is exposed to highly disturbing evidence of atrocities such as maiming, murder, dismemberment, child rape, etc., but must manage the semblance of impartiality. A judge must face the task of acknowledging and managing such feelings as horror, outrage, indignation, pity, all without seeming to do so.[4] Indeed, in leaders we admire, research shows, we seek signs of both a capacity to feel and to regulate those feelings – witnessed by the contempt shown for politicians who weep or panic.[5]

Emotional labor can be hard to recognize. We can, for example, feel *schadenfreude* – or pleasure at the misfortune of others, a feeling we may be ashamed to have. And our shame can get in the way of the very act of acknowledging that feeling. And that's important because it is the *pinch between* a real but disapproved feeling on one hand and an idealized one, on the other, that enables us to become aware of emotional labor. We may feel lonely at a joyous holiday party, relieved or indifferent at a funeral – and call on ourselves to correct our feelings. These kinds of pinches are of little consequence in certain cultures, and of great consequence in others, for cultures carry different feeling rules. "When I talked about emotional labor to Japanese people, they didn't know what I was talking about," Batja Mesquita, a psychologist at Leuven University in Belgium, and contributor to this book (Mesquita & Delvaux, 2012, Chapter 11), told me.[6] The Japanese highly value the capacity to relate to the feelings and needs of others.[7] So for the Japanese, emotional labor is more built in and so harder to see.

Cultural rules are seeing rules. And seeing is a matter of thinking about what we see. Based on our habits of thinking about emotion, we then recognize emotion in ourselves and others in an intricate variety of ways. Ironically, cultures that require the most emotional labor – and may be home to its most highly-trained practitioners – may also be those whose cultures inhibit the very recognition of it. Batja's observation leads us to the broader question of how cultural rules inhibit or highlight the very ways we see and think about emotion. Many Japanese recognize emotional labor, of course.[8] And as participants in a more relationship-oriented culture, they can perhaps better see the work it takes Americans to live in a more individualism-oriented one.

Tellingly, in the United States, the idea of emotional labor has been embraced by business advice gurus as an undiscovered resource and means of competitive advantage, and by labor unions as a cause of burnout deserving of financial compensation. And surely it is both. But questions remain. Do employees feel gratified by this work or strained by it? Does it alienate a person from him/herself or provide a deep expression of that self? Do workers experience more strain at work, or as one author here discovered, more at home (Lively, 2012, Chapter 10)? The chapters gathered here invite the scholar and general reader alike to delve deeper into the concept of emotional labor and to apply it to a wide and waiting world.

## ENDNOTES

1 Some parts of this preface overlap with the preface for the 2012 re-issue of *The Managed Heart*.
2 Cross, R., Baker, W., & Parker, A. (2003). What creates energy in organizations? *Sloan Management Review, 44*, 51–57.
3 Frost, P. J., & Robinson, S. (1999). The toxic handler: Organizational hero and casualty. *Harvard Business Review, 77*, 96–106.
4 See Terry A. Maroney, Emotional Regulation and Judicial Behavior, California Law Review (forthcoming 2012) and Terry A. Maroney, The Persistent Cultural Script of Judicial Dispassion, California Law Review, *99*, 629 (2011) with defining "judicial dispassion."
5 Shields, S.A., Warner, L.R., & Zawadzki, M.J. (July, 2011). *Beliefs About Others' Regulation of Emotion*. Paper presented at the International Society for Research on Emotion. Kyoto, Japan.
6 Batja Mesquita (July, 2011). *Emoting as a Contextualized Process*. Paper presented at the International Society for Research on Emotion. Kyoto, Japan.
7 Yukiko Uchida (July, 2011). *Emotions as Within or Between People? Cultural Variation in Subjective Well-being, Emotion Expression and Emotion Inference*. Paper presented at the International Society for Research on Emotion. Kyoto, Japan.
8 *The Managed Heart* has been translated and published in Japanese by Sekai Shisosha, Kyoto, Japan; in Chinese, by Laureate Books, Taipei, Taiwan; and in Korean by Image Books, Seoul, Korea.

Arlie Russell Hochschild
San Francisco, 2012

# About the Editors

**Dr. Grandey** is Associate Professor and Program Chair of Industrial-Organizational Psychology at The Pennsylvania State University. Dr. Grandey is especially interested in the performance-stress tradeoffs of Emotional Labor (EL) and the individual and contextual factors that influence those outcomes. Her EL work has been published in management and psychology journals such as *Journal of Applied Psychology (JAP)*, *Academy of Management Journal (AMJ)*, *Journal of Occupational Health Psychology (JOHP)*, *Organizational Behavior and Human Decision Processes*, and *Journal of Organizational Behavior*. Her EL research has earned Best Paper awards from the OB Division of Academy of Management, Emerald Publishing, and the JOHP editorial board. Dr. Grandey has also written review chapters on EL topics for the 2008 Sage *Handbook of Organizational Behavior* and the 2012 Routledge/Psychology Press book on *Relationships at Work* for the Frontiers Series. She has shared her EL findings internationally in a practitioner-oriented article for the Korean Labor Institute and at the International Summer School in Affective Sciences (ISSAS) in Switzerland. Dr. Grandey serves on the editorial board of *JAP, AMJ, JOHP, Journal of Management,* and is on the inaugural board of *Organizational Psychology Review*.

**Dr. Diefendorff** is Associate Professor of Industrial-Organizational Psychology at The University of Akron. His research interests include emotion management at work, emotional display rules, work motivation, and self-regulation. Dr. Diefendorff's work has been funded by the National Science Foundation and his publications have appeared in leading journals such as *Journal of Applied Psychology, Personnel Psychology, Journal of Management, Organizational Behavior and Human Decision Processes, Journal of Organizational Behavior,* and *Journal of Occupational Health Psychology*. Dr. Diefendorff recently completed a term as associate editor of *Journal of Business and Psychology* and is currently on the editorial boards of *Journal of Applied Psychology, Organizational Behavior and Human Decision Processes, Personnel Psychology,* and *Journal of Vocational Behavior.* Prior to joining the faculty at The University of Akron, Dr. Diefendorff served on the faculty in the psychology department at Louisiana State University and in the business school at The University of Colorado at Denver. He also has been a visiting scholar at Singapore Management University, University of Osnabrück, and Hong Kong Polytechnic University.

**Dr. Rupp** is the William C. Byham Chair in Industrial/Organizational Psychology in the Department of Psychological Sciences at Purdue University. She received her PhD in Industrial/Organizational Psychology from Colorado State University in 2002. She has two major research areas. The first explores phenomena related to employee justice, behavioral ethics, emotions at work, and corporate social responsibility. This is focused on isolating the motivations behind individuals' justice concerns, and the extent to which the experience of fair treatment at work influences the development of strong, lasting, socio-emotional ties between employees and employers; and argues that behavior at work is driven not by self-interest alone, but also by moral reasoning and a universal concern that justice is a fundamental human right. Her second major research area focuses on behavioral assessment and development. This work was a focus of the Thornton and Rupp (2005) text (which was cited in the Supreme Court proceedings for *Ricci v. DeStefano et al.*) and was a component of the revised Guidelines and Ethical Considerations for Assessment Center Operations (2009). Rupp's work has appeared in outlets such as *Journal of Applied Psychology, Academy of Management Review, Personnel Psychology,* and *Organizational Behavior and Human Decision Processes.* She is currently serving as Editor-in-Chief of *Journal of Management.*

# Contributors

Blake E. Ashforth, Department of Management, Arizona State University, USA

Neal M. Ashkanasy, UQ Business School, The University of Queensland, Australia

Daniel J. Beal, Department of Psychology, University of Texas at San Antonio, USA

David Cameron, Department of Psychology, Sheffield University, UK

Stéphane Côté, Rotman School of Management, University of Toronto, Canada

Jason J. Dahling, Department of Psychology, College of New Jersey, USA

Catherine S. Daus, Department of Psychology, Southern Illinois University-Edwardsville, USA

Ellen Delvaux, Department of Psychology, University of Leuven, Belgium

James M. Diefendorff, Department of Psychology, University of Akron, USA

Rebecca J. Erickson, Department of Sociology, University of Akron, USA

Alicia A. Grandey, Department of Psychology, The Pennsylvania State University, USA

James J. Gross, Department of Psychology, Stanford University, USA

Markus Groth, Australian Business School, University of New South Wales, Australia

Thorsten Hennig-Thurau, Marketing Center Muenster, University of Muenster, Germany and Department of Management, Cass Business School, City University, London, UK

David Holman, Manchester Business School, University of Manchester, UK

Ronald H. Humphrey, Department of Management, Virginia Commonwealth University, USA

Hazel-Anne M. Johnson, Department of Human Resource Management, Rutgers University, USA

Kathryn J. Lively, Department of Sociology, Dartmouth College, USA

Batja Mesquita, Department of Psychology, University of Leuven, Belgium

Christina M. Moran, Department of Psychology, University of Akron, USA

Karen Niven, Manchester Business School, University of Manchester, UK

Winifred R. Poster, Brown School of Social Work, Washington University at St. Louis, USA

S. Douglas Pugh, Department of Management, Virginia Commonwealth University, USA

Anat Rafaeli, Industrial Engineering & Management, Technion - Israel Institute of Technology, Israel

Deborah E. Rupp, Department of Psychology, Purdue University, USA

Clare L. Stacey, Department of Sociology, Kent State University, USA

Thomas Sy, Department of Psychology, University of CA-Riverside, USA

Peter Totterdell, Department of Psychology, University of Sheffield, UK

John P. Trougakos, Department of Management, University of Toronto-Scarborough, Ontario, Canada

Danielle van Jaarsveld, Sauder School of Business, University of British Columbia, Canada

Gerben A. Van Kleef, Department of Psychology, University of Amsterdam, The Netherlands

Karyn Wang, Australian School of Business, University of New South Wales, Australia

Amy S. Wharton, Department of Sociology, Washington State University Vancouver, USA

# *Acknowledgements*

We thank the School of Labor and Employment Relations at the University of Illinois at Urbana-Champaign, as well as Psychology Press, for sponsoring the research incubator that catalyzed this book. We also extend our sincere gratitude to Jean Drasgow, Jing Guo, Meghan Thornton, Megan Peters, and Eddie Gosselin for their enormous coordination efforts. Anne Duffy and Art Brief have our sincere appreciation for believing in and supporting our vision for this project. Finally, we thank the Cohort Researching Emotions at Work, some of whose fine work appears in this volume, and some who were unable to contribute, for being an ongoing source of support and inspiration.

# PART I
# Overview

# Bringing Emotional Labor into Focus

## A Review and Integration of Three Research Lenses

ALICIA A. GRANDEY • JAMES M. DIEFENDORFF • DEBORAH E. RUPP

I have to have a smile on my face. Some mornings that's a little difficult
. . . You're concentrating on what you're doing. It's a little difficult to have
that smile all the time. I have one particular girl who says to me, 'What? No
smile this morning?' So I smile. Clerks are really underpaid people.
(A hotel clerk, Terkel, 1972, p. 247)

Approximately 30 years ago, sociologist Arlie Russell Hochschild (1979)
published an article on emotion management in work and family roles,
followed by her groundbreaking book in 1983: *The Managed Heart:
Commercialization of Human Feeling*. In this work she proposed that the
rise of the service sector was creating a new form of labor – emotional
labor (EL) – where the worker manages feelings and expressions to help
the organization profit. Such labor is illustrated in the quote above, from
Studs Terkel's (1972) acclaimed book, *Working*. What is clear from
Hochschild's book, and the above quote, is that a personal and enjoyable
behavior – a smile – can also be a product available for public consumption in exchange for a wage.

Hochschild's (1983) naming of this form of labor sparked several lines of research over the last three decades. In fact, close to 10,000 articles have referred to EL; notably, over *half* of those articles were published since 2006, showing exponential growth in the attention to this concept (see Figure 1.1). In the broader context, EL is part of the growth of attention to emotions in sociology (Thoits, 2004; Wharton, 2009), psychology (Gross, 1998b), and the "affective revolution" in organizational behavior (Ashforth & Humphrey, 1995; Ashkanasy, Härtel, & Daus, 2002; Barsade, Brief, & Spataro, 2003). In sociology and organizational behavior (OB) particularly, the interest in EL is linked to the growth of the service sector worldwide (see www.cia.gov, The World Factbook), and more attention to interpersonal job demands (e.g., teams, client contact) (Humphrey, Nahrgang, & Morgeson, 2007). Though the service sector is often the focus of EL research (e.g., health care provider, teacher, paralegal, call center worker, fast-food cashier), many researchers consider EL to be a central component of any job requiring interpersonal contact (Diefendorff, Richard, & Croyle, 2006; Sloan, 2004). Thus, the ideas of EL can be applied to a majority of the current workforce.

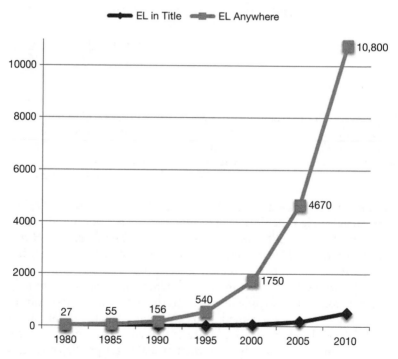

**Figure 1.1** Growth of published academic research on "emotional labor/labour".

With three decades of study, we consider the time to be right to take stock
of the emotional labor field by gathering the perspectives of experts from
a variety of disciplines and theoretical orientations. The chapters of this
book are intended to recognize the diverse research perspectives of EL
(e.g., psychology, sociology, management, marketing) and the different
ways of conceptualizing and investigating EL (e.g., event/episode, individual, group, organization, culture). These chapters review past research
and identify key issues for future work to consider. The chapters outline
methodological, theoretical, and practical issues in the literature as well as
asking new questions in each of these areas. For example: How do personal
abilities versus interpersonal power influence the way emotions are managed at work (Part 1)? How does physically proximal versus technology-
mediated service differ in the management and performance of emotions
(Part 2)? How does the global service economy – and the culturally diverse
interactions that occur – change the experience of EL (Part 3)?

As a starting point, this introductory chapter focuses on defining EL.
As the concept of EL has become more popular, its definition has
broadened and the boundaries between the construct and other related
constructs have become blurred. So, we start by asking the question: What
exactly is EL, or perhaps more importantly, what is it *not*? In the present
chapter, we review the conceptual development and measurement of EL
over time and then propose a framework aimed at differentiating the
concept of EL from other related concepts. We hope that some consensus
can be reached regarding the definition and conceptualization of EL and
that an agenda for future research on this increasingly relevant and
important topic can be developed.

## EMOTIONAL LABOR CONCEPT: THREE FOCAL LENSES

The answer to the question "what is EL?" is more complex than it may
seem. We propose that there are three main "lenses" or perspectives that
researchers use to "see" EL, but that using all three will result in the
clearest vision. In Table 1.1, we compare the definitions, measurement,
and outcomes of the three lenses: EL as Occupational Requirements, EL
as Emotional Displays, and EL as Intrapsychic Processes. Though all three
were originally part of Hochschild's (1983) original conceptualization,
different lenses tended to be used by different disciplines. The lens of *EL
as Occupational Requirements* tends to be the focus in sociology (e.g.,
Lively & Powell, 2006; Wharton, 1993); the lens of *EL as Emotional
Displays* tends to be the focus in organizational behavior (e.g., Ashforth
& Humphrey, 1993; Rafaeli & Sutton, 1987), and *EL as Intrapsychic*

TABLE 1.1  Viewing Emotional Labor (EL) Through Three Focal Lenses

| | EL as Occupational Requirements | EL as Emotional Displays | EL as Intrapsychic Processes |
|---|---|---|---|
| EL Definition | Jobs that require managing feelings to create an emotional display in exchange for a wage | Expressions of work role-specified emotions that may or may not require conscious effort | Effortfully managing one's emotions when interacting with others at work |
| Key Publications | Hochschild (1979, 1983) Wharton (1993) | Rafaeli & Sutton (1987, 1989) Ashforth & Humphrey (1993) | Morris & Feldman (1996) Zerbe (2000) Grandey (2000) |
| Central Concepts | *Emotion work* or *management* = done in private for personal motives<br><br>*EL Jobs* = frequent interactions with public, must induce feelings in others, and management controls emotion<br><br>*Feeling/Display Rules* = norms for how one should feel/display with others | *Emotional harmony* = feelings, displays and emotional expectations are congruent (i.e., "affective delivery")<br><br>*Emotional deviance* = expressions are incongruent with expectations (i.e., "breaking character")<br><br>*Authenticity* = extent to which expressions appear to be genuine | *Surface acting* = way of modifying *expressions* to meet job expectations (i.e., suppress, fake)<br><br>*Deep acting* = way of modifying *feelings* to meet job expectations (i.e., refocus, reappraise)<br><br>*Emotional dissonance* = state of tension when there is a discrepancy between feelings and displays |
| Measurement Approach | Qualitative (interviews, observation); O*Net | Observer ratings of expressive behavior | Actor's self-reports |
| Proposed Outcomes | EL is functional for the organization but dysfunctional for the employee | EL is functional for organization and employee; only dysfunctional if highly effortful and inauthentic | EL as deep acting is functional to organization and employee; surface acting and dissonance are dysfunctional |

*Processes* tends to be the focus in psychology (e.g., Grandey, 2000; Morris & Feldman, 1996). These disciplinary roots explain why the lenses are often used separately rather than in combination, and contribute to the blurring of the EL concept. Our goal is to make transparent the assumptions of these lenses, so that future researchers can see EL more clearly.

## Focal Lens #1: Emotional Labor as Occupational Requirements

In the first focal lens, EL is a type of occupation, a parallel concept to physical labor or cognitive labor. Hochschild (1983) suggested that the shift toward services, rather than goods, created jobs that required the task of pleasing customers to turn a profit. EL was proposed to be distinct from *emotion management* (i.e., *emotion regulation, emotion work*), which was performed in a private context for personal use. In viewing EL through this lens, certain jobs require EL and others (i.e., those lacking frequent customer interaction) do not.

### Focal Definition and Measurement

The central tenet of EL within this perspective was that it occurred in jobs requiring the managing of emotions in exchange for a wage. High EL jobs were defined by Hochschild (1983) as having three characteristics: 1) frequent interactions with the public (i.e., customers), 2) the expectation of inducing emotions in others, and 3) the management or control of these emotional interactions. Jobs with all three characteristics are clearly EL jobs, though others may be argued to be EL jobs if they have one or two of these characteristics (see Table 1.2). Based on this definition, Hochschild (1983) provided a list of "high EL jobs" in the appendix of her book, which she acknowledged was "no more than a sketch, a suggestion of a pattern that deserves to be examined more closely" (p. 234). Caring work (i.e., nurses), professional services (i.e., paralegals), and enforcement services (i.e., bill collector, police) have all been studied as EL jobs but do not have the same level of the three characteristics (Thoits, 2004; Wharton, 2009).

With its roots in sociology, qualitative research approaches are often used to provide rich descriptions of specific job contexts and employee experiences within this domain. Hochschild (1983) conducted observations and interviews with flight attendants and bill collectors, illustrating the variety of emotion expectations (i.e., warmth and calm versus anger and intimidation), and identifying how management socialized emotional norms. Sociologists have conducted in-depth observational studies of emotional labor in prototypical low-status jobs such as fast-food server and cashier (Leidner, 1993; Tolich, 1993) as well as professional jobs such as police detective and paralegal (Lively, 2000; Stenross & Kleinman, 1989).

## Focal Concepts

The qualitative approaches used in conjunction with this lens have yielded key EL concepts. Hochschild (1983) found that people working in EL occupations are socialized into certain *feeling rules*, or norms about how employees "should" feel when interacting with customers, clients, and patients. Others began to focus on *display rules*, or the expressive requirements of the job (Thoits, 2004). Wharton and Erickson (1993) reviewed three types of display rules: 1) *Integrative display rules:* the requirement to show positive emotions (e.g., liking, empathy) that "bind groups together" (p. 463); 2) *Differentiating display rules:* the requirement to show negative emotions (e.g., hostility, contempt) to create differences between others; and 3) *Masking display rules:* the requirement to show neutral emotions (e.g., calm) to convey impartiality and authority.

Status and gender were also central concepts within this perspective. The basic assumption of Hochschild's (1983) work was that there is an imbalance of power in EL jobs with higher power (and often male) customers being able to act more freely on their feelings than lower power (and often female) employees (Hochschild, 1983; Thoits, 2004). As a result, employees in EL jobs were found to experience a loss of personal control resulting in self-alienation, emotional estrangement, and a host of social- and health-related problems. This may be particularly problematic in contexts with integrative (or deferential) display rules which also tend to be lower status and female-gendered jobs (Thoits, 2004). Occupations with differentiating (bill collectors, drill sergeants; Sutton, 1991) or masking (surgeons, police; Stenross & Kleinman, 1989) display rules tend to be more male-dominated and higher status.

Emotional display rules have been commonly studied as individuals' *perceptions* of job requirements with customers (Diefendorff & Richard, 2003; Gosserand & Diefendorff, 2005; Schaubroeck & Jones, 2000) and other interaction partners (Diefendorff & Greguras, 2009; Sloan, 2004; Tschan, Rochat, & Zapf, 2005), permitting quantitative comparisons of EL requirements across jobs (e.g., Brotheridge & Grandey, 2002; Lively & Powell, 2006). This approach captures variation in the EL required of jobs, rather than categorizing jobs dichotomously as EL or not. In recent years, research has operationalized display rules as a) manipulated job requirements (Goldberg & Grandey, 2007; Trougakos, Jackson, & Beal, 2011), b) shared in work units (Diefendorff, Erickson, Grandey, & Dahling, 2011); and c) expert-coded descriptions of emotional demands by job title (Glomb, Kammeyer-Mueller, & Rotundo, 2004).

## Focal Outcomes and Evidence

A key assumption of this lens is that requiring emotions in exchange for a wage is uniquely distressing to employees. This is examined in two broad ways: 1) comparing outcomes for employees in high-EL and low-EL occupations, and 2) comparing financial motives versus other motives for performing emotion work.

Hochschild stated that "emotional labor is sold for a wage . . . I use the synonymous terms emotion work or emotion management to refer to these same acts done in a private context" (p. 7). She recognized that emotional displays are used strategically in many social contexts (Goffman, 1959); however, when emotions are used for financial gain "feelings are commoditized" (1979, p. 569), and this has unique effects on the employee. Lively and Powell (2006) found that emotion display requirements were more rigidly held at work (for pay) but this was unrelated to strain; this is in comparison to emotion display requirements held *at home*, which have, in contrast to Hochschild's proposal, been argued to be less rigidly held but more contributive to job strain (Wharton & Erickson, 1995). Surprisingly little research has assessed the assumption that performing emotion management for financial gain has personal costs (Wharton, 2009). Across occupations, EL demands are *negatively related* to wages, except for in professional jobs with higher cognitive demands (Glomb, et al., 2004); thus, the financial outcome of performing EL depends on job status. Financial motives for engaging in EL, however, may depend on the type of occupation. Sociologists have argued that *caring professionals* have a unique experience with regard to emotional labor (see Erickson & Stacey, 2013). Specifically, they are more likely to engage in EL for professional (to uphold professional norms of conduct) or philanthropic (to provide a "gift" to the patient) motives, rather than presentational (to conform to broadly held social norms), or pecuniary (to obtain financial benefits) motives (Bolton & Boyd, 2003). That said, research comparing motives for engaging in EL is still forthcoming.

There has been mixed support for stress-related differences in high versus low EL jobs. In support of the view that EL jobs involve an imbalance of power, increasing levels of EL job requirements have been equated to more frequent abusive customer interactions (Grandey, Kern, & Frone, 2007), which has been linked to unfair treatment and more distress from performing EL (Rupp & Spencer, 2006). However, low-status service employees can also "turn the tables" and use their emotions to influence the customers in ways that might level power differentials. Additionally, scripts for "controlling" workers in EL jobs may decrease stress for entry-level workers (i.e., Leidner, 1993) and interactions with the public can provide a break in monotony (Tolich, 1993). Overall, employees categorized as working in high EL jobs ("high contact with public", positive display requirements) were *not* more likely to feel burned out than employees in other jobs (Brotheridge & Grandey, 2002; Wharton, 1993), and there is some evidence that the effects of EL requirements vary as a function of gender and the associated "status shield" differences between men and women (Erickson & Ritter, 2001; Wharton, 2009).

Because occupation-level differences do not yield much support, researchers have turned to using variations in display rules to classify EL jobs. For instance, such work has shown that masking display rules (e.g., requiring employees to suppress negative emotions) are linked to negative well-being outcomes (Trougakos, et al., 2011). In contrast, integrative display requirements (e.g., "service with a smile") have shown mixed relationships with job satisfaction and employee health (Brotheridge & Grandey, 2002; Côté & Morgan, 2002; Diefendorff, et al., 2006; Schaubroeck & Jones, 2000). Overall, researchers must recognize EL differences within occupations (Wharton, 2009); simply focusing on EL requirements may not be sufficient for understanding and predicting employee outcomes (Meanwell, Wolfe, & Hallett, 2008). This brings us to our second lens focusing on employee behaviors rather than job requirements.

## Focal Lens #2: EL as Emotional Displays at Work

OB theorists have tended to look at EL through the lens of role-congruent emotional displays or expressions toward others, consistent with Hochschild's point that EL jobs involve requirements to influence the emotions of others. The early work by Rafaeli and Sutton (1987, 1989) drew heavily on Goffman's (1959) ideas surrounding the strategic use of emotional expressions in social interactions, and proposed that emotional displays are part of job performance. This lens is more attentive to how emotional expressions influence the target (usually a customer), a factor often missing from early research (Meanwell, et al., 2008).

### Focal Definitions and Measurement

Rafaeli and Sutton's work on emotions (1987, 1989) "considers work settings in which employees display emotions in order to fulfill role expectations" (1987, p. 24), particularly with persons outside the organization (i.e., customers). Rafaeli and Sutton (1987) emphasized observable expressions instead of internal feelings (see Table 1.1), and thus specified the importance of *display rules* rather than feeling rules. They recognized that display rules are influenced by organizational and occupational norms, as well as social norms, and discussed real-world examples of how organizations attempt to "create and maintain expectations about emotional expressions" (1987, p. 26). Building on this work, Ashforth and Humphrey (1993) defined EL as the act of *displaying* the emotions specified by the organization. They pointed out that EL can be conceptualized as displays that meet organizational expectations, regardless of whether they require effort on the part of the employee.

As such, this focal lens assumes that *observations* of emotional expressions within the work context are the most promising way to study EL. Early on, Rafaeli and Sutton (Rafaeli, 1989; Sutton & Rafaeli, 1988) conducted a series of studies where observers coded the presence of verbal (i.e., greeting, farewell) and non-verbal (i.e., smile, eye contact) cues of convenience store clerks, as well as the more subjective *pleasantness* of expressions. More recent approaches contrast "affective delivery" to the more task-based "service delivery" (Tsai & Huang, 2002), and expand this lens to include neutral and negative displays as well (Côté, Van Kleef, & Sy, 2013; Trougakos, et al., 2011).

### Focal Concepts

A key concept according to this lens is that EL (as organizationally-required displays) can be achieved actively *or effortlessly* (Ashforth & Humphrey, 1993; Diefendorff, Croyle, & Gosserand, 2005). Rafaeli and Sutton (1987) noted that three primary variables are involved in emotional displays at work: emotion requirements, feelings, and expressions. When feelings and displays match role expectations, this results in *emotional harmony*. This is likely when there is good person–job fit or, more specifically, emotional demands–ability fit (Arvey, Renz, & Watson, 1998). In fact, whether the displays are *authentic* is central to whether EL is beneficial for both the employee and the organization (Ashforth & Humphrey, 1993; Côté, 2005; Groth, Hennig-Thurau, & Wang, 2013).

A discrepancy between feelings and display expectations, or what is sometimes referred to as *emotional dissonance* (see more detailed explanation in the next section), may result in *emotional deviance*, when emotional expressions do not match work expectations. Rafaeli and Sutton (1987) argued that employees may avoid emotional deviance by "faking in bad faith" (i.e., faking emotional expressions, but not believing this should be part of the job), or by "faking in good faith" (i.e., faking, but believing it should be part of the job due to internalized role expectations). Ashforth and Humphrey (1993) linked these forms of faking to Hochschild's (1983) original concepts of surface and deep acting as 'active' management approaches.

Focal Outcomes and Evidence

Central to this lens is the idea that expressing emotions that are congruent with role expectations can be beneficial to the organization and employee. Rafaeli and Sutton (1987) discussed how role-congruent displays result in *immediate gains* (e.g., perceiver's mood, making a sale), *encore gains* (e.g., repeat business) and *contagion gains* (e.g., word-of-mouth to other customers) for the business. Research has supported these ideas such that expressing positive emotions in service contexts results in improved customers' moods, higher performance ratings, and intentions to return (Mattila & Enz, 2002; Pugh, 2001; Tsai & Huang, 2002). Though the theoretical basis of *primitive emotional contagion* is often used, the evidence suggests that customers cognitively appraise the positive displays as meeting role expectations rather than simply 'catching' the mood expressed (Barger & Grandey, 2006). However, there is very little evidence that positive displays improve sales (Tsai, 2001). In fact, studies of cashiers have found that the relationship between emotional expressions and store sales was negative. This has been explained as store busyness reducing display expectations while increasing sales (Sutton & Rafaeli, 1988). Moreover, research viewing EL through this lens suggests that customer reactions depend on the *authenticity* of emotion expressions. This notion has received some empirical support in service contexts (Grandey, Fisk, Mattila, Jansen, & Sideman, 2005). Thus, EL as displays improves customer affect and intentions, though there is less evidence for actual return or purchasing behaviors. Note that most of this research is on *customer* reactions (Groth, et al., 2013), but there is growing attention to how role-congruent emotional expressions influence co-workers (see Côté, et al., 2013; Niven, Totterdell, Holman, & Cameron, 2013; Spencer & Rupp, 2009). In fact, although their emphasis was on customers, Rafaeli and Sutton (1987) acknowledged that emotional expressions can be role-prescribed for interactions among employees *within* the organization.

This focal lens specifically diverges from the first focal lens by proposing benefits of EL to the employee. Though potential costs to *mental and physical well-being* are acknowledged, Rafaeli and Sutton (1989) argued that employees who display role-congruent positive emotions improve their well-being through facial feedback (a within-person mechanism) and social feedback (a between-person mechanism) (Beal & Trougakos, 2013; Côté, et al., 2013). However, though laboratory research suggests that positive expressions should enhance the actor's well-being, it is unclear if this holds in a work setting where the expressions are explicitly required (and potentially carried out for a wage). In fact, caring behaviors toward patients (including positive displays) were *negatively* related to well-being (Drach-Zahavy, 2010). There is even less attention to how role-congruent *neutral or negative* expressions influence the employee, but recent research is beginning to assess these displays in service and other interpersonal work contexts (Sy, Cote, & Saavedra, 2005; Trougakos, et al., 2011; Van Kleef, et al., 2006). Moreover, though Rafaeli and Sutton proposed enhanced *financial well-being* as an outcome of EL (and the associated promotions, tips and commissions), few studies have provided evidence that observable expressions improve employees' financial outcomes (Tidd & Lockard, 1978). Again, employees' authenticity may determine whether such gains occur, and also whether the displays harm or benefit their own well-being (Erickson & Ritter, 2001).

Current research applying this lens builds on a central premise of Rafaeli and Sutton's (1987) early work: that organizations manage employee emotional displays through formal and informal practices. Though there are many case studies and qualitative investigations (Martin, Knopoff, & Beckman, 1998; Theodosius, 2008; Van Maanen & Kunda, 1989), little quantitative research has explored how organizational practices shape EL processes (see van Jaarsveld & Poster, 2013). One hospital study found that service climate (e.g., perceived practices that reward and support service) buffered the strain of service behaviors with patients (Drach-Zahavy, 2010) and other research suggests that management practices may support, rather than control and coerce, EL processes (Pugh, Diefendorff, & Moran, 2013). Current research also supports that well-being and financial benefits of EL are more likely when there is personality match to the job's emotional requirements (Bono & Vey, 2007; Chi, Grandey, Diamond, & Krimmel, 2011; see Dahling & Johnson, 2013), suggesting support for the value of "emotional harmony" and authenticity as a key determinant of whether EL is costly to the individual.

### Focal Lens #3: EL as Intrapsychic Experiences

A major part of Hochschild's 1983 book was the description of the intrapsychic experiences of the flight attendants and bill collectors she interviewed. Hochschild described how employees experienced emotive dissonance from the incongruence of feeling rules and negative exchanges, with employees coping by changing expressions (e.g., surface acting) or feelings (e.g., deep acting). Drawing on psychological literatures of dissonance theory and emotion regulation (Festinger, 1954; Gross, 1998a), dissonance, surface acting, and deep acting became a defining focus of EL (Grandey, 2000; Morris & Feldman, 1996; Zerbe, 2000).

Focal Definition and Measurement.

Hochschild (1983) states in a footnote that EL "is the management of feeling to create a publicly facial and bodily display" (p. 7). Rather than focusing on display requirements, or the displays themselves, researchers using this third lens focus on *the internal experience* of managing emotions at work. This is therefore a person-focused view of EL (Brotheridge & Grandey, 2002). In one of the earliest papers to take this approach, Morris and Feldman (1996) defined EL as "the effort, planning and control needed to express organizationally desired emotion during interpersonal transactions" (p. 987). They defined EL as characteristic of a high frequency of interactions, a variety of emotions required, required attentiveness to emotional display rules, and dissonance (i.e., mismatch between feelings and emotional demands). These characteristics were then thought to result in the need to effortfully alter emotions and emotional expressions (i.e., deep acting and surface acting). Taking this further, Grandey (2000) defined EL as "the process of regulating both feelings and expressions for organizational goals" (p. 97), with a focus on deep and surface acting at the expense of emotion requirements and dissonance. In particular, she linked these forms of acting to emotion regulation (ER) strategies in psychological research (Gross, 1998a). Psychology-based EL scholars have tended to focus on emotional dissonance (Zerbe, 2000) or on effortful emotion management (Bono & Vey, 2005), though they are clearly related to each other (Hülsheger & Schewe, 2011).

Research viewing EL through this third lens tends to take a self-perception approach, asking respondents to report their experience of dissonance or the frequency with which they surface or deep act (typically with customers) (Brotheridge & Lee, 2003). Emotional dissonance has also been assessed as the calculated discrepancy between reported feelings and expressions (e.g., Zerbe, 2000). These experiences are assessed not only as an individual difference in work experience (see Dahling & Johnson, 2013), but also as something that varies at the event- or episodic-level (see Beal & Trougakos, 2013). Dissonance is likely experienced if one is surface acting, and the two (dissonance and surface acting) are strongly related (Hülsheger & Schewe, 2011; Pugh, Groth, & Hennig-Thurau, 2011). The dependence on self-reported EL has created measurement issues, since the outcomes (e.g., employee strain, attitudes) are also perceived. When scholars control for negative affectivity, the relationship between surface acting and stress decreases notably (Brotheridge & Grandey, 2002) though there still seems to be unique effects from surface acting itself (Diefendorff, et al., 2011; Grandey, Fisk, & Steiner, 2005). Deep acting measures seem to represent something quite different, since deep acting tends to relate inconsistently to well-being outcomes and is more likely to occur after *positive* events and for those with positive disposition (Hülsheger & Schewe, 2011; Totterdell & Holmann, 2003). Finally, it is unclear what a low level of surface and deep acting represents: a lack of motivation or lack of need to regulate? Evidence supports that expressing genuine emotions are a separate concept from surface or deep acting (Diefendorff, et al., 2005) suggesting that emotional harmony is not the opposite of high surface or deep acting. Research is needed that uncovers the role of effort and whether these strategies become unconscious and effortless with practice.

### Focal Concepts

There are three primary concepts inherent to this approach: dissonance, deep acting, and surface acting. Zerbe (2000) noted that *emotional dissonance* is used in two different ways in the literature – as the discrepancy between feelings and job requirements (Hochschild, 1983; Morris & Feldman, 1996) and the discrepancy between feelings and displays (Rafaeli & Sutton, 1987). More recently, Holman, Martinez-Ingo and Totterdell (2008b) identified *emotion–rule dissonance* as the first discrepancy, which comes prior to ER according to their model (see also Rubin, Tardino, Daus, & Munz, 2005; Totterdell & Holman, 2003). We use the label *emotion–display dissonance* to refer to the second discrepancy, which refers to the experience of feeling differently than one is expressing with others at work (e.g., Kruml & Geddes, 2000). Though emotion–rule dissonance is often the focus of theoretical description, studies tend to actually measure emotion–display dissonance.

*Deep acting*, in Hochschild's (1983) book, referred to employees who were trying to follow the feeling rules and "bring forth" the desired feelings in their interactions with others. Grandey (2000) linked deep acting to antecedent-focused ER strategies (Gross, 1998a), where people cognitively reappraise events or refocus attention to modify feelings before the feelings are fully present. *Surface acting* was conceptually aligned with response-focused ER, such that the emotion is in "full swing" internally, but the employee suppresses, amplifies or fakes the observable expression. Other authors have continued the application of Gross's (1998b) framework, showing that deep and surface acting are not the only means of emotion regulation at work (Diefendorff, Richard, & Yang, 2008).

### Focal Outcomes and Evidence

Researchers viewing EL according to the intrapsychic lens tend to focus on employee well-being (e.g., burnout, job satisfaction) as the primary outcome of interest (Hülsheger & Schewe, 2011). The theoretical assumption is that experiencing either type of dissonance, or engaging in surface acting, is dysfunctional for both employee performance and well-being, while deep acting is functional or at least not distressing (Brotheridge & Lee, 2002; Côté, 2005; Grandey, 2000). This view is counter to Hochschild's original arguments, which suggested that deep acting was a form of self-deception that was the most likely to have personal costs in the long run. However, with current measurement approaches, high surface acting is almost always more problematic than high deep acting (Hülsheger & Schewe, 2011).

The mechanisms for these relationships are less clear (for reviews see Côté, 2005; Hülsheger & Schewe, 2011). Dissonance, and surface acting, might reduce well-being due to feelings of tension and inauthenticity. In fact, evidence supports that dissonance/surface acting is more distressing when there is a poor value- or personality-fit to the job demands for emotions (Chi, et al., 2011; Judge, Woolf, & Hurst, 2009; Pugh, 2001). However, Rafaeli and Sutton (1987) and dissonance theory (Festinger, 1954), suggest that incongruent displays could *improve* one's mood through facial feedback or self-perception, and be less distressing when there is justification (i.e., pay) for the incongruent behavior, consistent with recent evidence (Grandey, et al., under review).

Another proposed mechanism is the expended effort of acting, which contributes to the depletion of regulatory resources and fatigue. Grandey (2000) drew on the (primarily laboratory) emotion regulation research to make this case (Gross, 1998b), which shows that regulating emotions requires effort and self-control. Specifically, suppression or presenting oneself as friendly (i.e., surface acting) is more distressing and requires more attention than reappraisal (i.e., deep acting) or no emotion management (Vohs, Baumeister, & Ciarocco, 2005). Finally, others have suggested that the differential relationships for surface and deep acting are due to authenticity differences in their resulting expressions toward others, and the social resource losses (or gains) for that performance (Brotheridge & Lee, 2002; Côté, 2005). Some evidence supports the idea that surface acting is observable by others and can influence judgments of the actor (Grandey, 2003; Groth, Hennig-Thurau, & Walsh, 2009), but we know less about whether social *behaviors* in response to the surface actor are different than they are to the deep actor.

Though there has been a focus on dissonance and these two forms of acting, others have found that employees manage emotions with others in a variety of ways. The intrapsychic lens has led to identifying other strategies for EL (Diefendorff, et al., 2008), and with other targets besides customers (Tschan, et al., 2005). However, focusing on emotion management with anyone at work can also blur the boundaries between EL and coping or self-regulation in general.

## Summary: Integrating the Three Focal Lenses

Our intention in reviewing the above approaches to studying EL is to provide some conceptual context and discussion of the measurement, empirical evidence, and theoretical issues that will be discussed throughout the remainder of this book. Elements of all three approaches are, to varying degrees, represented in most theoretical treatments and empirical investigations of EL; what varies is the focal lens, and consequently, the focal concepts, mechanisms, and operationalizations used in specific studies. The problems begin when one lens is used to the exclusion of others. Emotional labor *per se* does not reside in any one set of constructs but rather is a result of the dynamic interactions among occupational requirements (Lens #1), emotional displays (Lens #2), and intrapsychic processes (Lens #3), as originally argued by Hochschild (1983). In other words, by merging the three lenses and "using trifocals," we believe that the concept of EL becomes clearer, and the parameters bolder and more distinct from other concepts, than using any one lens alone.

Various authors have attempted to integrate these three approaches (Grandey, 2000; Holman, Martinez-Inigo, & Totterdell, 2008a; Rubin, et al., 2005). For instance, Diefendorff and Gosserand adopted a self-regulatory perspective in which display rules are conceptualized as goals (Lens #1) that employees strive for over time and across circumstances. Employees are thought to constantly compare their emotions and displays (Lens #2) to the display rules so as to detect and remove discrepancies (i.e., emotion–rule dissonance). When no discrepancy is sensed, individuals have no need to actively regulate feelings/expressions and can continue to meet display rules through either genuine (Ashforth & Humphrey, 1993) or automatically-regulated (Gallo, Keil, McCulloch, Rockstroh, & Gollwitzer, 2009) expressions. When feelings differ from display rules (i.e., emotion–rule dissonance), individuals are expected to exert effort in the form of ER (Lens #3) aimed at altering subsequent emotional displays (either directly, via surface acting or indirectly, via deep acting). Further, the model accounts for environmental *disturbances* – dynamic and unplanned circumstances (i.e., hostile interaction) – that are known to relate to EL processes (Spencer & Rupp, 2009), as well as the links of EL to other work and personal regulatory goals. Consistent with our description of EL, this model suggests that EL does not reside in any particular construct, but rather emerges as a result of the dynamic interplay of occupational expectations, expressed emotions, and emotion regulation strategies. This is just one example of how researchers might use the three lenses, simultaneously, to understand EL. What we advise against is relying on one focal lens (e.g., emotion regulation at work) as "emotional labor."

Our review indicates that the predominant focus has been on interactions with the public (i.e., patients, customers) but there is interest in
applying EL to other employee interactions (e.g., Côté, et al., 2013), and
some evidence that the experience is unique by target (Bono, Foldes,
Vinson, & Muros, 2007). Given that most jobs have some interpersonal
requirements, whether with team members, supervisors, subordinates, or
the public, is every job "emotionally laborious" in one way or another?
Does every job, therefore require EL? Similarly, doesn't every employee
have to manage their expressions or put on a 'face' with someone, as
shown in impression management during interviews? Is that EL? Is it EL
if it is effortful emotional self-regulation that occurs at work? But why
does regulating at work make it distinct from what we do with our family
or friends, and if it is not, why does it need its own label? Using all three
lenses – our trifocals – we argue that what makes it "emotional labor" is
when emotion regulation is *performed in response to job-based emotional
requirements in order to produce emotion toward – and to evoke emotion from
– another person to achieve organizational goals*. This may or may not be
explicitly linked to financial rewards, but needs to be required of the work
role (i.e., not extra-role) to clearly be emotional labor rather than emotion
management at work.

Similarly, though Hochschild's (1983) original description of EL
implied a dichotomy of occupations (i.e., EL or not, see Wharton, 1993),
authors have argued that EL may vary in *degree* across occupations and
even across contexts within occupations. As such, we prefer to think
about EL as existing along a continuum ranging from "pure EL " contexts
on one end (in which all of Hochschild's stated attributes are present) and
"pure ER" (emotion regulation, or emotion work) contexts on the other
end (in which none, or almost none of the stated attributes are present).
Using what seem to be the most commonly recognized or mentioned
features of EL jobs, we describe how different roles/occupations might
reside somewhere between pure EL and pure ER (see Table 1.2). We
present this with the interest in helping future researchers make explicit
not only their focal lens, but also to frame the ways in which less traditional samples might well be considered to be "doing EL. "

Perhaps the most obvious feature for differentiating EL and ER contexts is that EL occurs "for a wage" (e.g., economic exchange) and "at
work" (e.g., physical boundary that delineates public space versus private).
First, this speaks to paid employment; however persons may have a formal
work role that requires emotion management but is volunteer work.
Similarly, others have raised the point that in some occupations, the
emotion work is motivated by non-financial factors (Bolton & Boyd,
2003). Moreover, Hochschild recognized that this differentiation of
public versus private interactions has become blurred, as for instance in

TABLE 1.2 Emotional Labor or Not? Illustrating the Fuzzy Boundary with Examples

| Hochschild's EL Criteria | Customer Service Agent | Home Health Aid | Volunteer Fundraiser | Unit Leaders | Human Resource Generalist | R&D Team Member | Construction Worker | Spouse/ Parent |
|---|---|---|---|---|---|---|---|---|
| Work Context (vs. Private Context)? | Yes | No | Maybe | Yes | Yes | Yes | Yes | No |
| Financial gains linked to emotion performance? | Yes | Yes | No | Maybe | Maybe | Maybe | No | No |
| Frequent interactions with the public? | Yes | Yes | Yes | Maybe | No | No | Maybe | No |
| Emotion performance is role requirement? | Yes | Yes | Yes | Yes | Maybe | Maybe | No | Maybe |
| Management monitors and evaluates emotion performance? | Yes | Maybe | Yes | Maybe | Maybe | No | No | No |

Emotional Labor → Not Emotional Labour

Note: "Not Emotional Labor" may be called emotion work, emotion management, or emotion regulation, which are used interchangeably to refer to modifying feelings and expressions in any context. R&D refers to Research and Development.

the case of home workers who perform EL (e.g., domestic help, home care aids; Wharton, 2009). Another component is the target: Hochschild's (1983) focus was on jobs with frequent "interactions with the public"; emotional regulation may be performed with anyone (e.g., supervisors, coworkers, internal customers) while at work (Côté & Morgan, 2002; Erickson & Ritter, 2001; Glomb & Tews, 2004; Schaubroeck & Jones, 2000). Consistent with our continuum in Table 1.2, emotional displays tend to be "required" with customers but are sometimes also required with coworkers or supervisors (Diefendorff & Greguras, 2009; Tschan et al., 2005). As Table 1.2 illustrates, there are many "gray areas" in terms of the distinction between emotional labor and emotion regulation that are in need of further study.

## Conclusions

Overall, EL is an exponentially growing research topic, as illustrated in Figure 1.1. Partially due to this proliferation, the concept of EL has come to mean many different things. Researchers *must* clearly communicate how they define and operationalize the concept, and make explicit the assumptions for why they are studying EL rather than emotion regulation or emotion work. We encourage researchers to consider how their work complements and extends research that has applied the three focal lenses (Table 1.1). We also caution researchers to be aware of the assumptions implicit with each of these lenses and encourage them to adopt approaches that transcend the boundaries between the lenses. Such approaches are more likely to yield knowledge with broad implications for the study of EL. We also encourage researchers to explicitly consider how their sample and interpersonal context might determine the placement of their research on the EL and ER continuum (Table 1.2), as well as the substantive implications for how their work contributes to these fields of study. In some instances, the results may transcend the EL and ER distinction, but in others, the results may be wholly dependent on the placement of the study on this continuum (i.e., this distinction may moderate the relationships among independent and dependent variables).

In addition to advocating for the use of "trifocals" in order to more clearly understand EL, this book explicitly calls for emotional labor to be studied at different levels of analysis (Ashkanasy, 2003): the individual (Chapters 2, 3), the dyad/group (Chapters 4, 5), the job/occupation (Chapters 6–8), and the social–cultural context (Chapters 9–11). Furthermore, we aim to help with cross-fertilization across disciplines and focal lenses by including chapters from leading researchers based in psychology, organizational behavior, marketing, and sociology. The final section of the book includes five essays by esteemed scholars who have been pioneers in developing the three focal lenses presented here and who represent these various disciplines: Ashforth and Humphrey, Ashkanasy and Daus, Gross, Rafaeli, and Wharton. We asked each of them to provide "reflections and projections" about the field of EL, and they have made many clear suggestions for the future.

Given the increased importance of interpersonally-based jobs and the growing realization that interpersonal interactions have implications for both effectiveness and well-being in many organizational settings, the need to understand EL processes and advance our understanding of them in the future is only going to grow. This is truly an exciting time to do work on EL. Overall, our hope is that the view using all three lenses – our "trifocals" – will sharpen the focus of emotional labor research in the years to come.

# REFERENCES

Arvey, R. D., Renz, G. L., & Watson, W. W. (1998). Emotionality and job performance: Implications for personnel selection. *Research in Personnel and Human Resources Management, 16,* 103–147.

Ashforth, B., & Humphrey, R. H. (1995). Emotion in the workplace – a Reappraisal. *Human Relations, 48*(2), 97–125.

Ashforth, B. E., & Humphrey, R. H. (1993). Emotional Labor in Service Roles – the Influence of Identity. *Academy of Management Review, 18*(1), 88–115.

Ashkanasy, N. M. (Ed.). (2003). *Emotions in organizations: A multilevel perspective.* (Vol. 2). Oxford, UK: Elsevier/JAI Press.

Ashkanasy, N. M., Härtel, C. E. J., & Daus, C. S. (2002). Diversity and Emotion: The new frontiers in organizational behavior research. *Journal of Management, 28*(3), 307–338.

Barger, P., & Grandey, A. (2006). "Service with a smile" and encounter satisfaction: Emotional contagion and appraisal mechanisms. *Academy of Management Journal, 49*(6), 1229–1238.

Barsade, S. G., Brief, A. P., & Spataro, S. E. (2003). The affective revolution in organizational behavior: The emergence of a paradigm. In J. Greenberg (Ed.), *Organizational behavior: the state of the science* (2nd ed., pp. 3–52). Mahwah, NJ: Lawrence Erlbaum Associates.

Beal, D. J., & Trougakos, J. P. (2013). Episodic intrapersonal emotion regulation: Or, dealing with life as it happens. In A. A. Grandey, J. M. Diefendorff & D. E. Rupp (Eds.), *Emotional labor in the 21st century: Diverse perspectives on emotion regulation at work.* New York, NY: Psychology Press/Routledge.

Bolton, S., & Boyd, C. (2003). Trolley dolly or skilled emotion manager? Moving on from Hochschild's Managed Heart. *Work, employment and society, 17*(2), 289–308.

Bono, J., & Vey, M. (2005). Toward understanding emotional management at work: A quantitative review of emotional labor research. In C. E. Härtel & W. J.

Zerbe (Eds.), *Emotions in organizational behavior.* (pp. 213–233). Mahwah, NJ: Lawrence Erlbaum Associates.

Bono, J. E., Foldes, H. J., Vinson, G., & Muros, J. P. (2007). Workplace emotions: The role of supervision and leadership. *Journal of Applied Psychology, 92*(5), 1357.

Bono, J. E., & Vey, M. A. (2007). Personality and emotional performance: Extraversion, neuroticism, and self-monitoring. *Journal of Occupational Health Psychology, 12*(2), 177–192.

Brotheridge, C., & Grandey, A. (2002). Emotional labor and burnout: Comparing two perspectives of "people work". *Journal of Vocational Behavior, 60,* 17–39.

Brotheridge, C., & Lee, R. T. (2002). Testing a conservation of resources model of the dynamics of emotional labor. *Journal of Occupational Health Psychology, 7*(1), 57–67.

Brotheridge, C., & Lee, R. T. (2003). Development and validation of the Emotional Labour Scale. *Journal of Occupational and Organizational Psychology, 76,* 365–379.

Chi, N.-W., Grandey, A., Diamond, J., & Krimmel, K. (2011). Want a tip? Service performance as a function of extraversion and emotion regulation. *Journal of Applied Psychology, 96*(6), 1337–1346.

Côté, S. (2005). A social interaction model of the effects of emotion regulation on work strain. *Academy of Management Review, 30*(3), 509–530.

Côté, S., & Morgan, L. (2002). A longitudinal analysis of the association between emotion regulation, job satisfaction, and intentions to quit. *Journal of Organizational Behavior, 23*(8), 947–962.

Côté, S., Van Kleef, G. A., & Sy, T. (2013). The social effects of emotion regulation in organizations. In A. A. Grandey, J. M. Diefendorff & D. E. Rupp (Eds.), *Emotional labor in the 21st century: Diverse perspectives on emotion regulation at work.* New York, NY: Psychology Press/Routledge.

Dahling, J. J., & Johnson, H. (2013). Motivation, fit, confidence, and skills: How do individual differences influence emotional labor? In A. A. Grandey, J. M. Diefendorff & D. E. Rupp (Eds.), *Emotional labor in the 21st century: Diverse perspectives on emotion regulation at work.* New York, NY: Psychology Press/Routledge.

Diefendorff, J., Croyle, M., & Gosserand, R. (2005). The dimensionality and antecedents of emotional labor strategies. *Journal of Vocational Behavior, 66*(2), 339.

Diefendorff, J., Erickson, R. J., Grandey, A., & Dahling, J. J. (2011). Emotional display rules as work unit norms: A multilevel analysis of emotional labor among nurses. *Journal of Occupational Health Psychology, 16*(2), 170–186.

Diefendorff, J. M., & Greguras, G. J. (2009). Contextualizing emotional display rules: Taking a closer look at targets, discrete emotions, and behavior responses. *Journal of Management, 35*(4), 880–898.

Diefendorff, J. M., & Richard, E. (2003). Antecedents and consequences of emotional display rule perceptions. *Journal of Applied Psychology, 88*(2), 284–294.

Diefendorff, J. M., Richard, E. M., & Croyle, M. H. (2006). Are emotional display rules formal job requirements? Examination of employee and supervisor perceptions. *Journal of Occupational and Organizational Psychology*, 79(2), 273–298.

Diefendorff, J. M., Richard, E. M., & Yang, J. (2008). Linking emotion regulation strategies to affective events and negative emotions at work. *Journal of Vocational Behavior*, 73(3), 498–508.

Drach-Zahavy, A. (2010). How does service workers' behavior affect their health? Service climate as a moderator in the service behavior–health relationships. *Journal of Occupational Health Psychology*, 15(2), 105–119.

Erickson, R., & Stacey, C. L. (2013). Attending to mind and body: Engaging the complexity of emotion practice among caring professionals. In A. A. Grandey, J. M. Diefendorff & D. E. Rupp (Eds.), *Emotional labor in the 21st century: Diverse perspectives on emotion regulation at work*. New York, NY: Psychology Press/Routledge.

Erickson, R. J., & Ritter, C. (2001). Emotional labor, burnout, and inauthenticity: Does gender matter? *Social Psychology Quarterly*, 64(2), 146–163.

Festinger, L. (1954). A theory of social comparison processes. *Human Relations*, 7, 117–140.

Gallo, I.S., Keil, A., McCulloch, K.C., Rockstroh, B., Gollwitzer, P.M. (2009). Strategic automation of emotion regulation. *Journal of Personality and Social Psychology*, 96(1), 11–31.

Glomb, T. A., Kammeyer-Mueller, J. D., & Rotundo, M. (2004). Emotional labor demands and compensating wage differentials. *Journal of Applied Psychology*, 89(4), 700–714.

Glomb, T. M., & Tews, M. J. (2004). Emotional labor: A conceptualization and scale development. *Journal of Vocational Behavior*, 64(1), 1–23.

Goffman, E. (1959). *Presentation of self in everyday life*. New York: Doubleday.

Goldberg, L., & Grandey, A. (2007). Display rules versus display autonomy: Emotion regulation, emotional exhaustion, and task performance in a call center simulation. *Journal of Occupational Health Psychology*, 12(3), 301–318.

Gosserand, R. H., & Diefendorff, J. M. (2005). Emotional display rules and emotional labor: The moderating role of commitment. *Journal of Applied Psychology*, 90(6), 1256–1264.

Grandey, A. (2000). Emotion regulation in the workplace: A new way to conceptualize emotional labor. *Journal of Occupational Health Psychology*, 5(1), 95–110.

Grandey, A. (2003). When "the show must go on": Surface and deep acting as predictors of emotional exhaustion and service delivery. *Academy of Management Journal*, 46(1), 86–96.

Grandey, A., Fisk, G., Mattila, A., Jansen, K. J., & Sideman, L. (2005). Is service with a smile enough? Authenticity of positive displays during service encounters. *Organizational Behavior & Human Decision Processes*, 96(1), 38–55.

Grandey, A., Fisk, G. M., & Steiner, D. D. (2005). Must "service with a smile" be stressful? The moderating role of personal control for American and French employees. *Journal of Applied Psychology*, 90(5), 893–904.

Grandey, A., Kern, J., & Frone, M. (2007). Verbal abuse from outsiders versus insiders: Comparing frequency, impact on emotional exhaustion, and the role of emotional labor. *Journal of Occupational Health Psychology, 12*(1), 63–79.

Gross, J. (1998a). Antecedent- and response-focused emotion regulation: Divergent consequences for experience, expression, and physiology. *Journal of Personality and Social Psychology, 74*(1), 224–237.

Gross, J. (1998b). The emerging field of emotion regulation: An integrative review. *Review of General Psychology, 2*(3), 271–299.

Groth, M., Hennig-Thurau, T., & Wang, K. (2013). The customer experience of emotional labor. In A. A. Grandey, J. M. Diefendorff & D. E. Rupp (Eds.), *Emotional labor in the 21ˢᵗ century: Diverse perspectives on emotion regulation at work*. New York, NY: Psychology Press/Routledge.

Groth, M., Hennig-Thurau, T., & Walsh, G. (2009). Customer reactions to emotional labor: The roles of employee acting strategies and customer detection accuracy. *Academy of Management Journal, 52*(5), 958–974.

Hochschild, A. R. (1979). Emotion work, feeling rules, and social-structure. *American Journal of Sociology, 85*(3), 551–575.

Hochschild, A. R. (1983). *The managed heart: Commercialization of human feeling*. Berkeley, CA: University of California Press.

Holman, D., Martinez-Inigo, D., & Totterdell, P. (2008a). Emotional labour and employee well-being: an integrative review. In N. M. Ashkanasy & C. L. Cooper (Eds.), *Research Companion to Emotion in Organizations* (pp. 301–359). Northampton, MA: Edward Elgar Publishing.

Holman, D., Martinez-Inigo, D., & Totterdell, P. (2008b). Emotional labour and employee well-being: an integrative review. In N. M. Ashkanasy & C. L. Cooper (Eds.), *Research Companion to Emotion in Organizations* (pp. 301–359). Northampton, MA: Edward Elgar Publishing.

Hülsheger, U. R., & Schewe, A. F. (2011). On the costs and benefits of emotional labor: A meta-analysis of three decades of research. *Journal of Occupational Health Psychology, 16*(3), 361–389.

Humphrey, S. E., Nahrgang, J. D., & Morgeson, F. P. (2007). Integrating motivational, social, and contextual work design features: A meta-analytic summary and theoretical extension of the work design literature. *Journal of Applied Psychology, 92*(5), 1332–1356.

Judge, T. A., Woolf, E. F., & Hurst, C. (2009). Is emotional labor more difficult for some than for others? A multi-level, experience sampling study. *Personnel Psychology, 62*, 57–88.

Kruml, S., & Geddes, D. (2000). Catching fire without burning out: Is there an ideal way to perform emotional labor? In N. M. Ashkanasy, C. E. J. Hartel & W. J. Zerbe (Eds.), *Emotions in the workplace: Research, theory and practice*. Westport, CT: Quorum.

Leidner, R. (1993). *Fast food, fast talk: Service work and the routinization of everyday life*. Berkeley, CA: University of California Press.

Lively, K. J. (2000). Reciprocal Emotion management: working together to maintain stratification in private law firms. *Work and Occupations, 27*, 32–63.

Lively, K. J., & Powell, B. (2006). Emotional expression at work and at home:

Domain, status or individual characteristics?". *Social Psychology Quarterly,* 69(1), 17–38.

Martin, J., Knopoff, K., & Beckman, C. (1998). An alternative to bureaucratic impersonality and emotional labor: Bounded emotionality at The Body Shop. *Administrative Science Quarterly, 43*(2), 429–469.

Mattila, A., & Enz, C. (2002). The role of emotions in service encounters. *Journal of Service Research, 4*(4), 268–277.

Meanwell, E., Wolfe, J. D., & Hallett, T. (2008). Old paths and new directions: Studying emotions in the workplace. *Sociology Compass, 2*(2), 537–559.

Morris, J. A., & Feldman, D. C. (1996). The dimensions, antecedents, and consequences of emotional labor. *Academy of Management Review, 21*(4), 986–1010.

Niven, K., Totterdell, P., Holman, D., & Cameron, D. (2013). Emotional labor at the unit-level. In A. A. Grandey, J. M. Diefendorff & D. E. Rupp (Eds.), *Emotional labor in the 21st century: Diverse perspectives on emotion regulation at work.* New York, NY: Psychology Press/Routledge.

Pugh, D., Groth, M., & Hennig-Thurau, T. (2011). Willing and able to fake emotions: A closer examination of the link between emotional dissonance and employee well-being. *Journal of Applied Psychology, 96*(2), 377–390.

Pugh, S. (2001). Service with a smile: Emotional contagion in the service encounter. *Academy of Management Journal, 44*(5), 1018–1027.

Pugh, S. D., Diefendorff, J. M., & Moran, C. M. (2013). Emotional labor: Organization-level influences, strategies, and outcomes. In A. A. Grandey, J. M. Diefendorff & D. E. Rupp (Eds.), *Emotional labor in the 21st century: Diverse perspectives on emotion regulation at work.* New York, NY: Psychology Press/Routledge.

Rafaeli, A. (1989). When clerks meet customers: A test of variables related to emotional expression on the job. *Journal of Applied Psychology, 74*(3), 385–393.

Rafaeli, A., & Sutton, R. I. (1987). Expression of Emotion as Part of the Work Role. *Academy of Management Review, 12*(1), 23–37.

Rafaeli, A., & Sutton, R. I. (1989). The expression of emotion in organizational life. *Research in Organizational Behavior, 11*, 1–42.

Rubin, R. S., Tardino, V. M. S., Daus, C. S., & Munz, D. C. (2005). A reconceptualization of the emotional labor construct: On the development of an integrated theory of perceived emotional dissonance and emotional labor. In C. E. J. Hartel, W. J. Zerbe & N. M. Ashkanasy (Eds.), *Emotions in organizational behavior* (pp. 189–211). Mahwah, New Jersey: Erlbaum.

Rupp, D. E., & Spencer, S. (2006). When customers lash out: The effects of customer interactional injustice on emotional labor and the mediating role of discrete emotions. *Journal of Applied Psychology, 91*(4), 971–978.

Schaubroeck, J., & Jones, J. R. (2000). Antecedents of workplace emotional labor dimensions and moderators of their effects on physical symptoms. *Journal of Organizational Behavior, 21*, 163–183.

Sloan, M. (2004). The effects of occupational characteristics on the experience and expression of anger in the workplace. *Work and Occupations, 31*(1), 38–72.

Spencer, S., & Rupp, D. (2009). Angry, guilty and conflicted: Injustice toward coworkers heightens emotional labor through cognitive and emotional mechanisms. *Journal of Applied Psychology, 94*(2), 429–444.

Stenross, B., & Kleinman, S. (1989). The highs and lows of emotional labor: Detectives' encounters with criminals and victims. *Journal of Contemporary Ethnography, 17*(4), 435–452.

Sutton, R. I. (1991). Maintaining Norms About Expressed Emotions - the Case of Bill Collectors. *Administrative Science Quarterly, 36*(2), 245–268.

Sutton, R. I., & Rafaeli, A. (1988). Untangling the relationships between displayed emotions and organizational sales: The case of convenience stores. [Article]. *Academy of Management Journal, 31*(3), 461.

Sy, T., Cote, S., & Saavedra, R. (2005). The contagious leader: Impact of leader's mood on the mood of group members, group affective tone, group processes. *Journal of Applied Psychology, 90*(2), 295–305.

Terkel, S. (1972). *Working.* New York: The New Press.

Theodosius, C. (2008). *Emotional labour in health care: The unmanaged heart of nursing.* London: Routledge.

Thoits, P. A. (2004). Emotion norms, emotion work, and social order. In S. R. Manstead, N. Frijda & A. Fischer (Eds.), *Feelings and emotions* (pp. 359–378). Cambridge: Cambridge University Press.

Tidd, K. L., & Lockard, J. S. (1978). Monetary significance of the affiliative smile: A case for reciprocal altruism. *Bulletin of the Psychonomic Society, 11,* 344–346.

Tolich, M. B. (1993). Alienating and liberating emotions at work: Supermarket clerks' performance of customer service. *Journal of Contemporary Ethnography, 22*(3), 361–381.

Totterdell, P., & Holman, D. (2003). Emotion regulation in customer service roles: Testing a model of emotional labor. *Journal of Occupational Health Psychology, 8*(1), 55–73.

Trougakos, J. P., Jackson, C. L., & Beal, D. J. (2011). Service without a smile: Comparing the consequences of neutral and positive display rules. *Journal of Applied Psychology, 96*(2), 350–362.

Tsai, W.-C., & Huang, Y.-M. (2002). Mechanisms linking employee affective delivery and customer behavioral intentions. *Journal of Applied Psychology, 87*(5), 1001–1008.

Tsai, W. C. (2001). Determinants and consequences of employee displayed positive emotions. *Journal of Management, 27*(4), 497–512.

Tschan, F., Rochat, S., & Zapf, D. (2005). It's not only clients: Studying emotion work with clients and co-workers with an event-sampling approach. *Journal of Occupational and Organizational Psychology, 78,* 1–27.

van Jaarsveld, D., & Poster, W. (2013). Call centers: Emotional labor over the phone. In A. A. Grandey, J. M. Diefendorff & D. E. Rupp (Eds.), *Emotional labor in the 21st century: Diverse perspectives on emotion regulation at work.* New York, NY: Psychology Press/Routledge.

Van Kleef, G. A., Homan, A. C., Beersma, B., van Knippenberg, D., van Knippenberg, B., & Damen, F. (2006). *Understanding the effects of leader emotions on team performance. The effectiveness of angry versus happy leaders depends on followers' cognitive style*. Paper presented at the Annual Meeting of the Academy of Management.

Van Maanen, J., & Kunda, G. (1989). Real feelings: Emotional expression and organizational culture. *Research in organizational behavior* (Vol. 11, pp. 43–103). Greenwich, CT: JAI Press.

Vohs, K. D., Baumeister, R., & Ciarocco, N. J. (2005). Self-regulation and self-presentation: Regulatory resource depletion impairs impression management and effortful self-presentation depletes regulatory resources. *Journal of Personality and Social Psychology, 88*(4), 632–657.

Wharton, A. (2009). The sociology of emotional labor. *Annual Review of Sociology, 35,* 147–165.

Wharton, A. S. (1993). The affective consequences of service work: Managing emotions on the job. *Work and Occupations, 20*(2), 205–232.

Wharton, A. S., & Erickson, R. J. (1993). Managing emotions on the job and at home: Understanding the consequences of multiple emotional roles. *Academy of Management Review, 18*(3), 457–486.

Wharton, A. S., & Erickson, R. J. (1995). The consequences of caring: Exploring the links between women's job and family emotion work. *The Sociological Quarterly, 36*(2), 273–296.

Zerbe, W. (2000). Emotional dissonance and well-being. In N. M. Ashkanasy, C. E. J. Hartel & W. J. Zerbe (Eds.), *Emotions in the workplace: Research, theory and practice.* Westport, CT: Quorum.

# Person Perspectives: Within, Between, Dyadic and Group

# Episodic Intrapersonal Emotion Regulation

## Or, Dealing with Life as it Happens

DANIEL J. BEAL • JOHN P. TROUGAKOS

The regulation of emotion is a fundamental aspect of our social lives (Côté, 2005). It is particularly essential for interpersonal communication (Hareli & Rafaeli, 2008; Van Kleef, 2009), and there is perhaps no greater venue for human communication than our work lives. Consequently, to the extent that jobs involve regular contact with other people, they will necessarily involve the regulation of emotion. Although it is true that jobs in which employees interact with the public likely place greater importance on maintaining display rules (as being effective in these jobs is in some way defined by displaying the appropriate emotions to customers or clients), emotion regulation is likely important to virtually all jobs. As such, we view emotion regulation as a common, even quotidian aspect of our lives at work that impacts important outcomes for virtually all employees.

That said, we also assume that no workers are in a constant state of strenuous emotion regulation. For example, efforts directed at presenting a desired emotional expression – the form of emotion regulation on which we will place the greatest emphasis – are unlikely to occur when one's current affective state is congruent with the desired emotional display rules of the situation (Grandey, 2000; Hochschild, 1983). If emotion regulation is not happening all the time (i.e., is not a constant, stable effort), then time enters the picture as a potentially important factor. When do people engage in emotion regulation? For how long does it last? Given that there are different strategies used to regulate emotions (Gross, 1998a), how are these strategies implemented over time? Are multiple strategies used throughout the day? In response to the same emotion? At the same time? Our goal in this chapter is to provide answers – or at least plausible suggestions – to these questions. We do so by discussing *two major themes*:

First we will discuss the temporal structure of emotion regulation; in particular, when do instances of emotion regulation start and stop? Here, we draw on literature examining the episodic structure of our lives, noting that emotion regulation, like many other experiences, can be meaningfully constructed and discussed in terms of discrete, coherent episodes. Second, we dissect the thoughts and behaviors that occur during emotion regulation episodes, emphasizing the manner in which events unfold over time within a given episode. Having a precise understanding of what occurs on these occasions is fundamental. Fortunately, these processes have been discussed by others (e.g., Grandey, 2000; Gross, 1998a), and so our efforts will integrate and clarify several perspectives and add our own temporal considerations.

Although emotion regulation is an experiential process occurring at the intrapersonal level of analysis, often it is aggregated to higher levels of analysis in emotional labor research, such as the individual, dyad, or group. This is not to say that such shifts in level-of-analysis should not occur, but typically when this happens there is little consideration of whether the construct is isomorphic across levels or if its meaning and function change when moving from the intrapersonal level to higher levels (Kozlowski & Klein, 2000). It is not our intention to discuss how intrapersonal emotion regulation emerges at higher levels of analysis (see Dahling & Johnson, 2013; Côté, vanKleef & Sy, 2013; Niven, Totterdell, Holman & Cameron, 2013), but it is our contention that before such aggregation can be credibly articulated, one must first have a firm grasp of what occurs in the immediate intrapersonal context.

## EMOTION REGULATION EPISODES

In discussing emotion regulation episodes, our focus is on immediate intrapersonal contexts in naturalistic workplace settings. There are at least two reasons for our preference of naturalistic over experimental settings. First, the fixed time course introduced by the experimental context may match well neither with how people perceive their own naturally occurring emotional experiences nor the manner in which they would ordinarily regulate them. If emotions vary tremendously in intensity and duration (Frijda, 1993), then it is likely that emotion regulation does as well. Accordingly, the time limits of an experimental session hinder the ability to assess the full implications of emotion experience and regulation. Second, a naturalistic setting implies a larger context in which the experience and regulation of emotion takes place. Examinations in laboratory settings are limited in their capacity to examine the influence of interesting contextual factors. For example, how does emotion regulation change as a result of one's prior experiences at work? How does an instance of emotion regulation influence subsequent thoughts, behaviors, and feelings? To provide answers to these questions, we must understand how people experience and make sense of their emotional lives as they are lived.

To that end, we have emphasized the notion of episodes as units of time that are useful in capturing immediate subjective processes (Beal, Trougakos, Weiss, & Green, 2006; Beal & Weiss, in press; Beal, Weiss, Barros, & MacDermid, 2005). The idea of an episodic structure to our lives begins by looking to how we subjectively partition the stream of our daily experiences. Memory researchers conclude that we often chunk our experiences in multiple ways, typically in a hierarchical fashion (Conway & Pleydell-Pearce, 2000), with specific events nested within broader episodes. Recent research by Zacks and his colleagues (Kurby & Zacks, 2008; Zacks, Speer, Swallow, Braver, & Reynolds, 2007; Zacks & Tversky, 2001) suggests that there is a functional reason why people tend to chunk streams of experience into cohesive episodes: doing so helps one encode and consolidate memories of the events that took place during the episode, providing meaning to an otherwise overwhelming stream of experience (Swallow, Zacks, & Abrams, 2009).

If we use an episodic structure to make sense of our experiences, then what serves as the basis for such a structure? By way of example, our earlier work identified and examined a particular type of episode that was relevant for understanding the interface of emotions and effectiveness at work. These performance episodes were defined as "behavioral segments that are thematically organized around organizationally relevant goals or objectives" (Beal et al., 2005, p. 1055). This definition makes it clear that goals reflect one of the most common bases for the creation of episodic boundaries. When we engage in some activity, we do so commonly through the invocation and implementation of goals associated with the activity. As a result, when we reflect back on our day, we can easily describe it in terms of discrete, coherent activities. In this way, goals serve to structure our daily experiences into episodes.

We suggest that goals can also provide structure to episodes of emotion regulation. In an attempt to preempt potential confusion, we will note here that performance episodes and emotion regulation episodes need not reflect independent segments of experience. Each type of episode merely reflects one way of parsing the stream of experience. Toward that end, and analogous to performance episodes, we can define emotion regulation episodes as segments of experience that are thematically organized around goals for regulating our emotional experiences and expressions.

Evidence for the existence of such goals is abundant. In workplace contexts, emotion regulation goals often are borne out of organizational display rules (Diefendorff & Richard, 2003). If a service organization explicitly requires employees to appear enthusiastic and friendly toward customers, then employees are likely to implement goals of achieving this sort of emotional display when interacting with customers. Of course, there are many other sources for emotion regulation goals as well. Individuals might have personal standards for the expression of particular emotions (Diefendorff & Gosserand, 2003; Gross & John, 2003), or there might be aspects of a dyadic interaction that initiate regulation goals (Côté, 2005). Although the particular goals that are relevant to controlling one's emotions certainly are important and a topic to which we return later in the chapter, for now we are primarily interested in their capacity to provide structure to emotion regulation episodes.

Given the potential boundary conditions in identifying an emotion regulation episode, how do we know one when we see one? As the definition offered above suggests, the two necessary features of an emotion regulation episode include an active goal and a coherent set of experiences related to that goal. Such episodes necessarily emphasize an experienced or anticipated discrepancy between display rule goals (including personal standards for expressing emotions) and experienced emotions. Those familiar with control theory will note a large degree of similarity in the language and concepts discussed here as well as in the next few sections. This is not accidental; the similarities of some aspects of control theory and the episodic structure of experience speak to the powerful organizing function of goals in our daily lives (Kruglanski et al., 2002). Emotion regulation goals likely reflect what control theorists would call principle controls. They do not specify an exact course of action, but rather guide the choices of actions that we make (Carver & Scheier, 1998). We suggest that the dynamic changes in active principle controls may also serve the function of chunking the stream of our experience into discernible and memorable episodes.

At this point, we can take a glimpse at the manner in which emotion regulation might progress episodically over the course of a day. Imagine, for example, a random day in the life of a retail customer service worker. That worker might break down his or her day in any number of ways. As we've discussed elsewhere (Beal & Weiss, in press, Beal et al., 2005), one possible way is based on task-related goals, or performance episodes; here, however, we emphasize a structure based on emotion regulation goals: emotion regulation episodes. A visual presentation of this hypothetical workday appears in Figure 2.1. Note that we have portrayed display rule goals in this figure as constant within a given episode. In truth, display rule goals are likely to fluctuate within an episode in accordance with multiple factors, such as current affective state, difficulty of the goal, or slight changes in the environment (e.g., presence/absence of others). To simplify our exposition, however, we will maintain the hypothetical fiction of display rule constancy.

Several features of Figure 2.1 are worth noting. First, there are occasions where display rules may not be a salient aspect of one's experience, such as during a break from work or when working alone. The result is periods of time that are not considered emotion regulation episodes. Furthermore, occasions can occur where goals are in place, but an emotion regulation episode is not occurring. These instances reflect the fact that regulation episodes are a function of goal discrepancies: when one's affective state is consistent with display rule goals, regulation is not a defining feature of the experience. Finally, although emotion regulation episodes may often align with performance episodes, it does not need to be the case. One might not have a strong display rule goal while opening the store if, for example, relatively few customers are present. Nevertheless, these two levels of display rules may be incorporated into a single performance episode. Furthermore, one might have similar display rule goals across multiple sequential performance episodes, giving at least the potential for a single emotion regulation episode to cross multiple performance episodes.

## WITHIN AN EMOTION REGULATION EPISODE

Now that we have discussed the manner in which emotion regulation proceeds throughout the workday, we will next delve with greater precision into the processes occurring within a particular emotion regulation episode. A great deal of research and theory currently exists that either touches on or explicitly addresses the topic of what regulatory activities occur as a discrepant affective event approaches or is experienced. As such, our goal here is not to reinvent a set of processes for regulating one's emotions; rather, it is to reorganize and clarify the range of processes that are likely to occur in an experiential, intrapersonal manner, using the episode as the unit of time over which these processes occur. As discussed above, an emotion regulation episode commences when a discrepancy is noted between current or anticipated emotions and the goals in place that

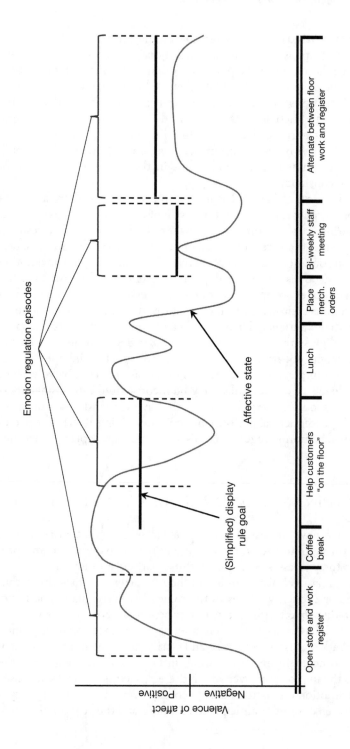

**Figure 2.1** Emotion regulation episodes during a day in the life of a hypothetical retail customer service employee.

dictate what emotions should be expressed. This discrepancy, which marks the beginning of the negative feedback loop described in control theory (Carver & Scheier, 1998), is based on the awareness of one's current emotions as well as the existence of a target emotion.

## The Targets and Timing of Emotion Regulation Discrepancies

Emotion regulation carries with it notions of both emotion experience and emotion expression. Complicating matters, these two concepts can be applied both to the awareness of one's current (or anticipated) emotions as well as to the goal of desired emotions. In the current chapter, we will focus on goals related to desired emotional expressions as opposed to emotional states (cf., Larsen, 2000). It is not that efforts to achieve a desired emotional state are not germane to workplace contexts; indeed, the areas of occupational stress, health, and well-being often focus on such efforts (Diefendorff & Gosserand, 2003; Edwards, 1992). The purpose of this volume, however, is concerned with emotional labor, and emotional labor specifically involves the individually and organizationally mandated display rules that are in place at work. It is true that attempts to improve affective states at work relate strongly to emotional labor (Pugliesi, 1999), but we see our purview as focused on the ways individuals achieve desired expressions at work.

Though we have singled out emotion expression as the goal state to be examined, there still is the distinction between perceptions of one's current experience or perceptions of one's current expression. We suggest that this distinction has important implications for the types of regulatory efforts that are undertaken to reduce the discrepancy. In particular, a focus on one's current emotional state is likely to result in efforts to change that state to be more in line with the desired expressions. Early research in emotional labor referred to these efforts as *deep acting* (Hochschild, 1983), a category of strategies paralleling the Stanislavski system of acting wherein actors would strive to achieve the same emotional state as their characters, with the presumption that an earnest and inspiring performance would follow. In contrast to altering one's emotional state, a focus on current expressions is likely to result in efforts to change those expressions to be more in line with what is desired. In the emotional labor literature, these efforts to alter the physical expression of emotion have been termed *surface acting*, and used as a counterpoint to deep acting.

In addition to this distinction concerning the object of focus in perceiving a discrepancy, there also is the notion of *when* the discrepancy is noticed and acted upon. Gross (1998a) has developed an extensive model based on when these regulatory efforts are initiated during the emotion generation process. Given the specificity of this model and our similar emphasis on the time course of such processes, we will borrow extensively from this work. Although Gross included strategies that extended far backward in time from the affective event (e.g., situation selection), we will emphasize the strategies people employ in the near-term, beginning with the initiation of the regulatory episode. We do so in an effort to match what is likely to occur during a single episode of emotion regulation, in which one or many affective events may be experienced.

## Appraisal Strategies

To set the stage for how these processes unfold, consider the manner in which prototypical emotions are experienced. First, there is an initiating affective event that carries with it some sort of object of attention (Weiss & Cropanzano, 1996). Many emotion theorists suggest that such events set off a cascade of fast- and slow-acting processes of appraisal (Lazarus, 1991). Once these appraisals have culminated in the initial experience of a particular emotion, the nature of this experience transmutes as continuing reappraisals of the event occur (Frijda, 1993). For example, the initial experience of envy often is followed by further appraisals of unfairness (i.e., as someone else has the object of envy), resulting in a transmutation into hostility (Sundie, Ward, Beal, Chin, & Geiger-Oneto, 2009). If, however, the individual appraises the event as reflecting his or her own shortcomings, then envy can transmute into depression (Miceli & Castelfranchi, 2007).

Given the reliance of emotional experience on initial and subsequent appraisals of the affective event, it seems obvious that one way to alter the resulting emotion and its expression is to first alter the manner in which it is appraised. Gross (1998a) termed such efforts *cognitive reappraisal* and stressed the potentially beneficial aspects of implementing these strategies (see Butler et al., 2003; Gross & John, 2003; and Richards & Gross, 2000 for more on these benefits).

Gross (1998a) also suggested that these efforts emphasized elements of experience that occur prior to the emotion, including them in the broader category of antecedent-focused strategies. Our discussion diverges somewhat from this categorization to emphasize that there are multiple opportunities throughout a particular episode to accomplish such modifications of appraisals. For example, much like antecedent-focused strategies, a yet-to-be-experienced discrepant emotion could be anticipated and interpretations of the upcoming event could be altered before it occurs. We refer to this as *anticipatory appraisal strategies*. If such anticipation did not occur, one could still alter the way the event is being appraised as it occurs. We term these efforts *concurrent appraisal strategies*. Finally, once the emotion arrives in full force, it is still possible to temper one's reactions through subsequent *reappraisal strategies*. These distinctions acknowledge factors that are likely in play during different phases of an emotion regulation episode and highlight the importance of temporal considerations in the unfolding of an emotion regulation episode. It is also worthy of note that within a given work context (e.g., a particular job, a particular set of co-workers, a particular affective climate, etc.) all three of these strategies are likely to begin as relatively controlled, deliberative processes, but given some level of consistency in the features of one's work context, may slowly become automatized, requiring little conscious reflection. Here, we discuss the more controlled forms of these processes, but will return to the idea of automatic emotion regulation afterward.

### Anticipatory appraisal strategies

Imagine that you are a graduate student whose advisor is notorious for her tendency to berate students when they hand in what she perceives to be work of low quality. You are about to go in to a meeting with this advisor after having turned in what you know to be less than your best effort. As you mull over the array of potential insults that seem imminent, you coach yourself by saying "It's just the way she is, it's nothing personal. It'll help me to handle difficult audiences in future meetings and presentations." The anticipation of future unwanted emotional states is the defining feature of this form of reappraisal. The example involves alterations of different components of the appraisal process. The first statement attenuates any potential self-blame by suggesting that there is no way that the situation can be controlled and by noting that it's not really a personal attack. Appraisals of self-blame tend to result in guilt or shame (Lazarus, 1991), which may also lead to feelings of personal distress (Tangney, 1991), so interpreting the impending interaction in this way will help eliminate these emotions. The second statement helps alter the valence of the event and is consistent with popular notions of putting a positive spin on something. In addition to altering the valence, it allows the person to incorporate greater levels of personal control over the positive event by suggesting that it is a learning experience that, if undertaken, will improve one's character (Seery, Holman, & Silver, 2010).

Admittedly, this example is only one of the many ways in which a particular negative event might be reinterpreted. In addition to the unique qualities of any given event, there are many potential components of the appraisal process that could be altered in an effort to reduce an upcoming discrepancy between how someone will feel and what that person wishes to express. For example, Scherer's (2001) component process model of emotion appraisal mentions more than a dozen potential components of appraisal, leaving innumerable options for exactly how one might reappraise an event that likely differ in their effectiveness.

Up to now, we have described aspects of anticipatory appraisal strategies that are more or less common across each of the appraisal strategies we discuss. What makes anticipatory appraisal strategies unique, however, is that the emotion has yet to be experienced. As a result, any efforts undertaken are done so at the behest of an experience that has only been forecasted. One important aspect of such forecasts that is now well-known in the psychological literature is that people are fairly poor at making them (Wilson & Gilbert, 2003), particularly for complex situations that often arise at work (Woodzicka & LaFrance, 2001).

As such, one conclusion would simply be that the increased inaccuracy of the forecasted emotion will lead to less effective regulation of emotion once the event has taken place. Another common bias in affective forecasting – the overestimation of the event's impact on one's emotional state (Wilson, Meyers, & Gilbert, 2003) – suggests that potential inaccuracies might be magnified as the actual event will be less severe than the anticipated experience. It is worth mentioning, however, that some dimensions of appraisal are predicted with greater accuracy, such as valence (Wilson & Gilbert, 2003). In addition, there are some situational factors that might serve to mitigate inaccuracies. For example, if the anticipated event is relatively common, then inaccuracy seems less likely. As we will see later, the relative frequency or novelty of the event may represent an important factor in not only the success of emotion regulation, but also the manner in which it occurs.

## Concurrent appraisal strategies

Putting aside for a moment the upstream influence of engaging in some form of anticipatory appraisal strategy, an individual also may alter the manner in which he or she appraises the affective event as it is being experienced. Although the process is essentially the same as what was described above for anticipatory appraisal strategies, there are aspects of the concurrent timeline that merit consideration. Many emotion scholars converge in their descriptions of the timing of the appraisal process, with primary appraisals (e.g., valence, importance) occurring very quickly and automatically, followed by slower, more deliberative secondary appraisals (e.g., locus of control, coping potential, normative consistency; see Lazarus, 1991 or Scherer, 2001 for examples). It is important to remember, however, that these are not the only processes occurring as reactions to an affective event progress. In particular, numerous events will coincidentally trigger changes in one's physiological functioning, facial and postural configurations, and action tendencies (Mauss, Levenson,

McCarter, Wilhelm, & Gross, 2005). Moreover, these corollaries do not occur in isolation of each other; rather, they represent elements of an integrated system of responses (Izard, 2007).

That said, specific emotional experiences vary in just how integrated these responses are; furthermore, research suggests that some elements of the emotional response may influence other elements of the response. For example, we know that physiological states can have a provocative influence on emotion appraisals (Schachter & Singer, 1962), and that facial configurations influence subjectively experienced states (Zajonc, Murphy, & Inglehart, 1989). Unfortunately, our understanding of these complex interrelations is nascent at best, and so it is difficult to know exactly how the alteration of the appraisals that immediately follow an affective event might influence and be influenced by other elements of the emotional response. One simple supposition, however, is that altering one's default appraisals of an affective event might be made more difficult by relatively fast-acting physiological reactions. For example, if a rude comment from a customer creates rapid activation of the autonomic nervous system (Levenson, 1992), it might be more difficult to select an appraisal that is consistent with the desired emotion, as heightened arousal often impairs the breadth of cognitive functioning (Easterbrook, 1959).

### Reappraisal strategies

Though an affective event has been appraised and the initial emotional response has taken place, this does not mean that the course of emotion is set. As the episode continues, people often will reinterpret the events that have just occurred and arrive at a new set of appraisals. This process can serve to soften, intensify, eliminate, or even transmute the initial emotional response. As with concurrent appraisals, some residual effects of other elements of the emotional response (e.g., heightened physiological arousal) may still exist, potentially hindering attempts to reappraise, but barring reappraisals that serve to intensify the initial response, continued reflection carries with it the possibility of successful regulation of one's emotional expressions. Indeed, the typical form of an emotional experience suggests that a quick peak intensity decays thereafter until awareness of the experience ceases (Sonnemans & Frijda, 1994). To the extent that intensity interferes with attempts to alter appraisals, the prototypical form of an emotion's intensity suggests that reappraisals may occur in more favorable (i.e., less intense) circumstances than during anticipatory or concurrent appraisals (i.e., when experiences are more intense).

Such success depends on a number of factors, many of which are unique to the particular circumstances of the affective event; however, some research speaks to the utility of continued reappraisal of emotional events. For example, research on rumination suggests that continuing to think about a negative event is harmful for well-being. More recent findings, however, suggest that it depends on the type of appraisals that are emphasized when engaging in ruminative thought. If these reappraisals emphasize self-blame, then the initiating negative events are heightened, leading to depressive symptoms (Treynor, Gonzalez, & Nolen-Hoeksema, 2003). If ruminators instead engage in more constructive reflective thought, then negative outcomes are mitigated (Watkins, 2008).

## Distraction Strategies

Moving away from the appraisal class of regulatory strategies, another option available for reducing discrepancies between experienced or anticipated emotions and desired expressions is to distract one's attention away from the affective event. Gross (1998a) included distraction alongside concentration and rumination as a family of strategies termed *attentional deployment*. Here, we focus exclusively on distraction, construed broadly as focusing attention on something other than the affective event. This construal encompasses Gross' (1998a) discussion of concentration yet excludes rumination, as rumination refers to focusing attention on the affective event itself rather than on something other than the affective event (Martin & Tesser, 1996).

This treatment of distraction is consistent with our other work on performance episodes, which emphasizes the discrete categorization of attention as either on-task or off-task (Beal et al., 2005). Here, however, the focus of attention is on the current or anticipated affective event. For example, when individuals perceive that a future event is likely to create an emotion regulation discrepancy, they may select another topic that will absorb their attention, allowing this new focus to drive their affective state. Obviously, the characteristics of such distractions are innumerable; nevertheless, to the extent that they take one's attention away from the perceived source of the emotion regulation discrepancy, they will eliminate its influence. In this way, all distractions have the potential to be effective means of emotion regulation.

Clearly there must be differences, however, in how well distractions function as regulation strategies. Indeed, Gross' (1998a) discussion of concentration alludes to the fact that topics of distraction that tend to draw attention and keep it focused for an extended period of time might be among the most effective means of distraction. This quality of attentional pull represents one important dimension that will determine the effectiveness of a distraction strategy. If, as an affective event transpires, people choose to think about the relative standing of their favorite Midwestern football team (e.g., "how 'bout them Bears?"), only to find that a brief consideration yields a fairly quick end to the distraction, then the affective event is likely to regain control of one's attentional focus. As we have discussed elsewhere (Beal & Weiss, in press; Beal et al., 2005), there are a number of characteristics that can serve to increase the attentional pull of a potential topic of distraction. Engaging in a task where skills and challenges are high (Csikszentmihalyi & LeFevre, 1989), having high levels of intrinsic motivation toward a topic or activity (Gagné & Deci, 2005), the creation of difficult, yet obtainable goals (Locke & Latham, 1990), or the inertia created by engaging in simple repetitive activities (Baldamus, 1961) all are characteristics of distractions that would be effective in grabbing and holding on to one's attention, allowing the affective event to have little to no influence.

The second important characteristic of distraction that is needed for it to be an effective regulation strategy concerns the affective implications of the distraction itself. Choosing a topic of distraction that will also create a discrepancy between one's current and desired states is obviously a faulty strategy. Therefore, to be effective, emotion regulators must have some idea as to how the distraction will affect their feelings. Once again, this involves some amount of affective forecasting and will consequently be fraught with error. Much like its role in anticipatory appraisal, however, fairly simple valence considerations often will be accurate and may represent a relatively quick and easy guide to selecting a topic of distraction. So far, the strategies we have discussed involve efforts to change the emotional experience, with the assumption or perhaps hope that the expression will follow. As such, both appraisal strategies and distraction strategies would be considered *deep acting* in the dramaturgical model of emotional labor (Hochschild, 1983). Next we turn to what this model would consider *surface acting* strategies.

## Expression-Focused Strategies

Here, we refer to attempts to modify the expression of emotion, independent of any attempts to modify the experienced emotion. Gross (1998a) also incorporated this notion in his model and referred to it as response-focused strategies. Our slight modification of the terminology is an attempt to place the spotlight on the key component of these strategies: the expression of emotion. We feel that the term *response* might create confusion, as there are a number of responses possible to an affective event, and only some of them involve the expression of emotion. For example, reappraisal or concurrent appraisal strategies could also be described as being focused on the emotional response.

## Suppression Strategies

Attempts to alter facial expressions or postural configurations away from undesired expressions fall into this category. Suppression typically refers both to completely hiding one's emotional expression as well as intermediate efforts that simply mitigate the unwanted emotion (e.g., the slight stifling of a smile when enjoyment is inappropriate). A great deal of research supports the notion that this strategy is one of the most socially and cognitively challenging (Butler et al., 2003; Richards & Gross, 2000), and results in a decrease in subsequent energy and effortful activities (Muraven & Baumeister, 2000; Trougakos, Jackson, & Beal, 2011). Part of the difficulty in suppressing one's expressions likely occurs as a result of the natural expressive tendencies that exist in social interactions (Hareli & Rafaeli, 2008). For example, research demonstrates that inhibiting the tendency to mimic another's facial expressions requires the recruitment of a large array of neural mechanisms and results in delays in coordinating the appropriate facial muscles (Lee, Dolan, & Critchley, 2008).

Given this burdensome view of suppression, one might wonder why individuals would ever choose such a strategy. Cursory introspection of our own experiences at work makes the answer to this quandary quite clear: often, one cannot anticipate the occurrence of an affective event in our work environment, nor can we always decide on the appropriate response ahead of time. Furthermore, the presence of complex workplace display rules combined with other potential emotion display goals at work (e.g., personal standards for emotion expression) paints a picture of great complexity in navigating one's emotional environment while at work, and leads to an important conclusion: although suppression is likely the most difficult emotion regulation strategy, carrying with it numerous negative outcomes, it may be a common or even necessary strategy to employ. That is, if people cannot accurately anticipate their emotion display context and often are inaccurate in anticipating their future affective states, then expression-focused strategies such as suppression may represent the default mode of emotion regulation. We will discuss this point shortly, but first stop to describe a final form of emotion regulation: faking.

### Faking Strategies

Instead of selecting a suppression strategy involving the inhibition of emotion expressions, one might instead choose to actively fake an emotional expression that is desirable for the particular episode. Just as suppression included even minor efforts at reducing unwanted expressions, faking includes amplifications of desired expressions. The difference between suppression and faking is subtle, yet potentially important. For example, Côté and Morgan (2002) found that although suppression was associated with subsequent decreases in job satisfaction, amplification of positive emotions led to increases in job satisfaction, presumably due to more pleasant interactions with co-workers. It does appear, however, that the exaggeration of some emotions carries with it difficulties similar to those of suppression. For example, Schmeichel and colleagues (Schmeichel, Demaree, Robinson, & Pu, 2006) found that the exaggeration of disgust led to increased depletion on a subsequent cognitive task.

Presumably, faking strategies are enacted to express a particular emotion to one or more observers. What happens, then, if the "performance" seems insincere? A number of studies have demonstrated that observers can detect true or "Duchenne" smiles from smiles that are inauthentic (e.g., Frank, Ekman, & Friesen, 1993), and that, at least in customer service contexts, the faking of positive emotions may be unlikely to succeed due to perceptions of inauthenticity (Grandey, Fisk, Mattila, Jansen, & Sideman, 2005). Further complicating matters is research suggesting that such surface acting *can* be effective in communicating the desired expressions to observers, at least for brief episodes (Beal et al., 2006; Gross, 1998b). Suffice it to say that further research is needed to fully understand the effects of faking relative to suppression of specific emotions in specific contexts.

## *Simultaneous or Sequential Strategies*

Throughout the discussion so far, we have described each strategy as if it were the sole strategy in use, or at least as if each strategy was orthogonal to the use of other strategies. Although this approach allows us to simplify our discussion, it ignores what is likely the more common practice: individuals will use multiple regulation strategies during a given episode. Consider, for example, the second emotion regulation episode depicted in Figure 2.1. It commences when the employee encounters a particularly obnoxious customer and anticipates that the previously pleasant state is quickly deteriorating, making it increasingly at odds with the desired positive display rule goal. To combat this discrepancy, the employee attempts to think about something other than the customer's bad behavior (distraction). At some point, however, it becomes clear that this strategy is not working. Given the difficulties noted with many of the strategies described earlier, this situation is not unlikely, and it seems probable that employees will often switch to a new strategy to reduce the display rule discrepancy. In our example, it appears that this second attempt was more successful as the employee experiences improving mood as lunch approaches.

Our contention that individuals often use multiple strategies during a single episode comes from an emerging literature that examines emotion regulation using a within-person, experiential approach (see Beal, 2012). For example, Bono, Foldes, Vinson, and Muros (2007) examined emotion regulation in health care professionals four times a day over a two-week period. Although only expression-focused strategies were examined (i.e., hiding negative and faking positive), the within-person correlation was .88, suggesting that these two strategies are almost always enacted together. In our own work (e.g., Beal, Trougakos, Dalal, & Weiss, 2011), we asked restaurant servers at multiple times during their shifts to report the extent to which they had faked, hidden, or reappraised emotions. Results again suggested a strong within-episode correspondence between the strategies (within *r*'s ranged from .35 to .61).

Interestingly, other research suggests that strategy use is less interconnected when examined over intervals that encompass multiple episodes. For example, two studies (Judge, Woolf, & Hurst, 2009; Scott & Barnes, 2011) have examined the use of deep and surface acting strategies at the daily level of analysis (i.e., respondents estimated the extent to which they used the strategies throughout each day for multiple days). At this level of aggregation, the relation appears to diminish greatly (.20 in one study and .07 in the other). One possibility that would produce this pattern is if multiple strategies are attempted during each episode, but when reflecting back on the episodes of that day, only the most salient strategies are recalled (e.g., ones that seemed most, or perhaps least, effective).

Although research examining simultaneous strategy use is only just surfacing, our control theory perspective suggests that its occurrence is likely. As we noted earlier, if anticipatory appraisal strategies have inherent inaccuracies, then it seems likely that perceived discrepancies will not be prevented (or reduced) from the use of this strategy. As a result, once the emotion occurs, another form of appraisal strategy – or some other strategy altogether – will likely be implemented. This reasoning brings us back to a point made earlier. We suspect that expression-focused strategies represent a common addition to the emotion regulation arsenal. If early, antecedent-focused strategies are ineffective, then the continued presence of an emotion regulation discrepancy would appear to make attempts to modify expressions a frequent last resort to displaying inappropriate emotions.

A final possibility is that rather than sequentially – or perhaps in addition to sequential adoption of regulation strategies – multiple strategies might be implemented simultaneously. We suggest, however, that the consciously controlled strategies outlined above are unlikely to be implemented in tandem. First, all of these strategies require some amount of cognitive resources, making simultaneous strategy use somewhat prohibitive given limited cognitive capacity. Of course, some strategies, such as those that are expression-focused, require relatively greater amounts of cognitive resources (Richards & Gross, 2000), but even those that are less cognitively burdensome require one to focus the content of thought on a specific subject, and these subjects are at odds with each other.

## Automatic Emotion Regulation

Throughout the above discussion of regulation strategies, we have purposely focused on situations where individuals are consciously aware of the discrepancy between current or anticipated state and an emotion expression goal. Furthermore, we have portrayed the above strategies as deliberative, controlled processes that individuals willingly enact to attain these goals. Although we do not wish to undermine the value of this representation, we should acknowledge that these controlled processes are not the only manner in which emotions are regulated; indeed, such deliberative efforts potentially may reflect a less common set of processes. There is an emerging consensus in the social cognitive literature that many, if not most, regulatory processes can be engaged automatically and that such automatic processes are commonly operating in the background of our consciously experienced lives (Bargh & Chartrand, 1999).

Take, for example, goals. Numerous studies now have demonstrated that goals can be implemented automatically (Bargh, Gollwitzer, Lee-Chai, Barndollar, & Trötschel, 2001), operate automatically (Custers & Aarts, 2005), do not occupy attentional resources (Deshon, Brown, & Greenis, 1996), and can trigger overt behavior (Chartrand & Bargh, 1996). Furthermore, the pervasive nature of these nonconscious goals extends into the emotion regulation domain (Mauss, Bunge, & Gross, 2007), and can reflect at least some of the particular aspects of specific controlled strategies (e.g., Williams, Bargh, Nocera, & Gray, 2009). Although space limitations and the infancy of the applicable literature prohibit a detailed explanation of such automatic processes in emotion regulation, there are a few issues that are relevant here.

First, there is the question of which aspects of emotion regulation can be nonconsciously activated. In terms of perceiving discrepancies, control theorists have always contended that negative feedback loops often operate outside of conscious awareness (Carver & Scheier, 1998). This would suggest not only that one can perceive discrepancies automatically, but that one can also engage in discrepancy reduction processes outside of awareness. Indeed, Mauss and colleagues (Mauss et al., 2007) suggest that most, if not all, of the conscious strategies at our disposal also can operate automatically. To some extent, this is unsurprising. Although individuals tend to emphasize some regulation strategies over others (Gross & John, 2003), most of us are at least familiar with the full complement of strategies and undoubtedly have tried all of them at some point in our lives. As a result, and much like the manner in which many other processes move from deliberative, controlled efforts to acquired, automatic skills (Kanfer & Ackerman, 1989), emotion regulation strategies may attain a certain level of automaticity through repeated use (Mauss et al., 2007). Examining how and to what degree different strategies can be successfully implemented outside of our awareness would seem like an interesting and important direction for future research in this area.

## FACTORS AFFECTING REGULATORY PROCESSES

Moving away from the regulatory processes themselves that occur during an emotion regulation episode, we now discuss what we see as several important factors that may influence the manner in which such episodes progress.

### *Immediate Regulatory Capacity*

To the extent that regulation requires effort (i.e., is a more controlled process), it will require and consume regulatory resources (Muraven & Baumeister, 2000). Therefore, it is important to know the nature and extent of earlier regulatory efforts in order to know the likelihood of successfully meeting the regulatory goal for the current episode. Similarly, understanding the nature and extent of emotion regulation in the current episode will be telling of what is to come in future episodes – not just emotion regulation episodes, but any episode involving the effortful regulation of thought or behavior. A series of episodes at work all involving intense regulatory efforts could result in a failure to regulate emotions during a critical emotion regulation episode at the end of this series.

This scenario begs the question of what happens exactly when someone "fails" to regulate? The somewhat absurd extreme interpretation of this idea conjures up images of people blurting out whatever comes to mind along with whatever expressions are desired. Despite the often compelling urge to do just that, we suggest that instead of adopting a stream of consciousness-style lack of regulation, people may simply abandon the current regulatory goal in lieu of a more desirable or more easily obtainable goal. That is, the expectancy and value of an emotion regulation goal may decrease as difficulties are encountered, resulting in either the abandonment of the goal or switching to a new goal (Klein, Austin, & Cooper, 2008). For example, if, while experiencing a difficult customer service encounter, the employee lacks the regulatory strength to maintain perfect composure (i.e., maintain the ideal organizational display rule goal), he or she might instead adopt a "fallback position" involving a more easily maintained emotional expression. Thus, rather than always expressing genuine emotions consistent with display rules, employees may adopt a sarcastically positive demeanor, or a confused expression as if they are having difficulty understanding what the customer is saying, or any of a number of other display goals that do not require the strength required by the initial ideal goal. Note that this idea brings up another issue: it is likely that multiple goals will almost always exist and may vie for attention and implementation during a particular episode of emotion regulation.

## Dueling Goals

If a given episode involves the possibility of multiple, potentially conflicting regulatory goals, then what determines which goals are favored and implemented? One mechanism that is clearly relevant in answering this question is one of the core tenets of control theory: goals are arranged hierarchically, and this hierarchical organization helps determine which goals become salient in any particular situation (Carver & Scheier, 1998). For example, while at work, we may consider the somewhat lofty and higher-order goal of career success. The activation of this goal hierarchy makes subservient goals more likely to also become active (Klein et al., 2008). So, in order to achieve career success, we might try hard to complete the day's work activities as expeditiously and effectively as possible. If these activities involve maintaining organizational display rules, then these too will be increasingly salient during any given episode at work. Through this process, many goals are shunted off to the back of our minds as they are irrelevant to meeting the currently active higher-order goal of career success. For example, goals involving romantic relationships may be less likely to govern our behavior during this time, as the goals of career success and romantic success often do not overlap.

In addition, early introductions of control theory into the psychological literature emphasized what might be considered goal inertia. That is, once a goal is salient and has been implemented, it has relative priority over other goals (Carver & Scheier, 1998). Recent research on goal systems suggests that this effect likely occurs for several reasons. For example, goals that are unfulfilled tend to maintain greater activation relative to other competing goals (Förster, Liberman, & Higgins, 2005), and once a goal is implemented, other competing goals are actively inhibited (Shah, Friedman, & Kruglanski, 2002). Indeed, recent research on goals suggests that when behavior is directed by an active, implemented goal, a variety of factors converge to give that goal priority and inertia in the face of other relevant goals (Förster, Liberman, & Friedman, 2007; Kruglanski et al., 2002).

## Quality of Experienced Emotion

One area that is quite relevant to emotional labor but has, to our knowledge, not received thorough examination, is the potential effects of the emotion itself on regulatory processes. First, emotions obviously vary in their relative intensity (Sonnemans & Frijda, 1994). The general assumption of emotion regulation scholars is that more intense emotions will be more difficult to regulate, but the precise nature of this relation is less clear. For example, is there a simple linear function where more intense emotions gradually become less likely to be regulated, or is there a critical point somewhere along the continuum? In this case, once the intensity of the emotion passes a certain mark, then successful regulation would be nearly impossible. A further question involves the role of self-regulatory strength in setting this hypothetical cut-point. For example, an individual may have a typical range of intensity at which regulatory efforts fail, but this range is modified based upon immediate levels of regulatory strength.

A second aspect of the emotion itself is its duration. Much like intensity, it seems reasonable to suspect that longer emotional experiences may pose a problem for regulatory efforts, as they generate a continual drain on immediate levels of regulatory resources. Indeed, it seems likely that the controlled process of continued reappraisal of the emotion and its consequences may serve as the source of this depletion. There may be other reasons for difficulties in successfully regulating emotions of greater duration. In particular, the specific appraisals that have occurred throughout the experience may themselves contribute to the emotion's duration. For example, if the event is appraised as negative and appraisals of blame focus on the self, then there is a greater likelihood that ruminative, brooding responses will occur (Watkins, 2008). Such responses may then result in a vicious cycle where negative affect leads to brooding, and brooding prolongs negative affect (Moberly & Watkins, 2008). Hopefully, the reverse of this scenario may also occur. That is, it seems plausible that different appraisals may not end or alter the initial experience, but may simply abbreviate it. We see this as another avenue for future research that has yet to be well explored.

## CONCLUSION

In this chapter, we have introduced the concept of an emotion regulation episode as a useful timeframe for understanding more immediate emotion regulation processes. In addition, we described the nature of these processes and explored some of the issues we see as interesting and unanswered. Furthermore, we have identified some of the factors that may serve to alter the typical set of processes that unfold when a discrepancy is perceived between one's current or anticipated emotional experience and what emotions one would ideally like to express. Although our description of these processes is necessarily brief, we hope that it will provide readers with a basic understanding of how individuals regulate their emotions on a day-to-day basis.

# REFERENCES

Baldamus, W. (1961). *Efficiency and effort: An analysis of industrial administration.* London, England: Tavistock.

Bargh, J. A., & Chartrand, T. L. (1999). The unbearable automaticity of being. *American Psychologist, 54,* 462–479.

Bargh, J. A., Gollwitzer, P. M., Lee-Chai, A., Barndollar, K., & Trötschel, R. (2001). The automated will: nonconscious activation and pursuit of behavioral goals. *Journal of Personality and Social Psychology, 81,* 1014–1027.

Beal, D. J. (2012). Industrial/Organizational Psychology. In M. R. Mehl & T. S. Conner (Eds.), *Handbook of research methods for studying daily life* (pp. 601–619). New York, NY: Guilford Press.

Beal, D. J., & Trougakos, J. P. (2013). Episodic intrapersonal emotion regulation: Or, dealing with life as it happens. In A. A. Grandey, J. M. Diefendorff & D. E. Rupp (Eds.), *Emotional Labor in the 21st Century: Diverse Perspectives on Emotion Regulation at Work.* New York, NY: Psychology Press/Routledge.

Beal, D. J., Trougakos, J. P., Dalal, R. S., & Weiss, H. M. (2011). *Episodic emotion regulation processes in restaurant servers.* Unpublished raw data.

Beal, D. J., Trougakos, J. P., Weiss, H. M., & Green, S. G. (2006). Episodic processes in emotional labor: perceptions of affective delivery and regulation strategies. *Journal of Applied Psychology, 91,* 1053–1065.

Beal, D. J., & Weiss, H. M. (in press). The episodic structure of life at work. In A. B. Bakker & K. Daniels (Eds.), *A day in the life of a happy worker.* Psychology Press.

Beal, D. J., Weiss, H. M., Barros, E., & MacDermid, S. M. (2005). An episodic process model of affective influences on performance. *Journal of Applied Psychology, 90,* 1054–1068.

Bono, J. E., Foldes, H. J., Vinson, G., & Muros, J. P. (2007). Workplace emotions: the role of supervision and leadership. *Journal of Applied Psychology, 92,* 1357–1367.

Butler, E. A., Egloff, B., Wilhelm, F. H., Smith, N. C., Erickson, E. a, & Gross, J. J. (2003). The social consequences of expressive suppression. *Emotion, 3,* 48–67.

Carver, C. S., & Scheier, M. F. (1998). *On the self-regulation of behavior.* New York: Cambridge University Press.

Chartrand, T. L., & Bargh, J. A. (1996). Automatic activation of impression formation and memorization goals: Nonconscious goal priming reproduces effects of explicit task instructions. *Journal of Personality and Social Psychology, 71,* 464–478.

Conway, M. A., & Pleydell-Pearce, C. W. (2000). The construction of auto-biographical memories in the self-memory system. *Psychological Review, 107,* 261–288.

Csikszentmihalyi, M., & LeFevre, J. (1989). Optimal experience in work and leisure. *Journal of Personality and Social Psychology, 56,* 815–822.

Custers, R., & Aarts, H. (2005). Positive affect as implicit motivator: on the non-conscious operation of behavioral goals. *Journal of Personality and Social Psychology, 89,* 129–142.

Côté, S. (2005). A social interaction model of the effects of emotion regulation on work strain. *Academy of Management Review, 30,* 509–530.

Côté, S., & Morgan, L. M. (2002). A longitudinal analysis of the association between emotion regulation, job satisfaction, and intentions to quit. *Journal of Organizational Behavior, 23,* 947–962.

Côté, S., Van Kleef, G. A., & Sy, T. (2013). The social effects of emotion regulation in organizations. In A. A. Grandey, J. M. Diefendorff & D. E. Rupp (Eds.), *Emotional Labor in the 21st Century: Diverse Perspectives on Emotion Regulation at Work.* New York, NY: Psychology Press/Routledge.

Dahling, J. J., & Johnson, H. (2013). Motivation, fit, confidence, and skills: How do individual differences influence emotional labor? In A. A. Grandey, J. M. Diefendorff & D. E. Rupp (Eds.), *Emotional Labor in the 21st Century: Diverse Perspectives on Emotion Regulation at Work.* New York, NY: Psychology Press/Routledge.

Deshon, R. P., Brown, K. G., & Greenis, J. L. (1996). Does self-regulation require cognitive resources? Evaluation of resource allocation models of goal setting. *Journal of Applied Psychology, 81,* 595–608.

Diefendorff, J. M., & Gosserand, R. H. (2003). Understanding the emotional labor process: a control theory perspective. *Journal of Organizational Behavior, 24,* 945–959.

Diefendorff, J. M., & Richard, E. M. (2003). Antecedents and consequences of emotional display rule perceptions. *Journal of Applied Psychology, 88,* 284–294.

Easterbrook, J. A. (1959). The effect of emotion on cue utilization and the organization of behavior. *Psychological Review, 66,* 183–201.

Edwards, J. R. (1992). A cybernetic theory of stress, coping, and well-being in organizations. *Academy of Management Review, 17,* 238–274.

Frank, M. G., Ekman, P., & Friesen, W. V. (1993). Behavioral markers and recognizability of the smile of enjoyment. *Journal of Personality and Social Psychology, 64,* 83–93.

Frijda, N. H. (1993). Moods, emotion episodes, and emotions. In M. Lewis & J. M. Haviland (Eds.), *Handbook of emotions* (1st ed., pp. 381–403). New York, NY: Guilford Press.

Förster, J., Liberman, N., & Higgins, E. (2005). Accessibility from active and fulfilled goals. *Journal of Experimental Social Psychology, 41,* 220–239.

Förster, J., Liberman, N., & Friedman, R. S. (2007). Seven principles of goal acti-vation: a systematic approach to distinguishing goal priming from priming of non-goal constructs. *Personality and Social Psychology Review, 11,* 211–233.

Gagné, M., & Deci, E. L. (2005). Self-determination theory and work motivation. *Journal of Organizational Behavior, 26,* 331–362.

Grandey, A. A. (2000). Emotion regulation in the workplace: A new way to conceptualize emotional labor. *Journal of Occupational Health Psychology, 5,* 95–110.

Grandey, A. A., Fisk, G. M., Mattila, A., Jansen, K., & Sideman, L. (2005). Is "service with a smile" enough? Authenticity of positive displays during service encounters. *Organizational Behavior and Human Decision Processes, 96,* 38–55.

Gross, J. J. (1998a). The emerging field of emotion regulation: An integrative review. *Review of General Psychology, 2,* 271–299.

Gross, J. J. (1998b). Antecedent- and response-focused emotion regulation: divergent consequences for experience, expression, and physiology. *Journal of Personality and Social Psychology, 74,* 224–237.

Gross, J. J., & John, O. P. (2003). Individual differences in two emotion regulation processes: Implications for affect, relationships, and well-being. *Journal of Personality and Social Psychology, 85,* 348–362.

Hareli, S., & Rafaeli, A. (2008). Emotion cycles: On the social influence of emotion in organizations. *Research in Organizational Behavior, 28,* 35–59.

Hochschild, A. R. (1983). *The managed heart: Commercialization of human feeling.* Berkeley, CA: University of California Press.

Izard, C. E. (2007). Basic emotions, natural kinds, emotion schemas, and a new paradigm. *Perspectives on Psychological Science, 2,* 260–280.

Judge, T. A., Woolf, E. F., & Hurst, C. (2009). Is emotional labor more difficult for some than for others? A multilevel, experience-sampling study. *Personnel Psychology, 62,* 57–88.

Kanfer, R., & Ackerman, P. L. (1989). Motivation and cognitive abilities: An integrative/aptitude-treatment interaction approach to skill acquisition. *Journal of Applied Psychology, 74,* 657–690.

Klein, H. J., Austin, J. T., & Cooper, J. T. (2008). Goal choice and decision processes. In R. Kanfer, G. Chen, & R. Pritchard (Eds.), *Work motivation: Past, present, and future* (pp. 101–150). New York: Routledge.

Kozlowski, S. W. J., & Klein, K. J. (2000). A multilevel approach to theory and research in organizations: Contextual, temporal, and emergent processes. In Katherine J. Klein & S. W. J. Kozlowski (Eds.), *Multilevel theory, research, and methods in organizations: Foundations, extensions, and new directions* (pp. 3–90). San Francisco: Jossey-Bass.

Kruglanski, A.W., Shah, J. Y., Fishbach, A., Friedman, R., Chun, W. Y., & Sleeth-Keppler, D. (2002). A theory of goal systems. *Advances in Experimental Social Psychology, 34,* 331–378.

Kurby, C. A., & Zacks, J. M. (2008). Segmentation in the perception and memory of events. *Trends in Cognitive Sciences, 12,* 72–79.

Larsen, R. J. (2000). Toward a science of mood regulation. *Psychological Inquiry, 11,* 129–141.

Lazarus, R. S. (1991). *Emotion and adaptation.* New York, NY: Oxford University Press.

Lee, T.-W., Dolan, R. J., & Critchley, H. D. (2008). Controlling emotional expression: behavioral and neural correlates of nonimitative emotional responses. *Cerebral Cortex, 18,* 104–113.

Levenson, R. W. (1992). Autonomic nervous system differences among emotions. *Psychological Science, 3,* 23–27.

Locke, E. A., & Latham, G. P. (1990). *Theory of goal setting and task performance.* Englewood Cliffs, NJ: Prentice Hall.

Martin, L. L., & Tesser, A. (1996). Some ruminative thoughts. *Advances in Social Cognition, 9,* 1–47.

Mauss, I. B., Bunge, S. A., & Gross, J. J. (2007). Automatic emotion regulation. *Social and Personality Psychology Compass, 1,* 146–167.

Mauss, I. B., Levenson, R. W., McCarter, L., Wilhelm, F. H., & Gross, J. J. (2005). The tie that binds? Coherence among emotion experience, behavior, and physiology. *Emotion, 5,* 175–190.

Miceli, M., & Castelfranchi, C. (2007). The envious mind. *Cognition & Emotion, 21,* 449–479.

Moberly, N. J., & Watkins, E. R. (2008). Ruminative self-focus and negative affect: an experience sampling study. *Journal of Abnormal Psychology, 117,* 314–323.

Muraven, M., & Baumeister, R. F. (2000). Self-regulation and depletion of limited resources: Does self-control resemble a muscle? *Psychological Bulletin, 126,* 247–259.

Pugliesi, K. (1999). The consequences of emotional labor: Effects on work stress, job satisfaction, and well-being. *Motivation and Emotion, 23,* 125–154.

Richards, J. M., & Gross, J. J. (2000). Emotion regulation and memory: the cognitive costs of keeping one's cool. *Journal of Personality and Social Psychology, 79,* 410–424.

Schachter, S., & Singer, J. (1962). Cognitive, social, and physiological determinants of emotional state. *Psychological Review, 69,* 379–399.

Scherer, K. R. (2001). Appraisal considered as a process of multi-level sequential checking. In K. R. Scherer, A. Schorr, & T. Johnstone (Eds.), *Appraisal processes in emotion: Theory, methods, research* (pp. 92–120). New York, NY: Oxford University Press.

Schmeichel, B. J., Demaree, H., Robinson, J., & Pu, J. (2006). Ego depletion by response exaggeration. *Journal of Experimental Social Psychology, 42,* 95–102.

Scott, B. A., & Barnes, C. M. (2011). A multilevel field investigation of emotional labor, affect, work withdrawal, and gender. *Academy of Management Journal, 54,* 116–136.

Seery, M. D., Holman, E. A., & Silver, R. C. (2010). Whatever does not kill us: Cumulative lifetime adversity, vulnerability, and resilience. *Journal of Personality and Social Psychology, 99,* 1025–1041.

Shah, James Y., Friedman, R., & Kruglanski, A. W. (2002). Forgetting all else: On the antecedents and consequences of goal shielding. *Journal of Personality and Social Psychology, 83,* 1261–1280.

Sonnemans, J., & Frijda, N. H. (1994). The structure of subjective emotional intensity. *Cognition & Emotion, 8,* 329–350.

Sundie, J. M., Ward, J. C., Beal, D. J., Chin, W. W., & Geiger-Oneto, S. (2009).

*Schadenfreude* as a consumption-related emotion: Feeling happiness about the downfall of another's product. *Journal of Consumer Psychology, 19,* 356–373.

Swallow, K. M., Zacks, J. M., & Abrams, R. A. (2009). Event boundaries in perception affect memory encoding and updating. *Journal of Experimental Psychology: General, 138,* 236–257.

Tangney, J. P. (1991). Moral affect: The good, the bad, and the ugly. *Journal of Personality and Social Psychology, 61,* 598–607.

Treynor, W., Gonzalez, R., & Nolen-Hoeksema, S. (2003). Rumination reconsidered: A psychometric analysis. *Cognitive Therapy and Research, 27,* 247–259.

Trougakos, J. P., Jackson, C. L., & Beal, D. J. (2011). Service without a smile: Comparing the consequences of neutral and positive display rules. *Journal of Applied Psychology, 96,* 350–362.

Van Kleef, G. A. (2009). How emotions regulate social life: The emotions as social information (EASI) model. *Current Directions in Psychological Science, 18,* 184–188.

Watkins, E. R. (2008). Constructive and unconstructive repetitive thought. *Psychological Bulletin, 134,* 163–206.

Weiss, H. M., & Cropanzano, R. (1996). Affective events theory: A theoretical discussion of the structure, causes, and consequences of affective experiences at work. *Research in Organizational Behavior, 18,* 1–74.

Williams, L. E., Bargh, J. A., Nocera, C. C., & Gray, J. R. (2009). The unconscious regulation of emotion: nonconscious reappraisal goals modulate emotional reactivity. *Emotion, 9,* 847–854.

Wilson, T. D., & Gilbert, D. T. (2003). Affective forecasting. *Advances in Experimental Social Psychology, 35,* 346–411.

Wilson, T. D., Meyers, J., & Gilbert, D. T. (2003). "How happy was I, anyway?" A retrospective impact bias. *Social Cognition, 21,* 421–446.

Woodzicka, J. A. & LaFrance, M. (2001). Real versus imagined gender harassment. *Journal of Social Issues, 57,* 15–30.

Zacks, J. M., Speer, N. K., Swallow, K. M., Braver, T. S., & Reynolds, J. R. (2007). Event perception: a mind-brain perspective. *Psychological Bulletin, 133,* 273–293.

Zacks, J. M., & Tversky, B. (2001). Event structure in perception and conception. *Psychological Bulletin, 127,* 3–21.

Zajonc, R. B., Murphy, S. T., & Inglehart, M. (1989). Feeling and facial efference: Implications of the vascular theory of emotion. *Psychological Review, 96,* 395–416.

# 3

# *Motivation, Fit, Confidence, and Skills*

## How Do Individual Differences Influence Emotional Labor?

JASON J. DAHLING • HAZEL-ANNE M. JOHNSON

In her seminal work on emotional labor, Hochschild (1983) described how airline stewardesses at Delta Airlines needed to have the right "Delta personality" (p. 98) to generate convincing emotional displays, which consisted of qualities like emotional stability, interpersonal warmth, and a collective orientation. Nearly 30 years later, many researchers are still focused on identifying the individual differences that are predictive of success in the emotional labor process (e.g., Grandey, 2000). This focus involves adopting a between–person perspective on emotional labor, in contrast to the within–person research described by Beal and Trougakos (2013, Chapter 2). Rather than attempting to explain variability in emotional labor within–persons and over time, our focus in this chapter is on understanding the variability in emotional labor that is observed between different people based on their stable characteristics. Accordingly, this chapter approaches emotional labor in terms of the third lens described by Grandey, Diefendorff, and Rupp (2013, Chapter 1); our focus is on emotional labor as an intrapsychic process, and we seek to explain between–person variability in the use of different strategies, invested effort to perform emotional labor, and the self-regulatory outcomes experienced from emotional labor.

A substantial amount of recent research has sought to identify many individual differences that are relevant to emotional labor, such as the Big Five model of personality (i.e., extraversion, agreeableness, conscientiousness, openness to experience, and neuroticism; Diefendorff, Croyle, & Gosserand, 2005), emotional intelligence (Johnson & Spector, 2007; Joseph & Newman, 2010), religious values (Syed, 2008), and self-efficacy (Pugh, Groth, & Hennig-Thurau, 2011). Unfortunately, much of this research is construct-driven rather than theory-driven, justifying hypothesized relationships in terms of the operant definitions of traits rather than elaborating on the theoretical mechanisms that may explain the observed effects (Sutton & Staw, 1995). A major shortcoming of this approach is that emotional labor scholars may be "reinventing the wheel" by studying different traits that impact emotional labor through the same theoretical mechanisms. Consequently, we know a great deal about *what* individual differences are important in the emotional labor process, but we know far less about *why* these qualities matter and *how* these findings fit together within shared theoretical frameworks. Therefore, our objective in this chapter is to organize the literature on emotional labor and individual differences in order to identify a set of major theories that can be used to organize existing findings and guide future research in this area.

As a starting point, our review of the literature yielded four general perspectives about the relevance of individual differences to the emotional labor process. These perspectives include (1) *motivational* explanations that state that certain employees are more receptive to organizational display standards and more willing to put effort into emotional labor; (2) explanations in terms of *congruence* or *fit* between emotional labor strategies that naturally correspond with employees' dispositional tendencies; (3) explanations that stress the importance of *confidence* in terms of emotional labor-related self-efficacies; and (4) *skill-based* explanations, which focus on individual differences that convey particular skills or abilities that make employees more capable of effective emotional labor.

For each of these basic explanations, we have identified a generalizable theory that can be used to elaborate on the causal mechanisms that underlie the observed relationships in each area. Specifically, the motivational explanations can be organized in terms of control theory (Carver & Scheier, 1998), a self-regulatory theory that has already been successfully integrated into the emotional labor literature (Diefendorff & Gosserand, 2003). The effects attributed to congruence can be explained in terms of the behavioral concordance model (Bono & Vey, 2007; Moskowitz & Côté, 1995), which elaborates on the consequences of expressing trait-inconsistent behaviors. Effects that are attributed to confidence or perceived agency are best explained in terms of social cognitive theory (Bandura, 1989; 2012), which highlights the importance of self-efficacy as a determinant of behavior and performance. Lastly, skill-based explanations are best approached in terms of trait theory (Buss; 1989; McCrae & John, 1992), which elaborates on how stable traits consistently elicit particular types of behaviors with which people become comfortable and skilled over time.

In the sections that follow, we expand on each perspective and the associated theory that we believe offers causal mechanisms that can be used to better understand the observed results in each area. This literature is summarized in Table 3.1. We then describe some representative findings from the emotional labor literature and potential directions for new research in each area. We ultimately conclude with some implications of this chapter for shaping the trajectory of future research concerning individual differences in the emotional labor process.

TABLE 3.1 Overview of Theoretical Perspectives and Individual Differences in the Emotional Labor Literature

| Common Explanations for Effects of Individual Differences on Emotional Labor | Related Theoretical Perspectives |
|---|---|
| 1. *Motivational* explanations state that certain employees are more receptive to organizational display standards and more willing to put effort into emotional labor. | *Control theory* (Carver & Scheier, 1998; Diefendorff & Gosserand, 2003) explains how employees self-regulate their performance through comparisons with organizational standards and dynamic feedback loops. |
| 2. Explanations made in terms of *congruence* or *fit* state that certain emotional labor strategies naturally correspond with employees' dispositional tendencies. | The *behavioral concordance model* (Bono & Vey, 2007; Moskowitz & Côté, 1995) elaborates on the negative consequences of expressing trait-inconsistent behaviors. |
| 3. *Confidence-based* explanations stress the importance of social self-efficacies to performing effective emotional labor. | *Social cognitive theory* (Bandura, 1989; 2012) highlights the importance of self-efficacy as a determinant of agentic behavior and performance. |
| 4. *Skill-based* explanations focus on individual differences that convey particular skills or abilities that make employees more capable of effective emotional labor. | *Trait theory* (Buss; 1989; McCrae & John, 1992) elaborates on how stable traits consistently elicit particular types of behaviors with which people become comfortable and skilled over time. |

TABLE 3.1 continued

| Individual Differences Related to Emotional Labor | Representative Studies |
| --- | --- |
| Trait Positive and Negative Affect | Bono & Vey, 2005; Brotheridge & Lee, 2003; Dahling & Perez, 2010; Diefendorff, Erickson, Grandey, & Dahling, 2011; Gosserand & Diefendorff, 2005; Liu, Prati, Perrewé, & Ferris, 2008; Schaubroeck & Jones, 2000 |
| Big Five Traits (i.e., Extraversion, Conscientiousness, Openness, Agreeableness, and Neuroticism) | Chi, Grandey, Diamond, & Krimmel, 2011; Diefendorff, Croyle, & Gosserand, 2005; Diefendorff & Richard, 2003; Judge, Woolf, & Hurst, 2009; Kiffin-Petersen, Jordan, & Soutar, 2011; Kim, 2008 |
| Self-Monitoring | Bono & Vey, 2005; Bono & Vey, 2007 |
| Proactive Personality | Randolph & Dahling, 2011 |
| Self-Efficacies | Heuven, Bakker, Schaufeli, & Huisman, 2006; Pugh, Groth, & Hennig-Thurau, 2011; Wilk & Moynihan, 2005 |
| Spirituality and Religiosity | Byrne, Morton, & Dahling, 2011; Syed, 2008 |
| Customer Service Orientation | Allen, Pugh, Grandey, & Groth, 2010 |
| Display Rule Commitment | Diefendorff & Croyle, 2008; Gosserand & Diefendorff, 2005 |
| Emotional Intelligence | Austin, Dore, & O'Donovan, 2008; Cheung & Tang, 2009; Gardner, Fischer, & Hunt, 2009; Giardini & Frese, 2006; Giardini & Frese, 2008; Johnson & Spector, 2007; Joseph & Newman, 2010 |
| Political Skill | Liu, Perrewé, Hochwarter, & Kacmar, 2004 |
| Perspective-Taking Ability | Rupp, McCance, Spencer, & Sonntag, 2008 |

## CONTROL THEORY AND MOTIVATIONAL DIFFERENCES IN EMOTIONAL LABOR

Many studies have offered motivational explanations for the effects of individual differences on emotional labor, and perceptual control theory (Carver & Scheier, 1998) provides a useful framework to organize this research. Control theory describes how people self-regulate their pursuit of goals through dynamic feedback loops. In brief, self-regulation begins with an input function, some perceived information about one's current performance. This information is then compared to a goal/standard for performance that has been internalized. If one's performance is acceptable and consistent with the standard, no adjustments are needed and goal pursuit continues without the dedication of any conscious resources. However, behavioral adjustments are required if one's performance is discrepant from the goal or standard. These adjustments take the form of output functions, new behaviors that are intended to have a changed effect on the external environment. The environmental effect then serves as a source of new input feedback about performance that can be used to make additional behavioral changes, if needed.

Diefendorff and Gosserand (2003) adapted the basic control theory model to the emotional labor process. In their model, organizational display rules, the organizational standards for emotions to show or hide from others, serve as the behavioral standards. Employees compare their emotional displays (inputs) to the display rule standard and evaluate their performance. If their emotional displays are discrepant from the display rules, then employees are motivated to engage in emotional labor strategies to bring forth an alternative display that does satisfy the display rule (outputs). Lastly, affective events, like an interaction with a rude customer, serve as environmental disturbances that can impact the appropriateness of the emotional display, resulting in new self-regulatory demands.

Control theory offers several mechanisms through which motivation-related individual differences can affect emotional labor. First, research indicates that some individual differences impact the extent to which organizational display rules are internalized as valid behavioral standards that will be used to guide emotional labor outputs. For example, display rule commitment and customer service orientation are both individual differences that speak to evaluating organizational standards as important, and both constructs moderate the relationship between display rule perceptions and emotional labor strategies (Allen, Pugh, Grandey, & Groth, 2010; Diefendorff & Croyle, 2008; Gosserand & Diefendorff, 2005). Specifically, the relationships between display rules and emotional labor are weaker for those employees with low commitment and customer service orientation, presumably because these employees have not accepted and internalized the organizational standards that they would use to evaluate and change their emotional displays.

Second, other individual differences shape employees' responsiveness to perceived discrepancies between their own behaviors and these internalized organizational goals. For example, some research on the Big Five model of personality has highlighted how conscientious and agreeable employees are particularly responsive to display rules and engage in good-faith emotional labor in the form of deep acting (Diefendorff et al., 2005). Recent work on proactive personality suggests that proactive employees are also very sensitive to behavior-standard discrepancies, and that proactive employees are highly likely to respond with emotional labor strategies that are aligned with the display rules that they perceive (Randolph & Dahling, 2011).

Lastly, individual differences in personal goal structures may explain why employees sometimes disregard organizational standards for emotional labor due to conflicting motivations with other goals. Control theory proposes that goals exist in hierarchies, with higher-level, more important goals being managed with superordinate feedback loops that take priority over lower-level goals that are governed by subordinate feedback loops (Carver & Scheier, 1998). Consequently, when lower-level organizational goals conflict with higher-level personal goals, the theory states that preservation of the higher-level personal goal takes precedence; the lower-level organizational goal of performing emotional labor consistent with display rules will be abandoned. Consistent with this idea, some emotional labor researchers have suggested that employees who possess strong religious values will struggle with conforming to certain organizational display rules (Byrne, Morton, & Dahling, 2011; Syed, 2008). For example, almost all religions call for the expression of integrative, supportive emotions toward others, and honoring these values is often a high-level personal goal for people who are very religious. If a deeply-religious employee is confronted with a display rule that calls for the expression of negative, differentiating emotions, control theory would accordingly predict that the employee would disregard the organizational goal in the interest of maintaining successful pursuit of the superordinate, personal religious goal.

Goal hierarchies are also important theoretical mechanisms for explaining the proposed effects of employee identification in emotional labor. Ashforth and Humphrey (1993) proposed that performing emotional labor, and deep acting in particular, is likely to contribute to increased identification with the service role. Further, as identification with the role increases, emotional labor is expected to become more personally important and an authentic expression of one's true self that leads to improved psychological well-being. In terms of control theory, this process implies that employees with high identification have internalized organizational display rules and merged these organizational goals with their own personal goal structure. Providing high-quality emotional labor thus becomes a part of fulfilling an important personal goal (e.g., to be a great salesperson), and employees with this level of role identification should be deeply motivated to self-regulate their emotional displays at work without experiencing adverse personal outcomes as a consequence (Ashforth & Tomiuk, 2000). To summarize, control theory offers a useful framework for organizing motivation-related explanations for the effects of individual differences on emotional labor. Within this framework, the key causal mechanisms used in hypothesis-building are goal adoption, responsiveness to goal-behavior discrepancies, and hierarchical goal conflicts, all of which impact the type and extent of emotional labor performed by employees. To date, the most under-studied extension of this theory is the impact of goal conflicts, which represents an important future research direction. Current research on conflicting goal hierarchies is non-empirical and has focused predominately on personal religious values and internalized societal values (e.g., Byrne et al., 2011; Syed, 2008). Some limited empirical evidence for the importance of goal conflicts was reported by Sutton (1991) in his study of bill collection agents, who reported conflict and discomfort when expected to express negative emotions toward debtors who were kind and likeable. Presumably, this conflict arose because the organizational display rule was in conflict with other high-level goals held by the collections agents (e.g., internalized societal values to reciprocate kindness, or personal goals to be seen as a good person). However, future empirical research is needed to explicitly test these ideas.

## THE BEHAVIORAL CONCORDANCE MODEL AND TRAIT-BEHAVIOR CONGRUENCE IN EMOTIONAL LABOR

Another key explanation offered for the effect of individual differences on emotional labor concerns behavioral congruence. From this perspective, employees are inclined to regulate their emotional displays with particular behavioral strategies that are congruent with their broad dispositional tendencies. The key theoretical explanation that underlies these findings is the behavioral concordance model (Moskowitz & Côté, 1995). The behavioral concordance model assumes that traits predispose people to act in particular ways that become their natural, primary responses to situations, and behaving in these trait-congruent ways results in positive feelings. Although people are certainly capable of committing trait-incongruent behaviors, doing so will generate more stress and negative emotions that people try to avoid. For example, highly-conscientious people are predisposed to engage in organizing and planning behaviors. Although conscientious people are capable of responding to a work demand in an unorganized, spontaneous fashion, the behavioral concordance model would predict that these employees will experience more stress and discomfort when forced to act out-of-character without the structured behaviors that they prefer to express.

The behavioral concordance model is not the only theoretical perspective that makes these predictions. For example, similar ideas are evident in Little's (2000) free trait theory. Little distinguished between "free" trait expressions, which are socially- or situationally-driven patterns of expressed behavior, and "fixed" trait expressions, which are patterns of expressed behavior that do not vary across situations. A key proposition of free trait theory is that free trait expressions that are incongruent with a person's typical fixed trait expressions increase stress and detract from a person's well-being. For example, a highly-introverted person might respond to the situational cue of a party with sociable behavior and expressions, but doing so is likely to be highly taxing because this behavior is discordant from her natural, fixed trait expressions. More frequent and extreme discordance with fixed traits results in increasingly severe detrimental effects on people, particularly when they do not have private moments of restoration in which they can act genuinely in ways that are congruent with their fixed, true dispositions. Recent work by Trougakos and colleagues on the importance of work breaks to service workers performing emotional labor further emphasizes the need for these private, restorative moments when people can express their authentic, fixed traits (Trougakos, Beal, Green, & Weiss, 2008; Trougakos & Hideg, 2009).

Thus, the key causal mechanism offered by the behavioral concordance model (and free trait theory) is the experience of, or freedom from, stress. When people act in ways that are trait-incongruent, they consume self-regulatory resources and become stressed, uncomfortable, and exhausted. In contrast, trait-congruent behavior results in less stress and a positive feeling of fit or "rightness" that enables greater persistence in performing the behavior. These intra-individual consequences guide people to select trait-congruent behaviors whenever they have the option to do so.

There is considerable support for these ideas in the emotional labor literature, most notably with respect to trait positive and negative affect as predictors of emotional labor strategies. A consistent body of research indicates that employees with high negative affect are more likely to report surface acting, whereas employees with high positive affect are more likely to report deep acting or the expression of naturally-felt emotions without modification when emotional labor requirements are present (Bono & Vey, 2005; Brotheridge & Lee, 2003; Dahling & Perez, 2010; Diefendorff, Erickson, Grandey, & Dahling, 2011; Gosserand & Diefendorff, 2005; Liu, Prati, Perrewé, & Ferris, 2008). The behavioral concordance model posits that employees with high positive affect, who are prone to experience more positive emotions, would find it most trait-congruent to use emotional labor strategies that align with approaching and actually feeling positive emotions, namely deep acting and expressing naturally-felt emotions. In contrast, employees with high negative affect, who typically experience more negative emotions, would find attempts to feel positive trait-incongruent. Consequently, these employees are more likely to keep their negative feelings intact and suppress them during the course of surface acting. Parallel findings have been reported with respect to extraversion and neuroticism, which represent similar patterns of affective experiences as positive and negative affect, respectively (e.g., Lucas & Baird, 2004). Highly-extraverted employees use more deep acting and express more naturally-felt emotions, whereas highly-neurotic employees use more surface acting when presented with emotional labor demands (Diefendorff et al., 2005; Kiffin-Petersen, Jordan, & Soutar, 2011; Kim, 2008). However, the nature of the emotional labor being performed is also important; for example, extraverts experience less cardiovascular stress when showing enthusiasm, but *more* stress when asked to show anger toward others, a trait-incongruent expression (Bono & Vey, 2007).

Affectivity also influences the way that employees perceive display rules, again suggesting that when people have options in behavioral responses, they are likely to construe the situation in ways that allow them to express trait-congruent behaviors. Specifically, employees with high extraversion and/or trait positive affect are more likely to perceive display rules as mandating the expression of positive emotions, whereas employees with high neuroticism and/or trait negative affect are more likely to perceive display rules as mandating the suppression of negative emotions (e.g., Diefendorff & Richard, 2003; Schaubroeck & Jones, 2000). In aggregate, this body of research demonstrates that trait affect shapes situational perceptions, which in turn allows for the selection of trait-congruent emotional labor strategies to meet the display demand.

The behavioral concordance model has also been supported with respect to self-monitoring (Bono & Vey, 2005, 2007). For people high in self-monitoring, attentive self-regulation and responsiveness to social demands constitutes trait-congruent behaviors. Consequently, emotion regulation constitutes trait-congruent behavior for high self-monitors (Bono & Vey, 2005), and research demonstrates that high self-monitors experience less stress and better emotional performance when engaging in emotional labor, especially when deep acting, relative to low self-monitors (Bono & Vey, 2007).

Future research on the behavioral concordance model should focus on the affective experiences that are thought to arise from trait-congruent and -incongruent behaviors over time. The model proposes that acting in a trait-congruent manner should elicit positive feelings and low stress, outcomes that have special significance in the context of emotional labor. Specifically, we expect that the use of trait-congruent emotional labor strategies should make subsequent emotional labor interactions easier, whereas trait-incongruent strategies should elicit more stress that undermines employees' ability to continue to provide convincing expressions of the requisite emotions. Testing these ideas would involve within-person measurements of emotional labor over time (Beal & Trougakos, 2013, Chapter 2) while taking into account between-person traits to evaluate the trait-behavior congruency of the selected strategies.

## SOCIAL COGNITIVE THEORY AND SELF-EFFICACY IN EMOTIONAL LABOR

Of the perspectives that we discuss in this chapter, confidence-based explanations for the importance of individual differences to emotional labor have received the least research attention. However, this is an important perspective that complements the research on trait-behavior congruence and actual skills to present a full picture of why some employees are better able to perform emotional labor. The dominant theoretical perspective in this part of the literature is social cognitive theory (Bandura, 1986, 1990, 1997). Social cognitive theory explains that human functioning is reciprocally determined by personal factors (e.g., thoughts and feelings), environmental influences, and agentic behaviors. Thus, behavioral outcomes, like emotional labor, are impacted both by personal factors and environmental conditions, and most emotional labor research that adopts this theoretical framework takes into account both individual differences and job characteristics.

The most important personal factors in social cognitive theory are self-efficacy beliefs, which refer to judgments of one's capability to successfully complete domain-specific tasks (Bandura, 1986, 2012). People are thought to possess many self-efficacies for different types of tasks and behaviors (e.g., an employee might have high self-efficacy for interpersonal selling, but low self-efficacy for computer use), and having high self-efficacy for a particular behavior conveys several advantages to people (Bandura, 1997). First, high self-efficacy in a domain encourages people to seek out tasks in that domain, giving them more opportunities for practice and skill development. Second, self-efficacy enables people to persist and put in the necessary effort to succeed when faced with challenging obstacles to performance. Lastly, people with high self-efficacy experience constructive cognitions when presented with failure; they believe that they have control over future outcomes and that failure is a function of putting forth insufficient effort rather than lacking the necessary abilities to ever succeed at the particular task. Consistent with these propositions of social cognitive theory, research in industrial/

organizational psychology has documented that self-efficacy has beneficial effects on the performance of basic tasks, such as service work,
beyond the effects of other individual differences, such as cognitive ability
and the Big Five model of personality traits (Judge, Jackson, Shaw, Scott,
& Rich, 2007).

Thus, the causal mechanism implied by social cognitive theory is
personal agency over tasks, which should help people overcome environmental stressors and challenges to improve their well-being and general
functioning. In the context of emotional labor, employees who possess
high self-efficacy for emotional labor-related performance will be
expected to adopt strategies with which they feel confident, exert high
levels of effort and persistence when faced with emotion regulation
demands, and respond to challenges and failures in a constructive fashion.

To date, several different types of self-efficacy have been studied in the
emotional labor literature. Wilk and Moynihan (2005) studied general job
self-efficacy in a sample of call center employees with the expectation
that self-efficacy would moderate the relationship between interpersonal
job demands and emotional exhaustion. Although their hypothesis was
not supported, subsequent studies that have focused on more narrowly-
defined self-efficacies have yielded greater support. For example, Heuven,
Bakker, Schaufeli, and Huisman (2006) found that emotion work-related
self-efficacy buffered the relationships between several emotional job
demands (i.e., feelings rules and emotionally-charged interactions with
customers) and emotional dissonance. Further, they found that emotion
work-related self-efficacy weakened the negative relationship between
emotional dissonance and work engagement, and that self-efficacy had a
direct, negative effect on emotional exhaustion. Similarly, Pugh et al.
(2011) found that surface acting self-efficacy buffered the negative
relationship between surface acting and emotional exhaustion among
customer-contact employees, but it did not moderate the relationship
between surface acting and job satisfaction. Some limited evidence also
suggests that self-efficacy for emotion management is important to understanding the use of emotional labor for interpersonal gain in negotiating
contexts (Barry, 1999).

Two major issues strike us as important research directions in this
literature. First, the variety of self-efficacies that has been studied to
date points out a need to clarify exactly what self-efficacies are important
to develop in customer-contact employees. Specifically, researchers have
studied general work self-efficacy (Wilk & Moynihan, 2005), emotion
work self-efficacies (Barry, 1999; Heuven et al., 2006), and strategy-
specific self-efficacies (Pugh et al., 2011). The domain-specific nature of
self-efficacy in social cognitive theory (Bandura, 1997) has forced emotional labor researchers to define and measure new self-efficacy constructs

in every study, which limits our ability to draw comparisons across findings. Additionally, emotional labor researchers have focused on self-efficacies that pertain to work tasks rather than social self-efficacies that might be more relevant to understanding emotional labor outcomes (e.g., Di Guntia et al., 2010).

The second major research need is to identify the sources of emotional labor-related self-efficacies. Social cognitive theory points to four types of domain-specific learning experiences that result in improved self-efficacy: performance proficiency (i.e., personal mastery experiences while working in the domain), vicarious learning by observing comparable others, social persuasion in the form of realistic encouragement, and physiological experiences (i.e., stress and tension; Bandura, 1988). We know virtually nothing about the types of learning experiences that result in emotional labor-related self-efficacy, and understanding how people develop this sense of personal agency over emotion regulation is a critical future research direction.

## TRAIT THEORY AND INTERPERSONAL SKILLS IN EMOTIONAL LABOR

The final perspective we explore examines skill-based explanations for the effects of individual differences in the emotional labor process. Although we generally expect that self-efficacy for a behavior and proficiency at performing that behavior should be positively related, self-efficacy only reflects beliefs about self-competence rather than objective truths about competence (Bandura, 1997). Consequently, people can have self-efficacy for a task that is higher or lower than their actual skill at the task (Bandura, 1986). Our focus in this section is therefore on traits that convey actual skills, abilities, or competencies that enable employees to persist at emotional labor longer than others, to perform emotional labor convincingly, or to persevere in the face of particularly challenging instances of self-regulation (e.g., dealing with a rude customer).

Trait theory (Boyle, Matthews, & Saklofske, 2008; Buss, 1989; McCrae & John, 1992) provides a useful framework for approaching this section of the literature. Trait theory organizes personality in terms of relatively-stable, consistent patterns of affect, behavior, and cognition (Pervin, 1994) that are multiply-determined by biological and environmental factors, resulting in trait taxonomies like the Big Five model of personality (McCrae & John, 1992). Thus, while there are many trait theories that offer competing taxonomies or lists of specific traits, all trait theories have several core principles (Boyle et al., 2008). The most important principle with respect to the emotional labor literature is the idea that traits result in the consistent expression of particular behaviors, and that people become more skilled and effective at performing those behaviors over time. For example, the trait of extraversion (McCrae & John, 1992) describes a consistent pattern of being warm, sociable, and cheerful in interpersonal contexts, and extraverted people tend to become more interpersonally skilled as a consequence of these dispositional tendencies. Consistent with this idea, recent research shows that the interpersonal skills associated with extraversion have been shown to improve the consequences associated with surface acting for customer-contact employees (Chi, Grandey, Diamond, & Krimmel, 2011; Judge, Woolf, & Hurst, 2009). Thus, from the perspective of trait theory, the causal mechanisms through which individual differences impact emotional labor is the development of skills and competencies that make employees more effective at regulating emotions and interacting with other people.

Emotional intelligence is the most widely-studied individual difference that is thought to convey a skill-based advantage to service employees when performing emotional labor (e.g., Austin, Dore, & O'Donovan, 2008; Cheung & Tang, 2009; Gardner, Fischer, & Hunt, 2009; Johnson & Spector, 2007; Joseph & Newman, 2010; Liu et al., 2008; Opengart, 2005). Emotional intelligence (EI) can be broadly defined as a set of abilities involving emotion in the self and others (Mayer & Salovey, 1997). However, despite its popularity with scientists and practitioners, emotional intelligence research continues to struggle with measurement and construct definition challenges. To date, researchers have delineated two models of emotional intelligence: (1) the ability-model measured with both objective items (Salovey & Mayer, 1990; Mayer & Salovey, 1997; Mayer, Salovey & Caruso, 2000) and with self-report or peer-report measures (Wong & Law, 2002; Law, Wong & Song, 2004); (2) mixed-model EI self-report measures (Bar-On, 2000). These multiple conceptualizations of emotional intelligence make it difficult to draw conclusions about its influence on the emotional labor process, although meta-analytic evidence shows that the emotion regulation facet of emotional intelligence is related to job performance for positions that have high emotional labor requirements after controlling for cognitive ability, conscientiousness, and emotional stability (Joseph & Newman, 2010). However, a variety of conflicting explanations have been offered for exactly how emotional intelligence influences the process of emotional labor.

First, some studies position emotional intelligence as an antecedent of emotional labor strategies (Gardner et al., 2009). For example, emotional intelligence has a direct, negative effect on surface acting (Austin et al., 2008) and a direct, positive effect on deep acting (Liu et al., 2008). Further, two facets of emotional intelligence, regulation of emotions and use of emotions, interact with positive affect to have a positive effect on deep acting and the expression of naturally-felt emotions, and a negative effect on surface acting (Cheung & Tang, 2009). Totterdell and Holman (2003) also found that emotionally-intelligent employees were more likely to utilize positive refocusing, an emotion regulation strategy that is conceptually a component of deep acting. Thus, overall, emotional intelligence seems to be positively related to deep acting and negatively related to surface acting, suggesting that strategy selection is an important reason that emotionally-intelligent employees perform more effective emotional labor.

However, emotional intelligence may contribute to effective emotional labor in alternative ways. One potential mechanism is through emotional contagion; some evidence suggests that emotionally-intelligent employees tend to regulate their own emotions to experience more positive affect, which subsequently spreads to customers and encourages them to appraise the transaction favorably (Giardini & Frese, 2008). There is also some mixed evidence that emotional intelligence may buffer the relationships between emotional labor and subsequent outcomes. For example, emotional intelligence weakens the positive relationship between emotional demands and emotional dissonance, and weakens the negative relationships between dissonance and subsequent criteria (general well-being and job satisfaction; Giardini & Frese, 2006). Johnson and Spector (2007) hypothesized a similar buffering role, with emotional intelligence expected to moderate the relationships between emotional labor strategies and a variety of outcomes (job satisfaction, general well-being, and emotional exhaustion). However, they found no support for these hypotheses, pointing to a need for more research in this area.

To summarize the findings on emotional intelligence, it seems that the emotion use and regulation skills developed by emotionally-intelligent employees result in several advantages when performing emotional labor. Employees with high emotional intelligence tend to deep act rather than surface act, and this choice of strategy subsequently results in more favorable outcomes for the employee and the organization. The positive emotions experienced as a consequence of effective emotion regulation can also contribute to favorable outcomes through contagion mechanisms, and there is some evidence that emotional intelligence buffers employees from the experience and consequences of emotional dissonance. However, there are many inconsistencies and questions that must be resolved in this section of the literature; as Joseph and Newman (2010) compellingly demonstrated, different facets of emotional intelligence sequentially cascade to impact job performance, and the manner in which emotional intelligence is defined and measured (e.g., self-report versus performance tests) can have a considerable impact on the observed results of any individual study. Much additional research is needed to clarify what aspects of emotional intelligence are most important to the performance of emotional labor and what measures of these aspects are most valid. Although most research focused on skills in emotional labor has involved emotional intelligence, some other traits that convey skills or abilities to remain resilient in the face of challenges have also received research attention. For example, Rupp, McCance, Spencer, and Sonntag (2008) showed that perspective-taking ability was an important quality that enabled employees to continue to surface act when faced with unjust treatment by customers. Perspective-taking ability enables employees to understand another person's point of view, and Rupp et al.'s findings demonstrate that employees who lack this ability suffer a breakdown in their ability to self-regulate emotional displays in the face of incivility from others. Similarly, Härtel, Hsu, and Boyle (2002) proposed that individual differences pertaining to emotional dissonance tolerance, hassle tolerance, and emotional uplift reactivity should be important to understand the development and consequences of emotional dissonance among service employees who are faced with negative affective events. Lastly, there is scant evidence that political skill may be an antecedent of emotional labor, with more politically-skilled employees exhibiting more effective emotional labor in political climates (Liu, Perrewé, Hochwarter, & Kacmar, 2004).

Clearly, there are several important research directions for skill-based perspectives on emotional labor. As we previously noted, we echo Joseph and Newman's (2010) cautions about facet-level analyses and measurement concerns when evaluating the influence of emotional intelligence on performance in jobs with high emotional labor requirements. Much additional research is needed to build upon the clear findings of their meta-analysis. We also note that many other traits thought to convey skills to employees performing emotional labor have been examined only in single studies (e.g., political skill; Liu et al., 2004). Replication is needed to confirm these findings and elaborate on the boundary conditions that may facilitate or hinder the expression of these skills and abilities.

## DISCUSSION AND FUTURE RESEARCH DIRECTIONS

Given the rapid proliferation of research on individual differences and emotional labor, our intent in this chapter was to identify the major theories that fill in the causal "black box" linking personal characteristics to emotional labor constructs. Although other theories may certainly prove important as the field moves forward, control theory, the behavioral concordance model, social cognitive theory, and trait theory offer key explanations that can be used to organize and summarize the bulk of research on this topic.

We caution that the theoretical explanations we have offered are not mutually exclusive, and we expect that most broad traits will influence emotional labor through multiple theoretical mechanisms. For example, across a variety of studies, extraversion seems to be consistently associated with more effective emotional labor. Extraversion may yield this effect partly because expressing enthusiastic, integrative emotions is behaviorally congruent for extraverts, resulting in less stress and better emotional performance (Bono & Vey, 2007). Because of their dispositional tendency to be sociable, extraverts become skilled at interpersonal interaction, which also makes their attempts at emotional labor more convincing (Chi et al., 2011). Further, research shows that highly extraverted people report higher social self-efficacy (Di Giunta et al., 2010), which likely encourages them to approach situations that require emotional labor with greater confidence. Lastly, extraverts may appraise organizational standards for behavior differently than introverts, which impacts the way in which they self-regulate their emotional labor (Diefendorff & Gosserand, 2003; Diefendorff & Richard, 2003). Thus, the effects of extraversion on emotional labor can be explained in terms of fit, skill, confidence, and motivation, and researchers could focus on any or all of these causal mechanisms when developing hypotheses. Our point is simply that the relevant theoretical mechanisms need to be carefully articulated and tested by emotional labor researchers in the interest of moving forward with trait research and making meaningful comparisons across studies. We stress that scholars interested in pursuing a line of research on individual differences and emotional labor should not just consider whether or not the trait in question has been studied before, but should instead determine the theoretical mechanism at work and whether or not it has been sufficiently tested in previous research.

Future research should also draw on new theoretical perspectives or elaborate on additional elements of previously identified theories that explain novel ways in which individual differences impact emotional labor. For example, some of our recent work (Dahling & Johnson, 2010) draws on regulatory focus theory to elaborate on motivational explanations for emotional labor. We showed that the manner in which employees self-regulate goal pursuit (i.e., as an approach goal to be promoted or an avoidance anti-goal to be prevented) impacts the emotional labor strategies that they select and the service outcomes that they experience. This work complements other motivational findings that are grounded in control theory by demonstrating that different outcomes are attained when employees self-regulate with promotion-oriented feedback loops versus prevention-oriented feedback loops.

Lastly, we note that there are important demographic differences related to emotional labor that we did not discuss in this chapter, such as age (Dahling & Perez, 2010), gender (Johnson & Spector, 2007; Schaubroeck & Jones, 2000), and race (Harlow, 2003). We excluded these topics because our focus is at the person level of analysis, and the effects of demographic characteristics on emotional labor are typically explained in terms of societal pressures and expectations that yield differential demands for particular groups to regulate emotions to a greater degree (e.g., Wharton & Erickson, 1993). We refer interested readers to a more detailed discussion by Lively (2013, Chapter 10) on the sociological mechanisms that result in stricter emotional labor expectations for people from minority demographic groups.

In conclusion, it is clear that understanding the role of individual differences in emotional labor is an important research direction, but more attention is needed to integrate and ground this section of the literature in generalizable theories. We offered several broad theories that we believe can explain much of the literature in this chapter, and we encourage future research that identifies new theoretical mechanisms. Moreover, we stress that multi-level research that draws on both between-person differences and within-person, transaction-level phenomena (Beal & Trougakos, 2013, Chapter 2) will offer the most insight into how individual differences translate into more effective emotional labor in the workplace.

# REFERENCES

Allen, J.A., Pugh, S.D., Grandey, A.A., & Groth, M. (2010). Following display rules in good or bad faith? Customer orientation as a moderator of the display rule–emotional labor relationship. *Human Performance, 23,* 101–115. doi: 10.1080/08959281003621695

Ashforth, B.E., & Humphrey, R.H. (1993). Emotional labor in service roles: The influence of identity. *Academy of Management Review, 18,* 88–115. doi: 10.2307/258824

Ashforth, B.E., & Tomiuk, M.A. (2000). Emotional labour and authenticity: Views from service agents. In S. Fineman (Ed.), *Emotion in organizations* (2nd ed., pp. 184–203). Thousand Oaks, CA: Sage.

Austin, E.J., Dore, T.C.P., & O'Donovan, K.M. (2008). Associations of personality and emotional intelligence with display rule perceptions and emotional labour. *Personality and Individual Differences, 44,* 679–688. doi: 10.1016/j.paid.2007.10.001

Bandura, A. (1986). *Social foundations of thought and action: A social cognitive theory.* Englewood Cliffs, NJ: Prentice Hall.

Bandura, A. (1988). Organizational applications of social cognitive theory. *Australian Journal of Management, 13,* 275–302.

Bandura, A. (1989). Human agency in social cognitive theory. *American Psychologist, 44,* 1175–1184.

Bandura, A. (1990). Reflections on non-ability determinants of competence. In

R.J. Sternberg & J. Kolligian (Eds.), *Competence considered* (pp. 315–362). New Haven, CT: Yale University Press.

Bandura, A. (1997). *Self-efficacy: The exercise of control.* New York, NY: Freeman Press.

Bandura, A. (2012). On the functional properties of perceived self-efficacy revisited. *Journal of Management, 38,* 9–44.

Bar-On, R. (2000). Emotional and social intelligence: Insights from the Emotional Quotient Inventory (EQ-I). In R. Bar-On & J. D. Parker (Eds.), *Handbook of emotional intelligence* (pp. 363–388). San Francisco, CA: Jossey-Bass.

Barry, B. (1999). The tactical use of emotion in negotiation. In R.J. Bies, R.J. Lewicki, & B.H. Sheppard (Eds.), *Research in negotiation in organizations* (Vol. 7, pp. 93–121). Stamford, CT: JAI Press.

Beal, D. J., & Trougakos, J. P. (2013). Episodic intrapersonal emotion regulation: Or, dealing with life as it happens. In A. A. Grandey, J. M. Diefendorff & D. E. Rupp (Eds.), *Emotional labor in the 21st century: Diverse perspectives on emotion regulation at work.* New York, NY: Psychology Press/Routledge.

Bono, J.E., & Vey, M.A. (2005). Toward understanding emotional management at work: A quantitative review of emotional labor research. In C.E.J. Hartel, W.J. Zerbe, & N.M. Ashkanasy (Eds.), *Emotions in organizational behavior* (pp. 213 - 233). Mahwah, NJ: LEA Publishers.

Bono, J.E., & Vey, M.A. (2007). Personality and emotional performance: Extraversion, neuroticism, and self-monitoring. *Journal of Occupational Health Psychology, 12,* 177–192. doi: 10.1037/1076-8998.12.2.177

Boyle, G.J., Matthews, G., & Saklofske, D.H. (2008). Personality theories and models: An overview. In G.J. Boyle, G. Matthews, & D.H. Saklofske (Eds.), *The SAGE handbook of personality theory and assessment* (Vol. 1, pp. 1–30). Thousand Oaks, CA: Sage.

Brotheridge, C.M., & Lee, R.T. (2003). Development and validation of the Emotional Labour Scale. *Journal of Occupational and Organizational Psychology, 76,* 365–379. doi: 10.1348/096317903769647229

Buss, A.H. (1989). Personality as traits. *American Psychologist, 44,* 1378–1388. doi: 10.1037/0003-066X.44.11.1378

Byrne, C.J., Morton, D.M., & Dahling, J.J. (2011). Spirituality, religion, and emotional labor in the workplace. *Journal of Management, Spirituality, & Religion, 8,* 299–315. doi: 10.1080/14766086.2011.630169

Carver, C.S., & Scheier, M.F. (1998). *On the self-regulation of behavior.* New York, NY: Cambridge University Press.

Cheung, F.Y., & Tang, C.S. (2009). The influence of emotional intelligence and affectivity on emotional labor strategies at work. *Journal of Individual Differences, 30,* 75–86. doi: 10.1027/1614-0001.30.2.75

Chi, N.-W., Grandey, A.A., Diamond, J.A., & Krimmel, K.R. (2011). Want a tip? Service performance as a function of emotion regulation and extraversion. *Journal of Applied Psychology, 96,* 1337–1346. doi: 10.1037/a0022884

Dahling, J.J., & Johnson, H.M. (2010). Promoting good service: The effects of trait and state regulatory focus on emotional labor. Paper presented at the 25ᵗʰ Annual Conference of the Society for Industrial and Organizational Psychology, Atlanta, GA.

Dahling, J.J., & Perez, L.A. (2010). Older worker, different actor? Linking age and emotional labor strategies. *Personality and Individual Differences, 48,* 574–578. doi: 10.1016/j.paid.2009.12.009

Di Giunta, L., Eisenberg, N., Kupfer, A., Steca, P., Tramontano, C., & Caprara, G.V. (2010). Assessing perceived empathic and social self-efficacy across countries. *European Journal of Psychological Assessment, 26,* 77–86. doi: 10.1027/1015-5759/a000012.

Diefendorff, J.M., & Croyle, M.H. (2008). Antecedents of emotional display rule commitment. *Human Performance, 21,* 310–332. doi: 10.1080/z08959280802137911

Diefendorff, J.M., Croyle, M.H., & Gosserand, R.H. (2005). The dimensionality and antecedents of emotional labor strategies. *Journal of Vocational Behavior, 66,* 339–357. doi: 10.1016/j.jvb.2004.02.001

Diefendorff, J.M., & Gosserand, R.H. (2003). Understanding the emotional labor process: A control theory perspective. *Journal of Organizational Behavior, 24,* 945–959. doi: 10.1002/job.230

Diefendorff, J.M., Erickson, R.J., Grandey, A.A., & Dahling, J.J. (2011). Emotional display rules as work unit norms: A multilevel analysis of emotional labor among nurses. *Journal of Occupational Health Psychology, 16,* 170–186. doi: 10.1037/a0021725

Diefendorff, J.M., & Richard, E.M. (2003). Antecedents and consequences of emotional display rule perceptions. *Journal of Applied Psychology, 88,* 284–294. doi: 10.1037/0021-9010.88.2.284

Gardner, W.L., Fischer, D., & Hunt, J.G. (2009). Emotional labor and leadership: A threat to authenticity? *The Leadership Quarterly, 20,* 466–482. doi: 10.1016/j.leaqua.2009.03.011

Giardini, A., & Frese, M. (2006). Reducing the negative effects of emotion work in service occupations: Emotional competence as a psychological resource. *Journal of Occupational Health Psychology, 11,* 63–75. doi: 10.1037/1076-8998.11.1.63

Giardini, A., & Frese, M. (2008). Linking service employees' emotional competence to customer satisfaction: A multilevel approach. *Journal of Organizational Behavior, 29,* 155–170. doi: 10.1002/job.509

Gosserand, R.H., & Diefendorff, J.M. (2005). Emotional display rules and emotional labor: The moderating role of commitment. *Journal of Applied Psychology, 90,* 1256–1264. doi: 10.1037/0021-9010.90.6.1256

Grandey, A.A. (2000). Emotion regulation in the workplace: A new way to conceptualize emotional labor. *Journal of Occupational Health Psychology, 5,* 95–110. doi: 10.1037/1076-8998.5.1.95

Grandey, A. A., Diefendorff, J. M., & Rupp, D. E. (2013). Emotional labor: Overview of definitions, theories, and evidence. In A. A. Grandey, J. M. Diefendorff & D. E. Rupp (Eds.), *Emotional labor in the 21st century: Diverse perspectives on emotion regulation at work.* New York, NY: Psychology Press/Routledge.

Harlow, R. (2003). "Race doesn't matter, but . . .": The effect of race on professors' experiences and emotion management in the undergraduate college classroom. *Social Psychology Quarterly, 66,* 348–363. doi: 10.2307/1519834

Härtel, C.E.J., Hsu, A.C.F., & Boyle, M.V. (2002). A conceptual examination of the causal sequences of emotional labor, emotional dissonance, and emotional exhaustion: The argument for the role of contextual and provider characteristics. In N.M. Ashkanasy, W.J. Zerbe, & C.E.J. Härtel (Eds.), *Managing emotions in the workplace* (pp. 251–275). Armonk, NY: M.E. Sharpe.

Heuven, E., Bakker, A.B., Schaufeli, W.B., & Huisman, N. (2006). The role of self-efficacy in performing emotion work. *Journal of Vocational Behavior, 69*, 222–235. doi: 10.1016/j.jvb.2006.03.002

Hochschild, A. R. (1983). *The managed heart: Commercialization of human feeling.* Berkeley, CA: University of California Press.

Johnson, H.M., & Spector, P.E. (2007). Service with a smile: Do emotional intelligence, gender, and autonomy moderate the emotional labor process? *Journal of Occupational Health Psychology, 12*, 319–333. doi: 10.1037/1076-8998.12.4.319

Joseph, D.L., & Newman, D.A. (2010). Emotional intelligence: An integrative meta-analysis and cascading model. *Journal of Applied Psychology, 95*, 54–78. doi: 10.1037/a0017286

Judge, T.A., Jackson, C.L., Shaw, J.C., Scott, B.A., & Rich, B.L. (2007). Self-efficacy and work-related performance: The integral role of individual differences. *Journal of Applied Psychology, 92*, 107–127. doi: 10.1037/0021-9010.92.1.107

Judge, T.A., Woolf, E.F., & Hurst, C. (2009). Is emotional labor more difficult for some than others? A multilevel, experience-sampling study. *Personnel Psychology, 62*, 57–88. doi: 10.1111/j.1744-6570.2008.01129.x

Kiffin-Petersen, S.A., Jordan, C.L., & Soutar, G.N. (2011). The Big Five, emotional exhaustion, and citizenship behaviors in service settings: The mediating role of emotional labor. *Personality and Individual Differences, 50*, 43–48. doi: 10.1016/j.paid.2010.08.018

Kim, H.J. (2008). Hotel service providers' emotional labor: The antecedents and effects on burnout. *International Journal of Hospitality Management, 27*, 151–161. doi: 10.1016/j.ijhm.2007.07.019

Law, K.S., Wong, C.S., & Song, L.J. (2004). The construct and criterion validity of emotional intelligence and its potential utility for management studies. *Journal of Applied Psychology, 89*, 483–496.

Little, B.R. (2000). Free traits and personal contexts: Expanding a social ecological model of well-being. In W.B. Walsh & K.H. Craik (Eds.), *Person–environment psychology: New directions and perspectives* (2ⁿᵈ ed., pp. 87–116). Mahwah, NJ: LEA.

Lively, K. J. (2013). Social and cultural influencers: Gender/work-work. In A. A. Grandey, J. M. Diefendorff & D. E. Rupp (Eds.), *Emotional labor in the 21st century: Diverse perspectives on emotion regulation at work.* New York, NY: Psychology Press/Routledge.

Liu, Y., Perrewé, P.L., Hochwarter, W.A., & Kacmar, C.J. (2004). Dispositional antecedents and consequences of emotional labor at work. *Journal of Leadership and Organizational Studies, 10*, 12–25. doi: 10.1177/107179190401000402

Liu, Y., Prati, L.M., Perrewé, P.L., & Ferris, G.R. (2008). The relationship between emotional resources and emotional labor: An exploratory study. *Journal of Applied Social Psychology, 38,* 2410–2439. doi: 10.1111/j.1559-1816.2008. 00398.x

Lucas, R.E., & Baird, B.M. (2004). Extraversion and emotional reactivity. *Journal of Personality and Social Psychology, 86,* 473–485. doi: 10.1037/0022-3514.86.3.473

Mayer, J.D., & Salovey, P. (1997). What is emotional intelligence? In P. Salovey & D. J. Sluyter (Eds.), *Emotional development and emotional intelligence* (pp. 3–31). New York: Basic Books.

Mayer, J.D., Salovey, P., & Caruso, D. R. (2000). Models of emotional intelligence. In R. J. Sternberg (Ed.), *Handbook of intelligence* (pp. 392–420). Cambridge, England: Cambridge University Press.

McCrae, R.R., & John, O.P. (1992). An introduction to the five-factor model and its applications. *Journal of Personality, 60,* 175–215. doi: 10.1111/j.1467-6494.1992.tb00970.x

Morris, J.A., & Feldman, D.C. (1996). The dimensions, antecedents, and consequences of emotional labor. *Academy of Management Review, 21,* 986–1010. doi: 10.2307/259161

Moskowitz, D.S., & Côté, S. (1995). Do interpersonal traits predict affect? A comparison of three models. *Journal of Personality and Social Psychology, 69,* 915–924. doi: 10.1037/0022-3514.69.5.915

Opengart, R. (2005). Emotional intelligence and emotion work: Examining constructs from an interdisciplinary framework. *Human Resource Development Review, 4,* 49–62. doi: 10.1177/1534484304273817

Pervin, L.A. (1994). A critical analysis of current trait theory. *Psychological Inquiry, 5,* 103–113. doi: 10.1207/s15327965pli0502_1

Pugh, S.D., Groth, M., & Hennig-Thurau, T. (2011). Willing and able to fake emotions: A closer examination of the link between emotional dissonance and employee well-being. *Journal of Applied Psychology, 96,* 377–390. doi: 10.1037/a0021395

Randolph, K.L., & Dahling, J.J. (2011, April). Proactive personality and task significance in the emotional labor process. Paper presented at the 26th Annual Conference of the Society for Industrial and Organizational Psychology, Chicago, IL.

Rupp, D.E., McCance, A.S., Spencer, S., & Sonntag, K. (2008). Customer (in)justice and emotional labor: The role of perspective taking, anger, and emotional regulation. *Journal of Management, 34,* 903–924. doi: 10.1177/0149206307309261

Salovey, P. & Mayer, J. D. (1990). Emotional intelligence. *Imagination, Cognition, and Personality, 9:* 185–211.

Schaubroeck, J., & Jones, J.R. (2000). Antecedents of workplace emotional labor dimensions and moderators of their effects on physical symptoms. *Journal of Organizational Behavior, 21,* 163–183. doi: 10.1002/(SICI)1099-1379 (200003)21:2<163::AID-JOB37>3.0.CO;2-L

Sutton, R.I. (1991). Maintaining norms about expressed emotions: The case of bill collectors. *Administrative Science Quarterly, 36,* 245–268. doi: 10.2307/2393355

Sutton, R.I., & Staw, B.M. (1995). What theory is not. *Administrative Science Quarterly, 40*, 371–384.

Syed, J. (2008). From transgression to suppression: Implications of moral values and societal norms on emotional labor. *Gender, Work, and Organization, 15*, 182-201. doi: 10.1111/j.1468-0432.2007.00356.x

Totterdell, P., & Holman, D. (2003). Emotion regulation in customer service roles: Testing a model of emotional labor. *Journal of Occupational Health Psychology, 8*, 55–73. doi: 10.1037/1076-8998.8.1.55

Trougakos, J.P., Beal, D.J., Green, S.G., & Weiss, H.M. (2008). Making the break count: An episodic examination of recovery activities, emotional experiences, and positive affective displays. *Academy of Management Journal, 51*, 131–146.

Trougakos, J.P., & Hideg, I. (2009). Momentary work recovery: The role of within-day work breaks. In S. Sonnentag, P.L. Perrewé, & D.C. Ganster (Eds.), *Current perspectives on job-stress recovery* (pp. 37–84). Bingley, UK: JAI Press.

Wharton, A.S., & Erickson, R.J. (1993). Managing emotions on the job and at home: Understanding the consequences of multiple emotional rules. *Academy of Management Review, 18*, 457–486. doi: 10.2307/258905

Wilk, S.L., & Moynihan, L.M. (2005). Display rule "regulators": The relationship between supervisors and worker emotional exhaustion. *Journal of Applied Psychology, 90*, 917–927. doi: 10.1037/0021-9010.90.5.917

Wong, C., & Law, K. S. (2002). The effects of leader and follower emotional intelligence on performance and attitude: An exploratory study. *Leadership Quarterly, 13(3)*, 243–274. doi: 10.1016/S1048-9843(02)00099-1

# The Social Effects of Emotion Regulation in Organizations

STÉPHANE CÔTÉ • GERBEN A. VAN KLEEF • THOMAS SY

Organization members often exert efforts to regulate their emotions during interpersonal work exchanges. Research has documented that these efforts have important intraindividual consequences – consequences for the individuals regulating the emotions, or regulators – in organizational settings. Specifically, this research has shown that how organization members choose to regulate their emotions predicts their own performance and levels of stress (see Bono & Vey, 2005; Côté, 2005; Grandey, 2008; Grandey, Diefendorff, & Rupp, 2013, for reviews).

Because emotion regulation influences displays of emotions, the efforts to regulate emotions also have interpersonal consequences – consequences for interaction partners, or perceivers. In a seminal qualitative study of emotion norms for bill collectors, Sutton (1991) found that to influence debtors to pay back their debts, bill collectors were encouraged to exert efforts to express anger and irritation when debtors appeared sad or friendly, and calmness when debtors appeared angry. In another seminal study, a "good-cop bad-cop" strategy in which police interrogators alternated between displays of negative and positive emotions elicited more confessions from criminal suspects than displays of positive or negative emotions alone (Rafaeli & Sutton, 1991). This is because suspects were inclined to admit wrongdoings to the good cop to escape dealings with the bad cop, or to reciprocate the perceived kindness of the good cop.

Despite these advances, little is known about the social effects of emotion regulation in organizations – the effects of organization members' regulation of emotions on the attitudes, inferences, and behaviors of perceivers both inside and outside of the organization. Displays of emotions have important effects on other people's behaviors and attitudes (Keltner & Haidt, 1999; Van Kleef, 2009). The effects of displayed emotions on the behaviors and attitudes of other people were part of Hochschild's (1983) original definition of emotional labor, but they have been mostly missing from the literature. We propose that a full understanding of the consequences of emotion requires attention to both intrapersonal and interpersonal effects.

The goal of this chapter is to present an integrative framework for the social effects of emotion regulation. The framework – depicted in Figure 4.1 – describes how emotion regulation strategies influence which displays of emotion are observed by others, and how these displays, in turn, change the attitudes and behaviors of others. These effects are moderated by power and epistemic motivation (how much a person is motivated to develop a complex understanding of situations; Kruglanski, 1989). After presenting the model, we demonstrate its applicability to three areas of investigation in organization science: customer service, negotiations, and leadership.

## Emotion Regulation

Emotion regulation includes all of the efforts to increase, maintain, or decrease one or more components of an emotion (Gross, 2002; Levenson,

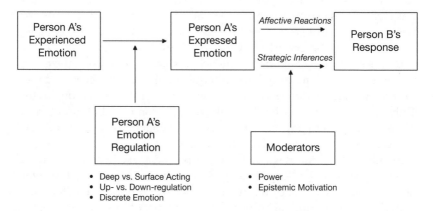

**Figure 4.1** A generic model of the social effects of emotion regulation.

1994). The components include facial displays, internal experiences, and physiological markers. Organization members may for example exert efforts to suppress the display of anxiety that they feel inside, or they may try to increase their enthusiasm. As described in the first chapter of this volume (Grandey et al., 2013), emotion regulation is a broad set of activities that may be labelled as emotional labor when certain criteria are met. Some instances of regulation do not fall within the realm of emotional labor, such as when negotiators modify their emotional displays for their own benefits. We focus on the construct at the highest level of abstraction (emotion regulation) to increase the breadth of the model.

There is a voluminous literature on emotion regulation in psychology and related fields (Gross, 2002). This research has focused on how these efforts change individuals' own internal experience of emotions, such as when one tries to cope with stressful events or suppress their anger. This research has identified an intimate connection between emotion regulation and emotion displays, demonstrating that when individuals change their internal experiences of emotion, changes to their facial displays ensue (Côté, 2005; Gross & Levenson, 1993). The effects of emotion regulation on emotion displays have attracted the attention of organizational scientists, because displays of emotion are thought to affect the quality of customer service and, in turn, company profits (Hochschild, 1983). The literature on the consequences of emotion regulation in the workplace is now substantial (Côté, 2005; Elfenbein, 2008; Grandey, 2008).

In this chapter, we extend this past theorizing by presenting an integrative model of how the emotion regulation of organization members shapes the attitudes and behaviors of their interaction partners. We extend past research on the effects of service agents' emotion regulation in customer service interactions (Grandey, 2003; Groth, Hennig-Thurau, & Walsh, 2009) by developing a model that subsumes all types of interactions in the workplace, including leader–follower interactions and negotiations. Our main proposal is that different emotion regulation strategies have different implications for the emotional displays of regulators and, in turn, for the behaviors that perceivers perform and the attitudes that perceivers hold.

## A SOCIAL FUNCTIONAL MODEL OF THE EFFECTS OF EMOTION REGULATION

Our model builds on past research on the social functions of emotions. Social functional accounts posit that emotions serve important interpersonal functions that facilitate interactions between people. Specifically, public displays of emotion communicate rich and important information about one's attitudes, goals, and intentions to those who observe these displays (Frijda & Mesquita, 1994; Keltner & Haidt, 1999; Van Kleef, 2009). For example, displays of enthusiasm by customer service agents communicate their intentions to be helpful to customers.

Social functional accounts of emotions also posit that individuals attend to others' emotions because these displays provide them with important information about the behavior they might expect from others. Individuals rapidly identify and respond to others' displays of emotions, suggesting that the process of identifying others' emotions is an evolutionary adaptation (Öhman & Mineka, 2001). For example, employees consult their leader's displays of emotions to obtain useful information about how their leader will act. In some instances, perceivers may respond quickly and automatically to the emotions that other people display. Followers may quickly catch the emotions of their leaders, and caught emotions, in turn, may affect how followers work (Sy, Côté, & Saavedra, 2005). In addition, perceivers may draw inferences from others' displays of emotions, and these inferences may, in turn, shape how perceivers think, act, and feel. When employees draw the inference that their leader is unsatisfied with the state of affairs because the leader is showing anger, employees may exert more effort.

Social functional accounts of emotions are supported by considerable evidence. First, evidence suggests that when individuals feel emotions internally, these feelings are displayed publicly (Cacioppo, Petty, Losch, & Kim, 1986). In addition, basic emotions are characterized by specific facial displays that involve distinct muscle movements (Ekman, 2003) and specific vocal expressions that involve distinct acoustic features (Juslin & Scherer, 2005). These displays are similar across cultures, although cultures have emotional dialects that shape, to some degree, how emotions are expressed (Elfenbein, Beaupré, Lévesque, & Hess, 2007).

There is also evidence for the basic premise that individuals are attuned to identify information about emotions in their environments in particular. In the laboratory, researchers have shown, using reaction time and neurophysiological measures, that participants are better able to process a target when it is linked to an emotional stimulus than when it is linked to a neutral stimulus (MacLeod, Mathews, & Tata, 1986; Mogg & Bradley, 1999). Displays of emotions that are shown subliminally – outside of the conscious awareness of observers – elicit corresponding muscle movements in observers (Dimberg, Thunberg, & Elmehed, 2000). These studies reveal that people pay special attention to emotional cues in their environment, presumably because these cues have evolutionary significance.

Another basic premise of social functional accounts of emotions is that displays of emotions have systematic effects on the attitudes and behaviors of people who observe them. Evidence for this premise comes from basic psychological research. Knutson (1996) showed that people infer the dispositions of others and, particularly, their trait dominance and affiliation, from their displays of emotions. More specifically, all else equal, people who display anger or disgust are perceived to be high in dominance and low in affiliation, those who display happiness are thought to be high on both traits, and those who display fear or sadness are believed to be low on both traits. Other research has shown that people who commit a social transgression are more likely to be forgiven if they display embarrassment (Keltner & Buswell, 1997) or guilt (Baumeister, Stillwell, & Heatherton, 1994). There is also evidence of social effects of positive emotions. In one study, displays of positive emotions in yearbook photographs of women graduating from a private college were associated with naïve observers' evaluations of both competence and affiliation and with the women's marital satisfaction and well-being, forty years later (Harker & Keltner, 2001).

## THE SOCIAL EFFECTS OF EMOTION REGULATION IN ORGANIZATIONS

We extend past research on the social effects of emotion by describing how efforts to regulate emotions, which have implications for regulators' displays of emotions, influence the behaviors and attitudes of perceivers. At the core of our model is the notion that emotion regulation can take different forms that have implications for how emotions are displayed and, in turn, the reactions that they elicit in observers. Past theory and research suggest that different emotion regulation efforts in organizations vary on three key dimensions: the form of regulation, direction of regulation, and discrete emotion that is regulated (Côté, 2005; Levenson, 1994).

### *The form of regulation: Deep versus surface acting*

At a broad level, researchers identified two forms of emotion regulation that differ in their timing during the unfolding of an emotion: antecedent-focused regulation, or deep acting, and response-focused regulation, or surface acting (Gross, 1998; Hochschild, 1983). Deep acting occurs before an emotion is fully under way. For example, leaders may think about uplifting moments to amplify both their subjective experience and their public display of confidence. By contrast, surface acting occurs once an emotion is fully under way. For instance, leaders may pretend to be excited about a change in the organization while leaving their subjective experience of doubt intact.

Laboratory studies show that deep and surface acting have different consequences for emotional displays and, in particular, the authenticity of the displays (Gross, 1998). Deep acting changes both the internal experience and the public display of emotion, while surface acting changes only the public display (Gross, 1998). For this reason, deep and surface acting produce displays that differ in their authenticity. Displays of emotions are authentic when they match other aspects of emotions, such as subjective experiences and physiological markers (Côté, 2005). Displays are inauthentic when they do not closely correspond to other aspects. The best known distinction between authentic and inauthentic displays is between Duchenne smiles, which involve muscle contractions around the eyes and the mouth, and non-Duchenne smiles (Ekman & Friesen, 1982). Deep acting produces more authentic displays of emotions, and surface acting produces more inauthentic displays (Côté, 2005; Grandey, 2003).

Different strategies to regulate emotion may have different social consequences because of differences in the authenticity of the displays that they generate. However, with the exception of research on customer service (e.g., Grandey, Fisk, Mattila, Jansen, & Sideman, 2005; Groth et al., 2009), the research on the social effects of emotion regulation to date has implicitly assumed that emotions were displayed authentically. Yet, inauthentic displays of emotions may be prevalent in organizations. Organization members may often try to show emotions that they do not feel or hide emotions that they do feel in efforts to influence others, because it is demanded by the organization, or to meet personal goals. We propose that the effects of emotion regulation differ depending on the authenticity of the displays that it produces. Unfortunately, there is a paucity of research about inferences that are drawn from inauthentic displays of various emotions and how those inferences, in turn, influence behavior in most organizational contexts. In the absence of research that explicitly examines the authenticity of displayed emotions, our understanding of the social effects of emotion regulation will remain incomplete.

### *The direction of regulation: Up- versus down-regulation.*

There are two directions in which organization members can regulate their emotions: (1) emotion amplification and (2) emotion suppression (Hochschild, 1983; Levenson, 1994). Emotion amplification (or the up-regulation of emotion) consists of initiating or enhancing public displays of emotion. For example, leaders may exert effort to enhance their public displays of enthusiasm about an organizational change. Emotion suppression (or the down-regulation of emotion) consists of reducing or eliminating public displays of emotion. For instance, leaders may exert effort to reduce their public displays of anxiety about an upcoming change. The social consequences of emotion regulation may depend on the direction in which emotion is regulated. For example, amplifying anger should have different consequences than suppressing anger. Thus, models of the social effects of emotion should identify the direction of interest.

### The discrete emotion that is regulated

Organization members can regulate a variety of discrete emotions (Glomb & Tews, 2004). Research on the social functions of emotions has revealed that different emotions communicate different attitudes, goals, and intentions to others (Morris & Keltner, 2000; Van Kleef, De Dreu, & Manstead, 2010). In addition, when emotional contagion occurs, observers catch the specific emotions that others show (Hatfield, Cacioppo, & Rapson, 1994). We propose that investigations of the social effects of emotions must precisely identify the emotion of interest, rather than assume that regulating different emotions has the same effects.

The notion that the social effects of emotion regulation will vary depending on these factors – the form of regulation, the direction of regulation, and the discrete emotion regulated – is intuitive yet important to consider in future research in this field. But what are the mechanisms by which these effects occur? In the following section, we describe mechanisms by which emotion regulation may exert social effects in organizations.

## THEORETICAL MECHANISMS UNDERLYING THE SOCIAL EFFECTS OF EMOTION REGULATION

We extend past research that investigated the mechanisms by which displays of emotions influence the behaviors and attitudes of others. Van Kleef (2009) parsimoniously organized the mechanisms into two broad categories: affective reactions and inferential processes. Here, we describe how these mechanisms underlie social effects of emotion regulation.

### Affective Reactions Mechanisms

The first category of mechanisms by which emotion regulation shapes the behaviors and attitudes of observers concerns the affective reactions of observers, which shape how observers think, feel, and act during social interactions (Van Kleef, 2009; Van Kleef et al., 2010). Affective reactions refer to the emotions that are elicited in observers and the liking that observers develop as a result of observing others' displays of emotions.

Affective reactions may be elicited in observers via the process of emotional contagion, a two-step process in which observers catch the emotion of displayers (Hatfield et al., 1994). Observers first unintentionally mimic others' public displays of emotion and, then, afferent feedback from facial, postural, or vocal mimicry produces a corresponding emotional response (Strack, Martin, & Stepper, 1988). The emotions that perceivers catch via emotional contagion, in turn, influence perceivers' attitudes and behaviors. Subordinates who catch their leaders' positive emotions, in turn, exhibit more cooperation (Sy et al., 2005).

Perceivers may also have affective reactions when others' displays of emotion themselves constitute emotionally-evocative stimuli. For instance, a display of disappointment elicited by an opponent may be an event that elicits happiness in a negotiator. In particular, in distributive negotiations in which parties can only gain at the expense of the other, displayed disappointment may indicate that the opponent is not satisfied and, thus, that one is doing well in the negotiation. Conversely, signs of happiness on the part of the opponent may indicate that the opponent is winning at one's own expense, which may trigger negative feelings (Thompson, Valley, & Kramer, 1995; Van Kleef et al., 2010).

A third type of affective reaction, liking, may also result from observing the emotions that others show. Past research has found that reports of how much people like others depend, in part, on the emotions that others express. Not surprisingly, people judge individuals who display happiness as likable and trustworthy (Clark, Pataki, & Carver, 1996), while individuals who display anger are liked less than individuals who display no emotion (Glomb & Hulin, 1997).

Here, we propose that different types of emotion regulation strategies, which are differentiated in their form, direction, and discrete emotion, produce different affective reactions in others. It is impractical to cover all combinations of form, direction, and discrete emotion, but we cover some illustrative combinations below. Observers may have different affective reactions when people display authentic emotions (as a result of deep acting) than when they display inauthentic emotions (as a result of surface acting). Observers may be able to detect that the displays of emotions that stem from surface acting are inauthentic, in that external displays do not perfectly correspond to internal experiences (Grandey et al., 2005; Groth et al., 2009). Detecting inauthenticity may produce a distinct set of affective reactions that is characterized by dislike and frustration because the interaction partner is not presenting his or her true self.

There could also be more nuanced effects of deep and surface acting in specific contexts. For instance, a customer service agent who is hiding frustration because of a previous upsetting customer may be particularly liked by the following customer, because the agent is trying his or her best to pay attention to that customer within unpleasant circumstances. In this situation, up-regulating enthusiasm via surface acting may generate more positive responses than no regulation. In the sections below, we present more specific examples of how emotion regulation strategies that differ in their form, direction, and discrete emotions elicit different affective reactions in the domains of customer service, negotiation, and leadership.

There may be mechanisms other than affective ones that drive the social effects of emotion regulation. Although emotional contagion models are popular in applied psychological research, not all studies have identified a role for them in mediating the social effects of emotions. In some studies, observers had affective reactions, but these reactions were not related to perceivers' attitudes and behaviors. For instance, research on distributive negotiation and bargaining has found that negotiators catch the emotions of their counterparts, but caught emotions do not drive their behavior (Van Kleef, De Dreu, & Manstead, 2004a). Instead, perceivers' inferences about the meaning of their counterparts' emotions guided their behavior. We now turn to this category of mechanisms.

## *Inferential Processes Mechanisms*

Displays of emotions stemming from regulation trigger inferential processes in observers by conveying information about expressers' attitudes, goals, and intentions (Keltner & Haidt, 1999). Observers' inferences, in turn, shape how they act during the interaction. Observers may infer, for instance, how much they trust those who express emotions, and whether these individuals are motivated by prosocial versus self-serving goals. Subordinates may infer from leaders' expressions of anger that their efforts are not meeting expectations, and that they need to increase their efforts to meet expected standards of performance (Sy et al., 2005; Van Kleef et al., 2009). Through this process, observers' inferences help them coordinate their behavior with the behavior of their interaction partners (Tiedens & Fragale, 2003).

We propose that different emotion regulation strategies that vary according to their form, direction, discrete emotion, and their various combinations produce different inferential processes in others. Observers will interpret the meanings of authentic and inauthentic displays of emotions to mean different things. We cover some illustrative combinations here. A negotiator who up-regulates anger via surface acting may be seen as particularly untrustworthy, as the negotiator is trying to attain a better negotiation position than he or she really has. A negotiator who uses surface acting to up-regulate happiness, however, may elicit different strategic inferences in others. This negotiator may be seen as making a particular effort to establish a cooperative climate in a setting that is typically associated with a competitive and tense atmosphere. We cover more specific instances of inferential processes from others' regulation of emotions in the sections below focused on the domains of customer service, negotiation, and leadership (see Figure 4.1).

## Moderators of the Social Effects of Emotion Regulation

We propose two important moderators of the social effects of emotion regulation, based on past findings from the literature of the social effects of emotion: power and epistemic motivation. Power is defined as "asymmetric control over valued resources in social relations" (Magee & Galinsky, 2008, p. 361). Research suggests that in negotiations, for instance, high power people are less affected by the emotions of others, presumably because they have substantial resources and hence can act at will without serious consequences (Sinaceur & Tiedens, 2006; Van Kleef & Côté, 2007).

Epistemic motivation is the degree to which a person is motivated to develop and maintain a complex understanding of situations (Kruglanski, 1989). When epistemic motivation is high, people expend more effort and process information about the situation more deliberately and systematically. Individuals with high epistemic motivation process emotional information in negotiation more thoroughly. Thus, they are more strongly influenced by inferential processes that are triggered by their counterparts' emotions, relative to those with low epistemic motivation (Van Kleef, De Dreu, & Manstead, 2004b).

# APPLICABILITY OF A MODEL OF THE SOCIAL EFFECTS OF EMOTION REGULATION IN ORGANIZATIONS

In the previous sections, we outlined a model by which the regulation of emotion exerts social effects by shaping the behaviors and attitudes of those who observe these efforts in organizations (see Figure 4.1). We propose that different emotion regulation efforts, characterized by different forms, directions, and discrete emotions, exert different effects via affective reactions and inferential processes. The effects are proposed to be moderated by power and epistemic motivation. In the sections below, we provide illustrative examples of how the model can be applied to understand the dynamics of interactions between people in the domains of customer service, negotiation, and leadership.

## Research on Customer Service

Research on customer service has examined whether the emotions expressed by service agents influence customer judgments such as service quality and customer behaviors such as purchases. Our model proposes that customer service agents can regulate their emotions in various ways, defined by the form, direction, and discrete emotion, and that these different ways of regulating emotions will have separate influences on the behavior and attitudes of customers. In customer service, agents will typically up-regulate positive emotions and down-regulate negative emotions, as past evidence suggests that customers are more satisfied with the quality of service and more likely to return to the store when agents express positive emotions (Tsai, 2001).

The studies of customer service have almost exclusively focused on displays of positive emotions. Several studies have found that displays of positive emotions by service agents have positive effects for organizations in various customer service settings. For example, Pugh (2001) found that bank tellers' positive emotional displays were related to clients' positive emotions following the service interaction and to positive customer evaluations of service quality. Research by Tsai (2001) and Tsai and Huang (2002) showed that retail employees' positive emotional displays increased customer willingness to return to the store and to make positive comments to friends.

Some studies have not found positive effects of service agents' displays of positive emotions. The positive displays of food service cashiers did not directly enhance customer mood, although they did enhance customers' service evaluations (Barger & Grandey, 2006). In the study by Tsai (2001), service agents' positive emotional displays were not related to customers' purchase decisions. Sutton and Rafaeli (1988) found that employees' displays of pleasant emotions were negatively related to sales in convenience stores. To further investigate this unexpected result, the authors conducted some qualitative analyses. These analyses showed that employees of stores with high levels of sales were busier and, in turn, less likely to display positive emotions than employees in slow-paced stores, who had time and resources to devote to displaying positive emotions.

These inconsistencies in the findings suggest possible moderating effects of the relation between displays of positive emotions and customer judgment and behavior. In one study, authentic displays of positive emotions resulted in perceptions of friendliness and performance judgments, but inauthentic displays of positive emotions did not show this effect (Grandey et al., 2005). Service agents who display authentic positive emotions are rated as performing better than those whose emotions are inauthentic (Grandey, 2003; Groth et al., 2009). These studies show that the authenticity of emotional expressions plays an important role.

These past divergent findings can be reconciled within our model. Specifically, when used to up-regulate positive emotions, deep acting should produce more authentic displays of positive emotions than surface acting. Thus, we should expect that when agents deep act positive emotions, customers should have more positive affective reactions and make more positive inferences about the service and the organization, and make more purchases, relative to when they surface act positive emotions. We should expect similar patterns when customer service employees hide negative emotions. When agents surface act, customers may recognize the discrepancy between what is publicly displayed and what is privately felt, and customers' affective reactions and inferences should be relatively negative.

An interesting boundary condition for this effect may be situations when customer service agents have obvious and reasonable reasons to be upset, yet are perceived to be making an effort to enhance the experience for customers. For instance, a customer who observes a service agent getting yelled at may react positively to any effort by the agent to up-regulate positive emotions, even if surface acting is used. Another possibility is when a service agent is obviously new and overwhelmed with the requirements of the job. A customer may appreciate any effort by the new service agent to up-regulate positive emotions.

## Research on Negotiations

In negotiations, just as in customer service, our model suggests that parties can regulate their emotions in various ways. The regulation strategies that negotiators choose are likely to depend on their ideas about the effectiveness of the various strategies (Thompson, Medvec, Seiden, & Kopelman, 2001). Some negotiators believe that a professional should maintain a poker face at all times. Such individuals can be expected to make attempts at down-regulating any emotion they may come to experience during negotiations, whether positive or negative. Other people believe that adopting a positive approach is most likely to yield good outcomes because it helps to create good rapport and puts the other party in a positive mood. Such people can be expected to down-regulate negative emotions and up-regulate positive emotions. Finally, a third group of negotiators believes that the best strategy is to express negative emotions such as anger during negotiations, because such emotions signal toughness and intransigence and may pressure the other party to concede. They may therefore be motivated to down-regulate positive emotions and "weak" negative emotions such as sadness or disappointment, and to up-regulate "strong" negative emotions such as anger and irritation.

There is empirical evidence for several of these intuitions. Most evidence points to the effectiveness of negative emotional expressions, but in some cases positive expressions appear to be more effective. Research has shown, for instance, that displayed emotions influence the attitudes and behaviors of counterparts. These studies suggest that expressions of anger communicate toughness and high limits (Sinaceur & Tiedens, 2006; Van Kleef et al., 2004a), whereas happiness communicates satisfaction with the current state of affairs (Van Kleef et al., 2004a). Thereby, expressions of anger elicit larger concessions and lower demands from counterparts, compared to neutral (Sinaceur & Tiedens, 2006) and happy emotional expressions (Van Kleef et al., 2004a).

Other studies have found that expressions of anger lead to unfavorable outcomes, and that expressions of positive emotions lead to favorable outcomes. Friedman, Anderson, Brett, Olekalns, Goates, and Lisco (2004) found that in online mediation of disputes, displays of anger reduced the other party's focus on dispute resolution, which in turn reduced the likelihood of settlement. In a series of studies, Kopelman, Rosette, and Thompson (2006) found that a) in a dispute setting, the counterparts of negotiators who displayed positive rather than negative or neutral emotions were more likely to desire future interaction; b) in an ultimatum setting, negotiators who displayed positive rather than negative emotions were more likely to close a deal; and c) in a distributive negotiation setting, negotiators placed higher demands on opponents displaying negative rather than positive emotions.

These studies indicate inconsistencies in findings regarding the effects of displaying negative emotions such as anger and positive emotions such as happiness in negotiations. Given these mixed findings, moderators of the relation between displayed emotion and opponents' demands and concessions have been examined, including power. Sinaceur and Tiedens (2006) found that displays of anger led to concessions in low-power, but not in high-power counterparts. Van Kleef and Côté (2007) showed how power and perceived justifiability of counterparts' displays of anger, together, guide negotiators' behavior. Low-power participants conceded when counterparts displayed anger, regardless of the perceived justifiability of the anger. By contrast, high-power participants ignored justifiable displays of anger and punished (by posing particularly high demands) unjustifiable displays of anger by their lower power counterparts.

In all these studies, it was unclear from the perspective of the participant whether the emotional expressions from the counterparts were authentic or not. That is, it was unclear whether the counterparts actually experienced the emotions that they expressed, or whether these expressions were strategically up-regulated. More recent research has addressed the question of how the way in which emotional expressions are regulated influences negotiation outcomes.

Côté, Hideg, and Van Kleef (2012) investigated the consequences of up-regulating anger during negotiation. In two experiments, participants engaged in a negotiation simulation with a (simulated) other person. As part of the negotiation, they saw a video clip of their supposed counterpart, who responded to the participant's last offer. The video clips showed an actor who had been trained to display different types of emotional expression. After seeing the clip, the participants made a new offer, which was the key variable of interest. One experiment showed that, relative to deep-acted anger (which was perceived as authentic by the participants), surface-acted anger (which was perceived as inauthentic) increased demands. This effect was mediated by reduced trust. The other experiment showed that, relative to a neutral emotion condition, surface acting anger increased demands (mediated by reduced trust), and deep acting anger decreased demands (mediated by increased perceptions of toughness). This study speaks to the first dimension of emotion regulation that we highlight here: deep acting versus surface acting.

It is possible that deep acting versus surface acting emotions have different effects depending on which emotion is regulated and expressed. This possibility calls for more research on the role of discrete emotions in emotion regulation. One possibility is that surface acted expressions of positive emotions are conducive to constructive interpersonal interactions and successful negotiation, because they suggest a prosocial motivation to invest in the relationship, whereas surface acted expressions of negative emotions are detrimental, because they suggest egoistic motives. In addition, past research does not speak to the second dimension of emotion regulation, namely up-regulation versus down-regulation. Future research is needed to shed light on the differences between up- and down-regulation of emotion in negotiations. Down-regulated negative emotions may be received more favorably than up-regulated negative emotions.

## Research on Leadership

The form of regulation is particularly relevant in the domain of leadership given that leaders are architects of emotional experiences at work (Brief & Weiss, 2002; Schneider & Bowen, 1985). While it is possible that other group members can shape emotional reactions, research suggests that leaders are most likely the agents shaping emotional reactions. Leaders are typically more powerful, and powerful others are more likely to shape the emotions of less powerful others. Less powerful others are more likely to pay attention to the emotions of powerful others (Fiske, 1993), including leaders (for a recent discussion of the interrelations between power and emotion, see Keltner, Van Kleef, Chen, & Kraus, 2008). Research has shown that leaders directly stimulate followers' emotions via contagion processes (Bono, Foldes, Vinson, & Muros, 2007; Sy et al., 2005). In addition, by expressing certain emotions, leaders model for followers what is appropriate to feel in a given situation (Lewis, 2000). Leaders may influence emotional experiences via deep acting or surface acting. Leaders may employ deep acting in several ways. Leaders often have significant control over their environment and can shape contextual features (e.g., norms, rules, routines, etc.) such that they (as well as their employees) are more inclined to experience certain emotions (Lord & Brown, 2004). Shaping emotional events reflects deep acting, in that this behavior is designed to induce certain emotional experiences from the outset. For example, establishing employee recognition programs is likely to influence both leaders' and followers' experience of positive emotions. Likewise, leaders may engage in practices such as team building activities that foster positive emotions, a process that may be facilitated by emotional intelligence (George, 2000).

Leaders may sometimes need to resort to surface acting. As architects of emotional experiences in the workplace, leaders are often required to react and respond to emotional experiences to maintain a healthy productive environment. Despite leaders' intentions and efforts in applying deep acting, leaders may not always be successful. At times, leaders may need to respond to unexpected emotional events, such as followers' sadness or anger stemming from unsatisfactory performance evaluations. In these unpredictable circumstances, leaders may have to resort to surface acting. Leaders may need to pretend to be sad externally (despite not experiencing sadness) as a way of expressing sympathy to establish a common bond and increase followers' receptiveness to performance feedback. Similarly, leaders may need to respond with calmness to diffuse followers' anger with the performance evaluation. Because of the immediacy of subordinates' reactions, leaders may not have the luxury of using deep acting, and surface acting may produce more favorable reactions than no regulation of emotion.

Research indicates that individuals have schemas associating certain emotions with certain jobs and roles (Briner & Totterdell, 2002), such as the leader role. Drawing from the implicit leadership theories literature, Sy, Côté, and van Knippenberg (2011) proposed that individuals have implicit theories about the emotions that leaders express, such that certain emotions are more relevant and prototypic of leaders, and others are less relevant and prototypic (Fitness, 2000; Glomb & Hulin, 1997; Lewis, 2000). This research demonstrates that implicit theories of leaders' emotions (ITLEs) – lay individuals' conceptions or schemas about the emotions of leaders – include the dimensions of Calm, Pride, Cheer, Fear, Anger, and Remorse. These ITLEs dimensions reflect the emotions that are associated with leaders in organizations. ITLEs may serve as a framework that influence leaders' up or down regulation of discrete emotions. Thus, emerging research indicates that leaders who endorse the Cheer dimension of ITLEs tend to up-regulate excitement (Sy et al., 2011). In a similar vein, ITLEs may serve as a framework through which followers interpret leaders' emotions and, thus, influence followers' liking for leader and evaluation of leader effectiveness.

Within the context of implicit theories of leader emotions, leaders' regulation of emotions (that vary according to their form, direction, and discrete emotion) may also have implications for leader–follower outcomes. Research examining the effect of leaders' emotions on subordinates' judgments and behaviors suggests a number of positive outcomes when leaders up-regulate displays of positive emotions. Bono and Ilies (2006) found that positive emotions displayed by leaders led to higher ratings of leader effectiveness, relative to neutral expressions. In addition, leaders' positive emotions are negatively related to groups' voluntary turnover rates (George & Bettenhausen, 1990) and positively associated with group performance (George, 1995). Leaders who display negative emotions when delivering feedback are perceived as less effective, and their subordinates perform worse on tasks (Gaddis, Connelly, & Mumford, 2004). Similarly, Glomb and Hulin (1997) found that supervisors who expressed anger were rated less favorably by observers, relative to unemotional supervisors and despite identical conversation.

Other research has identified some potential benefits of up-regulating displays of negative emotions. Lewis (2000) found that male leaders were rated as more effective when they displayed anger rather than neutral emotion or sadness. Sy and his associates (2005) found that groups with leaders in a negative mood showed more effort than groups with leaders in a positive mood, presumably because the negative mood indicated that the goal was not reached, and positive mood signaled that the state of affairs was satisfactory.

These mixed findings again suggest that some moderators of associations between leader emotion regulation and outcomes are at play. Whether emotion regulation produces authentic or inauthentic displays by leaders may have consequences. Leaders are evaluated negatively when their emotional displays are incongruent with their message content (Newcombe & Ashkanasy, 2002), suggesting that inauthentic displays may engender negative organizational outcomes.

Researchers have also investigated the role of epistemic motivation. Van Kleef and his associates (2009) found that teams with higher epistemic motivation performed better when the leader displayed anger rather than happiness, because such teams interpreted the leader's anger as a sign that the leader was not satisfied with the current progress. Teams with lower epistemic motivation, however, performed better when the leader displayed happiness rather than anger, because they caught positive emotions that, in turn, enhanced the degree to which they cooperated with each other.

Finally, a recent study reveals that the effectiveness of leader emotion regulation depends on followers' desire for social harmony, operationalized in terms of individual differences in agreeableness (Van Kleef, Homan, Beersma, & van Knippenberg, 2010). In this investigation, teams consisting of followers with high levels of agreeableness performed better when the leader expressed happiness, while teams consisting of low-agreeable followers performed better when the leader expressed anger.

## CONCLUSION

In this chapter, we presented a model of the social effects of emotion regulation. Emotion regulation is often done in the presence of others in the workplace, and how perceivers respond to emotion regulation may have various consequences for decisions to purchase products, concede or demand value in negotiations, and react to leadership.

We covered what is known so far about how organization members' efforts to regulate their emotions influence the attitudes and behaviors of those who observe displays of those emotions. We also identified several areas of future inquiry in this field. One critical question is whether the authenticity of the displays shapes how they are interpreted. There is research showing that inauthentic smiles reduce trust and cooperation (Johnston, Miles, & Macrae, 2010; Krumhuber, Manstead, Cosker, Marshall, Rosin, & Kappas, 2007). Similarly, inauthentic displays of other emotions could have very different effects than those found in past research on authentic displays. It is also important to investigate whether various aspects of the context shape observers' reactions to the same emotion displays. Displayed emotions may have different effects depending on whether the information exchange is immediate or not. For example, the reactions to inauthentic emotions may be less negative when organization members have not had the luxury of time to manage their emotions. Whether displays of emotions seem appropriate given the context or not may also moderate the effects of the displays (Van Kleef & Côté, 2007).

In addition, although several studies have examined the social effects of some emotions, other emotions have received little attention in the organizational research, and research on the social effects of regulating these emotions is needed. For instance, the regulation of embarrassment (Keltner & Buswell, 1997) and contempt (Melwani & Barsade, 2011) may have important social effects in organizations. Such research is needed to develop a complete understanding of the consequences of the regulation of emotions by organization members. Awaiting new research, we conclude that the consequences of emotion regulation occur as much *between* individuals as they occur within individuals. Emotion regulation is an inherently social process. Therefore, understanding its social consequences is vital for understanding emotional processes in organizations.

## REFERENCES

Barger, P. B., & Grandey, A. A. (2006). Service with a smile and encounter satisfaction: Emotional contagion and appraisal mechanisms. *Academy of Management Journal, 49*, 1229–1238.

Baumeister, R. F., Stillwell, A. M., & Heatherton, T. F. (1994). Guilt: An interpersonal approach. *Psychological Bulletin, 115*, 243–267.

Bono, J. E., Foldes, H. J., Vinson, G., & Muros, J. P. (2007). Workplace emotions: The role of supervision and leadership. *Journal of Applied Psychology, 92*, 1357–1367.

Bono, J. E., & Ilies, R. (2006). Charisma, positive emotions and mood contagion. *Leadership Quarterly, 17*, 317–334.

Bono, J. E., & Vey, M. A. (2005). Toward understanding emotional management at work: A quantitative review of emotional labor research. In C. E. Härtel, W.J. Zerbe & N. M. Ashkanasy (Eds.), *Emotions in organizational behavior* (pp. 213–233). Mahwah, NJ: Lawrence Erlbaum Associates.

Brief, A. & Weiss, H. (2002). Organizational behavior: Affect in the workplace. *Annual Review of Psychology, 53*, 279–307.

Briner, R., & Totterdell, P. (2002). The experience, expression and management of emotion at work. In P. Warr (Ed.), *Psychology at work* (pp. 229–252). New York, NY: Penguin Press.

Cacioppo, J. T., Petty, R. E., Losch, M. E., & Kim, H. S. (1986). Electromyographic activity over facial muscle regions can differentiate the valence and intensity of affective reactions. *Journal of Personality and Social Psychology, 50*, 260–268.

Clark, M. S., Pataki, S. P., & Carver, V. H. (1996). Some thoughts and findings on self-presentation of emotions in relationships. In G. J. O. Fletcher, & J. Fitness (Eds.), *Knowledge structures in close relationships: A social psychological approach* (pp. 247–274). Hillsdale, NJ: Lawrence Erlbaum Associates.

Côté, S. (2005). A social interaction model of the effects of emotion regulation on work strain. *Academy of Management Review, 30*, 509–530.

Côté, S., Hideg, I., & Van Kleef, G. A. (2012). *The consequences of faking anger in negotiations*. Manuscript submitted for publication.

Dimberg, U., Thunberg, M., & Elmehed, K. (2000). Unconscious facial reactions to emotional facial expressions. *Psychological Science, 11*, 86–89.

Ekman, P. (2003). *Emotions revealed: Recognizing faces and feelings to improve communication and emotional life*. New York: Henry Holt.

Ekman, P., & Friesen, W. V. (1982). Felt, false, and miserable smiles. *Journal of Nonverbal Behavior, 6,* 238–258.

Elfenbein, H. A. (2008). Emotion in organizations: A review and theoretical integration. In J. P. Walsh & A. P. Brief (Eds.), *Academy of management annals* (Vol. 1., pp. 315–386.) New York, NY: Taylor & Francis Group/Lawrence Erlbaum Associates.

Elfenbein, H. A., Beaupré, M., Lévesque, M., & Hess, U. (2007). Toward a dialect theory: Cultural differences in the expression and recognition of posed facial expressions. *Emotion, 7,* 131–146.

Fiske, S. T. (1993). Controlling other people: The impact of power on stereotyping. *American Psychologist, 48,* 621–628.

Fitness, J. (2000). Anger in the workplace: An emotion script approach to anger episodes between workers and their superiors, co-workers and subordinates. *Journal of Organizational Behavior, 21,* 147–162.

Friedman, R., Anderson, C., Brett, J., Olekalns, M., Goates, N., & Lisco, C. C. (2004). The positive and negative effects of anger on dispute resolution: Evidence from electronically mediated disputes. *Journal of Applied Psychology, 89,* 369–376.

Frijda, N. H., & Mesquita, B. (1994). The social roles and functions of emotions. In S. Kitayama & H. R. Markus (Eds.), *Emotion and culture: Empirical studies of mutual influence* (pp. 51–87). Washington, DC: American Psychological Association.

Gaddis, B., Connelly, S., & Mumford, M. D. (2004). Failure feedback as an affective event: Influences of leader affect on subordinate attitudes and performance. *Leadership Quarterly, 15,* 663–686.

George, J. M. (1995). Leader positive mood and group performance: The case of customer service. *Journal of Applied Social Psychology, 25,* 778–794.

George, J. M. (2000). Emotions and leadership: The role of emotional intelligence. *Human Relations, 53,* 1027–1055.

George, J. M., & Bettenhausen, K. (1990). Understanding prosocial behavior, sales performance, and turnover: A group-level analysis in a service context. *Journal of Applied Psychology, 75,* 698–709.

Glomb, T. M., & Hulin, C. L. (1997). Anger and gender effects in observed supervisor–subordinate dyadic interactions. *Organizational Behavior and Human Decision Processes, 72,* 281–307.

Glomb, T. M. & Tews, M. J. (2004). Emotional labor: A conceptualization and scale development. *Journal of Vocational Behavior, 64,* 1–23.

Grandey, A. A. (2003). When "the show must go on": Surface acting and deep acting as determinants of emotional exhaustion and peer-rated service delivery. *Academy of Management Journal, 46,* 86–96.

Grandey, A. A. (2008). Emotions at work: A review and research agenda. In C. Cooper & J. Barling (Eds.), *Handbook of organizational behavior* (Vol. 1, pp. 234–261). Thousand Oaks, CA: Sage.

Grandey, A. A., Diefendorff, J. M., & Rupp, D. E. (2013). Emotional labor: Overview of definitions, theories, and evidence. In A. A. Grandey, J. M. Diefendorff & D. E. Rupp (Eds.), *Emotional labor in the 21st century: Diverse perspectives on emotion regulation at work.* New York, NY: Psychology Press/Routledge.

Grandey, A. A., Fisk, G. M., Mattila, A. S., Jansen, K. J., & Sideman, L. A. (2005). Is "service with a smile" enough? Authenticity of positive displays during service encounters. *Organizational Behavior and Human Decision Processes, 96*, 38–55.

Gross, J. J. (1998). The emerging field of emotion regulation: An integrative review. *Review of General Psychology, 2*, 271–299.

Gross, J. J. (2002). Emotion regulation: Affective, cognitive, and social consequences. *Psychophysiology, 39*, 281–291.

Gross, J. J., & Levenson, R. W. (1993). Emotional suppression: Physiology, self-report, and expressive behavior. *Journal of Personality and Social Psychology, 64*, 970–986.

Groth, M., Hennig-Thurau, T., & Walsh, G. (2009). Customer reactions to emotional labor: The roles of employee acting strategy and customer detection accuracy. *Academy of Management Journal, 52*, 958–974.

Harker, L., & Keltner, D. (2001). Expressions of positive emotion in women's college yearbook pictures and their relationship to personality and life outcomes across adulthood. *Journal of Personality and Social Psychology, 80*, 112–124.

Hatfield, E., Cacioppo, J. T., & Rapson, R. L. (1994). *Emotional contagion*. New York: Cambridge University Press.

Hochschild, A. (1983). *The managed heart: Commercialization of human feeling*. Berkeley, CA: University of California Press.

Johnston, L., Miles, L., & Macrae, C. N. (2010). Why are you smiling at me? Social functions of enjoyment and non-enjoyment smiles. *British Journal of Social Psychology, 49*, 107–127.

Juslin, P. N., & Scherer, K. R. (2005). Vocal expression of affect. In J. A. Harrigan, R. Rosenthal & K. R. Scherer (Eds.), *The new handbook of methods in nonverbal behavior research* (pp. 65–135). New York: Oxford University Press.

Keltner, D., & Buswell, B. N. (1997). Embarrassment: Its distinct form and appeasement functions. *Psychological Bulletin, 122*, 250–270.

Keltner, D., & Haidt, J. (1999). Social functions of emotions at four levels of analysis. *Cognition and Emotion, 13*, 505–521.

Keltner, D., Van Kleef, G. A., Chen, S., & Kraus, M. (2008). A reciprocal influence model of social power: Emerging principles and lines of inquiry. *Advances in Experimental Social Psychology, 40*, 151–192.

Knutson, B. (1996). Facial expressions of emotion influence interpersonal trait inferences. *Journal of Nonverbal Behavior, 20*, 165–182.

Kopelman, S., Rosette, A. S., & Thompson, L. (2006). The three faces of Eve: Strategic displays of positive, negative, and neutral emotions in negotiations. *Organizational Behavior and Human Decision Processes, 99*, 81–101.

Kruglanski, A. W. (1989). *Lay epistemics and human knowledge: Cognitive and motivational bases*. New York: Plenum Press.

Krumhuber, E., Manstead, A. S. R., Cosker, D., Marshall, D., Rosin, P. L., & Kappas, A. (2007). Facial dynamics as indicators of trustworthiness and cooperative behavior. *Emotion, 7*, 730–735.

Levenson, R. W. (1994). Human emotions: A functional view. In P. Ekman & R. J.

Davidson (Eds.), *The nature of emotion* (pp. 123–126). New York: Oxford University Press.

Lewis, K. M. (2000). When leaders display emotion: How followers respond to negative emotional expression of male and female leaders. *Journal of Organizational Behavior, 21*, 221–234.

Lord, R. G., & Brown, D. J. (2004). *Leadership processes and follower identity.* New Jersey: Lawrence Erlbaum Associates.

MacLeod, C., Mathews, A., & Tata, P. (1986). Attentional bias in emotional disorders. *Journal of Abnormal Psychology, 95*, 15–20.

Magee, J. C., & Galinsky, A. D. (2008). Social hierarchy: The self-reinforcing nature of power and status. *Academy of Management Annals, 2*, 351–398.

Melwani, S., & Barsade, S. G. (2011). Held in contempt: The psychological, inter-personal, and performance consequences of contempt in a work context. *Journal of Personality and Social Psychology, 101*, 503–520.

Mogg, K., & Bradley, B. P. (1999). Orienting of attention to threatening facial expressions presented under conditions of restricted awareness. *Cognition and Emotion, 13*, 713–740.

Morris, M. W., & Keltner, D. (2000). How emotions work: The social functions of emotional expressions in negotiations. *Research in Organizational Behavior, 22*, 1–50.

Newcombe, M., & Ashkanasy, N. M. (2002). The role of affect and affective congruence in perceptions of leaders: An experimental study. *Leadership Quarterly, 13*, 601–614.

Öhman, A., & Mineka, S. (2001). Fears, phobias, and preparedness: Toward an evolved module of fear and fear learning. *Psychological Review, 108*, 483–522.

Pugh, S. D. (2001). Service with a smile: Emotional contagion in the service encounter. *Academy of Management Journal, 44*, 1018–1027.

Rafaeli, A., & Sutton, R. I. (1991). Emotional contrast strategies as means of social influence: Lessons from criminal interrogators and bill collectors. *Academy of Management Journal, 34*, 749–775.

Schneider, B., & Bowen, D. E. (1985). Employee and customer perceptions of service in banks: Replication and extension. *Journal of Applied Psychology, 70*, 423–433.

Sinaceur, M., & Tiedens, L. Z. (2006). Get mad and get more than even: When and why anger expression is effective in negotiations. *Journal of Experimental Social Psychology, 42*, 314–322.

Strack, F., Martin, L. L., & Stepper, S. (1988). Inhibiting and facilitating conditions of the human smile: A nonobtrusive test of the facial feedback hypothesis. *Journal of Personality and Social Psychology, 54*, 768–777.

Sutton, R. I. (1991). Maintaining norms about expressed emotions: The case of bill collectors. *Administrative Science Quarterly, 36*, 245–268.

Sutton, R. I., & Rafaeli, A. (1988). Untangling the relationship between displayed emotions and organizational sales: The case of convenience stores. *Academy of Management Journal, 31*, 461–487.

Sy, T., Côté, S., & Saavedra, R. (2005). The contagious leader: Impact of the leader's mood on the mood of group members, group affective tone, and group processes. *Journal of Applied Psychology, 90*, 295–305.

Sy, T., Côté, S., & van Knippenberg, D. (2011). The emotional leader: Implicit theories of leader emotions and consequences for leader–follower outcomes. Unpublished manuscript.

Thompson, L., Medvec, V. H., Seiden, V., & Kopelman, S. (2001). Poker face, smiley face, and rant 'n' rave: Myths and realities about emotion in negotiation. In M. A. Hogg & R. S. Tindale (Eds.), *Blackwell handbook of social psychology: Group processes* (pp. 139–163). Malden, MA: Blackwell.

Thompson, L., Valley, K. L., & Kramer, R. M. (1995). The bittersweet feeling of success: An examination of social perception in negotiation. *Journal of Experimental Social Psychology, 31*, 467–492.

Tiedens, L. Z., & Fragale, A. R. (2003). Power moves: Complementarity in dominant and submissive nonverbal behavior. *Journal of Personality and Social Psychology, 84*, 558–568.

Tsai, W. (2001). Determinants and consequences of employee displayed positive emotions. *Journal of Management, 27*, 497–512.

Tsai, W., & Huang, Y. (2002). Mechanisms linking employee affective delivery and customer behavioral intentions. *Journal of Applied Psychology, 87*, 1001–1008.

Van Kleef, G. A. (2009). How emotions regulate social life: The emotions as social information (EASI) model. *Current Directions in Psychological Science, 18*, 184–188.

Van Kleef, G. A., & Côté, S. (2007). Expressing anger in conflict: When it helps and when it hurts. *Journal of Applied Psychology, 92*, 1557–1569.

Van Kleef, G. A., De Dreu, C. K. W., & Manstead, A. S. R. (2004a). The interpersonal effects of anger and happiness in negotiations. *Journal of Personality and Social Psychology, 86*, 57–76.

Van Kleef, G. A., De Dreu, C. K. W., & Manstead, A. S. R. (2004b). The interpersonal effects of emotions in negotiations: A motivated information processing approach. *Journal of Personality and Social Psychology, 87*, 510–528.

Van Kleef, G. A., De Dreu, C. K. W., & Manstead, A. S. R. (2010). An interpersonal approach to emotion in social decision making: The emotions as social information model. *Advances in Experimental Social Psychology, 42*, 45–96.

Van Kleef, G. A., Homan, A. C., Beersma, B., & van Knippenberg, D. (2010). On angry leaders and agreeable followers: How leaders' emotions and followers' personalities shape motivation and team performance. *Psychological Science, 21*, 1827–1834.

Van Kleef, G. A., Homan, A. C., Beersma, B., van Knippenberg, D., van Knippenberg, B., & Damen, F. (2009). Searing sentiment or cold calculation? The effects of leader emotional displays on team performance depend on follower epistemic motivation. *Academy of Management Journal, 52*, 562–580.

CHAPTER
# 5

# Emotional Labor at the Unit-level

KAREN NIVEN • PETER TOTTERDELL •
DAVID HOLMAN • DAVID CAMERON

Early years of research concerning emotional labor were dominated by a
focus on the role of the employee who is required to perform emotional
labor (e.g., Hochschild, 1983). More recent dyadic models (e.g., Côté,
2005), discussed in the previous chapter (Côté, Van Kleef, & Sy, 2013),
also recognize the role played by the person towards whom the emotional
labor is directed. In this chapter, we seek to further expand the understanding of who is involved in and affected by emotional labor, by
broadening our focus to the unit (i.e., the collective or group), within
which emotional labor occurs. Within organizational contexts, employees
and their managers typically form units within which they work, and we
argue that it is important to consider emotional labor from a unit-level
perspective. To do this, we begin by outlining the traditional understanding of emotional labor, then go on to explain how this understanding
might be extended in light of recent avenues of organizational, psychological, and sociological research and theory. In our Framework for Unit-level
Emotional Labor (FUEL), we consider the roles played by individuals
within a unit and the unit as a whole. By broadening our focus to the unit,
we explain how the emotions, attitudes, and behaviors of whole units of
people can become affected by emotional labor, and discuss the methods
necessary for investigating these effects.

# TRADITIONAL UNDERSTANDING
# OF EMOTIONAL LABOR

Hochschild (1983) originally defined emotional labor as the management of feelings for commercial purposes. She explained how employees in service organizations are often required to produce particular affective states (e.g., happiness, calmness) in their customers. Hochschild (1983) argued that organizations require employees to manage their own emotional displays in order to achieve changes in customer affect, referring to this requirement as *The Managed Heart*. In her theoretical model, Grandey (2000) built on Hochschild's work by connecting emotional labor to the psychological process of *emotion regulation*. Emotion regulation has been defined as "the process of initiating, maintaining, modulating, or changing the occurrence, intensity, or duration of . . . feeling states" (Eisenberg, Fabes, Guthrie, & Reiser, 2000, p. 137) and Grandey (2000) argued that emotional labor could be understood as emotion regulation performed to achieve organizational goals.

Hochschild's and Grandey's works have prompted hundreds of subsequent studies, theories, and reviews of emotional labor as a form of emotion regulation. There are assumptions inherent within this body of literature about who is involved in the process of emotional labor and the nature of these parties' roles. In particular, the employee who is required by the organization to perform emotional labor (referred to herein as the 'agent') is seen as the key figure involved in emotional labor. The primary role played by the agent is thought to be to control his or her own emotions in order to express emotions that are considered appropriate by the organization. Hence, researchers have tended to highlight organizational rules and norms about employees' expressed emotions and the self-regulatory strategies used to meet these rules and norms, including antecedent-focused regulation (or deep acting) and response-focused regulation (or surface acting) (e.g., Diefendorff, Croyle, & Gosserand, 2005; Grandey, 2003; Totterdell & Holman, 2003).

As discussed in the previous chapter (Côté et al., 2013), more recent models (e.g., Côté, 2005) suggest that emotional labor is enacted within a dyadic context, in which the agent controls his or her emotions for the benefit of someone else (a customer, client, coworker, or manager; see Tschan, Rochat, & Zapf, 2005). Accordingly, these models recognize this 'target' as a second important figure in emotional labor. The agent's expressed emotion is thought to affect the target's emotions, attitudes, and behavior, via inferential processing and emotional contagion mechanisms (Van Kleef, 2009); in turn, the affective reactions of the target influence the agent (Côté, 2005). Changes in the target's emotions are therefore assumed to arise as a result of the agent's regulation of his or her own emotional expression and the target does not intentionally engage in any form of emotion regulation.

Thus, emotional labor has largely been studied as a dyadic process in which a single employee regulates his or her own expressed emotions for the benefit of an observing customer, client, coworker, or manager. As such, while effects of emotional labor on individual agents (e.g., for their well-being, job satisfaction, and job performance; Grandey, 2003; Totterdell & Holman, 2003) and individual targets (e.g., for their emotions, perceptions of service quality, and tipping; Barger & Grandey, 2006; Pugh, 2001) have been established, to date research has typically not considered effects beyond the interpersonal dyad. In the following sections of the paper, we draw on recent advances in theory and research to present a broader, unit-level perspective of who is involved in emotional labor and the emotion regulatory roles these parties play. Later in the chapter, we discuss the implications of this broader understanding for researchers studying emotional labor.

## A BRIEF NOTE ABOUT TERMINOLOGY

In this chapter, we refer to three key parties who we argue to be involved in the emotional labor process: the 'agent', the 'target', and 'third parties'. Like other researchers in this area we view the agent as an employee who is expected to perform emotion regulation in order to fulfil organizational norms or rules. The target is the person for whom the agent performs emotional labor. Third parties are individuals who become indirectly or directly involved in the emotional labor interaction between agent and target.

In line with the episodic understanding of emotional labor (see Beal & Trougakos, 2013), we view emotional labor as occurring within goal-directed episodes; each episode is directed by an agent's goal to fulfil his or her role requirements. Because the episode is defined and characterized by the agent's emotional labor goal, we differentiate the three key parties according to the roles they play *at the start* of an episode. Thus, even though, as we discuss later, all parties may hold goals that drive emotion regulation and may actively engage in emotion regulation at points during the episode, each party is referred to by the term that is designated at the start of the episode.

## THE AGENT OF EMOTIONAL LABOR

As the employee who is required by the organization to perform emotional labor, the agent is indisputably a key unit-member in the emotional labor process. Traditionally, researchers have viewed the agent as an individual whose role is to self-regulate his or her own emotions for the benefit of a given target. Here, we extend this view in two ways. First, we advance another type of emotion regulation that employees may also engage in as part of emotional labor. Second, we consider whether whole units as well as single individuals may act as agents in the emotional labor process.

## The Agent's Emotion Regulatory Role

There is little doubt that agents' attempts to self-regulate their emotions are a core feature of their role in the emotional labor process. Outside of the organizational literature, however, researchers have long-recognized that there are two main forms of emotion regulation: the regulation of one's own emotions and the regulation of other people's emotions. The latter process, *interpersonal emotion regulation*, involves deliberate attempts to shape the feelings of another person or persons (Niven, Totterdell, & Holman, 2009). It is somewhat similar to processes such as impression management (Goffman, 1955) and interpersonal influence (Kipnis, Schmidt, & Wilkinson, 1980), because it entails the use of deliberate strategies to try to influence someone else. However, unlike these other processes, interpersonal emotion regulation is primarily directed towards influencing others' emotions. Changes to attitudes and behaviors *can* arise as a result of interpersonal emotion regulation, but these changes occur via the effects on emotions, whereas impression management and influence tactics can affect others' attitudes and behaviors independently of their emotions.

Interpersonal emotion regulation can be considered as distinct from the self-regulatory processes typically studied in the emotional labor literature. Although, as the previous chapter (Côté et al., 2013) suggests, emotion self-regulation is part of a dyadic interaction, the regulation itself is self-directed, with the employee controlling his or her own emotions; any impact on the other person then occurs through the social information value of emotion (Kelly & Barsade, 2001; Parkinson, 1996; Van Kleef, 2009). In contrast, with interpersonal emotion regulation, the employee seeks to directly control someone else's emotions. Nevertheless, there are clear links between the processes, which can be understood with reference to a control theory perspective (Carver & Scheier, 1998). Taking this perspective, agents need to fulfill the goal of creating particular emotions in targets (i.e., interpersonal emotion regulation) in order to achieve the highest-level goal of meeting their role requirements, and this can be done by displaying positive emotions towards those targets (i.e., emotion self-regulation) (see Diefendorff & Gosserand, 2003). Thus, exaggerating or suppressing one's own displayed emotions is one way in which interpersonal emotion regulation can be achieved (Rafaeli & Sutton, 1991; Sutton, 1991), although it should be noted that: a) there are many other ways in which people can deliberately influence others' emotions, including complimenting, criticizing, listening, ignoring, humor, rationalizing, and giving advice (Niven et al., 2009); and b) people may engage in emotion self-regulation to fulfill other higher-level goals that do not involve interpersonal emotion regulation (e.g., to be happy).

The literature concerning interpersonal emotion regulation first emerged within the areas of developmental psychology and sociology (e.g., Francis, 1997; Gianino & Tronick, 1988; Niven, Holman, & Totterdell, in press; Thoits, 1996), but the process is now recognized to be a highly prevalent feature of everyday social relationships (Niven et al., 2009). Over the last twenty or so years, there has been an upsurge in evidence for employees' use of interpersonal emotion regulation within organizational contexts, including hospitals, law firms, prisons, and debt collection agencies (Francis, Monahan, & Berger; 1999; Lively, 2000; Locke, 1996; Niven, Totterdell, & Holman, 2007; Pierce, 1999; Rafaeli & Sutton, 1991; Sutton, 1991). The ability to manage others' emotions is thought to be a key contributing factor towards effective leadership (George, 2000), negotiation (Morris & Keltner, 2000), and trust building across organizational boundaries (Williams, 2007). Moreover, studies suggest that people may play specific roles within organizations relating to the type of interpersonal emotion regulation they typically perform. Toxin handlers attempt to reduce the stress and negative emotions that their coworkers experience (Frost & Robinson, 1999), while energizers attempt to inject happiness and enthusiasm into those around them (Cross, Baker, & Parker, 2003).

A notable feature of this mounting body of evidence is that much of the interpersonal emotion regulation that employees engage in at work is done to comply with organizational rules or norms. For example, in the studies of Francis and colleagues (1999) and Locke (1996), alleviating patients' distress was considered a central part of the role of medical professionals, and in Pierce's (1999) study she explained how the paralegals she studied perceived that they were expected to bolster their managers' affect as part of their job. Ashforth, Kreiner, Clark, and Fugate's (2007) research highlights how managers in stigmatized organizations (e.g., abortion clinics) see it as part of their job to normalize the work done by their staff to prevent employees from internalizing negative emotions and to restore pride and happiness. The debt collectors and criminal interrogators described in Sutton (1991) and Rafaeli and Sutton (1991), respectively, even received training about how best to manage the emotions of their debtors and suspects. In these cases, interpersonal emotion regulation may be seen as a form of emotional labor, in keeping with

Hochschild's (1983) original conceptualization, which had at its center the notion of employees being required by their organization to produce particular affective states in other people. We therefore propose that agents engage in two forms of emotion regulation to fulfill their job's emotional labor requirements: i) emotion self-regulation, where they attempt to manage their own feelings; and ii) interpersonal emotion regulation, where they attempt to manage the feelings of their customers, clients, patients, or managers.

## The Agent as a Whole Unit

Recently, it has been suggested that the norms and rules that govern the emotional labor process may best be conceptualized at the whole unit-rather than the individual-level. Diefendorff, Erickson, Grandey, and Dahling (2011) argued that the organizational rules and norms that prompt employees' use of emotion regulation (e.g., about the emotions it is appropriate to display) are adopted and modified within particular work units, via socialization and interactions, and should therefore be shared amongst members of the same work unit. In a study involving work units of hospital nurses, Diefendorff and colleagues found support for this assertion. They reported high levels of consensus within whole work units regarding the extent to which members believed that they were expected to perform emotion regulation during their interactions with patients, and reliable between-unit differences in these beliefs, concluding that "display rule perceptions exhibit group-level properties" (p. 181). Similarly, Martínez-Iñigo, Totterdell, Alcover, and Holman (2009) found that perception of display rule requirements in primary health care teams varied according to professional group, work team, and even district. Norms about emotion regulation during interactions with coworkers and managers may also reside at the unit-level. For example, Bartel and Saavedra's (2000) study of work teams highlighted shared norms within whole units about the emotions considered appropriate to express and elicit during interactions with group members.

Not only are there likely to be unit-level norms about which emotions one should express towards or elicit in others, but there may also be shared norms about *how* to express or elicit these emotions. For example, in Francis et al.'s (1999) study of providers in hospitals, there were clear shared norms about the use of humor as interpersonal emotion regulation (e.g., 'dark humor' was considered a functional strategy with coworkers, but not usually with patients or their families).

While the extent to which norms are shared within units may depend on the characteristics of unit members (e.g., gender, status, and race) and the mix of members in the unit (see Erickson & Stacey, 2013), broadly speaking, if norms about the performance of emotional labor can be understood at the whole unit-level, then it seems likely that the emotion regulation that takes place to meet these norms may also be conceptualized at the whole unit-level. In other words, as a result of socialization processes, shared norms concerning the emotions it is appropriate to display and elicit in others and the strategies that should be used to achieve these emotions likely develop within work units. In turn these norms should lead to consistency within whole units regarding employees' use of emotion self-regulation and interpersonal emotion regulation. In the Diefendorff et al. (2011) study, evidence for this proposition was found with relation to the self-regulation strategy of surface acting, where a significant amount of variance was attributable to the unit-level, although it should be noted that no such support was found for the strategy of deep acting.

As well as unit-level consistency regarding the use of emotion regulation to fulfill shared emotional labor norms, there may also be instances when whole units act together to try to regulate the feelings of target individuals. It appears that one of the key factors that drives whole units to act together in emotion regulation is norm violation; when a unit member violates the emotion norms that have developed within a unit, the rest of the unit might act in concert to 'correct' this breach. For example, research suggests that work units sometimes stage emotion-focused interventions to tackle a 'bad apple' in the team by influencing the poor workmate's emotions (Felps, Mitchell, & Byington, 2006). An additional factor that might underlie the performance of emotion regulation as a whole unit might be the need to exert a strong change in a target's emotions. The assumption underlying this factor is that regulation performed by a group of people will have a more powerful impact on a target's feelings than that performed by an individual agent. For example, outside of the work arena, Thoits's (1996) research with a psychodrama group (a type of support group that acts out members' problems) highlighted how the group collaboratively engaged in interpersonal emotion regulation to influence the clinically significant emotions of its members, for instance by performing group enactments of a member's trauma. To date, little research has examined whether the emotion regulation strategies employed by whole units differ from those used by individual agents, although some strategies by their very nature require cooperation from a whole unit (e.g., creating a sense of belonging to or being rejected from the unit). Nevertheless, it is apparent that the agent in the emotional labor process can be meaningfully conceptualized as a whole unit as well as an individual unit member.

# THE TARGET OF EMOTIONAL LABOR

In the previous section, we focused on the key figure within a unit involved in emotional labor, the agent. In this section, we turn our attention to the second party in the emotional labor process: the 'target'. The traditional view of the target is as an individual who plays a relatively passive, i.e., non-deliberate, emotion regulatory role. We seek to expand this view in two ways. First, we argue that the target is likely to play an active role in emotional labor, engaging in both emotion self-regulation and interpersonal emotion regulation during an episode. Second, we suggest that, like agents, targets may be whole units as well as individuals.

## *The Target's Emotion Regulatory Role*

By definition, the target is the person for whom emotional labor is performed. The target's main role to date has therefore been conceived as the 'receiver' of the emotion regulation efforts of the agent, but we contend that the target may play a more active role in the emotional labor process. Consistent with earlier theoretical work (Côté, 2005; Rafaeli & Sutton, 1987), we suggest that the episodic interaction between agent and target parties should be viewed as a two-way transaction. As such, the verbal and non-verbal cues sent out by the target party play an important role in influencing the emotions that are felt and displayed by the agent party and the emotion regulation that is necessary to achieve these experienced and expressed states. Moreover, just as the agent (or agents) engages in emotional labor with the goal of fulfilling the requirements of a job, the target of regulation will also have goals or intentions that may drive his or her own use of emotion regulation. A customer at a retail outlet may wish to make a purchase or obtain a discount or refund; a patient may desire reassurance; a criminal suspect may wish to be seen as innocent; and a debtor may want to gain extra time for a payment. Likewise, a coworker may want the agent to help with his or her work, and a manager might seek confirmation and acknowledgment of his or her status.

The target can engage in emotion regulation to achieve these goals during an emotional labor episode. For example, a customer aiming to get a refund might express regret about buying the item to try to elicit pity and compassion in the employee. In fact, the target's use of emotion regulation might be one of the factors prompting the agent's need to engage in emotional labor in the first place. For instance, in the case of a patient who desires reassurance, the medical professional may only engage in interpersonal emotion regulation to fulfill his or her role requirements of maintaining positive affect in patients when the patient communicates a worry in order to elicit the medic's concern. In this case, the emotional labor episode is still defined by the goal of the agent (it is only the agent who is performing *emotional labor* per se), yet the target is clearly acting in a goal-driven manner. Similarly, the target may engage in emotion regulation in response to the agent's emotional labor; Lively's (2000) work with paralegals even suggests that some employees' use of interpersonal emotion regulation is driven in part by the expectation that this effort will be reciprocated by a given target.

In recognizing the target as an active emotion regulator, the emotional labor process can be seen as an interactive episode between two parties. This echoes recent theoretical work by Hareli and Rafaeli (2008), which presents a model of emotions as cycles. As they argue, "social and organizational interactions are rarely one-shot unidirectional interactions, and typically involve multiple iterations, meaning that emotion episodes constantly surface" (p. 53). Likewise, emotional labor is not just a 'one-shot' process whereby an employee engages in emotion regulation in the presence of, or directed towards, a passive target. Instead, both the employee *and* target actively engage in emotion self-regulation and interpersonal emotion regulation, and the regulatory efforts and expressed emotions of both parties feed forward to influence their own emotions and regulatory behaviors and those of the other party involved.

## The Target as a Whole Unit

Just as the agent in the emotional labor process may be viewed as a whole unit, so might the target. When employees perform emotion self-regulation in line with shared unit-level norms, this regulation is directed broadly towards customers, coworkers or managers. In other words, the emotions they express outwardly may be controlled for the benefit of whole units, rather than single individuals.

Interpersonal emotion regulation may also be performed to regulate the emotions of whole units of people. There is strong evidence that emotions can be shared by whole units, and can therefore be seen as a meaningful whole unit-level construct. For example, research by George (1990) and Tanghe, Wisse, and van der Flier (2010), amongst others, has highlighted robust consistencies in the emotions of employees within whole work units. In addition, there is evidence that observers can reliably detect emotion at the whole unit-level (Bartel & Saavedra, 2000). As such, there are likely to be occasions where individual employees will try to regulate the emotions of a whole work unit as part of their job roles. For instance, leaders often try to inspire positive emotion in their work units (George, 2000; Sy, Côté, & Saavedra, 2005). Similarly, individuals who want to sell an idea may try to energize their whole work unit (Cross et al., 2003) and people working in high stress units may try to 'detoxify' the negative emotions of the unit as a whole (Frost & Robinson, 1999). Research has not yet identified what types of strategies are used to regulate the emotions of a whole unit and whether these might differ from those used to regulate the emotions of individual targets. Nonetheless, in line with the above discussion, we contend that targets, as well as agents, may be conceptualized at both individual and unit levels.

## THIRD PARTY INVOLVEMENT
## IN EMOTIONAL LABOR

Accounts of emotional labor typically restrict their focus to two individuals that comprise the emotional labor dyad: the agent and the target. In the two previous sections, we have expanded this understanding by considering the possibility that each of these parties can be a whole unit rather than a single individual. Here, we go beyond the idea that there are only two parties involved. We suggest that it is relatively rare that interactions within organizations are confined to just two parties and that even episodes that are initially dyadic may draw other parties in. Thus, even in cases where a single agent performs emotional labor for the benefit of a single target, other individuals within as well as outside the work unit, and even whole units, may become involved in and affected by emotional labor.

There are three main ways in which third parties can become involved in emotional labor. First, third parties can observe emotional labor in action. For example, at a store's customer service desk, customers waiting in the line and coworkers on duty may witness the employee's regulatory attempts and the customer's responses. In non face-to-face encounters (e.g., over the telephone in a customer contact center), third parties may similarly overhear the emotional labor interaction, at least from one side.

Second, third parties may be told about an emotional labor interaction by either of the two parties who is initially involved or even someone who witnessed the interaction. According to Rimé, Finkenauer, Luminet, Zech, and Philippot (1998), when people experience emotional events, they often feel compelled to share "the emotional circumstances and their feelings and reactions" with other people (p. 145). Certainly when it comes to emotional labor, social sharing of emotions seems likely. For example, an employee who has struggled to perform emotion regulation while serving a rude customer may feel the need to vent about this experience with a coworker. Likewise, customers who are served by surly employees will probably tell their friends about the experience.

A third way that third parties may be drawn into emotional labor is if an agent or target uses them as a part of an emotion regulation strategy.

Many interpersonal emotion regulation strategies necessarily involve third parties to be present. For example, strategies used to elicit social emotions may require an audience (e.g., strategies to make a person feel proud or embarrassed; Niven et al., 2009). Moreover, third parties may be directly co-opted into the emotion regulation process. For instance, Smith's (2008) research with professional wrestlers highlighted that the objective of a wrestler "is not to win the match, but rather, to attain a strong emotional reaction from the audience" (p. 157), and that the wrestlers use their 'opponents' as tools to help achieve the regulation of the audience's emotions.

## The Role of Third Parties

As we discuss later in this chapter, through the relatively passive role they play in emotional labor, third parties may become affected by the process. However, third parties can also play a more active role in emotional labor. They may be used to help an agent regulate a target's emotions during the initial emotion regulation attempt, as described earlier. Alternatively, as a result of witnessing or being told about emotional labor, third parties may choose to get directly involved in an episode. For example, witnessing or being told about a coworker struggling to control his or her emotions while dealing with a difficult client might provoke an employee to engage in interpersonal emotion regulation towards the coworker or client or both in an act of solidarity or caring (Hill & Bradley, 2010; Kahn, 1993).

One reason why third parties might choose to get directly involved in an emotional labor episode is goal contagion, a phenomenon whereby people automatically make inferences about others' goals and in turn come to initiate and pursue these goals themselves (Aarts, Dijksterhuis, & Dik, 2008). In the case of emotional labor, an employee might witness a coworker trying to down-regulate his or her emotions during a meeting to maintain a neutral façade and might infer from this that it is important to display neutral emotion in meetings. Thus, the employee may down-regulate his or her own enthusiasm in line with this inferred goal. Another reason why third parties might choose to get directly involved is that they may consider it to be part of their job role. For example, employees in customer service contact centers often call on their team leaders to deal with difficult customers, and this is considered part of the team leader job role. Employees may even come to rely on the involvement of third parties in emotional labor. In a series of studies, Fitzsimons and Finkel (2011) demonstrated the phenomenon of 'self-regulatory outsourcing', whereby simply thinking of a helpful and supportive other reduces the effort people expend on self-regulation, especially when their resources are depleted. Their findings suggest that close coworkers in the same work unit might develop a shared regulatory system such that when employees' resources are depleted, other unit members may step in to help them perform the emotion regulation necessary for their job. Thus, third parties may often get directly drawn into the process of emotional labor, leading to their own use of emotion regulation.

## Third Parties as Whole Units

Similar to agents and targets, third parties can be conceptualized at the unit-level as well as the individual-level. Whole units may witness emotional labor. For example, a whole unit might observe an employee struggling to control his or her emotions when being shouted at by a manager. Similarly, agents and targets may choose to socially share their emotions with a whole work unit, for instance during a team meeting. Whole units can also be used to help in the regulatory process; for example, trying to improve a target's mood by making him or her feel socially included or trying to worsen a target's mood by making the target feel socially excluded may require the help of a whole unit (Niven et al., 2009). Even in cases where the third party is a single individual, this third party may draw in others from a unit (e.g., via social sharing of emotions; Rimé et al., 1998), or may go on to initiate further emotional labor episodes. Thus, emotional labor and its effects may spread and propagate around whole networks.

## FRAMEWORK FOR UNIT-LEVEL EMOTIONAL LABOR (FUEL)

In this chapter so far, we have expanded the understanding of who is involved in emotional labor and the emotion regulatory roles they play by broadening our focus to the unit or units within which emotional labor occurs. We present our expanded understanding in the FUEL model (see Figure 5.1). As can be seen in the model, there are two key parties ('agent' and 'target') who are directly involved in the initial emotional labor episode, both of whom may be individuals or whole units. Both of these parties can actively self-regulate their emotions and can also attempt to regulate each other's emotions. There are also direct links between the emotions of the agent(s) and target(s), which represent how one party's expressed emotions can serve to influence another party's feelings, via inferential processing and emotional contagion. The FUEL model illustrates that individual or even whole unit third parties may become indirectly involved in emotional labor as a result of witnessing or being told about emotional labor. They too may become actively involved,

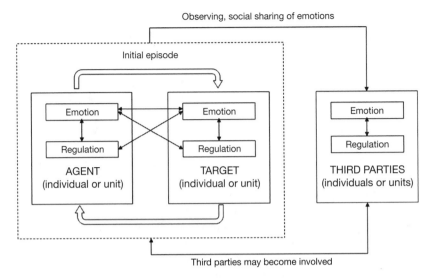

**Figure 5.1** Framework for Unit-level Emotional Labor (FUEL).

regulating their own emotions or those of either the agent(s) or target(s). Hence, emotional labor is a dynamic and cyclical process that involves individuals within units as well as whole units of people.

## IMPLICATIONS FOR EMOTIONAL LABOR RESEARCHERS

In this final section of the chapter, we consider the implications of the unit-level understanding of emotional labor for researchers. In particular, we discuss implications in terms of the effects that emotional labor can have within organizations and implications for how researchers should investigate emotional labor.

### *Implications for the Effects of Emotional Labor*

Expanding our understanding of the role played by agents in the emotional labor process to include their use of interpersonal emotion regulation has implications for the effects that we can expect emotional labor to have on agents. To date, research on the effects of interpersonal emotion regulation is in its infancy. However, studies have demonstrated that strategies used to improve others' emotions may positively influence the agent's emotions, and strategies used to worsen others' emotions may negatively influence the agent's emotions (Niven, Totterdell, Holman, &

Headley, 2012). Similar mechanisms to those involved in the effects of emotion self-regulation are thought to underlie these effects. Specifically, effects on agents' emotions are thought to result from actual and anticipated emotional and behavioral feedback from the targets of regulation (Niven et al., 2012). Via these observed effects on emotions, it is likely that changes to agents' attitudes and behaviors will arise (Schwarz & Clore, 1983; Van Kleef, 2009). Thus, like emotion self-regulation, interpersonal emotion regulation may influence outcomes like satisfaction, motivation, commitment and performance. Certainly, there is preliminary evidence to support a performance link; Seiter and Dutson (2007) found that hairdressers received higher tips from customers who they complimented (a commonly-used strategy to improve others' emotions) compared to customers who they did not compliment. However, additional evidence suggests that, like emotion self-regulation, interpersonal emotion regulation may be effortful and depleting for agents to perform (Pugliesi, 1999). As such, future research should consider the simultaneous effects of interpersonal emotion regulation *and* emotion self-regulation on agents, to determine whether both types of regulation draw on the same limited energy resource (Baumeister, Bratlavsky, Muraven, & Tice, 1998) and so compound each other's effects.

Expanding our understanding of the role played by targets in the emotional labor process also has implications for the expected effects of emotional labor. Specifically, as targets may actively engage in emotion self-regulation and interpersonal emotion regulation during emotional labor episodes, it is possible that targets may experience similar consequences to agents when performing these types of emotion regulation. However, a key difference between the role of the agent and target is that agents' use of emotion regulation is prompted by the external norms and rules of the organization; hence, it is considered emotional labor. For targets, while they *may* use emotion regulation to fulfil emotional labor goals, in many cases they will use emotion regulation to help achieve their own personal goals. As such, it is possible that targets' use of emotion regulation may not always threaten their self-determination, meaning that they might not experience regulation as depleting (Deci & Ryan, 2000). Future studies should therefore investigate differences in the effects of emotion regulation when used to fulfill emotional labor requirements versus to achieve personal goals.

Recognizing the involvement of third parties in the emotional labor process further has implications for the effects of emotional labor. Observing an emotional labor interaction between an agent and target may influence the emotions, attitudes, and behaviors of third parties via mechanisms of empathizing with one or both parties involved, emotional contagion (Côté et al., this volume; Van Kleef, 2009), and goal contagion

(Aarts et al., 2008). Observers may also make inferences about the power, competence, credibility and likeability of both parties involved (Hareli & Rafaeli, 2008) and this too may affect their emotions, attitudes, and behaviors. Witnessing another person perform emotion self-regulation may even deplete people; across two laboratory-based studies, Ackerman, Goldstein, Shapiro, and Bargh (2009) demonstrated that taking the perspective of a person exercising self-regulation resulted in depletion. Our own research further suggests that others' use of interpersonal regulation vicariously depletes people; in an applied study of hospital workers, we found that observing interpersonal emotion regulation was associated with one's own emotional exhaustion and that this effect was heightened when the observer engaged in perspective taking (Totterdell, Hershcovis, Niven, Reich, & Stride, in press). Likewise, social sharing of the emotional labor incident can affect the third party listener. Research has shown that social sharing of emotions typically results in emotional convergence, more often than not with the listener empathically taking on the sharer's emotions (Rimé et al., 1998).

Thus, third parties become affected by emotional labor simply by virtue of their indirect involvement in the process. In addition to these relatively passive effects, as discussed earlier, third parties may be actively involved in the process, either because they are initially co-opted into the regulation effort, or later get involved once they observe or hear about the emotional labor episode. Once a third party takes on this active role, he or she may engage in emotion self-regulation or interpersonal emotion regulation and, as such, may experience the effects of these regulatory efforts. Through this route as well then, third parties can be affected by emotional labor. As such, the effects of emotional labor on third parties as well as the two parties initially involved should be studied. Moreover, as mentioned earlier, third parties (and targets) may initiate emotional labor episodes as agents later down the line which, in turn, may have implications for other targets and third parties. The networks of spreading emotional labor processes (e.g., emotions, emotion regulation) throughout organizations may therefore be important to examine.

Viewing agents, targets, and third parties as units rather than individuals has further implications in terms of the effects of emotional labor. As discussed earlier, emotions may be shared within whole work units (e.g., George, 1990), and so it is likely that emotion regulation performed by or directed towards a whole unit will have implications for the emotions of the unit as a whole. Other phenomena might also meaningfully present at the whole unit-level. For example, the unit's performance (or individual perceptions of the unit's performance) might be affected by emotional labor. In support of this, Sy et al. (2005) reported evidence that leaders' emotions can affect the coordination and effort levels of their followers as a unit, and Pugh (2001) suggested that the emotions expressed by a service employee could affect the customer's generalized evaluations of the organization's service quality. Similarly, exhaustion and strain can conceivably be shared at the whole unit-level and influenced by whole unit regulation; certainly, exhaustion and strain are thought to converge within close relationships as a result of contagion and empathy (e.g., Bakker, Demerouti, & Schaufeli, 2005). Based on Tanghe et al. (2010) and Diefendorff et al. (2011), it seems likely that more cohesive work units and those units that have stronger shared emotion regulation norms may be most affected, as a whole, by emotional labor.

In addition to highlighting the potential for the effects of emotional labor to manifest at the unit-level, viewing agents, targets, and third parties as units raises the question of whether the effects of emotional labor vary depending on whether the parties involved are individuals or whole units. The idea that emotion regulation is easier and more effective when performed by a whole unit rather than an individual agent is intuitively appealing, and from the research on self-regulatory outsourcing (Fitzsimons & Finkel, 2011) we know that involving others in regulation reduces the efforts we make, suggesting that 'many hands make light work'. However, whether some members of the unit take on the bulk of the regulatory effort (e.g., toxin handlers and energizers; Cross et al., 2003; Frost & Robinson, 1999) and so still experience depletion while others manage to avoid the effort and depletion associated with emotional labor (e.g., social loafers; Karau & Williams, 1993) is yet to be explicitly tested. In addition, it is possible, although as yet untested, that it may be more effortful or difficult to regulate the emotions of a whole unit rather than an individual target. In sum, recognizing that the parties involved in an emotional labor episode may be units as well as individuals highlights the need for the effects of emotional labor to be studied at the whole unit-level as well as the individual-level, especially within cohesive units, and for the differential effects of unit-level regulation on all unit-members to be investigated.

## *Implications for the Methods Used to Study Emotional Labor*

In the section above, we explained how the effects of the two regulatory processes involved in emotional labor may extend to third parties and may even be shared across whole work units. This presents some unique challenges to researchers with respect to the methods that are required to study emotional labor and its effects. Here, we highlight four key methodological advances that help to meet some of these challenges.

First, self-report measures are now available that allow researchers to measure interpersonal emotion regulation. Our own recently-developed scale (Niven, Totterdell, Stride, & Holman, 2011) provides a quantitative self-report measure that assesses the use of strategies to improve and to worsen others' emotions, either in general or within specific interactions (e.g., with a customer), and has been validated using organizational samples. The measure includes items such as "I gave someone (person x) helpful advice to improve their feelings", and forms part of the wider 'Emotion Regulation of Others and Self (EROS)' scale, in which the use of both interpersonal emotion regulation and emotion self-regulation strategies are assessed. Other measures also enable researchers to measure people's ability to regulate others' emotions. For example, the emotion regulation in others subscale assesses this ability as part of a larger measure of emotional intelligence (Tett, Fox & Wang, 2005; e.g., "Usually, I know what it takes to turn someone else's boredom into excitement").

Second, longitudinal, in-situ methods have been developed, allowing researchers to capture emotional labor and its effects as they unfold. Video-observation methods in particular enable researchers to capture emotional interactions within their full social context (as opposed to just one person's perspective) (e.g., Maitlis & Liu, 2009). Such methods therefore provide the opportunity to examine the regulatory inter-changes between agents and targets and to investigate changes in each party's emotions and regulatory behaviors, to map fluctuations and dynamics over time. One way of analyzing such data is using video-cued recall, where parties who are involved in a video-recorded incident are asked to watch the incident back and describe it from their perspective (Simons & Parkinson, 2009). Researchers using this method can ask participants to rate their own emotions, their perceptions of others' emotions, and their regulatory intent, at various times during a video-recorded interaction.

Third, advances in multilevel analysis techniques have enabled researchers to investigate phenomena at multiple levels of analysis (e.g., the individual-level and the unit-level). Such advances include different types of compositional models that give researchers options with respect to the ways in which they measure and aggregate individual-level constructs (e.g., emotions, perceptions of display rules, emotion regula-tion) to higher levels (e.g., Chan, 1998), and statistical packages that allow researchers to analyze data at multiple levels (e.g., Hierarchical Linear Modeling; Raudenbush, Bryk, & Congdon, 2004). Together, these advances help researchers to consider whether there are differences in the nature and effects of individual- and unit-level emotion regulation, and whether unit composition (e.g., in terms of dispersion and agreement) influences the effects of emotional labor.

Fourth, social network methods have been developed that enable researchers to map interactions and emotions across whole networks of individuals. Social network methods view organizations as systems of 'actors' (i.e., individuals or whole work units) joined by relationships or 'ties', and recognize the socially embedded and constrained nature of actors and their actions (Tichy, Tushman, & Fombrun, 1979). Network studies are usually conducted by administering surveys to actors within a given network (e.g., to employees in a whole work unit or to the manager of each whole unit within an organization) and asking about their interactions with other actors and attributes like emotions over a specified time period. This therefore allows researchers to see which individuals or units are involved in and affected by an emotional labor incident, to determine which third parties get drawn into the process. Indeed, researchers have already used social network methods to map the spread of affect (Totterdell, Wall, Holman, Diamond, & Epitropaki, 2004) and energy (Cross et al., 2003) throughout networks and work units. Network methods further allow researchers to identify groups (known as 'cliques') within networks who share similarities, for example in terms of their emotions or emotion regulation use (Totterdell et al., 2004); thus, network methods can be used to determine whether informal groups as well as more formal work units experience emotional labor at the unit-level.

## CONCLUSION

In *The Managed Heart*, Hochschild (1983) described the requirement for service employees to manage their own expressed emotions in order to produce desirable changes in their customers' feelings. We now revisit an example given in Hochschild's work, to demonstrate how taking a unit-level perspective can cast a different light on emotional labor. The example we take regards the overworked flight attendant who responds to a passenger's request to give him a smile by saying: "I'll tell you what. You smile first, then I'll smile . . . Good . . . Now freeze, and hold that for fifteen hours" (Hochschild, 1983, p. 127).

In this scenario, the flight attendant is the party who is expected to perform emotion regulation as part of her job role, i.e., the agent. We can see that the flight attendant used an interpersonal emotion regulation strategy towards the passenger that did not involve emotional expression. The passenger is the target but he is also an active participant in the emotional labor process, as he actively tried to get the attendant to regulate her emotions. Moreover, other people on the aeroplane were likely to be involved and affected by the episode. Other passengers and flight attendants were likely to have witnessed the interaction, which may have affected their emotions and attitudes, and some may have chosen to get involved, for example, by laughing in league with or reprimanding the attendant. These third parties, as well as the attendant and the passenger, might also have shared what they saw or experienced with other passengers or staff members. Ultimately, these processes could have led to consistency within the whole work unit or the unit of passengers regarding emotion and emotion regulation, and hence could have affected the level of service throughout the flight, along with future attitudes and behaviors towards other service staff.

By broadening our focus to the unit or units within which emotional labor is enacted, we have therefore illustrated how a simple episode involving two individuals can take a different form to that traditionally studied by emotional labor researchers, and can draw in and affect multiple individuals and even whole units of people. It may therefore be fruitful to study emotional labor beyond the individual- and dyadic-levels, as a unit-level phenomenon that has implications throughout and beyond the work unit in which it is enacted.

# REFERENCES

Aarts, H., Dijksterhuis, A., & Dik, G. (2008). Goal contagion: Inferring goals from other's actions – and what it leads to. In J. Y. Shah & W. L. Gardner (Eds.), *Handbook of motivation science*. New York: Guilford Press.

Ackerman, J. M., Goldstein, N. J., Shapiro, J. R., & Bargh, J. A. (2009). You wear me out: the vicarious depletion of self-control. *Psychological Science, 20,* 326–332.

Ashforth, B. E., Kreiner, G. E., Clark, M. A., & Fugate, M. (2007). Normalizing dirty work: Managerial tactics for countering occupational taint. *Academy of Management Journal, 50,* 149–174.

Bakker, A. B., Demerouti, E., & Schaufeli, W. B. (2005). The crossover of burnout and work engagement among working couples. *Human Relations, 58,* 661–689.

Barger, P. B. & Grandey, A. A. (2006). Service with a smile and encounter satisfaction: Emotional contagion and appraisal mechanisms. *Academy of Management Journal, 40,* 1220–1238.

Bartel, C. A., & Saavedra, R. (2000). The collective construction of workgroup moods. *Administrative Science Quarterly, 45,* 197–231.

Baumeister, R. F., Bratslavsky, E., Muraven, M., & Tice, D. M. (1998). Ego depletion: Is the active self a limited resource? *Journal of Personality and Social Psychology, 74,* 1252–1265.

Beal, D. J., & Trougakos, J. P. (2013). Episodic intrapersonal emotion regulation: Or, dealing with life as it happens. In A. A. Grandey, J. M. Diefendorff & D. E. Rupp (Eds.), *Emotional labor in the 21st century: Diverse perspectives on emotion regulation at work*. New York, NY: Psychology Press/Routledge.

Carver, C. S., & Scheier, M. F. (1998). *On the self-regulation of behavior*. Cambridge, NY: Cambridge University Press.

Chan, D. (1998). Functional relations among constructs in the same content domain at different levels of analysis: A typology of composition models. *Journal of Applied Psychology, 83,* 234–246.

Côté, S. (2005). A social interaction model of the effects of emotion regulation on work strain. *Academy of Management Review, 30,* 509–530.

Cote, S., Van Kleef, G., & Sy, T. (2013). The social effects of emotion regulation in organizations. In A. A. Grandey, J. M. Diefendorff & D. E. Rupp (Eds.), *Emotional labor in the 21st century: Diverse perspectives on emotion regulation at work.* New York, NY: Psychology Press/Routledge.

Cross, R., Baker, W., & Parker, A. (2003). What creates energy in organizations? *Sloan Management Review, 44,* 51–57.

Deci, E. L., & Ryan, R. M. (2000). The 'what' and 'why' of goal pursuits: Human needs and the self-determination of behavior. *Psychological Inquiry, 11,* 227–268.

Diefendorff, J. M., Croyle, M. H., & Gosserand, R. H. (2005). The dimensionality and antecedents of emotional labor strategies. *Journal of Vocational Behavior, 66,* 339–357.

Diefendorff, J. M., & Gosserand, R. H. (2003). Understanding the emotional labor process: A control theory perspective. *Journal of Organizational Behavior, 24,* 945–959.

Diefendorff, J. M., Erickson, R. E., Grandey, A. A., & Dahling, J. J. (2011). Emotional display rules as work unit norms: A multi-level analysis of emotional labor among nurses. *Journal of Occupational Health Psychology, 16,* 170–186.

Eisenberg, N., Fabes, R. A., Guthrie, I. K., & Reiser, M. (2000). Dispositional emotionality and regulation: Their role in predicting quality of social functioning. *Journal of Personality and Social Psychology, 78,* 136–157.

Erickson, R. & Stacey, C. (2013). Attending to mind and body: Engaging the complexity of emotion practice among caring professionals. In A. A. Grandey, J. M. Diefendorff & D. E. Rupp (Eds.), *Emotional labor in the 21st century: Diverse perspectives on emotion regulation at work.* New York, NY: Psychology Press/Routledge.

Felps, W., Mitchell, T. R., & Byington, E. (2006). How, when, and why bad apples spoil the barrel: Negative group members and dysfunctional groups. *Research in Organizational Behavior, 27,* 181–230.

Fitzsimons, G. M., & Finkel, E. J. (2011). Outsourcing self-regulation. *Psychological Science, 22,* 369–375.

Francis, L. E. (1997). Ideology and interpersonal emotion management: Redefining identity in two support groups. *Social Psychology Quarterly, 60,* 153–171.

Francis, L. E., Monahan, K., & Berger, C. (1999). A laughing matter? The uses of humor in medical interactions. *Motivation and Emotion, 23,* 154–177.

Frost, P. J., & Robinson, S. (1999). The toxic handler: Organizational hero and casualty. *Harvard Business Review, 77,* 96–106.

George, J. M. (1990). Personality, affect and behavior in groups. *Journal of Applied Psychology, 75,* 107–116.

George, J. M. (2000). Emotions and leadership: The role of emotional intelligence. *Human Relations, 53,* 1027–1055.

Gianino, A., & Tronick, E. Z. (1988). The mutual regulation model: The infant's self and interactive regulation and coping defense capacities. In T. Field, P. McCabe, & N. Schneiderman (Eds.), *Stress and coping across development* (pp. 47–68). Hillsdale, NJ: Erlbaum.

Goffman, E. (1955). On face-work: An analysis of ritual elements in social interaction. *Psychiatry, 18,* 213–231.

Grandey, A. A. (2000). Emotion regulation in the workplace: A new way to conceptualize emotional labor. *Journal of Occupational Health Psychology, 5,* 95–110.

Grandey, A. (2003). When 'the show must go on': Surface and deep acting as determinants of emotional exhaustion and peer-rated service delivery. *Academy of Management Journal, 46,* 86–96.

Hareli, S., & Rafaeli, A. (2008). Emotion cycles: On the social influence of emotions in organizations, *Research in Organizational Behavior, 28,* 35–59.

Hill, T. D., & Bradley, C. (2010). The emotional consequences of service work: An ethnographic examination of hair salon workers. *Sociological Focus, 43,* 41–60.

Hochschild, A. R. (1983). *The managed heart: Commercialization of human feeling.* Berkeley, CA: University of California Press.

Kahn, W. A. (1993). Caring for the caregivers: Patterns of organizational caregiving. *Administrative Science Quarterly, 38,* 539–563.

Karau, S., & Williams, K. (1993). Social loafing: A meta-analytic review and theoretical integration. *Journal of Personality and Social Psychology, 65,* 681–706.

Kelly, J. R., & Barsade, S. G. (2001). Mood and emotions in small groups and work teams. *Organizational Behavior and Human Decision Processes, 86,* 99–130.

Kipnis, D., Schmidt, S. M., & Wilkinson, I. (1980). Intraorganizational influence tactics: Exploration of getting one's way. *Journal of Applied Psychology, 65,* 440–452.

Lively, K. J. (2000). Reciprocal emotion management: Working together to maintain stratification in private law firms. *Work and Occupations, 27,* 32–63.

Locke, K. (1996). A funny thing happened: The management of consumer emotions in service encounters. *Organization Science, 7,* 40–59.

Maitlis, S. & Liu, F. (2009). Exploring emotions in the practice of strategy: A video-based analysis of top team meetings. *Academy of Management Annual Meeting,* Chicago, USA.

Martínez-Iñigo, D., Totterdell, P., Alcover, D. M., & Holman, D. (2009). The source of display rules and their effects on primary health care professionals' well-being. *Spanish Journal of Psychology, 12,* 618–631.

Morris, M. W., & Keltner, D. (2000). How emotions work: An analysis of the social functions of emotional expression in negotiations. *Research in Organizational Behavior, 22,* 1–50.

Niven, K., Holman, D., & Totterdell, P. (in press). How to win friendship and trust by influencing people: An investigation of interpersonal affect regulation and the quality of relationships. *Human Relations.*

Niven, K., Totterdell, P., & Holman, D. (2007). Changing moods and influencing people: The use and effects of emotional influence behaviours at HMP Grendon. *The Prison Service Journal, 173,* 39–45.

Niven, K., Totterdell, P., & Holman, D. (2009). A classification of controlled interpersonal affect regulation strategies. *Emotion, 9,* 498–509.

Niven, K., Totterdell, P., Stride, C. B., & Holman, D. (2011). Emotion Regulation of Others and Self (EROS): The development and validation of a new individual difference measure. *Current Psychology, 30,* 53–73.

Niven, K., Totterdell, P., Holman, D., & Headley, T. (2012). Does regulating others' feelings influence people's own affective well-being? *Journal of Social Psychology, 152,* 246–260.

Parkinson, B. (1996). Emotions are social. *British Journal of Psychology, 87,* 663–683.

Pierce, J. L. (1999). Emotional labor among paralegals. *Annals of the American Academy of Political and Social Science, 561,* 127–142.

Pugh, S. D. (2001). Service with a smile: Emotional contagion in the service encounter. *Academy of Management Journal, 44,* 1018–1027.

Pugliesi, K. (1999). The consequences of emotional labor: Effects on work stress, job satisfaction, and well-being. *Motivation and Emotion, 23,* 135–154.

Raudenbush, S. W., Bryk, A. S., & Congdon, R. (2004). *HLM 6: Hierarchical linear and nonlinear modelling.* Lincolnwood, IL: Scientific Software International.

Rafaeli, A., & Sutton, R. I. (1987). Expression of emotion as part of the work role. *Academy of Management Review, 12,* 23–37.

Rafaeli, A., & Sutton, R. I. (1991). Emotional contrast strategies as means of social influence: Lessons from criminal interrogators and bill collectors. *Academy of Management Journal, 34,* 749–775.

Rimé, B., Finkenauer, C., Luminet, O., Zech, E., & Philippot, P. (1998). Social sharing of emotion: New evidence and new questions. In W. Stroebe & M. Hewstone (Eds.), *European Review of Social Psychology* (pp.145–189). Chichester, UK: Wiley.

Schwarz, N., & Clore, G. L. (1983). Mood, misattribution, and judgments of well-being: Informative and directive functions of affective states. *Journal of Personality and Social Psychology, 45,* 513–523.

Seiter, J. S., & Dutson, E. (2007). The effect of compliments on tipping behavior in hairstyling salons. *Journal of Applied Social Psychology, 37,* 1999–2007.

Simons, G., & Parkinson, B. (2009). Time-dependent observational and diary methodologies for assessing social referencing and interpersonal emotion regulation. *Contemporary Social Science: Journal of the Academy of Social Sciences, 4,* 175–186.

Smith, R. T. (2008). Passion work: The joint production of emotional labor in professional wrestling. *Social Psychology Quarterly, 71,* 157–176.

Sutton, R. I. (1991). Maintaining norms about expressed emotions: The case of bill collectors. *Administrative Science Quarterly, 36,* 245–268.

Sy, T., Côté, S., & Saavedra, R. (2005). The contagious leader: Impact of the leader's mood on the mood of group members, group affective tone, and group processes. *Journal of Applied Psychology, 90,* 295–305.

Tanghe, J., Wisse, B., & Van der Flier, H. (2010). The role of group member affect in the relationship between trust and cooperation. *British Journal of Management, 21,* 359–374.

Tett, R. P., Fox, K. E., & Wang, A. (2005). Development and validation of a self-report measure of emotional intelligence as a multidimensional trait domain. *Personality and Social Psychology Bulletin, 31*, 859–888.

Thoits, P. A. (1996). Managing the emotions of others. *Symbolic Interaction, 19*, 85–109.

Tichy, N. M., Tushman, M. L., & Fombrun, C. (1979). Social network analysis for organizations. *Academy of Management Review, 4*, 507–519.

Totterdell, P., Hershcovis, M. S., Niven, K., Reich, T. C., & Stride, C. B. (in press). Can employees be emotionally drained by witnessing unpleasant interactions between co-workers? A diary study of induced emotion regulaion. *Work and Stress.*

Totterdell, P., & Holman, D. (2003). Emotional regulation in customer service roles: Testing a model of emotional labor. *Journal of Occupational Health Psychology, 8*, 55–73.

Totterdell, P., Wall, T., Holman, D., Diamond, H., & Epitropaki, O. (2004). Affective networks: A structural analysis of the relationship between work ties and job-related affect. *Journal of Applied Psychology, 89*, 854–867.

Tschan, F., Rochat, S., & Zapf, D. (2005). It's not only clients: Studying emotion work with clients and co-workers with an event-sampling approach. *Journal of Occupational and Organizational Psychology, 78*, 195–220.

Van Kleef, G. A. (2009). How emotions regulate social life: The emotions as social information (EASI) model. *Current Directions in Psychological Science, 18*, 184–188.

Williams, M. (2007). Building genuine trust through interpersonal emotion management: A threat regulation model of trust and collaboration across boundaries. *Academy of Management Review, 32*, 595–621.

# Occupational Perspectives: Customer Service, Call Centers, Caring Professionals

# The Customer Experience of Emotional Labor

MARKUS GROTH • THORSTEN HENNIG-THURAU • KARYN WANG

The quality of interactions between frontline employees and their customers is an important determinant of service delivery outcomes. Researchers in management and marketing have examined the role of such interpersonal interactions for key service success variables such as customers' service quality perceptions of, satisfaction with, and loyalty to the service provider (Parasuraman, Zeithaml, & Berry, 1988; Rust & Oliver, 1994; Seth, Deshmukh, & Vrat, 2005). For customers, displays of valued emotions by service employees, such as a friendly smile, have a profound impact on their service quality perceptions, either by serving as substitutes for aspects of the core service that are too difficult to evaluate objectively (i.e., legal services, car repair) or by providing immediate social benefits to customers (Hennig-Thurau, Gwinner, & Gremler, 2002; Parasuraman et al., 1988). Likewise, the taste of a great steak in a restaurant or the excellent décor of a hotel can be drastically counteracted by employees who refrain from positive emotional displays, even to such an extent that the customer leaves the service provider unsatisfied and unlikely to return.

Organizations use explicit or implied norms as formal control mechanisms to ensure that employees display the emotions valued by customers (Hochschild, 1979, 1983; Leidner, 1999). Such norms have been labeled 'organizational display rules' by organizational behavior scholars investigating the role of such rules in delivering 'service with a smile' (e.g., Diefendorff, Richard, & Croyle, 2006; Rafaeli & Sutton, 1987). Employees often respond to such organizational control by engaging in emotional labor, a type of emotion regulation whereby service employees manage their emotions in order to match specific job-related display requirements (Hochschild, 1983)[1].

Previous research indicates that there are two prevailing emotional labor strategies used by frontline employees to regulate their emotions when serving customers: surface acting and deep acting (e.g., Brotheridge & Lee, 2003; Grandey, 2000). When employees engage in surface acting, they adjust only their outward display according to display rules, but not their inner feelings. Deep acting, in contrast, requires employees also to change their inner feelings during the service interaction in order to call forth emotional displays that are consistent with display rule requirements.

How does emotional labor and its strategic implementation by the frontline employee affect customers? Although it is the *customer's* reaction that should determine management's decision-making about emotional labor policies, the majority of research on emotional labor has been limited to conceptual issues and employee-related outcomes (e.g., Brotheridge & Grandey, 2002; Morris & Feldman, 1997; also see meta-analysis by Hülsheger & Schewe, 2011). Meanwhile, the effects of emotional labor on customers have remained, at least until recently, largely unexplored. This chapter aims to summarize the current state of knowledge on the relationship between employee emotional labor and customer outcomes. We offer a comprehensive framework that links emotion regulation among frontline employees with customer responses and discuss why, how, and when employee emotional labor affects reactions to service delivery. Given the gaps in the literature on the emotion regulation–customer outcome relationship, our discussion lays significant groundwork for future research.

## A FRAMEWORK: HOW EMOTIONAL LABOR IMPACTS CUSTOMERS

In this chapter, we focus on a theoretical framework linking emotional labor and customer outcomes, shown in Figure 6.1. Emotional labor and customer outcomes are linked by two key mechanisms or pathways: namely, an 'emotional display pathway' (emotional labor strategies trigger distinct emotional displays that result in corresponding customer outcomes) and an 'employee well-being pathway' (well-being outcomes

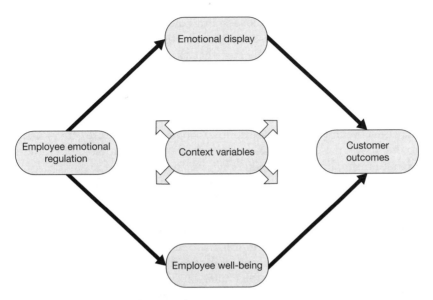

**Figure 6.1** Conceptual framework.

associated with certain emotional labor strategies impact customer reactions through service performance and service expectations). We will elaborate on these pathways and discuss the mechanisms as well as moderating forces that determine their strength and valence.

In our framework, the term 'customer' is not limited to the receivers of commercial services (e.g., hair salon patrons or airline passengers). Rather, it encompasses *any* receiver of a service provided by a professional organization or individual, and thus extends to health-care and educational service recipients (e.g., Erickson & Grove, 2008), among others. In the literature, the term customer is sometimes applied to actors in the internal processes of organizations (e.g., human resources). While we expect that the key pathways of our framework also apply to such groups, some differences exist (e.g., often limited management controls; Grandey, Diefendorff, & Rupp, 2013) that may require adjustments to the framework that are beyond the scope of this chapter.

## The Emotional Display Pathway of Emotional Labor

In service provision, emotional displays play an important role in influencing the customer's judgment of a service. The role of emotional display is crucial in leisure services such as those provided by bars, theme parks, hotels, and tour operators; customers spend money to 'have a good time,' which often includes the expectation that they will be treated kindly and in a friendly manner by employees. But emotional display is also important in other contexts, where positive emotional displays by employees are often taken to be an indicator that the company cares for its customers. This is especially true when customers are not equipped to judge the quality of the service, either in advance (e.g., being welcomed at a hotel) or after consumption (e.g., medical services, insurance). Emotions can also provide information about other dimensions of the service that may be difficult to judge. For example, people who smile are often judged to be more trustworthy and elicit greater cooperation from others (Scharlemann, Eckel, Kacelnik, & Wilson, 2001).

Despite psychological research showing that positive displays and authentic expressions are linked with interpersonal outcomes (Frank & Ekman, 1993; Surakka & Hietanen, 1998), empirical evidence showing relationships between employee displays and organizational outcomes has only recently emerged and is still in its infancy. The majority of this research has focused primarily on smiling and similar behavioral cues (e.g., Ford, 1995; Pugh, 2001; Tsai & Huang, 2002). Specifically, research has found that positive emotional displays such as maintaining eye contact, greeting customers, and smiling are associated with positive customer reports of positive mood, service quality, and positive behavioral intentions (i.e., willingness to return to the store and recommend it to others) (Ford, 1995; Mattila & Enz, 2002; Tsai, 2001). Consistent with this, Pugh (2001) and Tsai and Huang (2002) found positive displays by employees to be associated with service quality perceptions and positive behavioral intentions. This process may be mediated by customer affect and perceptions of the employee's friendliness, with the latter being a somewhat ill-defined and diffuse concept.

Some scholars have started to deconstruct the concept of positive display into its discrete components. For instance, Barger and Grandey (2006) reported a link between employee smiling and customer satisfaction in the context of coffee shop patrons. The findings indicate that the extent of employee smiling influenced customers' service quality appraisals (i.e., the extent to which employees were perceived as friendly, efficient, accurate, knowledgeable, and responsive), which consequently impacted overall customer satisfaction. However, given the unclear causal structure of service quality and satisfaction judgments (e.g., Hennig-Thurau & Klee, 1997), a reverse order of cause and effect could not be ruled out. Söderlund and Rosengren (2008) reported that employee smiling influenced customer satisfaction through changes in positive customer affect. The mediating role of positive customer affect between smiling and customer satisfaction was not observed by Barger and Grandey (2006). In addition, Hennig-Thurau et al. (2006), while controlling for employee authenticity, did not find a direct effect of the extent of employee smiling on customer satisfaction. These researchers also failed to find support for a mediating role of customer mood, though they did identify customer–employee rapport as a mediator.

In addition to the existence and extent of positive emotional displays (i.e., smiling), the authenticity of the emotional display plays an important role in the employee's performance and customer outcomes. Authenticity, describing an action that is sincere, genuine, and true to one's core sense of self (Kernis & Goldman, 2006; Salmela, 2005), is closely linked to emotional labor, with deep acting generally implying authentic display, while surface acting implies faking emotions. Given the social nature of service interactions, the interpersonal adversity associated with inauthentic expressions (which may communicate a lack of sincerity, individual attention, honesty, and trust) is likely to be associated with negative service quality judgments.

So far, relatively few studies have examined the effects of emotional labor and authenticity on service delivery. Ashforth and Humphrey (1993) were among the first to suggest that the employee's effort in displaying emotions and the quality of that effort may be related to customer service performance, arguing that genuine and authentic emotional displays may be important to external observers. Among the few studies that have directly modeled employee authenticity is one by Hennig-Thurau et al. (2006), who manipulated authenticity and the extent of smiling in a laboratory context and found that the impact of emotional labor authenticity on customer satisfaction and employee–customer rapport is much stronger than that of the extent of employee smiling.

Most other studies have measured the effects of employee authenticity only indirectly, for example by equating it with strategic deep acting, which is considered as authentic behavior in comparison to surface acting. Most of these studies have found that deep acting (as the more authentic emotional labor strategy) leads to better service outcomes. Specifically, Grandey, Fisk, Mattila, Jansen, and Sideman (2005) found that deep-acted smiles were associated with higher ratings of service employee friendliness and customer satisfaction. Groth, Hennig-Thurau, and Walsh (2009) similarly found that deep acting enhanced customer perceptions of employee customer orientation, while Chi, Grandey, Diamond, and Krimmel (2011) found that customers provide more tips to employees who engage in deep acting.

## *Underlying Mechanisms of the Emotional Display Pathway to Customer Outcomes*

The emotional display pathway assumes that the relationship between employee emotion regulation and customer outcomes is driven by customer perceptions of emotional display, triggered by emotion regulation. This relationship emphasizes not only the extent of emotional labor but also its quality in terms of its perceived authenticity and the effort behind it. Key to understanding this emotion regulation–customer outcomes relationship is an appreciation of the theoretical mechanisms that explain it.

One important theoretical mechanism is *emotional contagion* – the flow of emotions from one individual to another, with the receiver 'catching' the sender's displayed emotions (Schoenewolf, 1990). Research on emotional contagion posits customer emotions as a critical link between employee affective displays and service outcomes. Because customers 'catch' the positive emotions displayed by service employees during interactions, the resulting positive experience is a function of the positive change in emotions experienced by the customer (Hennig-Thurau et al., 2006; Pugh, 2001; Tsai & Huang, 2002).

The most prevalent kind of emotional contagion is *primitive emotional contagion*, which occurs through a two-stage process involving mimicry and feedback (Hatfield, Cacioppo, & Rapson, 1994). Mimicry refers to the process by which people unconsciously synchronize their facial expressions with those of others. Feedback refers to the experience of the mimicked emotions through facial feedback of "facial expressions, vocalizations, posture, and movements" (Hatfield et al., 1994). A second kind of contagion is *conscious emotional contagion*, whereby individuals deliberately adopt the emotional expressions of those around them or imagine how they would feel in another's position in order to facilitate social interactions, particularly in ambiguous social situations (Barsade, 2002; Hatfield et al., 1994). It is believed that assessments of others' emotional experiences trigger corresponding emotions in the observer through empathy or perspective-taking.

Researchers examining primitive contagion have turned to the literature on cognitive processes in explaining the mimicry of behaviors and emotions of others (e.g., Chartrand & van Baaren, 2009). For example, it has been argued that schema activation theories underlie mimicry effects (e.g., Bower, 1981). This explanation posits that interpretative cognitive schemas share considerable overlap with other schemas of similar semantic content, such as behavioral schemas, such that the perception of behaviors activates schema networks that trigger the behavior in the observer. This principle may also apply to emotional contagion, with the perception of a smiling employee triggering schematic networks associated with smiling, including the activation of behavioral schemas, which then cause smiling in the observer.

In service interactions, however, extant research suggests that conscious contagion is more effective for customer outcomes than primitive contagion processes. Specifically, Hennig-Thurau et al. (2006) compared conscious emotional contagion (based on the authenticity of the emotional displays in order to reduce ambiguity) and primitive emotional contagion (based on the extent or frequency of emotional displays). They found that it was the authenticity of the employee's emotional display rather than the extent of employee smiling which influenced changes in customer affect. Consistent with this line of research, Söderlund and Rosengren's (2004, 2008) finding that customer assessments of employee emotional states mediates the relationship between employee smiling and customer positive emotion also provides evidence that it is the evaluation of the employee's emotional state that elicits a similar emotional state in the customer (i.e., conscious emotional contagion). Hess and Blairy (2001), who also found no direct link between behavioral mimicry and emotional congruence, proposed that emotional contagion often occurs because individuals are motivated to understand the internal states of others.

But *how* do changes in customer mood caused by conscious contagion influence service evaluations? Research in social psychology shows that moods can 'color' thoughts, attitudes, and behaviors. That is, affective information can influence the judgment processes of other people and the outcomes to situations through a process known as *affect infusion* (Forgas, 1995). Forgas (1995) argues that when judgments operate in circumstances of little personal relevance that do not require in-depth consideration, people may use simple, heuristically based processing strategies that minimize effort. In these circumstances, people may use 'affect as information' (Schwarz & Clore, 1983) instead of using cues from the target. That is, people may ask themselves 'how do I feel about it' and interpret their existing moods as a reaction to the target (e.g., Barger & Grandey, 2006; Pugh, 2001).

Given that service quality judgments often occur in circumstances where heuristic processing is likely, especially in low-involvement services (Chowdhury & Miles, 2006), the affect infusion model may explain how customer mood mediates the relationship between employee smiling and service evaluation. Following emotional contagion mechanisms, whereby a customer 'catches' the emotions of the employee, customers may evaluate the service in terms of their own mood. If a customer's mood is improved, he or she may attribute this outcome to the service encounter, leading to enhanced customer service quality judgments.

Meanwhile, the endogenous nature of emotional contagion provides the answer for why emotional congruence is followed by higher service quality ratings. Researchers have suggested that the purpose of mimicry is to unconsciously convey liking, rapport, and the desire to continue communicating (Chartrand & van Baaren, 2009). Chartrand and Bargh

(1999) found that mimicry was related to liking and the smoothness of the transaction. Thus, employee–customer emotional contagion may not only cause enjoyment within the customer, but also result from the customer's enjoyment of the service interaction, which is then expressed in positive service quality judgments.

Another important theoretical mechanism of the emotional display pathway is the *emotion recognition* propensity of customers. The ability to recognize and detect others' emotions has been shown to be a valid predictor of important work outcomes (e.g., job performance) and is generally considered to be a key dimension of emotional intelligence (Elfenbein, Foo, White, Tan, & Aik, 2007; Elfenbein, Marsh, & Ambady, 2002).

Although research suggests that it is difficult to detect fake emotions and deliberate deception by others in real-life situations, Ekman and colleagues provide evidence that many people are able to correctly identify inauthentic emotions to some extent through the 'leaking' of felt emotions (Ekman & Friesen, 1969; Ekman & O'Sullivan, 1991; Ekman, O'Sullivan, & Frank, 1999). For instance, people rate authentic smiles ('Duchenne smiles', named after French 18th century neurologist Guillaume Duchenne de Boulogne) as more expressive, natural, outgoing, sociable, and pleasant (Frank, Ekman, & Friesen, 1993). Duchenne smiles also evoke stronger positive experiences such as perceived interest (Surakka & Hietanen, 1998).

To apply this idea to the context of employee emotional display, because internal feelings are misaligned with emotional displays in surface acting, customers may be better able to detect emotional leaks and thus be inclined to believe that the employee is inauthentic (Groth et al., 2009). On the other hand, because deep acting involves the effortful regulation of internal experiences to match emotional displays, the employee's felt emotions match those displayed to the customers, and thus customers may be more likely to perceive the employee's performance as authentic.

Of course the implications of this depend on the extent to which customers are even able to make these judgments. While Scherer and Ceschi's (2000) findings suggest that employees are able to detect the emotions of customers, the only empirical study providing evidence that customers are able to detect the emotions of employees is by Groth et al. (2009). Using matched surveys from employees and customers completed immediately after their interactions, these authors show that customers are, to a limited extent, able to detect whether an employee has deliberately engaged in inauthentic emotional display as opposed to authentic emotional display. Customers' accurate detection of surface acting has a negative impact on perceived customer orientation above and beyond a potential main effect of surface acting, and their accurate detection of deep acting has a positive impact on the same outcome above and beyond the main effect of deep acting.

In summary, there is a limited but growing body of research that supports the emotional display pathway of our framework. The emotion regulation strategies selected by frontline employees result in observable emotional displays that can be (but often are not) detected by customers. And through emotional contagion, affect infusion, and emotion recognition, the resulting displays have a strong potential to influence customer judgments of service delivery. However, the customer's perception of the employee's emotional display may be crucial in this process, although further empirical evidence is needed. Future research should investigate the impact of *negative* emotions displayed by employees on customers, as well as the possible reciprocal impact of customer emotions on employee emotional displays. The reciprocal links by which customer emotions may impact employee emotional displays may lead to potentially spiraling effects (Andersson & Pearson, 1999).

## *The Employee Well-Being Pathway of Emotional Labor*

The second pathway in our conceptual framework linking employee emotion regulation to customer outcomes is the employee well-being pathway. This pathway suggests that employees' emotion regulation efforts influence their well-being (see Erickson & Stacey, 2013, for a review of the impact of emotional labor on employees in caring professions), which subsequently affects their job performance (including service performance) and thus ultimately customer outcomes.

The link between emotional labor strategies and employee well-being was posited by Hochschild (1983) as a cornerstone of emotional labor theory and has since become one of the most frequently researched topics in the field (Grandey, 2000). The strategies of surface acting and deep acting have established relations to facets of employee well-being such as job satisfaction, burnout, organizational identity, turnover, and stress (Ashforth & Humphrey, 1993; Brotheridge & Grandey, 2002; Goodwin, Groth, & Frenkel, 2011; Grandey, 2003; Pugh, Groth, & Hennig-Thurau, 2011; Schaubroeck & J. R. Jones, 2000). In the literature, surface acting is associated with negative outcomes such as emotional exhaustion, depersonalization, and low job satisfaction, whereas deep acting is positively related to customer satisfaction and emotional performance (Brotheridge & Grandey, 2002; Holman, Chissick, & Totterdell, 2002; Hülsheger & Schewe, 2011).

According to the service marketing literature and the 'service–profit chain' framework (Heskett, Jones, Loveman, Sasser, & Schlesinger,

1994; Heskett, Sasser, & Schlesinger, 1997), reduced well-being and job satisfaction among frontline service employees will invariably lead to reduced job performance in their role of serving customers. Briefly, the service–profit chain describes how the internal structures of the work environment ('internal service quality') influence employee attitudes toward the organization, which themselves influence customer outcomes and, subsequently, the service company's financial performance. In this model, employee well-being is associated with higher organizational commitment and lower turnover (e.g., Cotton & Tuttle, 1986; Heskett et al., 1997; Mathieu & Zajac, 1990). In the long term, less burnt-out employees are likely to feel satisfied with their work, unlikely to leave the organization, and likely to gain experience in their roles and perform their jobs more effectively, all of which lead to higher customer satisfaction (Leiter, Harvie, & Fizzell, 1998; Parker & Kulik, 1995; Vahey, Aiken, Sloane, Clarke, & Vargas, 2004).

Although there is no empirical doubt of the linkage between employee well-being and customer outcomes (see Whitman, Van Rooy, & Viswesvaran, 2010), interesting questions have been raised about the causal nature of the service–profit chain (Dietz, Pugh, & Wiley, 2004; Schneider & D. E. Bowen, 1985). Overall, results indicate that employee attitudes affect service outcomes (Schneider, Hanges, Smith, & Salvaggio, 2003), with several meta-analyses supporting an overall positive influence of employee satisfaction on customer satisfaction as well as on service quality perceptions (Brown & Lam, 2008; Harter, Schmidt, & Hayes, 2002). However, correlations can be expected to be somewhat inflated by endogeneity, as positive customer outcomes are themselves known to foster employee well-being (e.g., through contagion; Luo & Homburg, 2007).

## Underlying Mechanisms of the Employee Well-Being Pathway to Customer Outcomes

Although the reasons for a negative relationship between surface acting and burnout have not been thoroughly explored within the literature, researchers believe that surface acting leads to diminished well-being among employees because the continuous regulation of emotions may be seen as a job demand that consumes one's personal resources (Brotheridge & Lee, 2002; Pugliesi, 1999) and can be emotionally taxing for the employee (Bakker & Demerouti, 2007). Why do higher levels of well-being, such as high employee satisfaction or low levels of employee burnout, lead to beneficial customer outcomes? Empirical evidence shows that service employees' emotional exhaustion, a key dimension of burnout, is a predictor of poor service performance (Cropanzano, Rupp,

& Byrne, 2003). Similarly, Singh (2000) found that stress experienced by service employees equally affects service performance. Again, this is consistent with theories of resource depletion; because employees have limited resources to perform effectively in their roles, employee burnout increases the likelihood of poor performance (Trougakos, Beal, Green, & Weiss, 2008; Wang, Liao, Zhan, & Shi, 2011).

A second mechanism of the employee well-being pathway is *extra-role behaviors* performed by service employees. Extra-role behaviors, such as organizational citizenship behaviors (OCB), are employee discretionary behaviors that are outside the scope of role expectations and which enhance organizational effectiveness (Organ, 1988, 1997). OCB captures behaviors that may be viewed by customers as exceeding expectations (Bell & Menguc, 2002). And because the nature of services is inherently social, engaging in OCB will elicit positive judgments among customers (George & Bettenhausen, 1990), translating to perceptions of better service quality. Furthermore, engagement in extra-role behaviors within the organization, such as assisting co-workers, is likely to bolster the functioning of the organizational unit, thus enhancing overall productivity (Bell & Menguc, 2002; Ryan, Schmit, & Johnson, 1996). According to Heskett et al. (1997), such productivity gains are likely to further contribute to perceptions of service quality and customer satisfaction.

In the customer service context, there is evidence of a link between employee well-being and OCB, whereby satisfied employees are more likely to engage in extra-role behaviors (LePine, Erez, & Johnson, 2002; Organ & Ryan, 1995; Whitman et al., 2010). Likewise, burnout has been shown to be a predictor of lower levels of OCB (Cropanzano et al., 2003) and higher levels of counterproductive workplace behaviors (Cropanzano, Howes, Grandey, & Toth, 1997). This is consistent with the norm of reciprocity, as employees are believed to engage in extra-role behaviors as a result of preferable treatment from the organization.

In sum, the service–profit chain framework suggests that one of the ways in which emotional labor affects customer outcomes is through employee well-being outcomes such as job satisfaction, burnout, and stress. Emotional labor, specifically surface acting, increases the chances that an employee will develop lower organizational well-being (in the form of higher burnout and lower job satisfaction), which is linked to lower performance and decreased engagement in extra-role behaviors due to resource depletion and the norm of reciprocity.

## CONTEXTUAL FORCES MODERATING
## THE EMOTION REGULATION–CUSTOMER
## OUTCOME RELATIONSHIP

As has become evident in this chapter, there is a limited amount of research on the importance of the link between frontline employees' emotion regulation strategies and customer reactions and experiences, and what little empirical evidence does exist is often inconclusive. Thus, an important avenue for future research is to examine this link using a variety of different research methods and to examine potential contextual variables impacting this relationship. Given the unique challenges often encountered in studying the customer service context, several contextual forces are likely to shape the relationships shown in our conceptual framework. The 'moment of truth' when an employee and customer interact does not occur in the same way across encounters, and is indeed subject to various contextual factors. Here, we discuss three contextual variables we believe are crucial for understanding heterogeneity in the link between employee emotions and customer outcomes: the type of service offered, the kind of customers involved, and the unique relationship between the organization and its customers. And because the literature examining these factors in relation to employee emotion regulation and customer outcomes is very limited, we consider these to be important avenues for future research.

### *Service Characteristics*

While there is agreement that services differ quite substantially from consumer products, the same is true for the character of the service sector overall. Comprising call centers, banks, hospitals, hair salons, supermarkets and universities, there is as much heterogeneity within the service sector as there is outside of it. This heterogeneity can have an impact on how and to what extent employee emotional labor affects customers and customer outcomes.

To capture the differences and similarities among a wide range of services, there has long been an interest in the development of service typologies. One typology developed by Price, Arnould, and Deibler (1995) suggests that services can be characterized by differences in duration, affective content, and special proximity. Another often-cited study that empirically integrates the meta-characteristics of services is by Bowen (1990), who identifies three service types distinguished by (a) the extent of contact with employees, (b) the level of customization, and (c) the object (or subject) that is integrated in the service process. In Bowen's typology, the extent of contact covers issues such as the length of time and communication richness of interactions with customers. Customization concerns the extent to which the service can be changed to meet a customer's needs. This dimension has often been regarded as a key distinguishing factor of service types, with some research showing that customized services are widely regarded as 'better' and more valuable by customers, even though they are often more expensive and require the service firm and frontline employees to relinquish some control to the customer (Surprenant & Solomon, 1987). Finally, the integration dimension distinguishes services that depend on the customer to provide information or other kinds of input from those services in which it is an object owned by the customer (e.g., the car) that is integrated.

Given the wide range of service types available to customers, it is possible that the effects of employee emotional behavior are context-specific and perhaps a direct function of the type of service. With regard to the defining characteristics of Bowen's (1990) typology, we argue that a higher degree of contact with the same employee will increase a customer's ability to correctly recognize the employee's emotional labor strategy (via the emotional display pathway), although some research suggests that frequent contact between employees and customers can be equally stressful or motivating, depending on the service context (Grandey & Diamond, 2010). Theoretically, increased contact between the employee and customer should strengthen the relationship between employee well-being and customer outcomes (the well-being pathway of our framework), as resource depletion and extra-role performance will become more visible to the customer and thus more salient in his or her overall evaluation of the service.

In testing the moderating impact of context, Groth et al. (2009) did not find differences between Bowen's service types with regard to the impact on customers' emotional labor detection accuracy. However, the authors of the study did not control for situational influences in their dyadic field study approach and did not examine the extent of customization and the object/subject of the service, which may play a decisive role in how emotional labor impacts customer outcomes.

Regarding customization, we similarly expect that higher customization will result in greater authentic emotional display by employees and therefore lead to greater likelihood of customers correctly identifying employee emotions. However, it is less clear whether higher customization will positively or negatively affect the customer experience via the employee well-being pathway; customization may lead to higher resource depletion but at the same time may result in more satisfied and engaged service employees due to the increased autonomy they enjoy.

Finally, regarding whether it is the customers or their possessions that are the target of service delivery (e.g., a health check as opposed to a dry cleaning service), we expect services involving direct physical contact (e.g., a visit to the dentist) to be more susceptible to the effects of emotional labor. We expect services directed at customers generally to be more susceptible to emotional contagion processes as a result of increased emotional arousal in the participating customers and that this may affect their ability to correctly read an employee's true emotions. Nevertheless, emotional display is likely a more important element of service quality judgments in these cases than in performance of services directed at a customer's possessions, which is more likely to be judged based on other, more objective cues.

Other service factors such as the level of experience qualities (i.e., aspects of services whose quality customers are able to appraise only *after* their delivery, such as a concert performance) versus credence qualities (i.e., aspects of services for which customers cannot truly evaluate the quality of the core service outcome even after its delivery, such as legal services), and the degree of customer involvement in the service delivery process might also moderate the role of emotional labor. For example, emotional display may be less important for the staff at a concert, whose core service (the performance itself) the customer is likely in a position to judge. On the other hand, customer expectations for authentic emotional display may be higher when receiving legal advice, the quality of which customers may have difficulty assessing. Regarding customer involvement, the choice of employees' emotion regulation strategies as well as the degree of importance customers place on the choice of such strategies might be quite different in sensitive service deliveries in which customers may be concerned for their personal safety (e.g., health care) than in quick transactions of low importance to the customer (e.g., buying a newspaper in a convenience store).

In short, a great variety of service types exist, and the strength and importance of the links in our conceptual framework likely depend on the type of service in which they occur. To date there has been insufficient research to provide answers even to fairly basic questions about the moderating role that service context may play in the relationship between the display and recognition of emotions (Brown & Lam, 2008; Groth et al., 2009), despite growing evidence that the service context plays a vital role in shaping the emotion regulation–customer outcome link. Thus, we hope that future research explores many of the potential service characteristics that have been identified in prior service management and marketing research.

## Customer Characteristics

A second category of contextual factors likely to influence some of the key relationships in our framework are individual differences among customers. It is important to note that service transactions are dyadic and reciprocal, such that customers can influence how the service employee acts and how the service transpires (Rafaeli & Sutton, 1989). Regardless of the service context itself, it is likely that customers will differ both in the degree to which they perceive emotional display and the level of expectations they have about service delivery processes, and thus they may react differently to the same service outcome.

The attitudes of the service employee toward customers in general can influence the two pathways shown in our model. For example, consider customer orientation – an employee's interest in and ability to fulfill customers' service-related needs (Brady & Cronin, 2001; Brown, Mowen, Donavan, & Licata, 2002). One study found that employees with lower customer orientation were more likely to fake their emotional displays, which resulted in a less favorable performance rating by customers (Allen, Pugh, Grandey, & Groth, 2010). In addition, perspective-taking, or the ability to put oneself in another person's shoes (Parker & Axtell, 2001), is likely to positively influence the quality of interactions between employees and customers (Rupp, McCance, Spencer, & Sonntag, 2008). Therefore, the ability and/or motivation to put oneself in the shoes of the exchange partner in order to understand his or her view is likely to improve an employee's service performance. Research shows that the ability to take the perspective of others is partly determined by one's exchange partner (i.e., customers), such that people are more likely to engage in perspective taking when they perceive others as similar to them (Cialdini, Brown, Lewis, Luce, & Neuberg, 1997; Davis, Conklin, Smith, & Luce, 1996). Thus, the characteristics of the customer can trigger processes that not only influence the emotional labor strategies employees choose but also how the emotional display pathway and the well-being pathway facilitate positive customer outcomes.

Customers' emotional intelligence – that is, their ability to recognize and regulate emotions in themselves and others (Salovey & Sluyter, 1997) – is likely to affect the way in which employee emotional labor influences customer outcomes. Emotional intelligence may affect customers' ability not only to detect inauthentic emotional displays on the part of service employees but also to regulate their emotions during extremely positive or extremely frustrating service experiences. For example, Elfenbein and Ambady (2002) concluded that the ability to recognize emotions varies within and across cultures such that people are better at recognizing the emotions of others when they belong to the same region (i.e., in-group bias). Thus it may be expected that customers will be more impervious to the effects of emotional labor when the employees are from a different region. In addition, it could be argued that females are more perceptive of the emotions of others (Brackett, Mayer, & Warner, 2004; Hall, 1978;

McClure, 2000) and therefore may be better able to detect inauthentic emotional expressions, making them more sensitive to the effects of employee emotional labor than males.

Tan, Foo, and Kwek (2004) found that customer traits such as agreeableness and negative affectivity influence the positive display of emotions by the service provider. A logical extension of their study is that customer characteristics also influence the way in which employees manage their displays to produce those positive displays. In addition, Tan et al. (2004) found that agreeableness directly influenced customer satisfaction with the service employee. They argue that those higher in agreeableness may be more tolerant of service employee behavior. It is therefore possible that those higher in agreeableness are also impervious to the effects of inauthentic emotions. In addition, extraversion, agreeableness, neuroticism, and conscientiousness are implicated in the development of trust, trustworthiness, and rapport, which influence the development of customer satisfaction (Barrick et al., 2012; Bernieri, Gillis, Davis, & Grahe, 1996; Evans & Revelle, 2008). The influence of emotional labor on customer outcomes may be different for customers who are more inclined to trust and develop rapport because they are more likely to sympathize with an employee engaging in emotional labor. Furthermore, the presence of trust and rapport may influence potential mechanisms underlying the emotional display pathway, such as emotional contagion between employees and customers.

A question of particular interest to the marketing perspective is whether customers with a high 'lifetime value' for the organization (e.g., high future spending) differ in their response to employee emotion regulation from those with a lower lifetime value. In the services marketing literature, satisfaction with service quality is determined by the disconfirmation paradigm, which suggests that customers are satisfied with service quality when service perceptions exceed expectations (Oliver, 1993; Parasuraman et al., 1988). Authentic employee displays, as discussed above, are a predictor of customer outcomes and would be expected to contribute to the perception of satisfactory service. However, it is not known whether customers with a high lifetime value have different expectations of service. If customers with higher lifetime value have higher expectations of the service, perhaps the display of inauthentic emotions by employees is more detrimental than for customers of lower lifetime value. On the other hand, it is possible that those with a higher lifetime value have a greater threshold for tolerating service failures, perhaps buffering the effects of inauthentic displays. Given the multitude of segmentation criteria used by marketers, it will be crucial to determine which of these criteria will moderate the employee emotions–customer outcomes link and whether new criteria should be considered when designing service offers.

## Relationship Characteristics

The nature of the relationship between the customer and employee is also expected to play an important role in explaining the service delivery context, likely acting as a moderator of some of the links in our conceptual framework.

A number of different conceptualizations of relationship types have been suggested in prior research. Gutek and colleagues distinguish between service relationships and service encounters (Gutek, Bhappu, Liao-Troth, & Bennett, 1999; Gutek, Groth, & Cherry, 2002). In service relationships, the customer and employee develop a shared history of interactions through repeated encounters, and over the course of developing the service relationship, customers and employees often get to know each other well, form personal bonds, and develop mutual respect for and trust in each other. Service relationship strength has been shown to have an impact even in service failures, with personal relationships mitigating the negative consequences of a failed service recovery, presumably because customers in long-term relationships with service providers might be more willing to give the providers another chance (Mattila, 2001). This has obvious implications for emotion regulation strategies and customer outcomes, as employees may not only be more likely to make an effort to display authentic emotions (i.e., deep acting) but the display of fake emotions, if detected by customers, may reduce perceptions of trust and respect more strongly than in more casual relationships.

Service encounters, on the other hand, are characterized as single interactions with no expectations of future interactions (Gutek et al., 1999). For example, customers in a convenience store often do not know the employee who serves them and do not expect to ever see that person again. The employee's choice of emotion regulation strategy may be less important in these types of interactions, as long as it does not interfere with the quick and efficient delivery of the service (Sutton & Rafaeli, 1988). Similarly, it can be assumed that customer expectations for emotional display may differ significantly based on whether the service is delivered in a relationship context or an encounter context.

It should be acknowledged that relationships and encounters are not static; a transactional customer can become a loyal patron for several reasons. Beatty, Mayer, Coleman, Reynolds, and Lee (1996) note that a range of factors will impact the likelihood of closer bonds between employees and customers developing over time and discuss a number of stages that such service relationships will likely go through in the long term. What is the role of employee emotion regulation in this dynamic process? Those more familiar with each other may have different expectations regarding emotional display, the degree of authenticity desired in interactions, and the customer's motivation and ability to judge the authenticity of the emotions displayed by the employee.

In sum, the level of interpersonal knowledge between employee and customer likely plays a significant role in shaping all aspects of our conceptual framework, from the choice of emotion regulation strategies by the employee to the customer's expectations and subsequent reactions to the emotion regulation and resulting display during the delivery. Again, the empirical literature on such contextual factors is limited, and future research is needed to further our understanding of the role that relationship characteristics play in the service delivery process.

## CONCLUSIONS

This chapter develops a conceptual framework that links employee emotion regulation and customer outcomes, an area which has received increasing empirical interest in the emotional labor and service management and marketing literatures. We reviewed a growing body of literature that demonstrates a relationship between the emotions displayed by frontline employees and customer reactions to the service delivery.

The theoretical framework we propose integrates the findings of previous studies into two key pathways which appear to facilitate the emotion regulation–customer outcomes relationship: an emotional display pathway and an employee well-being pathway. In addition to discussing these two pathways, we identify the critical role of service context as a potential moderator within our framework. Given the importance of context in arriving at service delivery outcomes, the scarcity of research that is available on service types, customer characteristics, and relationship characteristics suggests three promising avenues for future research.

Because customer outcomes are important for any service organization, we hope this chapter will stimulate further thinking and research in this area in order to increase our knowledge of how and why frontline employees' emotion regulation impacts the customer experience.

## ENDNOTES

1 Please note that a variety of theoretical approaches toward emotional labor exists; this chapter follows the original definition by Hochschild (1983) in that it focuses on the intrapsychological processes involved with the required matching of employee feelings with emotion-related organizational display rules. For an extensive discussion, see Grandey, Diefendorff, and Rupp (2013).

# REFERENCES

Allen, J. A., Pugh, S. D., Grandey, A. A., & Groth, M. (2010). Following display rules in good or bad faith?: Customer orientation as a moderator of the display rule–emotional labor relationship. *Human Performance, 23*(2), 101–115.

Andersson, L. M., & Pearson, C. M. (1999). Tit for Tat? The spiraling effect of incivility in the workplace. *Academy of Management Review, 24*(3), 452–471.

Ashforth, B. E., & Humphrey, R. H. (1993). Emotional labor in service roles: The influence of identity. *Academy of Management Review, 18*, 88–115.

Bakker, A. B., & Demerouti, E. (2007). The job demands–resources model: State of the art. *Journal of Managerial Psychology, 22*(3), 309–328.

Barger, P. B., & Grandey, A. A. (2006). Service with a smile and encounter satisfaction: Emotional contagion and appraisal mechanisms. *Academy of Management Journal, 49*(6), 1229–1238.

Barrick, M. R., Dustin, S. L., Giluk, T. L., Stewart, G. L., Shaffer, J. A., & Swider, B. W. (2012). Candidate characteristics driving initial impressions during rapport building: Implications for employment interview validity. *Journal of Occupational and Organizational Psychology, 85*, 330–352.

Barsade, S. G. (2002). The ripple effect: Emotional contagion and its influence on group behavior. *Administrative Science Quarterly, 47*, 644–675.

Beatty, S. E., Mayer, M., Coleman, J. E., Reynolds, K. E., & Lee, J. (1996). Customer-sales associate retail relationships. *Journal of Retailing, 72*, 223–247.

Bell, S. J., & Menguc, B. (2002). The employee–organization relationship, organizational citizenship behaviors, and superior service quality. *Journal of Retailing, 78*(2), 131–146.

Bernieri, F. J., Gillis, J. S., Davis, J. M., & Grahe, J. E. (1996). Dyad rapport and the accuracy of its judgment across situations: A lens model analysis. *Journal of Personality and Social Psychology, 71*(1), 110–129.

Bowen, J. (1990). Development of a taxonomy of services to gain strategic marketing insights. *Journal of the Academy of Marketing Science, 18*(1), 43–49.

Bower, G. H. (1981). Mood and memory. *The American psychologist, 36*(2), 129–148.

Brackett, M. A., Mayer, J. D., & Warner, R. M. (2004). Emotional intelligence and its relation to everyday behaviour. *Personality and Individual Differences, 36*(6), 1387–1402.

Brady, M. K., & Cronin Jr, J. J. (2001). Some new thoughts on conceptualizing perceived service quality: A hierarchical approach. *The Journal of Marketing, 65*(3), 34–49.

Brotheridge, C. M., & Grandey, A. A. (2002). Emotional labor and burnout: comparing two perspectives of "people work." *Journal of Vocational Behavior, 60*(1), 17–39.

Brotheridge, C. M., & Lee, R. T. (2002). Testing a conservation of resources model of the dynamics of emotional labor. *Journal of Occupational Health Psychology, 7*(1), 57–67.

Brotheridge, C. M., & Lee, R. T. (2003). Development and validation of the emotional labour scale. *Journal of Occupational and Organizational Psychology, 76*(3), 365–379.

Brown, S., & Lam, S. K. (2008). A meta-analysis of relationships linking employee satisfaction to customer responses. *Journal of Retailing, 84*(3), 243–255.

Brown, T. J., Mowen, J. C., Donavan, D. T., & Licata, J. W. (2002). The customer orientation of service workers: Personality trait effects on self- and supervisor performance ratings. *Journal of Marketing Research, 39*(1), 110–119.

Chartrand, T. L., & van Baaren, R. (2009). Human mimicry. *Advances in Experimental Social Psychology, 41*, 219–274.

Chartrand, T. L., & Bargh, J. A. (1999). The chameleon effect: The perception–behavior link and social interaction. *Journal of personality and social psychology, 76*(6), 893–910.

Chi, N. W., Grandey, A. A., Diamond, J. A., & Krimmel, K. R. (2011). Want a tip? Service performance as a function of emotion regulation and extraversion. *Journal of Applied Psychology, 96*, 1337–1346.

Chowdhury, S., & Miles, G. (2006). Customer-induced uncertainty in predicting organizational design: Empirical evidence challenging the service versus manufacturing dichotomy. *Journal of Business Research, 59*(1), 121–129.

Cialdini, R. B., Brown, S. L., Lewis, B. P., Luce, C, & Neuberg, S. L. (1997). Reinterpreting the empathy–altruism relationship: When one into one equals oneness. *Journal of Personality and Social Psychology, 73*(3), 481–94.

Cotton, J. L., & Tuttle, J. M. (1986). Employee turnover: A meta-analysis and review with implications for research. *The Academy of Management Review, 11*(1), 55–70.

Cropanzano, R., Howes, J. C., Grandey, A. A., & Toth, P. (1997). The relationship of organizational politics and support to work behaviors, attitudes, and stress. *Journal of Organizational Behavior, 18*(2), 159–180.

Cropanzano, R., Rupp, D. E., & Byrne, Z. S. (2003). The relationship of emotional exhaustion to work attitudes, job performance, and organizational citizenship behaviors. *Journal of Applied Psychology, 88*(1), 160–169.

Davis, M. H., Conklin, L., Smith, A., & Luce, Carol. (1996). Effect of perspective taking on the cognitive representation of persons: A merging of self and other observer. *Journal of Personality and Social Psychology, 70*(4), 713–726.

Diefendorff, J. M., Richard, E. M., & Croyle, M. H. (2006). Are emotional display rules formal job requirements? Examination of employee and supervisor perceptions. *Journal of Occupational and Organizational Psychology, 79*(2), 273–298.

Dietz, J., Pugh, S. D., & Wiley, J. W. (2004). Service climate effects on customer attitudes: An examination of boundary conditions. *Academy of Management Journal, 47*(1), 81–92. Academy of Management.

Ekman, P., & Friesen, W. V. (1969). The repertoire of non-verbal behavior: Categories, origins, useage, and coding. *Semiotica, 1*(1), 49–98.

Ekman, P., & O'Sullivan, M. (1991). Who can catch a liar? *American Psychologist, 46*(9), 913–920.

Ekman, P., O'Sullivan, M., & Frank, M. G. (1999). A few can catch a liar. *Psychological Science, 10*(3), 263–266.

Elfenbein, H. A., & Ambady, N. (2002). On the universality and cultural specificity of emotion recognition: A meta-analysis. *Psychological Bulletin, 128*(2), 203–235.

Elfenbein, H. A., Foo, M. D., White, J., Tan, H. H., & Aik, V. C. (2007). Reading your counterpart: The benefit of emotion recognition accuracy for effectiveness in negotiation. *Journal of Nonverbal Behavior, 31*(4), 205–223.

Elfenbein, H. A., Marsh, A. A., & Ambady, N. (2002). Emotional intelligence and the recognition of emotion from facial expressions. In L. F. Barrett & P. Salovey (Eds.), *The wisdom of feelings: psychological processes in emotional intelligence* (pp. 37–59). New York: Guilford Press.

Erickson, R. J., & Grove, W. C. J. (2008). Emotional labor and health care. *Sociology Compass, 2*(2), 704–733.

Erickson, R. & Stacey, C. (2013). Attending to mind and body: Engaging the complexity of emotion practice among caring professionals. In A. A. Grandey, J. M. Diefendorff & D. E. Rupp (Eds.), *Emotional labor in the 21st century: Diverse perspectives on emotion regulation at work.* New York, NY: Psychology Press/Routledge.

Evans, A. M., & Revelle, Q. R. (2008). Survey and behavioral measurements of interpersonal trust. *Journal of Research in Personality, 42*(6), 1585–1593.

Ford, W. S. Z. (1995). Evaluation of the indirect influence of courteous service on customer discretionary behavior. *Human Communication Research, 22,* 65–89.

Forgas, J. P. (1995). Mood and judgment: The affect infusion model (AIM). *Psychological Bulletin, 117*(1), 39–66.

Frank, M. G., & Ekman, P. (1993). Not all smiles are created equal: The difference between enjoyment and nonenjoyment smiles. *Humor, 6,* 9–26.

Frank, M. G., Ekman, P., & Friesen, W. V. (1993). Behavioral markers and recognizability of the smile of enjoyment. *Journal of Personality and Social Psychology, 64*(1), 83–93.

George, J. M., & Bettenhausen, K. (1990). Understanding prosocial behavior, sales performance, and turnover: A group-level analysis in a service context. *Journal of Applied Psychology, 75*(6), 698–709.

Goodwin, R. E., Groth, M., & Frenkel, S. J. (2011). Relationships between emotional labor, job performance, and turnover. *Journal of Vocational Behavior, 79*(2), 538–548.

Grandey, A. A. (2000). Emotion regulation in the workplace: A new way to conceptualize emotional labor. *Journal of Occupational Health Psychology, 5*(1), 95–110.

Grandey, A. A. (2003). When "the show must go on": Surface acting and deep acting as determinants of emotional exhaustion and peer-rated service delivery. *Academy of Management Journal, 46,* 86–96.

Grandey, A. A., & Diamond, J. A. (2010). Interactions with the public: Bridging job design and emotional labor perspectives. *Journal of Organizational Behavior, 31,* 338–350.

Grandey, A. A., Diefendorff, J. M., & Rupp, D. E. (2013). Emotional labor: Overview of definitions, theories, and evidence. In A. A. Grandey, J. M. Diefendorff & D. E. Rupp (Eds.), *Emotional labor in the 21st century: Diverse perspectives on emotion regulation at work.* New York, NY: Psychology Press/Routledge.

Grandey, A. A., Fisk, G. M., Mattila, A. S., Jansen, K. J., & Sideman, L. A. (2005). Is "service with a smile" enough? Authenticity of positive displays during service encounters. *Organizational Behavior and Human Decision Processes, 96*, 38–55.

Groth, M., Hennig-Thurau, T., & Walsh, G. (2009). Customer reactions to emotional labor: The roles of employee acting strategies and customer detection accuracy. *Academy of Management Journal, 52*(5), 958–974.

Gutek, B. A., Bhappu, A. D., Liao-Troth, M. A., & Bennett, C. (1999). Distinguishing between service relationships and encounters. *Journal of Applied Psychology, 84*(2), 218–233.

Gutek, B. A., Groth, M., & Cherry, B. (2002). Achieving service success through relationships and enhanced encounters. *The Academy of Management Executive, 16*(4), 132–144.

Hall, J. A. (1978). Gender effects in decoding nonverbal cues. *Psychological Bulletin, 85*(4), 845–857.

Harter, J. K., Schmidt, F. L., & Hayes, T. L. (2002). Business-unit-level relationship between employee satisfaction, employee engagement, and business outcomes: A meta-analysis. *Journal of Applied Psychology, 87*(2), 268-279.

Hatfield, E., Cacioppo, J. T., & Rapson, R. L. (1994). *Emotional contagion.* Cambridge: Cambridge University Press.

Hennig-Thurau, T., Groth, M., Paul, M., & Gremler, D. D. (2006). Are all smiles created equal? How emotional contagion and emotional labor affect service relationships. *Journal of Marketing, 70*(3), 58–73.

Hennig-Thurau, T., Gwinner, K. P., & Gremler, D. D. (2002). Understanding relationship marketing outcomes: an integration of relational benefits and relationship quality. *Journal of Service Research, 4*(3), 230–247.

Hennig-Thurau, T., & Klee, A. (1997). The impact of customer satisfaction and relationship quality on customer retention: a critical reassessment and model development. *Psychology & Marketing, 14* (December), 737-764.

Heskett, J. L., Jones, T. O., Loveman, G. W., Sasser, W. E. J., & Schlesinger, L. A. (1994). Putting the service–profit chain to work. *Harvard Business Review, 72*(2), 164–174.

Heskett, J. L., Sasser, W. E. J., & Schlesinger, L. A. (1997). *The service profit chain: How leading companies link profit and growth to loyalty, satisfaction, and value.* New York: The Free Press.

Hess, U., & Blairy, S. (2001). Facial mimicry and emotional contagion to dynamic emotional facial expressions and their influence on decoding accuracy. *International Journal of Psychophysiology, 40*, 129–141.

Hochschild, A. R. (1979). Emotion in work, feeling rules and social structure. *American Journal of Sociology, 85*, 551–575.

Hochschild, A. R. (1983). *The Managed Heart: Commercialization of human feeling.* California: University of California Press.

Holman, D., Chissick, C., & Totterdell, P. (2002). The effects of performance monitoring on emotional labor and well-being in call centers. *Motivation and Emotion, 26*(1), 57–81.

Hülsheger, U. R., & Schewe, A. F. (2011). On the costs and benefits of emotional labor: A meta-analysis of three decades of research. *Journal of Occupational Health Psychology, 16,* 361–89.

Kernis, M. H., & Goldman, B. M. (2006). A multicomponent conceptualization of authenticity: Theory and research. *Advances in Experimental Social Psychology, 38,* 283–357.

Leidner, R. (1999). Emotional labor in service work. *The Annals of the American Academy of Political and Social Science, 561,* 81–95.

Leiter, M. P., Harvie, P., & Fizzell, C. (1998). The correspondence of patient satisfaction and nurse burnout. *Social Science & Medicine, 47*(10), 1611–1617.

LePine, J. A., Erez, A., & Johnson, D. E. (2002). The nature and dimensionality of organizational citizenship behavior: A critical review and meta-analysis. *Journal of Applied Psychology, 87*(1), 52– 65.

Luo, X., & Homburg, C. (2007). Neglected outcomes of customer satisfaction. *Journal of Marketing, 71,* 133–149.

Mathieu, J. E., & Zajac, D. M. (1990). A review and meta-analysis of the antecedents, correlates, and consequences of organizational commitment. *Psychological Bulletin, 108*(2), 171–194.

Mattila, A. S. (2001). The impact of relationship type on customer loyalty in a context of service failures. *Journal of Service Research, 4*(2), 91–101.

Mattila, A. S., & Enz, C. A. (2002). The role of emotions in service encounters. *Journal of Service Research, 4*(4), 268–277.

McClure, E. B. (2000). A meta-analytic review of sex differences in facial expression processing and their development in infants, children, and adolescents. *Psychological Bulletin, 126*(3), 424–53.

Morris, J. A., & Feldman, D. C. (1997). Managing emotions in the workplace. *Journal of Managerial Issues, 9*(3), 257–274.

Oliver, R. L. (1993). Cognitive, affective, and attribute bases of the satisfaction response. *The Journal of Consumer Research, 20*(3), 418–430.

Organ, D. W. (1988). A restatement of the satisfaction–performance hypothesis. *Journal of Management, 14*(4), 547–557.

Organ, D. W. (1997). Organizational citizenship behavior: It's construct clean-up time. *Human Performance, 10*(2), 85–97.

Organ, D. W., & Ryan, K. (1995). A meta-analytic review of attitudinal and dispositional predictors of organizational citizenship behavior. *Personnel Psychology, 48,* 775–803.

Parasuraman, A., Zeithaml, V. A., & Berry, L. L. (1988). SERVQUAL: A multiple-item scale for measuring consumer perceptions of service quality. *Journal of Retailing, 64*(1), 12–40.

Parker, S. K., & Axtell, C. M. (2001). Seeing another viewpoint: Antecedents and outcomes of employee perspective taking. *The Academy of Management Journal, 44*(6), 1085–1100.

Parker, P. A., & Kulik, J. A. (1995). Burnout, self- and supervisor-rated job performance, and absenteeism among nurses. *Journal of Behavioral Medicine, 18*(6), 581–599. Price, L. L., Arnould, E. J., & Deibler L., S. (1995). Consumers' emotional responses to service encounters. *International Journal of Service Industry Management, 6,* 34–63.

Pugh, S. D. (2001). Service with a smile: Emotional contagion in the service encounter. *Academy of Management Journal, 44*, 1018–1027.

Pugh, S. D., Groth, M., & Hennig-Thurau, T. (2011). Willing and able to fake emotions: A closer examination of the link between emotional dissonance and employee well-being. *The Journal of Applied Psychology, 96*(2), 377–390.

Pugliesi, K. (1999). The consequences of emotional labor: Effects on work stress, job satisfaction, and well-being. *Motivation and Emotion, 23*(2), 125–154.

Rafaeli, A., & Sutton, R. I. (1987). Expression of emotion as part of the work role. *Academy of Management Review, 12*, 23–37.

Rafaeli, A., & Sutton, R. I. (1989). The expression of emotion in organizational life. *Research in Organizational Behavior, 11*, 1–42.

Rupp, D. E., McCance, S. A., Spencer, S., & Sonntag, K. (2008). Customer (in)justice and emotional labor: The role of perspective taking, anger, and emotional regulation. *Journal of Management, 34*(5), 903–924.

Rust, R. T., & Oliver, R. L. (1994). Service quality: Insights and managerial implications from the frontier. In R. T. Rust & R. L. Oliver (Eds.), *Service Quality: New Directions in Theory and Practice* (pp. 1–19). New York: SAGE Publications.

Ryan, A. M., Schmit, M. J., & Johnson, R. (1996). Attitudes and effectiveness: Examining relations at an organizational level. *Personnel Psychology, 49*(4), 853–882.

Salmela, M. (2005). What Is emotional authenticity? *Journal for the Theory of Social Behaviour, 35*(3), 209–230.

Salovey, P., & Sluyter, D. (1997). *Emotional development and emotional intelligence: educational implications.* (P. Salovey & D. J. Sluyter, Eds.) (Vol. 43, pp. 741–743). Basic Books. Retrieved from http://books.google.com/books?hl= en&lr=&id=P5oAE5wDwBIC&pgis=1

Scharlemann, J. P. W., Eckel, C. C., Kacelnik, A., & Wilson, R. K. (2001). The value of a smile: Game theory with a human face. *Journal of Economic Psychology, 22*(5), 617–640.

Schaubroeck, J., & Jones, J. R. (2000). Antecedents of workplace emotional labor dimensions and moderators of their effects on physical symptoms. *Journal of Organizational Behavior, 21*(2), 163–183.

Scherer, K. R., & Ceschi, G. (2000). Criteria for emotion recognition from verbal and nonverbal expression: Studying baggage loss in the airport. *Personality and Social Psychology Bulletin, 26*(3), 327–339.

Schneider, B., & Bowen, D. E. (1985). Employee and customer perceptions of service in banks: Replication and extension. *Journal of Applied Psychology, 70*(3), 423–433.

Schneider, B., Hanges, P. J., Smith, D. B., & Salvaggio, A. N. (2003). Which comes first: Employee attitudes or organizational financial and market performance? *The Journal of Applied Psychology, 88*(5), 836–851.

Schoenewolf, G. (1990). Emotional contagion: Behavioral induction in individuals and groups. *Modern Psychoanalysis, 15*(1), 49–61.

Schwarz, N., & Clore, G. L. (1983). Mood, misattribution, and judgments of well-being: Informative and directive functions of affective states. *Journal of Personality and Social Psychology, 45*(3), 513–523.

Seth, N., Deshmukh, S. G., & Vrat, P. (2005). Service quality models: A review. *International Journal of Quality & Reliability Management, 22*(9), 913–949.

Singh, J. (2000). Performance productivity and quality of frontline employees in service organizations. *Journal of Marketing, 64*(2), 15–34.

Surakka, V., & Hietanen, J. K. (1998). Facial and emotional reactions to Duchenne and non-Duchenne smiles. *International Journal of Psychophysiology, 29*(1), 23–33.

Surprenant, C. F., & Solomon, M. R. (1987). Personalization and predictability in the service encounter. *Journal of Marketing, 51*(2), 86–96.

Sutton, R. I., & Rafaeli, A. (1988). Untangling the relationship between displayed emotions and organisational sales: The case of convenience stores. *Academy of Management Journal, 31*(3), 461–487.

Söderlund, M., & Rosengren, S. (2004). Dismantling "positive affect" and its effects on customer satisfaction: An empirical examination of customer joy in a service encounter. *Journal of Consumer Satisfaction, Dissatisfaction and Complaining Behavior, 17*(1), 27–41.

Söderlund, M., & Rosengren, S. (2008). Revisiting the smiling service worker and customer satisfaction. *International Journal of Service Industry Management, 19*(5), 552–574.

Tan, H. H., Foo, M. D., & Kwek, M. H. (2004). The effects of customer personality traits on the display of positive emotions. *Academy of Management Journal, 47*(2), 287–296.

Trougakos, J. P., Beal, D. J., Green, S. G., & Weiss, H. M. (2008). Making the break count: An episodic examination of recovery activities, emotional experiences, and positive affective displays. *Academy of Management Journal, 51*(1), 131–146.

Tsai, W.-C. (2001). Determinants and consequences of employee displayed positive emotions. *Journal of Management, 27*, 497–512.

Tsai, W.-C., & Huang, Y.-M. (2002). Mechanisms linking employee affective delivery and customer behavioral intentions. *Journal of Applied Psychology, 87*, 1001–1008.

Vahey, D. C., Aiken, L. H., Sloane, D. M., Clarke, S. P., & Vargas, D. (2004). Nurse burnout and patient satisfaction. *Medical care, 42*(2 Suppl), 57–66.

Wang, M., Liao, H., Zhan, Y., & Shi, J. (2011). Daily customer mistreatment and employee sabotage against customers. *Academy of Management Journal, 54*(2), 312–334.

Whitman, D. S., Van Rooy, D. L., & Viswesvaran, C. (2010). Satisfaction, citizenship behaviors, and performance in work units: A meta-analysis of collective construct relations. *Personnel Psychology, 63*(1), 41–81.

# 7

# Call Centers

## Emotional Labor Over the Phone

DANIELLE VAN JAARSVELD • WINIFRED R. POSTER

Emotional labor is "the management of feeling to create a publicly observable facial and bodily display" occurring in face-to-face or voice-to-voice interactions with customers (Hochschild, 1983, p. 7). Service workers who interact with customers over the phone, namely the call center workforce, do not need to directly manage the visual cues they communicate to customers. Rather, their focus is primarily on communicating appropriate emotions via vocal cues, which presents some unique challenges for performing emotional labor. In this chapter, we focus on the call center context to underscore the unique aspects of emotional labor in voice interactions. First, we present an overview of working conditions in call centers, and the role of emotional labor in call center work. Second, we examine how organizational factors, extra-organizational factors (i.e., customers), and individual factors such as personality, gender, and race influence emotional labor. Finally, we consider the consequences of emotional labor for the call center workforce and suggest future research directions.

## WORKING CONDITIONS IN CALL CENTERS

Customers view call centers as a way for them to communicate with company representatives over the phone or via other communication channels such as instant messaging. Qualitative studies of call center work reveal a high pressure environment where customer service representatives cope with demands to deliver high quality customer service efficiently (Callaghan & Thompson, 2002; Taylor & Bain, 1998). On one hand, call centers are efficient alternatives to face-to-face customer service interactions. Management uses routinization through script use, and technological tools such as automatic call distribution systems and predictive dialers to control the work pace and to closely track the efficiency and accuracy of customer service interactions (Callaghan & Thompson, 2002). On the other hand, some researchers suggest that the climate of control these mechanisms create contributes to an unfavorable image that some describe as "electronic panopticons" (Fernie & Metcalf, 1998, p. 9) and "dark satanic mills" (p. 2).

These characterizations, however, overlook the extensive variation in job characteristics (e.g., length of calls, types of customers), organizational characteristics, and working conditions that exists across call centers (Bain & Taylor, 2000; Callaghan & Thompson, 2002; Frenkel, Korczynski, Shire, & Tam, 1999). Calls vary in length and complexity ranging from a directory assistance call to a pension plan inquiry. Some call centers handle inbound calls that customers initiate (e.g., billing, product or service information), while others handle outbound calls that the call center workforce initiates (e.g., telemarketing, surveys). Call centers can be in-house, serving the customers of their own firms (e.g. banking) or outsourced, serving customers of other companies. These outsourced call centers can be found in the same country as the customers they serve, or located offshore separating customers and the call center workforce geographically.

## DEFINING FEATURES OF EMOTIONAL
## LABOR IN CALL CENTERS

Call center work meets three criteria Hochschild (1983) describes as being characteristic of emotional labor jobs: (1) face-to-face or voice-to-voice contact with the public; (2) employees altering the customer's emotional state as part of their job; and (3) employers exerting control over employees through training and supervision. Some characteristics distinguish call center work from other frontline service occupations involving emotional labor such as the greater reliance on the voice and the absence of face-to-face contact with customers. In call centers, customers have no idea whether or not call center employees are smiling when they interact, and so, call center employees learn to "smile down the phone" or convey positive emotions through the tone or inflection of their voice (Marshall & Richardson, 1996, p. 1855).

Information and communication technologies figure prominently in these workplaces facilitating workflow and workforce management. The use of electronic performance monitoring metrics such as call handling time, after call time, compliance with schedule and script content, and customer satisfaction ratings is more intensive than in other frontline service workplaces (Bain & Taylor, 2000). Throughout the workday, managers also listen in on calls with customers, and review them with call center employees. In combination with the high level of control exercised in these workplaces, this boundary-spanning workforce interacts with the public more frequently than other service work occupations involving emotional labor (Frenkel, May, Korczynski, & Shire, 1998; Holman, 2003). Moreover, compared with other service occupations, the call center workforce is under more pressure to express fewer negative emotions (Zapf, Isic, Bechtoldt, & Blau, 2003). At a general level, the distinguishing characteristics of call center work, specifically, the use of voice in performing emotional labor, the extensive role of technology, and frequent interactions with customers, create a unique environment for studying emotional labor.

## ORGANIZATIONAL FACTORS: PERFORMANCE MONITORING AND DISPLAY RULES

Quantitative studies of call centers view emotional labor as an intrapsychic process focusing on how individuals manage their emotions (Grandey, Diefendorff, & Rupp, 2013). Constructs commonly examined in more general emotional labor research also appear in call center research on emotional labor, including: (1) display rules, (2) emotional dissonance, (3) surface acting and deep acting, and (4) the frequency, intensity, duration, and variety of interactions in the job (Morris & Feldman, 1996). In this section, we examine the influence of some organizational factors on emotional labor, specifically, performance monitoring and display rules in call center settings. Beyond these factors, we discuss how other choices regarding technology and how the workforce perceives them could influence emotional labor.

In call centers, performance monitoring offers a way for managers to track and document employee work behaviors (Stanton & Weiss, 2000). The performance of the call center workforce can be monitored electronically or in person by a supervisor who, for example, listens to call recordings. This data varies in its content (e.g. criteria for evaluation) and purpose (e.g. how the information is used). By reinforcing the emotions employees are required to display, performance monitoring can heighten emotional dissonance and employees' regulatory responses.

Holman, Chissick, and Totterdell (2002) evaluated the role of performance monitoring in the emotional labor process in call centers. How employees viewed the purpose of performance monitoring (i.e., perceived benefits) was related to surface acting via emotional dissonance. That is, if employees viewed performance monitoring as having a beneficial purpose, it reduced emotional dissonance and the perceived need to surface act. Moreover, emotional dissonance also mediated the relationship between employees' perceptions of the intensity of the monitoring and surface acting, such that if employees perceived the monitoring as especially intense they were more likely to be aware of emotional dissonance, and to regulate their emotions by surface acting.

Display rules, or the emotions management expects employees to express (Ekman & Friesen, 1975), are another relevant organizational factor crucial to understanding emotional labor in the call center context. Display rules vary across call centers. Those handling inbound inquiries (e.g. airline reservations) are expected to be friendly and courteous, whereas those who are convincing customers to pay bills may exhibit neutral or negative emotions (Sutton, 1991). To comply with display rules, employees may have to resort to self-regulatory behaviors (Diefendorff & Gosserand, 2003). When employees surface act, they can deplete their resources thereby affecting their ability to comply with the display rules. Alternatively, when employees deep act, they modify their feelings, removing the need to constantly monitor their feelings in response to display rules (Goldberg & Grandey, 2007). Deep actors are also able to narrow the difference between the display rules and their felt emotions enabling employees to replenish their resources.

The content of display rules can also influence the consequences of emotional labor. In an experimental study simulating a call center, Goldberg and Grandey (2007) compared the reactions of individuals who could freely express their emotions to customers with individuals who were required to display a specific type of emotion. Employees required to exhibit positive emotions to customers found display rule compliance more effortful and more emotionally exhausting compared to employees who were free to display their naturally-occurring emotions to customers. Moreover, surface acting explained the relationship between display rules and emotional exhaustion such that employees who were required to express positive emotions were more emotionally exhausted because they surface acted.

These findings indicate that display rule expectations can influence how employees regulate their emotions, as well as the consequences of their regulatory choices. While display rules can be presented through scripts and training, it is the responsibility of call center supervisors to enforce display rules on a daily basis. Yet, the emphasis call center supervisors place on display rules can vary. In a field study of call center employees, Wilk and Moynihan (2005) found that employees experienced higher levels of emotional exhaustion when they worked for a supervisor who placed more importance on display rules, and as a consequence, placed more pressure on employees to regulate their emotions. As such, supervisors in the call center context are "display-rule regulators" – a source of differentiation in how customer service representatives experience display rules.

## ORGANIZATIONAL FACTORS: INFORMATION AND COMMUNICATION TECHNOLOGIES

Research in call centers connecting technology and emotional labor primarily focuses on performance monitoring. However, call centers rely on other technologies that could also influence how employees manage their emotions. How employees view these various technological choices and whether these choices influence emotional labor warrants further research attention.

### Workflow and Interaction Automation Technologies

Workflow automation, and interaction automation are specific technologies that support the work process in call centers (Sieben, de Grip, Longen, & Sørensen, 2009). *Workflow automation* systems route specific types of calls to employees with specialized skills. For example, call centers may distribute calls to customer service representatives who specialize in handling business as opposed to mass market customers (Batt, 2002). From self-regulation theories, we know that employees have a certain amount of resources at their disposal. Demands such as display rules can deplete the resources individuals have to regulate their emotions. Centers with workflow automation could signal employees that the calls they receive will require their specialized skills and therefore have higher cognitive demands (Sieben et al., 2009). If employees perceive these technologies as increasing their specific workloads or the complexity of the calls they handle, this could increase the effort they have to exert to regulate their emotions.

*Interaction automation technologies* such as interactive voice response (IVR) automate simpler aspects of the customer interaction (Sieben et al.,

2009). IVR enables customers to input information using the telephone keypads or using speech recognition technology (Cena & Torre, 2006). Similar to workflow automation, reserving complex parts of calls for the call center workforce to handle could exacerbate discrepancies between their felt emotions and the emotions they are expected to display, thus requiring more regulatory effort. Alternatively, customers could become frustrated with the truncated nature of the interaction with the call center workforce, which in turn will require more emotional regulation from call center workers.

## Emotion Detection Systems

An emerging trend in call centers is the use of *emotion detection systems* to analyze the wave frequencies of a person's voice to detect a wide range of human emotions – irritation, duplicity, delight, or sexual arousal (Gurstelle, 2005). These systems can evaluate both word choice and emotions, using indicators such as pitch, tone, cadence, and pace for their emotional content. They can signal a supervisor to intervene when the emotional content of a call exceeds appropriate levels or if specific words are used in the interaction.

Emotion detection systems could influence how employees manage their emotions (Poster, 2011). On the one hand, employees' awareness that such systems are monitoring their emotions and word choice could heighten the pressure felt regarding compliance with display rules. Employees might compensate for this by engaging in higher levels of surface acting. On the other hand, emotion detection systems can alert supervisors to intervene when employees are experiencing an especially emotional customer, which could protect call center employees from draining their emotional regulation reservoir.

Supervisor intervention during especially stressful calls may also allow call center workers an opportunity for the regulatory recovery that breaks have been shown to provide (Trougakos, Beal, Green, & Weiss, 2008; Trougakos & Hideg, 2009). However, such recovery opportunities would be reduced if other technologies are simultaneously speeding up the work pace and thus deceasing the opportunities for such breaks. Research is needed that considers the cross-purposes of call center technologies in influencing emotion regulation processes.

## Enhanced Interaction Technologies

The call center context is also useful for examining how employees regulate their emotions using *enhanced interaction technologies*, which add to or replace telephone communication with email, electronic chat, or videoconferencing (van Jaarsveld, Frost, & Walker, 2007). Combining telephone contact with other communication channels expands the range of cues that the call center workforce can use to communicate with customers. At the same time, regulating emotions through multiple communication channels simultaneously could be more demanding for employees. Better understanding how employees regulate their emotions using various types of communication channels could offer important insights into the nature and consequences of emotional labor.

A few studies are beginning to examine whether the communication medium influences how employees regulate their emotions when interacting with customers. In an experimental study comparing employees who interacted with customers over the phone with those who interacted with them via video conference, Wegge, Vogt, and Wecking (2007) found that both groups experienced similar levels of emotional dissonance. Consistent with this pattern, in a field study comparing call center workers (e.g. voice interactions with customers) with cabin crew (e.g. face-to-face interactions), Kinman (2009) found that both groups experienced emotional labor, and that for both groups, emotional labor was associated with negative consequences (e.g., decreased job satisfaction, increased psychological distress, and increased work–life conflict). However, the specific components of emotional labor (e.g. emotional faking, emotional suppression, and perceptions of display rules) were shown to be differentially related to strain outcomes. For example, display rules were positively related to work–life conflict and negatively related to intrinsic job satisfaction for the cabin crew, but were only related to lower extrinsic job satisfaction for the call center workforce. Moreover, emotional suppression and display rules were positively related to work–life conflict for the cabin crew while emotional faking and emotional suppression were positively related to work–life conflict for the call center employees.

Employees and customers are now communicating through text-based communication (e.g. email, text messaging). Regulating emotions over email could be less effortful and could have less negative consequences for employees than phone interactions because employees have more time to respond to emails giving them the opportunity to recover regulatory resources before responding. Research suggests that customers appear to prefer authentic emotional expressions in text responses as much as they do in other types of communication (Turel, Connelly, & Fisk, 2011).

Initial investigations into the influence of communication mode on emotional labor reveal similar levels of emotional labor regardless of the service delivery mode. Yet the differential relationships between dimensions of emotional labor and its consequences reveal complexity in how employees experience emotional labor. Based on these findings, how front-line service workers engage in emotional labor and its effect on employees when different communication modes are in use requires further investigation. As the communication channels for customer service expand (e.g. co-browsing, Twitter, Facebook, instant chat, video conference), new avenues arise for emotional labor research in technology-mediated interactions.

## THE INFLUENCE OF CUSTOMERS
## ON EMOTIONAL LABOR

We now turn our focus to extra-organizational factors that can influence the emotional labor of call center employees. Recognizing that the call center workforce frequently interacts with difficult customers during the workday (Deery, Iverson, & Walsh, 2002; Grandey, Dickter, & Sin, 2004), researchers are beginning to examine the influence of customers on emotional regulation processes at work. In relation to emotional labor, negative interactions with customers can undermine employee compliance with display rules, and increase efforts to regulate emotions. Consistent with this reasoning, employees who feel mistreated by customers have been shown, in both laboratory and field research, to exert more effort in managing their emotions (Grandey et al., 2004; Rupp & Spencer, 2006).

How employees regulate their responses to customer mistreatment depends on the degree to which they view it as stressful or unfair. Grandey et al. (2004) showed that employees who were more threatened by customer verbal aggression surface acted or vented their emotions to customers whereas those who viewed it as less threatening were more likely to deep act. In a lab study, Goldberg and Grandey (2007) showed that negative encounters with customers were positively associated with emotional exhaustion, and surface acting partially mediated this effect.

Rupp and Spencer (2006) examined customer interactional injustice in a lab study simulating a call center and found that employees were angered by unfair treatment from customers and expended more effort regulating their emotions. In a follow-up study involving face-to-face interactions among service workers, perspective-taking, which is a person's cognitive skill to comprehend another person's position, buffered the negative effect of customer injustice on surface acting (Rupp, McCance, Spencer, & Sonntag, 2008). Perspective-taking could be useful to examine in call centers as well because call center employees are customers in other contexts and therefore can appreciate and sympathize with frustrations and customer complaints.

Most emotional labor studies investigate employee experienced emotional dissonance more generally, while overlooking the specific emotions that employees suppress or fake when interacting with customers. Investigating how call center employees react to customer mistreatment, Wegge, van Dick, and von Bernstorff (2010) depart from this approach by incorporating an emotion-specific dissonance measure derived from the EMO-16 (Schmidt-Atzert & Hüppe, 1996). They find that when interacting with customers, employees mask anger, boredom and affection. With this approach, they suggest that the consequences of emotional dissonance depend on whether the emotions that employees are suppressing or faking are positive or negative (Wegge et al., 2010). This approach is useful because it has the potential to resolve mixed findings regarding the consequences of emotional dissonance.

We know customer mistreatment influences emotional labor, yet we know less about the consequences of emotional labor when it is provoked by customer mistreatment. Customers, relative to the call center workforce, enjoy a fair amount of freedom in how they behave in the customer service interaction (Harris & Reynolds, 2003). Despite the extensive monitoring of the call center workforce, however, employees have some power in the face of customer mistreatment. Two studies of call center employees in Canada and China revealed that they react to customer mistreatment and in some cases, these reactions involve them sabotaging customers (Skarlicki, van Jaarsveld, & Walker, 2008; Wang, Liao, Zhan, & Shi, 2011). The call center workforce has also been shown to respond to customer mistreatment by being uncivil to customers (van Jaarsveld, Skarlicki, & Walker, 2010). These examples reveal that employees who view themselves as being unfairly treated can retaliate in response to injustice. Call center employees could engage in other types of dysfunctional workplace behaviors in retaliation for what they perceive as unfair emotional labor demands. Qualitative studies of the call center workforce provide some examples of undesirable retaliation behaviors, including the manipulation of performance monitoring systems by faking sales, failure to fulfill customer requests, and call avoidance (Mulholland, 2004).

Existing studies emphasize the interpersonal nature of the service interaction overlooking the call center worker as a representative of a company. Similar to counterproductive work behaviors, motivations for customer mistreatment could differ. Customers are sophisticated and can distinguish between the fault of the company and that of the employee. Motivations for customer mistreatment may be personal in nature because the call center representative was rude or could be incited by corporate policies.

Connecting this to emotional labor, employees could experience greater need to regulate their emotions when the customer mistreatment is perceived as a personal attack. When customer mistreatment is motivated by corporate policies and the target is the company as opposed to the employee, employees could exert less effort to manage their emotions in this context. Personal attacks could be viewed as being more unfair than attacking the company. Do customer service representatives surface act when they encounter customer mistreatment that is a personal attack and deep act when the content of the mistreatment is focused on the company? Research is needed to clarify these various motivations for customer mistreatment and their influence on emotional labor.

Negative interactions with customers clearly influence how employees choose to regulate their emotions, and in turn, the consequences associated with these choices. To date, customer mistreatment measures rely on self-report data from employees. Collecting data on actual customer behavior typified by Rafaeli and Sutton (1989) is a feasible research design in the call center setting because recordings of customer service interactions are available. This type of research could benefit our understanding of how customers react to employees when they surface or deep act. Moreover, this data could yield valuable insights about whether customers can detect when employees surface act and deep act over the phone (e.g., Rupp & Spencer, 2006).

## INDIVIDUAL FACTORS: PERSONALITY, GENDER AND RACE

Beyond organizational factors and discrete customer encounters, individual differences may influence the emotional labor process in call center settings. That is, certain individual characteristics might aid employees in coping with high levels of emotional dissonance, frequent interactions with customers, and aggressive customer behavior, all of which are common for call center employees.

### *Personality*

Several studies have examined whether personality characteristics are related to emotional labor, some of which have been undertaken in call centers (see Dahling & Johnson, 2013). Emotional intelligence, positive expressivity, negative affectivity, and positive affectivity have been examined as potentially influencing the emotional labor process (Grandey, 2000). Empirical research shows that call center workers are more likely to surface act if they score high on emotional intelligence, a set of abilities involving emotion in the self and others (Mayer & Salovey, 1997). Call center employees who score high on emotional intelligence have been shown to be more likely to deep act (Totterdell & Holman, 2003). Meanwhile, positive emotional expressivity, the degree to which employees find it difficult to hide their true emotions from customers, has been shown to be unrelated to the emotional labor of call center workers.

Negative affectivity (NA) is an especially relevant personality characteristic in the call center context. Trait negative affectivity has been shown to relate to emotional dissonance among call center employees (Wegge et al., 2010). Low NA individuals have been shown to be more likely to experience a dramatic increase in emotional dissonance when they encountered customer aggression than their high NA counterparts. Wegge et al. (2010) explain this finding as high NA individuals being more understanding of disgruntled customers than low NA individuals.

Beyond the personality characteristics Grandey (2000) identifies, self-efficacy, an evaluation of one's capability to successfully complete a task (Bandura, 1986, 2012) is another personality chacteristic that has been studied in relation to emotional labor in the call center context. Highlighting the importance of specifying what type of self-efficacy is relevant to the context being studied (Dahling & Johnson, 2013), Wilk and Moynihan (2005) found in a sample of call center employees that general job self-efficacy did not moderate the relationship between interpersonal job demands (display rules) and emotional exhaustion whereas Wang et al. (2011) found in a sample of call center employees in China that self-efficacy for regulating emotions moderated the relationship between daily customer mistreatment and employee sabotage such that higher scoring employees (versus lower) engaged in less sabotage.

Psychological hardiness and emotion recognition (a component of emotional intelligence involving the ability to interpret verbal cues) are other personality characteristics that could influence call center workers' ability to regulate their emotions (Elfenbein & Ambady, 2002; Kobasa, 1979). Important for call center contexts in particular, the Diagnostic Analysis of Nonverbal Accuracy Test (DANVA) measures emotion recognition with photographs and audio recordings (Nowicki Jr, 2000). In a study of police and nurses, Bechtoldt, Rohrmann, De Pater, and Beersma (2011) used this assessment to show that emotion recognition moderated the relationship between emotional labor and work engagement such that employees with high emotion recognition who engaged in emotional labor did not report lower work engagement whereas employees with low emotion recognition did. Call center workers who have better emotion recognition skills could more accurately assess customer emotions, and, based on this information, could exert less effort to respond with the appropriate emotions.

## Gender and race

Call center workers' demographic characteristics are generally treated as control variables in studies undertaken from the intrapsychic perspective. However, theory suggests these variables be considered as moderating the effects of emotional labor processes in call center settings, especially considering the prominent role of personal characteristics in shaping customer expectations in these contexts (Grandey et al., 2004; Totterdell & Holman, 2003).

Similar to other frontline service jobs involving emotional labor, the call center workforce is overwhelmingly female (with some exceptions, such as IT helpdesk employees; Belt, Richardson, & Webster, 1999; Lively, 2013). Despite this, sex differences have been found with regard to emotional labor processes. For example, Totterdell and Holman (2003) found that female call center employees engaged in higher levels of negative affect regulation and faking emotions compared with their male counterparts (in a call center where 72% of the workforce was female). This finding supports Hochschild (1983)'s assertion that women have lower status shields, meaning that they are more susceptible to anger, and lack necessary coping skills for dealing with negative emotion.

Gender differences in emotional labor could also be the result of different motivations for regulating emotions, with women striving for positive interpersonal relations and men striving for control (Grandey, 2000). An alternative to studying sex differences among this predominately female workforce might be to consider gender (i.e., the possession of masculine and feminine characteristics across the sexes; Bem, 1974; Kent & Moss, 1994). For example, a woman with masculine characteristics may exert less regulatory effort and be less affected by surface acting than a woman with feminine characteristics.

As is the case with gender, few quantitative call center studies focus explicitly on the relationship between race and emotional labor. The racial identity of a call center worker is only detectable on the phone via accents when speaking. Individuals with certain accents can be viewed as less competent (Atkins, 1993; Cargile, 2000), and those individuals with accents from countries viewed as having lower socio-economic status (e.g. Mexico, India; Lippi-Green, 1997) can experience discrimination. Grandey et al. (2004) showed that Hispanic call center employees reported more hostile callers in comparison to non-Hispanic employees, and explained this finding as a manifestation of aversive racism where people who have the opportunity to punish someone do so to a greater extent if the person is a minority member (Crosby, Bromley, & Saxe, 1980; Gaertner & Dovidio, 1986). Gender and race characteristics can also interact and, accordingly, we would expect minority women to engage in higher levels of surface acting.

## Nationality

Increasingly, the call center workforce is geographically separated from the customers they serve. For example, as a strategy to reduce labor costs, we see call center work moving, from the UK and the US to India, and from Canada to the Philippines (Dossani & Kenney, 2007). Performance monitoring is used more, and display rules are more intensely enforced in offshore call centers because they want to offer clients a competitive alternative to retaining work in-house (Mirchandani, 2008). Offshore call center employees are also put under great pressure to emulate the culture they are serving, for example, by adopting new names, altering their accents, and reciting scripts to reflect national identities that are reinforced through training (Noronha & D'Cruz, 2006; Poster, 2007). Poster refers to this practice as "national identity management."

On the one hand, from a conservation of resources (COR) perspective, intensive enforcement of display rules and performance monitoring in addition to organizational requirements to present an alternative national identity to customers could compound the depletion of resources that the offshore workforce has available to regulate their emotions (Hobfoll, 1989). The offshore call center workforce deceives customers regarding their location, nationality, and name as part of their job. Greater awareness about the organizational expectations for emotional expression and national identity management as a result of intensive monitoring could increase the efforts necessary to regulate emotions.

On the other hand, offshore call center work can (for example, in India) attract university educated job applicants who view such jobs as positive career opportunities – an attitude that may not be held by a similar onshore workforce (for example, in the US). These offshore call center employees may consequently have relatively more regulatory resources with which to cope with emotional challenges. Because the deceit inherent to offshore call center work (i.e., "national identity management," Poster, 2007) is organizationally sanctioned, employees might also feel more powerful and less vulnerable when interacting with hostile customers. Tenure might also moderate these processes, with lying replenishing resources in the short term, and depleting them over the long term.

Another useful perspective for considering how requiring offshore employees to present an alternative national identity could influence the emotional labor process is *national identity centrality*, or "the extent to which individuals define themselves by their citizenship or the subjective importance of one's national identity in the hierarchy of different social identities"(Das, Dharwadkar, & Brandes, 2008, p. 1507). Using data from a call center in India, Das et al. (2008) found that offshore call center workers with strong national identity centrality experienced more burnout, higher turnover intentions, and lower performance compared with those with weaker identity centrality. Applying this concept to emotional labor, national identity centrality could moderate the relationship between surface acting and outcomes such as emotional exhaustion. The dissonance offshore call center employees experience from managing their emotions could be compounded by the efforts they exert to present customers with an alternative national identity. A research design comparing two call centers, one located in the same country as its customers, and one offshore, would be useful for exploring such issues.

## THE CONSEQUENCES OF EMOTIONAL LABOR IN CALL CENTERS

Throughout this chapter, we identified several future research ideas to expand our understanding of how characteristics internal and external to call centers and their employees influence emotional labor processes. In this section, we turn to the consequences of emotional labor.

In general, the consequences of emotional labor in call centers are similar to those in other service occupations. Surface acting is generally associated with negative consequences for both individuals and organizations (e.g. employee well-being, performance, turnover intentions). Evidence from field research reveals that the relationship between surface acting, deep acting and performance is complicated by the use of different performance measures. In call center studies, Totterdell and Holman (2003) found no relationship between surface acting and self-reported performance whereas Goodwin, Groth, and Frenkel (2011) found that surface acting is indirectly related to supervisor ratings of performance. Although some have found that deep acting is positively related to self-reported job performance and laboratory-based measures of performance, others have found that deep acting is not related to supervisor-reported job performance (Goldberg & Grandey, 2007; Goodwin et al., 2011; Totterdell & Holman, 2003).

With respect to individual outcomes, the disconnect between employees' true feelings and the organizationally-sanctioned emotion display rules can be costly for employees. Surface acting is positively associated with stress, emotional exhaustion, psychological distress, psychosomatic complaints, and lower job satisfaction (Kinman, 2009; Totterdell & Holman, 2003; Zapf, Schmitte, Mertini, & Holz, 2001; Zapf, Vogt, Seifert, Mertini, & Isic, 1999). Emotional dissonance, sometimes used as a proxy for surface acting, is related to lower well-being, lower work motivation, and an increase in emotional exhaustion, health disorders, and work-family conflict (Kinman, 2009). Deep acting is negatively related to job satisfaction and positively related to a personal sense of accomplishment and displayed enthusiasm (Totterdell & Holman, 2003).

The majority of emotional labor studies examining the consequences of emotional labor involve call center samples from developed economies as opposed to offshore operations. Given the global nature of call center work, emotional labor researchers can use this context to examine whether the emotional labor process operates in the same way for the offshore workforce in, for example, India or the Philippines, as it does for call center samples in advanced economies. Call center work lends itself to addressing these questions because it is expanding in several countries, facilitating comparative studies using call centers in different countries to evaluate the influence of cultural and institutional differences on the experience of emotional labor (Batt, Holman, & Holtgrewe, 2009).

Some evidence suggests that the dynamics of emotional labor play out differently in offshore versus domestic call centers. One of the few studies examining the relationships between display rules and emotional exhaustion in an offshore call center found that call center employees in India reported lower levels of emotional exhaustion when their supervisors emphasized display rules (Little, Nelson, Quade, & Ward, 2011). This finding contrasts with Wilk and Moynihan (2005) who found that US call center employees experienced higher levels of emotional exhaustion when their supervisor emphasized display rules. Little et al. (2011) explain this difference as call center employees in India viewing display rules as helpful because they clarify job requirements as opposed to their US counterparts who view them as stressful and controlling.

Although India receives significant attention as an offshore destination for call center work, the Philippines, Canada, and Ireland are also offshoring destinations for English speaking work. Non-English speaking countries also offshore work to the following partnerships: Germany to Poland, France to Morocco, and Spain to Latin America (Batt et al., 2009). In circumstances where the offshoring dynamic involves two countries with considerable distance between their cultures such as the US and India (Hofstede, 1980), there may exist greater demands on the call center workforce and larger differences in the consequences associated with emotional labor. In contrast, when the offshore partnership involves countries with narrower cultural differences, such as the US and Canada, less effort is required to manage national identity and therefore we would expect smaller differences in the consequences of emotional labor.

This distinction in how call center workers in the US and India view display rules highlights the importance of taking cultural context into consideration when we evaluate theories about emotion work. Countries also differ on an institutional level (e.g. employment regulations and collective bargaining systems) with coordinated economies having stronger employment regulations than liberal market economies (Hall & Soskice, 2001). These institutional differences have been shown to influence working conditions (e.g. compensation, employment contracts) in call centers (Batt, Holman, & Holtgrewe, 2009; Batt & Nohara, 2009; van Jaarsveld, Kwon, & Frost, 2009). Institutional factors such as union density and whether collective agreements are sectoral could influence the degree of emotional labor that employees engage in. For example, Grandey, Rafaeli, Ravid, Wirtz, and Steiner (2010) found that unionization and policies that protect employees in France resulted in lower perceived status of customers and thus employees encountered fewer constraints and consequences for expressing negative emotions.

While the emotional labor process may vary depending on where the work is located, it could also vary across call centers within the same country depending on the human resource systems call centers choose to adopt (Batt, 2002; Frenkel et al., 1999; Houlihan, 2002). Some centers empower their employees by increasing job discretion, organizing them into teams, and paying them generously while others resemble Taylorized operations exercising control over employees through low levels of discretion, intense routinization, and low pay (Batt, 2002). Considering the connection between human resources practices and emotional labor, and whether the negative effects of emotional labor are buffered by the choices organizations make regarding their human resource practices warrants research attention. Matching data from a large sample of call centers measuring their human resource practices with individual level data from their call center employees about how they manage their emotions, and other relevant employee attitudinal, and behavioral data would help connect the macro and micro levels of analysis.

The general patterns in the consequences of emotional labor for the call center workforce are similar to what is found in other contexts. We have outlined some factors that warrant attention for emotional labor researchers who are studying the phenomenon in call centers. Given the context, acknowledging the global nature of call center work and evaluating whether variation in cultural and institutional characteristics should influence emotional labor theories is particularly important.

## Conclusion

Examining emotional labor in the call center context yields important insights about the unique challenges of voice interactions in an environment featuring intensive monitoring and routinization. Technology in call centers has a primary role in service delivery and as companies expand the means of delivering customer service beyond the phone to include other communication channels, this evolution could affect how employees perform emotional labor, as well as its consequences for employees. The geographic movement of call center work is also altering the locations of customers and customer service representatives in profound ways. This shift is exposing both parties to variations in cultural norms regarding emotional expression. Considering these dynamics, call centers will continue to be a fertile environment for the study of emotional labor.

# REFERENCES

Atkins, C. P. (1993). Do employment recruiters discriminate on the basis of nonstandard dialect? *Journal of Employment Counseling, 30*(3), 108–118.

Bain, P., & Taylor, P. (2000). Entrapped by the 'electronic panopticon'? Worker resistance in the call centre. *New Technology, Work and Employment, 15*(1), 2–18.

Bandura, A. (1986). *Social foundations of thought and action: A social cognitive theory*. Englewood Cliffs, NJ: Prentice-Hall.

Bandura, A. (2012). On the functional properties of self-efficacy. *Journal of Management, 38,* 9–44.

Batt, R. (2002). Managing customer services: Human resource practices, quit rates, and sales growth. *Academy of Management Journal, 45,* 587–597.

Batt, R., Holman, D., & Holtgrewe, U. (2009). The globalization of service work: Comparative institutional perspectives on call centers: Introduction to a special issue of ILRR. *Industrial & Labor Relations Review, 62*(4), 453–488.

Batt, R., & H. Nohara. (2009). How institutions and business strategies affect wages: A cross-national study of call centers. *Industrial & Labor Relations Review, 62*(4), 533–552.

Bechtoldt, M. N., Rohrmann, S., De Pater, I. E., & Beersma, B. (2011). The primacy of perceiving: Emotion recognition buffers negative effects of emotional labor. *Journal of Applied Psychology, 96*(5), 1087–1094.

Belt, V., Richardson, R., & Webster, J. (March 1999). *Smiling down the phone: Women's work in telephone call centers*. Paper presented at the Workshop on Telephone Call Centres, London School of Economics, London.

Bem, S. L. (1974). The measurement of psychological androgyny. *Journal of Consulting and Clinical Psychology, 42*(2), 155–162.

Callaghan, G., & Thompson, P. (2002). We recruit attitude: The selection and shaping of routine call centre labour. *Journal of Management Studies, 39*(2), 233–254.

Cargile, A. C. (2000). Evaluations of employment suitability: Does accent always matter? *Journal of Employment Counseling, 37*(3), 165–177.

Cena, F., & Torre, I. (2006). Adapting the interaction in a call centre system. *Interacting with Computers, 18*(3), 478–506.

Crosby, F., Bromley, S., & Saxe, L. (1980). Recent unobtrusive studies of Black and White discrimination and prejudice. *Psychological Bulletin, 87,* 546–563.

Dahling, J., & Johnson, H-A. (2013). Motivation, fit, confidence, and skills: How do individual differences influence emotional labor? In A. A. Grandey, J. M. Diefendorff & D. E. Rupp (Eds.), *Emotional labor in the 21st century: Diverse perspectives on emotion regulation at work*. New York, NY: Psychology Press/Routledge.

Das, D., Dharwadkar, R., & Brandes, P. (2008). The importance of being Indian: Identity centrality and work outcomes in an off-shored call center in India. *Human Relations, 61*(11), 1499–1530.

Deery, S., Iverson, R., & Walsh, J. (2002). Work relationships in telephone call centres: Understanding emotional exhaustion and employee withdrawal. *Journal of Management Studies, 39*, 471–496.

Diefendorff, J. M., & Gosserand, R. H. (2003). Understanding the emotional labor process: A control theory perspective. *Journal of Organizational Behavior, 24*(8), 945–959.

Dossani, R., & Kenney, M. (2007). The next wave of globalization: Relocating service provision to India. *World Development, 35*(5), 772–791.

Eckman, P., & Friesen, W. (1975). *Unmasking the face: A guide to recognizing emotions from facial clues*. Englewood Cliffs, NJ: Prentice Hall.

Elfenbein, H. A., & Ambady, N. (2002). Predicting workplace outcomes from the ability to eavesdrop on feelings. *Journal of Applied Psychology, 87*(5), 963.

Fernie, S., & Metcalf, D. (1998). (Not) hanging on the telephone: Payment systems in the new sweatshops. *Centrepiece, 3*, 7–11.

Frenkel, S., Korczynski, M., Shire, K., & Tam, M. (Eds.). (1999). *On the frontline: Organization of work in the information economy*. Ithaca, NY: Cornell University Press.

Frenkel, S., May, T., Korczynski, M., & Shire, K. (1998). Beyond bureaucracy? Work organization in call centres. *International Journal of Human Resource Management, 9*(6), 957–979.

Gaertner, S. L., & Dovidio, J. F. (1986). The aversive form of racism. In J. F. Dovidio & S. Gaertner (Eds.), *Prejudice, discrimination, and racism* (pp. 61–90). Orlando, FL: Academic Press.

Goldberg, L. S., & Grandey, A. A. (2007). Display rules versus display autonomy: Emotional regulation, emotional exhaustion, and task performance in a call center simulation. *Journal of Occupational Health Psychology, 12*, 301–318.

Goodwin, R. E., Groth, M., & Frenkel, S. (2011). Relationships between emotional labor, job performance, and turnover. *Journal of Vocational Behavior. 79*(2): 538–548.

Grandey, A. A. (2000). Emotional regulation in the workplace: A new way to conceptualize emotional labor. *Journal of Occupational Health Psychology, 5*(1), 95–110.

Grandey, A. A., Dickter, D. N., & Sin, H. P. (2004). The customer is not always right: Customer aggression and emotion regulation of service employees. *Journal of Organizational Behavior, 25*, 397–418.

Grandey, A. A., Diefendorff, J. M., & Rupp, D. E. (2013). Emotional labor: Overview of definitions, theories, and evidence. In A. A. Grandey, J. M. Diefendorff & D. E. Rupp (Eds.), *Emotional labor in the 21st century: Diverse perspectives on emotion regulation at work*. New York, NY: Psychology Press/Routledge.

Grandey, A. A., Rafaeli, A., Ravid, S., Wirtz, J., & Steiner, D. D. (2010). Emotion display rules at work in the global service economy: The special case of the customer. *Journal of Service Management, 21*(3), 388–412.

Gurstelle, W. (2005, June 13). Call now – robots are standing by. *Wired.*

Hall, P. A., & Soskice, D. (2001). *Varieties of capitalism: The institutional foundations of comparative advantage.* Oxford: Oxford University Press.

Harris, L. C., & Reynolds, K. L. (2003). The consequences of dysfunctional customer behavior. *Journal of Service Research, 6*(2), 144–161.

Hobfoll, S. E. (1989). Conservation of resources: A new attempt at conceptualizing stress. *American Psychologist, 44,* 513–524.

Hochschild, A. R. (1983). *The managed heart: Commercialization of human feeling.* Berkeley, CA: University of California Press.

Hofstede, G. (1980). *Cultures consequences: International differences in work-related values.* Beverly Hills, CA: Sage.

Holman, D. (2003). Call centres. In D. Holman, T. D. Wall, C. W. Clegg, P. Sparrow & A. Howard (Eds.), *The new workplace: A guide to the human impact of modern working practices* (pp. 115–134). Chichester, UK: Wiley.

Holman, D., Chissick, C., & Totterdell, P. (2002). The effects of performance monitoring on emotional labor and well-being in call centers. *Motivation and Emotion, 26*(1), 57–81.

Holman, D., Frenkel, S., Sørensen, O., & Wood, S. (2009). Work design variation and outcomes in call centers: Strategic choice and institutional explanations. *Industrial & Labor Relations Review, 62*(4), 510–532.

Houlihan, M. (2002). Tensions and variations in call centre management strategies. *Human Resource Management Journal, 12*(4), 67–85.

Kent, R. L., & Moss, S. E. (1994). Effects of sex and gender role on leader emergence. *Academy of Management Journal, 37*(5), 1335–1346.

Kinman, G. (2009). Emotional labour and strain in "front-line" service employees: Does mode of delivery matter? *Journal of Managerial Psychology, 24*(2), 118–135.

Kobasa, S. C. (1979). Stressful life events, personality, and health: An inquiry into hardiness. *Journal of Personality and Social Psychology, 37*(1), 1–11.

Lippi-Green, R. (1997). *English with an accent: Language, ideology, and discrimination in the United States*: Psychology Press.

Little, L. M., Nelson, D. L., Quade, M., & Ward, A. (2011). Stressful demands or helpful guidance? The role of display rules in Indian call centers. *Journal of Vocational Behavior 79*(3) 724–733.

Lively, K. J. (2013). Social and cultural influencers: Gender effects on emotional labor at work and at home. In A. A. Grandey, J. M. Diefendorff & D. E. Rupp (Eds.), *Emotional labor in the 21st century: Diverse perspectives on emotion regulation at work.* New York, NY: Psychology Press/Routledge.

Marshall, J. N., & Richardson, R. (1996). The impact of 'telemediated' services on corporate structures: The example of 'branchless' retail banking in Britain. *Environment and Planning A, 28*(10), 1843–1858.

Mayer, J. D., & Salovey, P. (1997). What is emotional intelligence? In P. Salovey & D. J. Sluyter (Eds.), *Emotional development and emotional intelligence.* New York: Basic Books.

Mirchandani, K. (2008). The call center: Enactments of class and nationality in transnational call centers. In S. Fineman (Ed.), *The emotional organization* (pp. 88–101). Malden, MA: Blackwell.

Morris, J. A., & Feldman, D. C. (1996). The dimensions, antecedents, and consequences of emotional labor. *Academy of Management Review, 21*(4), 986–1010.

Mulholland, K. (2004). Workplace resistance in an Irish call centre: Slammin', scammin' smokin' an' leavin'. *Work, Employment and Society, 18*(4), 709–724.

Noronha, E., & D'Cruz, P. (2006, May 27). Organising call centre agents: Emerging issues. *Economic and Political Weekly,* 2115–2121.

Nowicki Jr, S. (2000). *Manual for the receptive tests of the diagnostic analysis of nonverbal accuracy 2.* Atlanta, GA: Department of Psychology, Emory University.

Poster, W. (2007). Who's on the line? Indian call center agents pose as Americans for U.S.-outsourced firms. *Industrial Relations, 46*(2), 271–304.

Poster, W. (2011). Emotion detectors, answering machines and e-unions: Multisurveillances in the global interactive services industry. *American Behavioral Scientist, 55*(7), 868–901.

Rafaeli, A., & Sutton, R. I. (1989). The expression of emotion in organizational life. *Research in Organizational Behavior, 11*, 1–43.

Rupp, D. E., McCance, A. S., Spencer, S., & Sonntag, K. (2008). Customer (in)justice and emotional labor: The role of perspective taking, anger, and emotional regulation. *Journal of Management, 34*, 903–924.

Rupp, D. E., & Spencer, S. (2006). When customers lash out: The effects of customer interactional injustice on emotional labor and the mediating role of discrete emotions. *Journal of Applied Psychology, 91*, 971–978.

Schmidt-Atzert, L., & Hüppe, M. (1996). Ein Fragebogen zur Selbstbeschreibung des aktuellen emotionalen Gefühlszustandes. / Emotion Scales EMO 16: An inventory for the self-rating of actual emotional feelings. *Diagnostica 42*(3), 242–267.

Sieben, I., de Grip, A., Longen, J., & Sørensen, O. (2009). Technology, selection, and training in call centers. *Industrial & Labor Relations Review, 62*(4), 553–572.

Skarlicki, D. P., van Jaarsveld, D. D., & Walker, D. D. (2008). Getting even for customer mistreatment: The role of moral identity in the relationship between customer interpersonal injustice and employee sabotage. *Journal of Applied Psychology, 93*(6), 1335–1347.

Stanton, J., & Weiss, E. (2000). Electronic monitoring in their own words: An exploratory study of employees' experiences with new types of surveillance. *Computers in Human Behavior, 16*(4), 423–440.

Sutton, R. I. (1991). Maintaining norms about expressed emotions: The case of bill collectors. *Administrative Science Quarterly, 36*, 245–268.

Taylor, S., & Bain, P. (1998). 'An assembly line in the head': The call centre labour process. *Industrial Relations Journal, 30*(2), 101–117.

Thompson, P., & Callaghan, G. (2002). Skill formation in call centres. In U. Holtgrewe, C. Kerst & K. Shire (Eds.), *Re-organising service work: Call centres in Germany and Britain* (pp. 105–122). Aldershot: Ashgate.

Totterdell, P., & Holman, D. (2003). Emotion regulation in customer service roles: Testing a model of emotional labor. *Journal of Occupational Health Psychology, 8*(1), 55–73.

Trougakos, J. P., Beal, D. J., Green, S. G., & Weiss, H. M. (2008). Making the break count: An episodic examination of recovery activities, emotional experiences, and positive affective displays. *Academy of Management Journal, 51*(1), 131–146.

Trougakos, J. P., & Hideg, I. (2009). Momentary work recovery: The role of within-day work breaks. In S. Sonnentag, D. Ganster & P. Perrewe (Eds.), *Research in occupational stress & well-being* (Vol. 7, pp. 37–84). Bingley, UK: Emerald Research

Turel, O., Connelly, C. E., & Fisk, G. M. (2011). *Service with an e-smile: Employee authenticity and customer usage of web-based services.* Paper presented at the International Conference on System Sciences, Honolulu, HI.

van Jaarsveld, D. D., Frost, A. C., & Walker, D. D. (2007). The Canadian contact centre industry: Strategy, work organization, & human resource management. Vancouver, BC: University of British Columbia.

van Jaarsveld, D. D., Kwon, H., & Frost, A. C. (2009). The effects of institutional and organizational characteristics on work force flexibility: Evidence from call centers in three liberal market economies. *Industrial & Labor Relations Review, 62*(4) 573–601.

van Jaarsveld, D. D., Skarlicki, D. P., & Walker, D. D. (2010). The role of job demands and emotional exhaustion in the relationship between customer and employee incivility. *Journal of Management, 36*(6): 1486–1504.

Wang, M., Liao, H., Zhan, Y., & Shi, J. (2011). Daily customer mistreatment and employee sabotage against customers: Examining emotion and resource perspectives. *Academy of Management Journal, 54*(2), 312–334.

Wegge, J., van Dick, R., & von Bernstorff, C. (2010). Emotional dissonance in call centre work. *Journal of Managerial Psychology, 25*(6), 596–619.

Wegge, J., Vogt, J., & Wecking, C. (2007). Customer induced stress in call centre work: A comparison of audio and videoconference. *Journal of Occupational and Organizational Psychology, 80*(4), 693–712.

Wilk, S. L., & Moynihan, L. M. (2005). Display rule "regulators": The relationship between supervisors and worker emotional exhaustion. *Journal of Applied Psychology, 90*, 917–927.

Zapf, D., Isic, A., Bechtoldt, M., & Blau, P. (2003). What is typical for call centre jobs? Job characteristics, and service interactions in different call centres. *European Journal of Work and Organizational Psychology, 12*(4), 311–340.

Zapf, D., Schmitte, B., Mertini, H., & Holz, M. (2001). Emotion work and job stressors and their effects on burnout. *Psychology and Health, 16*, 527–545.

Zapf, D., Vogt, C., Seifert, C., Mertini, H., & Isic, A. (1999). Emotion work as a source of stress: The concept and development of an instrument. *European Journal of Work and Organizational Psychology, 8*, 370–400.

# 8

# *Attending to Mind and Body*

## Engaging the Complexity of Emotion Practice Among Caring Professionals

REBECCA J. ERICKSON • CLARE L. STACEY

> Rethinking care involves dismantling the dichotomies that have delimited care: private versus public, love versus money, and altruism versus self-interest.
>
> (Glenn, 2010, p. 10).

> There is a central paradox in this professionalization process. The accepted masculine emotion codes that make up the 'competent' and 'professional' teacher contradict the profession's fundamental reliance on feminine emotion codes such as nursing, caring, and so on.
>
> (Bolton, 2007, pp. 19–20).

This chapter examines the performance of emotion management in the context of occupations typified by expectations for "care." Focusing primarily on the field of health care, we explore the ways in which the complexity of emotion norms grounded in the "ethic of care" combine with calls for economic efficiency and standardized performance expectations to create unique challenges for caring professionals when compared

to their commercial counterparts. These challenges do not exempt helping professionals from the processes and outcomes of emotion regulation
that are commonly found among commercial service workers. However,
they do suggest that traditional approaches may be theoretically and
empirically insufficient for understanding the experience and effects of
managing emotion in caring contexts. Moreover, caring contexts themselves may be distinguished by differences between caring for the body
and for the mind. The complexities emerging from this analysis lead to
our initial outline of a theory of *emotion practice* that we believe can serve
as a useful framework for integrating the different paradigms within
emotion management theory and research.

Institutions typified by caring labor involve complex webs of emotional
experience. Subtly reproducing the paradoxical relationship between
mind and body, rationality and emotion, frontline (predominantly female)
human service workers (e.g., nurses, teachers, social workers) are expected
to be nurturing yet firmly "in charge" of their clients (e.g., patients, students). This type of relational complexity characterizes emotion management performed in caring contexts but not within most commercial
service work (Zapf, 2002). As Boler (1999) further suggests, the different
ways that emotions are controlled serve not only to structure interaction
in particular ways but also to reflect and shape social hierarchies of race,
class, and gender (among others; also see Lively, 2013). As such, studying
emotion management within human service contexts makes visible how
feeling and display rules are tied not only to one's occupational role but
also to *who* tends to perform the role.

Our centering of the *context* within which emotion management
takes place suggests the need to transcend the dualistic tendencies of
emotional labor research – emotion vs. rationality, males vs. females, care
vs. commerce, rules vs. relationships, experience vs. expression – through
the creation of a broader, dialectical frame that integrates competing
approaches and theorizes their complementarity. For example, in one of
the earliest and most influential essays on emotional labor, Ashforth and
Humphrey (1993) reject Hochschild's (1983) original focus on feeling
and replace it with their preference for expressive display. We suggest
that such a choice is feasible only when studying contexts in which the
internal experience of emotion is assumed to be irrelevant to producing
expressive displays. Others have raised concerns that focusing on the
performance of "emotional labor" misrepresents the experience of caring
professionals who offer their emotional displays as interactional gifts
or in an effort to behave consistently with the meanings underlying
professional identity (e.g., Bolton, 2000, 2005). Similarly, research on the
performance of caring labor raises concern that emotional labor scholarship often overlooks the ways in which emotion norms and processes are

linked to social hierarchies of status such as race, class, and gender (Stacey, 2005, 2011).

Based on these and other tendencies within the literature that we review below, the study of emotion management among caring laborers provides the foundation for an initial outline of a theory of emotion practice. Building on Bourdieu's (1977, 1990a, 1990b) general theory of practice, and consistent with Bolton's (2000, 2005) view that emotions embedded in social context cannot be "simplified and condensed" into one form (2005, p. 99), an *emotion practice* framework draws explicit attention to the ways that emotion operates at both the micro and macro levels of analysis. For example, it synthesizes Theodosius' (2008) examination of how emotion's physiological dimensions (not just their linguistic or cognitive ones) are central to understanding nurses' emotional practices with patients, Bolton's (2005) and Lopez's (2006) observations that individual emotion management practices both reflect and influence the structural (e.g., material and economic) and cultural (e.g., symbolic, noneconomic and philanthropic) dimensions of organizational contexts as well as the insights of caring labor scholars who point to the role emotion plays in the reproduction of status-based inequalities (e.g., Harvey Wingfield, 2010; Lively, 2000; Stacey, 2011). It does so through a critical or reflexive examination of the traditional concepts, relationships, and implications of emotional labor research.

Because caring labor contexts range from those characterized by heavily scripted, boundary-spanning emotional labor governed primarily by display rules to those typified by organized emotional care which seeks to enable the development of authentic relationships among workers and those with whom they interact (Dodson & Zincavage, 2007; Lopez, 2006), specifying which relationships hold across settings, and under what conditions, is no easy task. We hope to show how explicit consideration of different facets of caring contexts can initiate new ways of thinking about the emotional practices that contribute to differential individual and organizational outcomes (e.g., in terms of pay, advancement, productivity, retention, satisfaction, health), the reproduction of status-based inequalities, and the generation, maintenance, and change of emotion norms to which individuals hold themselves and others accountable during interaction.

## DEFINING CARING LABOR IN EMOTION PRACTICE TERMS

Defined as the "work of caring for others," carework or caring labor takes place informally in the home (the unpaid care of one's children, for example) or formally within the workplace (the paid care of children in a daycare). Although it is tempting to view caring labor as "natural" or "essential," scholars of carework are quick to point out that it is "hard physical, mental and emotional work, which is often unequally distributed" (Misra, 2011, p. 49). Women, for example, are disproportionately represented in caring fields like childcare, eldercare, nursing, social work, and teaching. Compared to Hochschild's (1983) original description of emotional labor, the type of high-intensity caring labor that takes place in these contexts is incompletely commodified (Radin, 1996). In today's caring labor contexts, the simultaneous influence of market and non-market (i.e., relational) forces is a critical part of what makes the emotion management experiences of these workers distinct. The term *caring labor* also signifies the complexity, ambiguity, and embedded contradictions that characterize the emotion management performed in human service jobs – jobs that exemplify the tension between "relationships versus rules" (Stone, 2000, p. 91).

Common origins of both the carework (Abel & Nelson, 1990) and emotional labor literatures (Hochschild, 1983) continue to influence each of the research traditions today. In both cases, feminist scholarship that advanced the study of women's labor in and outside the home was critical to these initial conceptualizations (Fenstermaker Berk, 1980; Hartmann, 1981). Both literatures emphasize that carework and emotional labor are often invisible, unrecognized, and unfairly compensated (if compensated at all) and socially undervalued (Belenky et al., 1986; Cancian, 2000; Daniels, 1987; England, 1992). Both also emphasize the meaning and consequences of relationality for those (primarily women) performing carework and/or emotional labor (Ehrenreich & Hochschild, 2002; Stacey, 2005, 2011; Twigg, 2000).

Despite these similarities, a number of differences also exist between the literatures on carework and emotional labor. Research on carework has stronger roots in feminist philosophy and places more attention on informal caregiving within private contexts (Abel & Nelson, 1990; England, 1992; Tronto, 1993). The emotional labor literature has a stronger connection to the political economy of emotions in which women are responsible for the reproduction of human feeling in others as part of a service-based capitalist economy (Bolton, 2005; Hochschild, 1983). The carework focus tends to be broader in scope – always emphasizing the combined physical and affective characteristics of the work and the importance of attending to another individual's personal needs or well-being. In this sense, an examination of work within the health care sector of the economy is the most closely associated with carework in that health care professionals must attend to the physical and emotional dimensions of their interactions with others (Dodson & Zincavage, 2007;

Theodosius, 2008). Physical care is not as central, however, to other helping professions in education (e.g., teachers), criminal justice (e.g., police officers), or other human service sectors (e.g., social workers) that may also require substantial amounts of emotion management. As noted above, focusing on these types of occupational contexts draws attention to the commonly gendered "ethic of care" that underlies many of the frontline jobs in these fields and to complementary aspects of occupational experience that much of the organizational literature published in the 20th century tended to overlook. Where carework scholars are attuned to how cultural emotion norms linked to hierarchies of status (e.g., gender, race, class, nationality) have "silently attached themselves to many a job description" (paraphrased from Hochschild, 1983, p. 170), emotional labor researchers have specified the complex stimuli, processes, and outcomes involved in providing service(s) to others. The insights gleaned from both areas of study fit well within a theory of emotion practice that seeks to account for how emotion (in both its embodied and symbolic forms) influences and reflects the interests of individuals within everyday interaction while, at the same time, (re)producing the broader structural and cultural conditions in which such interactions occur. In sum, although the carework and emotional labor literatures have different substantive starting points, considering them as complementary dimensions of emotion practice that are theoretically and empirically entwined holds great promise for researchers working in either area.

Despite the very unique forms of emotional and physical labor associated with caring, using an emotion practice framework – as we suggest – does not draw firm boundaries between the emotion management performed in commercial versus human sector service jobs. Instead, we propose that scholars explicitly incorporate considerations of context into emotion management research and theory. Such considerations are rarely included in studies of emotion management, even when there is empirical evidence of their importance. For example, Morris and Feldman (1997) collected data from three different service sector groups: debt collectors, military recruiters, and nurses.[1] Although they reported significant differences across job categories, Morris and Feldman did not discuss the implications of such differences or examine the possibility that the effects of their emotional labor variables were conditioned by occupational context. Instead, the assumption underlying this and other related work appears to be that any differences among human and commercial service work can be accounted for by assessing variations in the standard emotional labor variables (e.g., display rules, surface and deep acting; cf. Glomb, Kammeyer-Mueller & Rotundo, 2004).

Building on Bourdieu's (1977, 1990a, 1990b) general theory of practice, an emotion practice approach suggests that instead of considering display rules or surface acting as attributes of individuals and groups (e.g., work units, gender, occupational statuses, organizations), or considering the influence of service sector (or other social) contexts to have standardized the behavior of sector employees, researchers should pursue a more synthetic, relational approach. For example, characteristics, antecedents, and/or effects of display rules would be understood only in relation to the underlying structural (i.e., power) differences among those accountable to the rules and within a cultural context typified by the ethics of care.

Similarly, Brotheridge and Grandey's (2002) initial analyses show clear distinctions between high emotional labor jobs (commercial service) and high burnout jobs (human service or caring labor). In this case there was a "hierarchy of emotional labor expectations" where human service workers reported "the highest level of frequency, variety, intensity, and duration of emotional display and expectations for control over emotional expressions" (p. 31) along with the highest levels of deep acting and feelings of personal accomplishment and significantly lower levels of depersonalization. As the authors note, such workers are likely to operate in a context where the development of authentic relationships reflective of genuine caring is expected (by both the organization and one's self); expectations that are quite different from the normative goals underlying commercial service transactions where showing one's real feelings may violate professional norms (i.e., emotions are private) and jeopardize the ability of the organization to provide quality service (i.e., emotions are pathologized) (James, 1989; Morris & Feldman, 1997).

Given these findings, what other insights might be gained were future investigators to examine the experiences of these two occupational contexts separately rather than combining them into the more generic category of "people work (e.g., service, sales, caring professions)" (Brotheridge & Grandey, 2002, p. 20)? The basis for such a suggestion lies not only in prior empirical results but also in the ontological and epistemological implications of grounding one's work in the study of care (where human relationships are essential) or the study of commerce (where the demands of economic rationality prevail). The challenge facing those interested in studying the emotion management of caring laborers in the 21st century is that *both* sets of expectations are operating simultaneously. As such, the content of today's emotion management theories must recognize the differences across contexts while also working to avoid dualistic, either/or conceptualizations.

## CARING FOR MIND AND BODY: DISTINCTIONS IN HUMAN SERVICE AND EMOTION MANAGEMENT

Not long after Hochschild's original publications (1979, 1983), studies of the caring professions were incorporated into models and research on emotion management (e.g., James, 1989). Despite the tendency of researchers to concentrate their efforts on understanding emotion management within the context of commercial service work, authors frequently reference caring labor occupations in their descriptions of emotional labor performance. Such a connection is not surprising given the gendered aspects of the work (see Lively, 2013), its affinity with earlier descriptions of "sentimental work" within health care settings (e.g., Strauss, Fagerhaugh, Suczek, & Wiener, 1982), and the examination of burnout as a prominent outcome measure which, originally, was associated with the helping professions (Maslach, 1976, 1982; Maslach & Jackson, 1981).

Despite these connections, the underlying distinctions between the two types of service work become apparent in their discursive juxtaposition. For example, Ashforth and Humphrey (1993, p. 89) illustrate feeling rules by noting that "nurses are expected to feel empathetic and supportive" but that they prefer Ekman's (1973) concept of display rules because compliance with these behavioral rules is more easily observed by "customers, managers, and peers." In shifting the emphasis from an expectation for feeling – which does indeed characterize the professional norms underlying paid carework (Bolton, 2005; Cancian, 2000) – to a methodological preference for observable display, the authors have begun with care and finished with commerce. We believe that these types of a priori distinctions (e.g., that when studying display you can ignore feeling) are unnecessary and draw seemingly fixed boundaries where, in actual practice, they do not exist.

As noted above, a second tendency is for scholars to conflate human and commercial service under the umbrella of research on "emotional labor." For example, in Zapf's (2002) review of emotion management and well-being, the dynamics of interacting with different types of clients (e.g., customers, patients, and children) remain undifferentiated (p. 238; also see Erickson & Ritter, 2001; Gosserand & Diefendorff, 2005; Rafaeli & Sutton, 1987 for similar tendencies). And yet, section titles within Zapf's review are distinguished by whether they contain human service or commercial service examples. As a result, Zapf's piece is notable not only for the substance of its argument but also for the *pervasive yet unidentified differences* between emotion management occurring in human service contexts and that taking place within commercial sectors of the economy.

In sum, much of the literature on emotional labor has tended to conceptualize, model, and measure what is perceived to be common across occupational contexts without also fully examining what may distinguish them. Much has been gained by such an approach. At the same time, others who examine emotion management in caring labor contexts (Boler, 1999; Bolton, 2005; Erickson, 2008; Lopez, 2007; Stacey, 2011; Theodosius, 2008) might suggest that theory and research on this topic would be advanced by also attending to the potential distinctions between the social and economic contexts in which such work occurs. As Payne (2009, p. 359) suggests, one of the problems associated with the current research on emotional labor is the tendency to "lump all emotion workers and all jobs involving emotion work together." This restricts workers' ability to advocate for being seen (and paid) as "highly skilled" workers in that a cashier wishing a customer "have a nice day" has become equated with, for example, the emotional skills required to care for terminally ill patients and their families. We illustrate the potential utility of such differentiation, and some of the insights gained through an emotion practice approach, by exploring the contours of emotion management within health care contexts.

## Emotion Management in Health Care

Studies that have examined human service occupations have reaffirmed the utility of more general theoretical models of emotion management (e.g., Grandey, 2000) at the same time that they have illustrated the ways in which these traditional models may be limited. In what follows, we briefly review each strand of the literature in an effort to demonstrate that while there are common influences, processes, and outcomes across occupational contexts, other dimensions of emotion practice emerge when examining emotion in the context of the caring labor performed within health-related settings in particular, and human service contexts more broadly.

Using an evolutionary approach to understanding the development of research concepts, Huynh, Alderson, and Thompson (2008) trace the emergence of knowledge about the antecedents and consequences of emotional labor within nursing as well as the disciplines of management, psychology, and medicine.[2] Their analysis indicates that unlike other disciplinary approaches, few researchers who study nursing have used quantitative methodologies to measure and assess emotional labor processes. Nonetheless, their final conceptual model shares a great deal in common with others proposed by organizational psychologists (e.g., Grandey, 2000; Schaubroeck & Jones, 2000; Diefendorff, Croyle, & Gosserand, 2005). These include references to organizationally prescribed display rules, job characteristics (e.g., interactional frequency and duration, emotional variety; Erickson, 2005; Erickson & Grove, 2007, 2008; Morris & Feldman, 1996), individual characteristics (e.g., commitment, experience, affective disposition), management processes (e.g., surface and deep acting) and organizational and individual consequences. As with other studies that may have included health care workers in their samples, these studies tend to focus on the effects of organizationally imposed demands or display rules. Recently, researchers have begun to move beyond the individual-level of analysis to examine the impact of display rules at the level of the work unit or group. For example, Diefendorff, Erickson, Grandey, and Dahling (2011) demonstrated that unit-level display rules (i.e. rules regarding emotional expression that reflect the shared normative conceptions of nurses working on the hospital unit) are negatively related to nurses' job satisfaction. In addition, consistent with Grandey (2000), display rules were shown to affect burnout directly as well as being mediated by surface and deep acting which was also influenced by individual affective dispositions. Nurses who had high positive affectivity and who worked on a unit with high levels of shared integrative display rules tended to engage in more "good faith" (Rafaeli & Sutton, 1987) deep acting efforts. In contrast, nurses in similar unit-level contexts but who were high in negative affectivity, tended to engage in surface acting – which others have shown is associated with lower levels of well-being (Bono & Vey, 2005). Despite the consistency of these findings with others studies, the authors raise the possibility that such results may be more likely to emerge within occupational contexts that place a premium on the development of authentic relationships and would not be found within "occupations in which authenticity and caring are not central professional values (e.g., sales)" (p. 182).

This suggestion is consistent with results reported by Bakker and Heuven (2006) in their study of nurses and police officers – two high-intensity caring labor jobs with quite different emotional expectations. Bakker and Heuven (2006) examined the extent to which the effect of emotional job demands on burnout was mediated by the experience of emotional dissonance (i.e., experiencing a discrepancy between felt emotions and those required by occupational display rules). Although the data fit the proposed model adequately for both occupational groups, Bakker and Heuven report that, among nurses but not police officers, emotional demands had a direct effect on burnout over and above the effect of emotional dissonance. In other words, emotional dissonance fully mediated the effect of emotional demands on burnout for police but only partially for nurses. This result suggests that the type of emotional demands faced by health care workers may differ in kind (rather than merely degree) from those faced by other high-intensity emotional laborers.

Following the job-demands resources perspective (Bakker & Demerouti, 2007) and building on the work of others (Grandey, 2000; Kruml & Geddes, 2000) who have also suggested that different dimensions of emotional labor are likely to lead to different outcomes, Seery and Corrigal (2009) studied nurses' aides and child care workers to examine the effects of surface acting and emotional enhancement (i.e., attempts to make others feel increased self-worth, happiness or contentment; also see Himmelweit, 1999) on a range of individual outcomes. Explicitly bringing the "nurturing" concerns of family-based carework into their approach, Seery and Corrigal draw attention to aspects of emotion practice that are often neglected in traditional conceptualizations of the emotional labor process. By focusing on emotional enhancement, the authors illustrate sensitivity to the differences between self- and other-focused emotion management (Pugliesi, 1999; Thoits, 1996). Managing one's emotions in ways that are specifically targeted toward enhancing a particular other's well-being is common among caring labor occupations which depend on one's ability to understand another's situation or to empathize with their feelings. For Seery and Corrigal (2009), such distinctions are critical for understanding the outcomes of emotion management in that other-focused management is not considered to be as resource-depleting as the more self-focused process of surface acting. Such an argument is similar to those made below regarding the deep acting performed by teachers and what Rafaeli and Sutton (1987) refer to as "faking in good faith" (also see Ashforth & Humphrey, 1993). Despite such similarities, we suggest that the two strategies are not the same and that distinctions between them need to be maintained. One reason for this is that deep acting (like surface acting) is a self-focused process. As such, the effects of deep acting should not be as sensitive to who the target of emotion management is when compared to those for more interpersonal, or other-focused, processes such as surface acting. Indeed, Seery and Corrigal report that self-enhancement had a beneficial effect on workers' intentions to quit and emotional exhaustion, but only in the context of interactions with family members, rather than patients and children themselves. The negative effects of surface acting demonstrated no such sensitivity. Because enhancing others' well-being can provide workers with a sense of meaning and personal accomplishment, it may operate as a source of intrinsic motivation and thus be experienced as less resource-depleting (Muraven, 2008). These results suggest that conceptualizations of emotion practice need to include strategies that involve interpersonal processes (also see Niven, Totterdell, Holman, & Cameron, 2013) as well as intrapersonal ones and that account for how the target of one's emotion management efforts may condition its effects.

Although the preceding studies suggest that there are some common processes underlying micro-level strategies of emotion management in caring and commercial contexts, these studies and others have identified differences that deserve more theoretical and empirical attention (Bolton, 2005; Davies, 1995; James, 1992; Lopez, 2006; Theodosius, 2008). Mark (2005) suggests, for example, that part of the distinctiveness (and importance) of studying emotion within health care settings is that while contexts such as education are characterized by a culture of logic and rationality, the dominance of rationality within medicine serves not merely a scientific purpose but also an emotional one. Rationality

> provides the cognitive means by which emotionally unacceptable procedures and activities are allowed to occur to individuals as patients . . . Getting the emotional agenda wrong in health care becomes particularly worrying because of the nature of the activity, and the costs to both patients and staff.
>
> (Mark, 2005, p. 279).

Bolton's (2000, 2005, 2007) re-envisioning of emotion management in the context of nursing in the United Kingdom is perhaps the best known attempt to explain why Hochschild's original conceptualization of emotional labor is too limited for understanding the complexity of emotional processes within caring labor contexts. Bolton's (2005) argument is that the concept of "emotional labor" refers *only* to a form of emotion regulation that has commercial value and that underscores workers' relative lack of control over the management process. It is this pecuniary form of emotion management that emphasizes externally imposed display (as opposed to feeling) rules (e.g., Ashforth & Humphrey, 1993), draws on the materialist motivations underlying the commercial service sector, and is most often associated with cynical surface acting performances and resulting alienation. To be sure, this pecuniary form of emotion management – or emotional labor – has infiltrated the larger organizational contexts of human service work (Bone, 2002; Woodward, 1997), which are further complicated by the combined influence of masculine forms of professional practice (linked to patriarchal capitalism) and feminine cultures of care (Bone, 2002; Grumet, 1988; Jaggar, 1989; Phillips, 1996; Syed, 2008). Because of such complexity, Bolton argues that the experience of emotion management in health care contexts cannot be reduced to emotional labor.

As a result, Bolton (2005) proposes a set of emotion management processes that reflect health care's blurring of private and public emotion work and the boundaries between a workers' physical display and her personal emotional investment. In so doing, she introduces a typology of workplace emotion (Bolton, 2005, Table 5.1, p. 93) that distinguishes between pecuniary (focused on commercial gain), prescriptive (grounded in professional or organizational values), presentational (drawing on general social rules which may be linked to status characteristics), and philanthropic emotion management which is given as a "gift" to another and thus is not tied to social norms of reciprocity. Bolton's approach is motivated by the need to make sense of empirical results indicating that human service professionals often derive their greatest sense of personal satisfaction from their interactions with others (Boler, 1999; James, 1992; Smith, 1992). In her far-ranging discussion of theoretical foundations, Bolton's (2005) labor process approach draws on the same concerns that motivate our own proposal to use *emotion practice* as an overarching framework, noting that "divisions of emotion work have both symbolic and material dimensions" (p. 75), that the "status of participants in the interaction order will be a defining feature of how emotion work is to be distributed" (p. 75), but that individuals must also be seen as active agents whose everyday practices may also challenge existing material and moral orders in unique and creative ways. For Bolton, researchers need to move beyond the pecuniary-based concept of emotional labor to include consideration of the *emotion* management that may be guided by one's desire to fulfill self-values grounded in professional socialization, the presentational rules of emotion management guided by one's generally recognized status characteristics (e.g., gender, race–ethnicity, age), and/or the self-motivated gifts of emotional care that reinforce the basic humanity of another individual (also see Lopez, 2006; Stacey, 2005, 2011).

A key contribution of Bolton's approach is that it draws attention to issues of agency and power within paid employment in a way that is quite different than that of Hochschild (1983) and that shares concerns raised by carework scholars. Human service workers are neither "free-floating agents unconstrained by hierarchies and institutions" (Bolton, 2009, p. 554) nor are they "passive providers of an emotional labour/work which is determined by management or professional norms" (Lewis, 2005, p. 567). Although autonomy is frequently considered in studies of emotional labor, power is not. Yet, as Morris and Feldman (1997) recognized, processes of emotion and expression management are not only influenced by control over one's work but also by the relative power (and status) of the interactants involved (also see Diefendorff & Greguras, 2009). The power that caring providers have may be quite different than that of the frontline commercial service worker. In the helping professions, there is an underlying assumption that the clients served are more vulnerable and have relatively *less* power than the health care provider on whom they are dependent for their physical as well as emotional health. In her study of nurses, Theodosius (2008, p. 39, 41) notes that as the purveyors of health care, nurses hold power over their patients, whereas flight attendants are vulnerable to the consumer power of their customers . . . Emotional labour helps redress the balance of power held by health care professionals over those who are vulnerable and sick . . . It is fundamentally important when understanding emotional labour in health care not to underestimate the dependency that sick and vulnerable people have on their carers . . . The social values encapsulated in the Nightingale Ethic are essential to many of the interactions undertaken in health care because the belief that doctors and nurses act to save and preserve life is fundamental to society having the confidence to accept the care offered.

Sliter, Jex, Wolford, and McInnerney's (2010) study of bank tellers lends support to the distinctions drawn by Theodosius, noting that commercial service workers are particularly at risk for incivility because they have relatively low power in relation to their customers, and that this may be particularly problematic for women working in the commercial sector. These results suggest that an emotion practice theory must include consideration of actors' relative power and agency within interactional contexts, the possibility that power and agency may vary depending on the type and target of one's emotion management, and that it remains an empirical question whether particular emotional practices reinforce existing power structures or serve to challenge them.

Theodosius (2008) offers a typology of emotional labor among nurses that complements yet extends Bolton's (2005) in two critical ways. First, in her discussion of "instrumental emotional labor," Theodosius illustrates how caring for others' *physical* well-being fundamentally alters how scholars should think about the emotional labor experience, both as performers and recipients. Second, building on Archer's (2000) model of emotional experience and analyzing her narrative data though a unique application of identity-focused, sociological reflexivity (Bourdieu, 1992; Prus, 1996), Theodosius reminds us of the importance of something that has been missing from many studies of emotional labor, namely, the experience of *felt* emotion. In combination with the other points we have raised, Theodosius' work provides the strongest evidence yet for why a theory of emotion practice is preferable to frameworks grounded in either emotional labor or emotion management.

Theodosius (2008) reminds us that before any type of emotion management is possible, there first must be an emotional experience to manage. Theodosius (2008) criticizes the tendency of emotional labor researchers to emphasize the cognitive control of emotional experience to the relative neglect of neuroscientific evidence that emotions also can operate outside of cognitive appraisals (also see Turner, 2000; Zajonc, 1984). This tendency has led scholars to study *either* "emotion" *or* "emotion management," as if no understanding of the former was necessary for examining the latter. Theodosius provides convincing evidence that this tendency leads investigators to define away a significant dimension of what should be at the heart of emotion management theory and research.

We believe that the source of the problem lies with the use of the term "emotional labor" (Hochschild, 1983) for describing a field of study that incorporates a broad range of social scientific and business disciplines. Among those focusing primarily on human service work, the concept of emotional labor has been seen as problematic because it conveys an economically-based, scripted process that is at odds with the professional norms of service workers who pride themselves on subscribing to altruistic ethics of care and service to others (Bolton, 2005; Lopez, 2006). Using the term, "emotion management," rather than emotional labor addresses some of these concerns but it fails to explicitly recognize that embodied emotional experience (not just its management) is a fundamental part of the processes under consideration in both the human and commercial sectors (e.g., Erickson & Ritter, 2001; Sloan, 2007). In addition, shifting from "emotional labor" to "emotion management" sanitizes all occupational contexts as sites that both reproduce inequalities and serve as spaces for individual, structural and cultural change.

The concept of *emotion practice* has none of the above limitations. All of the concepts/processes usually examined by organizational psychologists in studies of emotional labor are easily accommodated within an emotion practice framework (e.g., display rules, surface and deep acting, etc.) as is the concern with emotional experience highlighted by Sloan (2007) or Theodosius (2008). Bolton's typology of emotion management also fits nicely into the practice framework as it specifies particular empirical variants (e.g., pecuniary, prescriptive, philanthropic) that may take on greater or lesser significance depending on the surrounding context. A theory of emotion practice enables each of these different (and potentially competing) approaches to emotion to be understood in light of one another. In so doing, any seeming oppositions that might be drawn between them are "transcended and integrated" in the broader theoretical frame of emotion practice (see Swartz, 1997, p. 55 for a discussion of this within Bourdieu's theory).

Focusing on emotion practice also overcomes problems associated with categorical (dualistic) theories of gender, race, and class. Existing research customarily compares the experiences of those holding different status characteristics (e.g., men vs. women or nurses vs. physicians) in an effort to generate information about group differences. Although this type of approach has benefits, it does not problematize the gendered/raced/ classed emotion norms (or emotional cultures) that contribute to the reproduction of inequalities (in terms of pay, advancement, retention, satisfaction, health) and to which status group members hold themselves and others accountable during interaction.

For example, we know that gender plays a role in shaping the contours of emotion practice (i.e. women are more likely to perform emotion work in caring contexts) and that, in so doing, women accrue considerable "emotional capital" (Nowotny, 1981; Reay, 2005; Virkki, 2007) but very little economic capital when laboring in caring contexts (England, Budig and Folbre, 2002; Glomb et al., 2004). Race, socioeconomic status (SES), and professional status also inform emotion practice in caring contexts, as evidenced by the relegation of low-income women of color to lower-skilled human service occupations, such as childcare worker or nursing assistant (Glenn, 1992, 2010; Stacey, 2011). As the sociological literature makes clear, it is not simply a question of *who* carries out caring work that makes race, class and gender relevant, but also *how the experience and enactment of emotion* on the job is shaped by social location. We suggest that a comprehensive understanding of emotion practice must not only take into account the context of care (human vs. commercial service work) but also consider how worker status shapes the experience of emotion management on the job.

## CARE AND COMMERCE, MIND AND BODY: EMOTION PRACTICE IN THE 21st CENTURY

Paid carework in the 21st century does not exist in a parallel universe outside the reach of Hochschild's (1983) original commodification process or the influence of pecuniary display rules that guide the emotional labor performed by commercial service workers; far from it. Instead, the antecedents, processes, and outcomes associated with the emotion management performed in commercial service work exist side-by-side with equally powerful demands to adhere to a professional (and often philanthropic) ethic of care. Thus, rather than understanding today's caring labor contexts as being antithetical or somehow outside the boundaries of traditional models of emotional labor, they should be seen as affected by such processes while simultaneously seeking adherence to a culturally-powerful set of social difference codes (Ridgeway, 2000). It is this complex set of potentially contradictory influences that renders caring labor contexts so full of theoretical and empirical possibility.

Himmelweit (1999) suggests that the relational connection between carer and caree can have a profound impact on whether the worker finds the work rewarding/satisfactory. This idea is consistent with the original argument made by Morris and Feldman (1996) that researchers need to measure characteristics of the interactional context. However, the approach one might take to these particular dimensions, along with their expected outcomes, is potentially different when considered in the context of caring labor. For example, citing Cordes and Dougherty (1993), Morris and Feldman argue that longer interactions with clients should be associated with higher levels of burnout. In addition, their approach captures the very real differences between commercial jobs and organizations that are governed by norms focused on display rules and the need for workers to "avoid showing their own personal feelings," and those of high-intensity, human service work in which job incumbents seek the development of meaningful relationships with others (Himmelweit, 1999; Lopez, 2006).

In the latter context, to the extent that interactions with clients are shaped by organizational norms supporting "emotional honesty and authentic relationship building" (Lopez, 2006, p. 157), frequency and length of contact would be expected to have the opposite effect. As Lopez observes, this does not mean that interactions between caring laborers and clients cannot be organized or managed, merely that such managers should not privilege adherence to specific feeling/display rules if they seek to enhance their employees' effectiveness, well-being, and retention. Within a caring labor context, the goal is not to achieve *individual* autonomy but to nurture the development and maintenance of authentic *relationships* (also see Godin, 2010). In other words, it is about the ability of workers to provide emotional care rather than to perform emotional labor (Lopez, 2006, p. 157). If workers are told they must bring their feelings and/or displays into line with managerial requirements, by definition, emotional labor is being performed and the behavior is therefore *not* autonomous. In contrast, if employees are permitted to act according to *their own evaluations* of what their work situations require in regard to their *relationships with others* then they are not doing emotional labor as Hochschild defined it but are more likely to be involved in organized emotional care. To the extent that emotional labor continues to be used as a catch-all term generically applied across human and commercial service sectors, these subtle yet fundamental empirical differences between the processes and potential outcomes of diverse caring labor contexts will remain unrecognized.

Instead, we have suggested that these multidimensional and, at times, seemingly contradictory processes and outcomes might be more fully understood within a theory of *emotion practice*. With its roots in Bourdieu's (1977, 1990b) general science of social practice, a theory of emotion practice is not hampered by linguistic and methodological assumptions in the same way as emotional labor and emotion management. Moreover, it provides a means of re-envisioning traditional concepts such as display rules and acting strategies in relation to concepts such as emotional capital that are tied to social location but, as relations of power (Bourdieu, 1986), may operate quite differently depending on the social or occupational context under consideration. Given that a theory of emotion practice encourages scholars to specify the material, symbolic, and individual or agentive dimensions of each concept or process examined, it also has the ability to provide insight into how micro-level strategies (e.g., deep acting) may benefit one's sense of self, identity, or well-being while it nonetheless reproduces the very systems of status- or occupationally-based inequality that put one's self at risk in the first place (e.g., Lively, 2000). In so doing, the approach stays true to the original theoretical and empirical goals set by Hochschild (1983) while recognizing that within today's caring labor contexts attending to mind *and* body, care *and* commerce, emotional experience *and* management are integral features of 21$^{st}$ century emotion practice.

## ENDNOTES

1 Among those studying emotional labor, this type of "mixed" sample is quite common (e.g., Brotheridge & Lee, 2002; Diefendorff & Richard, 2003; Erickson & Ritter, 2001; Erickson & Wharton, 1997; Gosserand & Diefendorff, 2005; Tschan, Rochat & Zapf, 2005; Zapf & Holz, 2006).
2 Because the vast majority of research on emotional labor within health care has focused on the experience of nurses, our discussion primarily reviews the literature on nurses as well.

## REFERENCES

Abel, E. K. & Nelson, M. K. (1990). Circles of care: An introductory essay. In *Circles of care: Work and identity in women's lives* (pp. 4–34). Albany, NY: State University of New York Press.

Archer, M. (2000). *Being human: The problem of agency*. Cambridge: Cambridge University Press.

Ashforth, B. E., & Humphrey, R. H. (1993). Emotional labor in service roles: The influence of identity. *Academy of Management Review*, 18, 88–115.

Bakker A. B., & Demerouti, E. (2007). The job demands–resources model: State of the art. *Journal of Managerial Psychology, 22*(3), 309–28.

Bakker, A. B., & Heuven, E. (2006). Emotional dissonance, burnout, and in-role performance among nurses and police officers. *International Journal of Stress Management, 13*(4), 423–440.

Belenky, M., Clinchy, B., Goldberger, N., & Tarule, J. (1986). *Women's ways of knowing: The development of self, voice, and mind*. New York, NY: Basic Books.

Boler, M. (1999). *Feeling power: Emotions and education*. New York, NY: Routledge.

Bolton, S. (2000). Who cares? Offering emotion work as a 'gift' in the nursing labour process. *Journal of Advanced Nursing, 32(3),* 580–586.

Bolton, S. (2005). *Emotion management in the workplace.* New York, NY: Palgrave Macmillan.

Bolton, S. (2007). Emotion work as human connection: Gendered emotion codes in teaching primary children with emotional and behavioural difficulties. In P. Lewis & R. Simpson (Eds.), *Gendering Emotions in Organisations* (pp. 17–34). London: Palgrave.

Bolton, S. (2009). The lady vanishes: Women's work and affective labour. *International Journal of Work, Organization and Emotion, 3*(1), 72–80.

Bone, D. (2002). Dilemmas of emotion work in nursing under market-driven health care. *The International Journal of Public Sector Management, 15*(2), 140–150.

Bono, J. E., & Vey, M. A. (2005). Toward understanding emotional management at work: A quantitative review of emotional labor research. In C. E. J. Härtel, W. J. Zerbe, & N. M. Ashkanasy (Eds.), *Emotions in Organizational Behavior* (pp. 213–233). New Jersey: Lawrence Erlbaum.

Bourdieu, P. (1977). *Outline of a theory of practice.* Cambridge: Cambridge University Press.

Bourdieu, P. (1986). The forms of capital. In J. G. Richardson (Ed.), *Handbook of Theory and Research for the Sociology of Education* (pp. 241–258). New York, NY: Greenwood Press.

Bourdieu, P. (1990a). *In other words:* Essays toward a reflexive sociology. Stanford, CA: Stanford University Press.

Bourdieu, P. (1990b). *The logic of practice.* Stanford, CA: Stanford University Press.

Bourdieu, P. (1992). *Invitation to a Reflexive Sociology.* Chicago: University of Chicago Press.

Brotheridge, C. M., & Grandey, A. A. (2002). Emotional labor and burnout: Comparing two perspectives of 'people work'. *Journal of Vocational Behavior, 60,* 17–39.

Brotheridge, C. M., & Lee, R. T. (2002). Testing a conservation of resources model of the dynamics of emotional labor. *Journal of Occupational Health Psychology, 7*(1), 57–67.

Cancian, F. M. (2000). Paid emotional care: Organizational forms that encourage nurturance. In M. H. Meyer (Ed.), *Carework: Gender, Labor, and the Welfare State* (pp. 136–148). New York, NY: Routledge.

Cordes, C. L., & Dougherty, T. W. (1993). A review and an integration of research on job burnout. *Journal of Academy of Management Review, 18,* 621–56.

Daniels, A. K. (1987). Invisible work. *Social Problems, 34,* 403–415.

Davies, C. (1995). Competence versus care? Gender and caring work revisited. *Acta Sociologica, 38,* 17–31.

Diefendorff, J. M., Croyle, M. H., & Gosserand, R. H. (2005). The dimensionality and antecedents of emotional labor strategies. *Journal of Vocational Behavior, 66,* 339–357.

Diefendorff, J. M., Erickson, R. J., Grandey, A. A., & Dahling, J. (2011). Emotional display rules as work unit norms: A multilevel analysis of emotional labor among nurses. *Journal of Occupational Health Psychology, 16*(2), 170–186.

Diefendorff, J. M., & Greguras, G. J. (2009). Contextualizing emotional display rules: Examining the roles of targets and discrete emotions in shaping display rule perceptions. *Journal of Management, 35*(4), 880–898.

Diefendorff, J. M., & Richard, H. M. (2003). Antecedents and consequences of emotional display rule perceptions. *Journal of Applied Psychology, 88*(2), 284–294.

Dodson, L., & Zincavage, R. M. (2007). 'It's like a family:' Caring labor, exploitation, and race in nursing homes. *Gender & Society, 21*(6), 905–928.

Ehrenreich, B., & Hochschild, A. R. (2002). *Global woman: Nannies, maids, and sex workers in the new economy*. New York: Henry Holt.

Ekman, P. (1973). Cross culture studies of facial expression. In Ekman P. (Ed.) *Darwin and facial expression: A century of research in review* (pp. 169–222). New York, NY: Academic Press.

England, P. (1992). *Comparable worth: Theories and evidence*. New York: Aldine de Gruyter.

England, P., Budig, M., & Folbre, N. (2002). Wages of virtue: The relative pay of care work. *Social Problems, 49*, 455–473.

Erickson, R. J. (2005). *Improving the context for CAARE*. Unpublished interim report, baseline data and initial recommendations.

Erickson, R.J. (2008). The context of care: Reconsidering culture, structure, and the performance of emotional labor. In D. T. Robinson & J. Clay-Warner (Eds.), *Social Structure and Emotion* (pp. 259–286). New York, NY: Elsevier.

Erickson, R, J., & Grove, W. J. C. (2007). Why emotion matters: Age, agitation, and burnout among registered nurses. *Online Journal of Issues in Nursing, 13*(1). Retrieved from http://nursingworld.org/MainMenuCategories/ANAMarketplace/ANAPeriodicals/OJIN/TableofContentsvol132008/No1 Jan08/ArticlePreviousTopic/WhyEmotionsMatterAgeAgitationandBurnout AmongRegisteredNurses.aspx.

Erickson, R. J., & Grove, W. J. C. (2008). Emotional labor and health care. *Sociology Compass, 2*(2), 704–733.

Erickson, R. J., & Ritter, C. (2001). Emotional labor, burnout, and inauthenticity: Does gender matter? *Social Psychology Quarterly, 64*, 146–163.

Erickson, R. J. & Wharton, A. S. (1997). Inauthenticity and depression: Assessing the consequences of interactive service work. *Work and Occupations, 24*(2), 188–213.

Fenstermaker Berk, S. (1980). *Women and household labor*. Thousand Oaks, CA: Sage Publications.

Glenn, E. N. (1992). From servitude to service work: Historical continuities in the racial division of paid reproductive labor. *Signs, 18*(1), 1–43.

Glenn, E. N. (2010). *Forced to care: Coercion and caregiving in America*. Cambridge, MA: Harvard University Press.

Glomb, T. M., Kammeyer-Mueller, J. D., & Rotundo, M. (2004). Emotional labor demands and compensating wage differentials. *Journal of Applied Psychology, 89*(4), 700–714.

Godin, S. (2010). *Linchpin: Are you indispensable?* New York: Portfolio Penguin.

Gosserand, R. H., & Diefendorff, J. H. (2005). Display rules and emotional labor: The moderating role of commitment. *Journal of Applied Psychology, 90*, 1256–1264.

Grandey, A. (2000). Emotional regulation in the workplace: A new way to conceptualize emotional labor. *Journal of Occupational Health Psychology, 5*(1), 95–110.

Grumet, M. (1988). *Bitter milk.* Amherst, MA: University of Massachusetts Press.

Hartmann, H. (1981). The family as a locus for gender, class and political struggle: The example of housework. *Signs, 6*(5), 366–394.

Harvey Wingfield, A. (2010). Are some emotions marked 'Whites Only'? Racialized feeling rules in professional workplaces. *Social Problems, 57*(2), 251–268.

Himmelweit, S. (1999). Caring labor. *The Annals of the American Academy of Political and Social Science, 561*, 27–38.

Hochschild, A. (1979). Emotion work, feeling rules, and social structure. *American Journal of Sociology, 85*(3), 551–575.

Hochschild, A. (1983). *The managed heart: Commercialization of human feeling.* Berkeley, CA: University of California Press.

Huynh, T., Alderson, M., & Thompson, M. (2008). Emotional labour underlying caring: An evolutionary concept analysis. *Journal of Advanced Nursing, 64*(2), 195–208.

Jaggar, Al. (1989). Love and knowledge: Emotion in feminist epistemology. *Inquiry, 32*(2), 151–176.

James, N. (1989). Emotional labour: Skill and work in the social regulation of feelings. *Sociological Review, 37*, 15–42.

James, N. (1992). Care = organization + physical labour + emotional labour. *Sociology of Health & Illness, 14*(4), 488–509.

Kruml, S. M., & Geddes, D. (2000). Exploring the dimensions of emotional labor: The heart of Hochschild's work. *Management Communication Quarterly, 14*(1), 8–49.

Lewis, P. (2005). Suppression or expression: An exploration of emotion management in a special care baby unit. *Work, Employment, and Society, 19*, 565–581.

Lively, K. J. (2000). Reciprocal emotion management: Working together to maintain stratification in private law firms. *Work and Occupations, 27*, 32–63.

Lively, K. J. (2013). Social and cultural influencers: Gender effects on emotional labor at work and at home. In A. A. Grandey, J. M. Diefendorff & D. E. Rupp (Eds.), *Emotional labor in the 21st century: Diverse perspectives on emotion regulation at work.* New York, NY: Psychology Press/Routledge.

Lopez, S. H. (2006). Emotional labor and organized emotional care: Conceptualizing nursing home care work. *Work and Occupations, 33*(2), 133–160.

Lopez, S. H. (2007). Efficiency and the fix revisited: Informal relations and mock routinization at a nonprofit nursing home. *Qualitative Sociology, 30*(3), 225–247.

Mark, A. (2005). Organizing emotions in health care. *Journal of Health Organization and Management, 19*(4), 277–289.

Maslach, C. (1976). Burned-out. *Human Behavior, 9*(5), 16–22.

Maslach, C. (1982). Understanding burnout: Definitional issues in analyzing a complex phenomenon. In W. S. Paine (Ed.), *Job stress and burnout* (pp. 29–40). Beverly Hills, CA: Sage Publications.

Maslach, C., & Jackson, C. E. (1981). The measurement of experienced burnout. *Journal of Occupational Behaviour, 2*, 99–113.

Misra, J. (2011). Carework. In G. Ritzer & J. M. Ryan (Eds.), *The Concise Encyclopedia of Sociology* (p. 49). Malden, MA: Wiley-Blackwell.

Morris, J. A., & Feldman, D. C. (1996). The dimensions, antecedents, and consequences of emotional labor. *Academy of Management Review, 21*(1), 986–1010.

Morris, J. A., & Feldman, D. C. (1997). Managing emotions in the workplace. *Journal of Managerial Issues, 9*(3), 257–274.

Muraven, M. (2008). Autonomous self-control is less depleting. *Journal of Research in Personality, 42*, 763–770.

Niven K., Totterdell, P., Holman, D., & Cameron, D. (2013). Emotional labor at the unit-level. In A. A. Grandey, J. M. Diefendorff & D. E. Rupp (Eds.), *Emotional labor in the 21st century: Diverse perspectives on emotion regulation at work*. New York, NY: Psychology Press/Routledge.

Nowotny, H. (1981). Women in public life in Austria. In C. F. Epstein & R. L. Coser (Eds.), *Access to power: Cross-national studies of women and elites* (pp. 178–192). London: George Allen & Unwin.

Payne, J. (2009). Emotional labour and skill: A reappraisal. *Gender, Work & Organization, 16*(3), 348–367.

Phillips, D. (1996). The internationalization of labour: The migration of nurses from Trinidad and Tobago (a case study). *International Sociology, 11*(1), 109–127.

Prus, R. (1996). *Symbolic interaction and ethnographic research*. Albany, NY: State University of New York Press.

Pugliesi, K. (1999). The consequences of emotional labor: effects on work stress, job satisfaction, and well-being. *Motivation and Emotion, 23*(2), 125–54.

Radin, M. J. (1996). *Contested commodities*. Cambridge, MA: Harvard University Press.

Rafaeli, A., & Sutton, R. I. (1987). The expression of emotion as part of the work role. *Academy of Management Review, 12*(1), 23–27.

Reay, D. (2005). Gendering Bourdieu's concepts of capitals? Emotional capital, women and social class. *The Sociological Review, 52*(2), 57–74.

Ridgeway, C. (2000). Social difference codes and social connections. *Sociological Perspectives, 43*, 1–11.

Schaubroeck, J., & Jones, J. R. (2000). Antecedents of workplace emotional labor dimensions and moderators of their effects on physical symptoms. *Journal of Organizational Behavior, 21*, 163–183.

Seery, B. L., & Corrigall, E. A. (2009). Emotional labor: Links to work attitudes and emotional exhaustion. *Journal of Managerial Psychology, 24*(8), 797–813.

Sliter, M., Jex, S., Wolford, K., & McInnerney, J. (2010). How rude! Emotional labor as a mediator between customer incivility and employee outcomes. *Journal of Occupational Health Psychology, 15*(4), 468–481.

Sloan, M. M. (2007). The "real self" and inauthenticity: The importance of self-concept anchorage for emotional experiences in the workplace. *Social Psychology Quarterly, 70*(3), 305–31.

Smith, P. (1992). *The emotional labour of nursing.* London: The Macmillan Press.

Stacey, C. L. (2005). Finding dignity in dirty work: The constraints and rewards of low-wage home care labor. *Sociology of Health and Illness, 27*(6), 831–854.

Stacey, C. L. 2011. *The caring self: The work experiences of home care aides.* Ithaca, NY: Cornell/ILR Press.

Stone, D. (2000). Caring by the book. In M. H. Meyer (Ed.), *Carework: Gender, labor, and the welfare state* (pp. 89–111). New York, NY: Routledge.

Strauss, A., Fagerhaugh, S., Suczek, B., & Wiener, C. (1982). Sentimental work in the technologized hospital. *Sociology of Health and Illness, 4,* 255–278.

Swartz, D. (1997). Culture & Power: The Sociology of Pierre Bourdieu. Chicago: The University of Chicago Press.

Syed, J. (2008). Societal norms and contextual emotional labor. In N. M. Ashkanasy, W.J. Zerbe, and C.E.J. Härtel (Eds.), *Research on emotion in organizations* (volume 4, pp. 241–258). Bingley, UK: Emerald.

Theodosius, C. (2008). *Emotional labour in health care: The unmanaged heart of nursing.* London: Routledge.

Thoits, P. A. (1996). Managing the emotions of others. *Symbolic Interaction, 19*(2), 85–109.

Tronto, J. C. (1993). An ethic of care. In A. Cudd & R. Andreason (Eds.), *Feminist Theory: A Philosophical Anthology* (pp. 251–263). Malden, MA: Blackwell Publishers Inc.

Tschan, F., Rochat, S., & Zapf, D. (2005). It's not only clients: Studying emotion work with clients and co-workers with an event-sampling approach. *Journal of Occupational and Organizational Psychology, 78,* 195–220.

Turner, J. H. (2000). *On the origins of human emotions: A sociological inquiry into the evolution of human affect.* Stanford, CA: Stanford University Press.

Twigg, J. (2000). *Bathing~the body and community care.* London: Routledge.

Virkki, T. (2007). Emotional capital in caring work. In C. E. J. Härtel, N. M. Ashkanasy, & W. J. Zerbe (Eds.) *Research on Emotion in Organizations, Volume 3: Functionality, Intentionality, and Morality* (pp. 265–285). Oxford: Elsevier.

Woodward, V. M. (1997). Professional caring: A contradiction in terms? *Journal of Advanced Nursing, 26,* 999–1004.

Zajonc, R. B. (1984). On the primacy of affect. *American Psychologist, 39*(2), 117–123.

Zapf, D. (2002). Emotion work and psychological well-being: A review of the literature and some conceptual considerations. *Human Resource Management Review, 12,* 237–268.

Zapf, D., & Holz, M. (2006). On the positive and negative effects of emotion work in organizations. *European Journal of Work and Organizational Psychology, 15*(1), 1–28.

PART IV

# Contextual Perspectives: Organization, Gender, Culture

# 9

# *Emotional Labor*

## Organization-level Influences, Strategies, and Outcomes

S. DOUGLAS PUGH • JAMES M. DIEFENDORFF •
CHRISTINA M. MORAN

Make eye contact and smile . . . Looking a Guest in the eye and smiling is
a positive interaction; Smile! We are famous for our courtesy and friendliness; Display appropriate body language . . . Don't lean. Smile and look
happy . . . Don't be preoccupied . . . Have a pleasant look on your face;
Thank every guest . . . Do it with sincerity and a smile.
(blog.leecockrell.com; retrieved May 15, 2011).

The quote above comes from Disney service guidelines which are taught
to every cast member. As stated, the emotions displayed by "cast members" (i.e., service employees) at work are a significant organizational
concern. In another example, from California's Memorial Medical Center,
standards of behavior emphasize, among other things, using "eye contact
and body language that displays respect" (Memorial Medical Center,
2008). Organizational expectations for the emotions displayed by
employees are a strategic business maneuver – Disney's friendly, smiling
employees are arguably *the* element that differentiates Disney from other
organizations. Given the market gains that are available to organizations
that are perceived to provide exceptional service (e.g., Heskett, Sasser, &
Schlesinger, 1997), it is no surprise that organizations have been known

to recruit, select, and train employees to achieve this goal, as well as to develop cultures that emphasize a particular type of displayed emotions (Hochschild, 1983; Van Mannen & Kunda, 1989).

The term *emotional labor* derives from the seminal work of Hochschild (1983), who described a type of work demand imposed on employees in service-based occupations. This form of labor requires the management of feelings and emotional displays as a means by which broader organizational objectives (e.g., to gain a competitive advantage, increase market share) could be attained. Hochschild (1983) described these emotional demands as an *occupational* requirement, occurring most often in jobs with a significant amount of face-to-face or voice-to-voice contact between employees and customers. Soon thereafter, Rafaeli and Sutton's (1987) work placed greater emphasis on role expectations prescribed by the *organization* as the source of emotional work demands. Both of these early emotional labor pieces discussed the role of organizational practices, such as selection, socialization, training, and performance management, in shaping employee emotional displays. Thus, since the beginning of emotional labor research, scholars have observed that (a) organizations place demands for particular displays of emotion on employees, (b) organizations differ in the nature and execution of these demands, and (c) organizations utilize both formal human resource management practices and informal expectations (e.g., norms, climate, culture) to better ensure that organizational members can and will show the expected emotions (e.g., Ashforth & Humphrey, 1993; Rafaeli & Sutton, 1987; Van Maanen & Kunda, 1989).

However, in the years that followed these early works, much of the focus of emotional labor research has been at the individual or dyadic levels of analysis and emphasized psychological and social processes. As a result, relatively little is known about how factors at higher levels of analysis (e.g., unit, department, organization) relate to emotional labor processes. The focus of this chapter is on the formal and informal organizational-level factors that shape and direct emotional labor processes. We contend that emotional display rules represent the point at which organizational objectives, policies, and practices interface with individual emotion management. In particular, we argue that organizational policies and practices are geared toward communicating, fostering commitment to, and enhancing capabilities in meeting the display rules of the job. Once perceived and adopted by employees, display rules then guide subsequent emotional displays and emotion regulation. Thus, individual emotional labor occurs in response to display rules that are implicitly or explicitly communicated by organizational norms, policies, and practices.

We note at the start of this chapter that we approach the issue of emotional labor through a lens of understanding how organizational practices (e.g. recruitment, selection) are used to shape employee emotional labor processes and outcomes in a manner that contributes to organizational effectiveness. We acknowledge, however, that a broader question, beyond the scope of this chapter but relevant at many points along the way, is whether organizations should be engaging in these practices at all. Hochschild's (1983) original work raised many concerns about the effects on employees when emotions are commoditized and sold for a wage, and a significant body of scholarship has continued to raise concerns about the effects of emotional labor on employee identity and well-being. Mumby and Putnam (1992), for example, describe emotional labor as a process that controls the heart, welds individuals to managerial interests, and in so doing "alienates and fragments the individual" (p. 472). The primary concern voiced in this research is that emotional labor creates dilemmas of identity and authenticity in workers (Erickson & Ritter, 2001; Leidner, 1993; Tracey, 2005). Other work has raised concerns that explicit demands for displayed emotions can decrease the intrinsic motivation of workers (Diefendorff & Gosserand, 2003). Overall, it is clear that certain types of emotional labor can have negative effects on employee well being (Hülsheger & Schewe, 2011). It is also clear, however, that the management of emotion, facilitated by organizational practices, also can bring benefits to employees (Leidner, 1993). Wharton (2009) concludes that it is not the emotional demands of work that are harmful per se, but rather it is the employee response to those demands that determine the psychological consequences of emotional labor. As we describe organizational practices that evoke and shape how employees engage in emotional labor, readers should consider the possibility of the detrimental *and* beneficial effects of these practices as avenues for future theory development and empirical research.

The chapter unfolds as follows. We first review research on emotional display rules, taking the view that these expectations are shaped, in part, by higher-level processes in organizations. Next, we turn to organization-level factors aimed at managing employee emotional displays so that they conform to display rules, including factors based in informal norms and processes (e.g., culture, climate) as well as formal human resource management practices (e.g., selection, training, performance management). Acknowledging a relative dearth of systematic research on this topic, we frame this section as a brief overview of extant work and propose an agenda for future research. The chapter concludes with a discussion of future directions and conceptual challenges for doing work in this area.

## EMOTIONAL DISPLAY RULES

In describing the emotional requirements of service work, Hochschild (1983) argued that employees engaged in emotional labor abide by "feeling rules" (p. 18) to know what emotions are "owed" in interactions. Rafaeli and Sutton (1989) adopted the term "display rules," which they preferred because it emphasized emotional expressions which are more amenable to organizational monitoring and control. Research shows that display rules matter: they relate to subsequent emotion regulation strategies, emotional displays, well-being outcomes, and job attitudes (Diefendorff & Richard, 2003; Gosserand & Diefendorff, 2005)

Emotional labor research has often treated display rules as attributes of specific occupations, with empirical research assuming that a given display rule applies to all members of an occupational sample under consideration (e.g., cashiers, Rafaeli, 1989; funeral directors, Smith et al., 2009; physicians, Smith & Kleinman, 1989). However, other research has argued that display rules may vary on a continuum across jobs within an occupation (e.g., Wilk & Moynihan, 2005) and across units within an organization (e.g., Diefendorff, Erickson, Grandey, & Dahling, 2011). This work conceptualizes display rules as norms or standards for appropriate expression on the job (Ashforth & Humphrey, 1993; Rafaeli & Sutton, 1987). The etiology of display rules as norms or job requirements suggests that they emanate from and have a foundation in macro-level structures. Understanding the sources and effects of higher level display rules is important to link macro- and micro-level processes in emotional labor research.

Alluding to macro-level factors that might impact emotional labor, Diefendorff and Richard (2003) found that job features (i.e., the amount of interpersonal demand in the job), social information (i.e., supervisor ratings of the emotional display rules expected of their employees), and employee personality all uniquely predicted employees' emotional display rule perceptions. These results suggest that the content of work and expectations of supervisors, both of which may derive from higher-level organizational factors, contribute to employee display rule perceptions beyond the influence of individual traits. Wilk and Moynihan (2005) found that supervisor expectations were more important for predicting emotion work than was one's job or level in the organization. Both studies thus show that managers, as a higher-level source of role expectations, can impact emotional labor processes. Similarly, Diefendorff, Richard, and Croyle (2006) found that the vast majority of employees in their sample considered the expression of positive emotions and suppression of negative emotions to be formally required in their jobs, that supervisors agreed with this assessment, and that these beliefs were predicted by their occupation's "contact with others" rating in the Occupational Information Network (O*NET; National Center for O*NET Development, 2011). Although it is established that display rules may be conceptualized as job, group, organizational, or occupational norms or standards (Becker & Cropanzano, under review), display rules are typically measured at the employee-level as individual perceptions. Employee perceptions of emotional demands are surely important, as these will likely predict individual employee behavior more proximally (e.g., Diefendorff et al., 2011), however, there is a need to better link theory and measurement by assessing display rules as an aggregate (e.g., group, team, organization) construct. In one of the only studies to use this approach, Diefendorff et al. (2011) found that nurses within units shared perceptions of display rule requirements and that these unit-level display rules influenced individual-level emotion regulation and well-being. It is surprising that Diefendorff et al. (2011) is the only study we are aware of to assess display rules at the unit level given that (a) theory clearly specifies display rules as norms that exist at a level above the individual (e.g., group, organization, or occupation; Rafaeli & Sutton, 1989) and (b) aggregation and analysis at the group/unit level is common in related areas such as service climate (e.g., Schneider & Bowen, 1985). Although significant qualitative work addresses display rules as organization-level norms (e.g., Van Maanen & Kunda, 1989), there is a need for quantitative research to examine antecedents and consequences of shared display norms in organizations.

We now turn our attention to macro-level factors aimed at encouraging people to conform to display rules. Sometimes these organizational influences are deliberate, top-down, and explicit (i.e., formal human resource management practices), but they can also be less intentional, bottom-up, and implicit (i.e., informal socialization, culture, or norms).

## FORMAL ORGANIZATIONAL PRACTICES: HUMAN RESOURCE MANAGEMENT

Formal, explicit organizational practices aimed at shaping employee emotional displays may fall under the general topic of *human resource management* (HRM). HRM practices are typically designed to give organizations a competitive advantage through the employment, management, and development of a capable and committed workforce (Storey, 1995). HRM practices generally include recruitment, selection, training, performance management, and compensation, among others. Rafaeli and Sutton (1987), for example, identify recruitment, selection, socialization, rewards, and punishments as features of the organizational context from which role expectations are derived (see also Ashforth & Humphrey,

1993; Hochschild, 1983). Van Maanen and Kunda (1989) describe top management as affecting the work culture by recruiting employees with homogenous backgrounds, putting them through intensive socialization, and monitoring adherence to corporate values, norms, and practices (e.g., through direct supervision of appropriate emotional displays). Accordingly, HRM practices are referred to as *cultural control* in the service management literature (Bowen & Schneider, 1988). We review how specific HRM practices can be used to impact emotional labor processes.

## Job Analysis

The starting point of all HRM practices is job analysis (Prien, Goodstein, Goodstein, & Gamble, 2009). Job analysis is a systematic attempt at (a) describing the major work behaviors and tasks performed by someone in a given job, (b) identifying the knowledge, skills, and abilities necessary to perform the job successfully, and (c) determining the minimum qualifications a person would need to perform the job (Sackett & Laczo, 2003). Arvey et al. (1998) suggested the utility of using job analysis to determine the emotional demands of a position. Steinberg and Figart (1999) are the only known authors who have published a job analysis specifically focused on emotional labor; interestingly, they found that the emotional labor required by nurses and police officers was similar, despite the apparent differences in work tasks. Other work also speaks to the utility of conducting emotion-focused job analyses; for example, Basch and Fisher (2000) developed an event-by-emotion matrix and found that specific types of events tended to correspond with certain types of emotional content. This finding suggests that understanding the frequency and importance of certain work activities may be useful for inferring the emotional demands of a particular position.

Although the discussion above might suggest the need to design new job analysis instruments to gauge the emotional demands of jobs, examination of many popular job analysis tools suggests that they already tap some of the emotional attributes of work, albeit in relatively coarse ways. For instance, the Functional Job Analysis (Fine & Wiley, 1971) includes a "people" dimension, which assesses the extent to which employees are required to use interpersonal resources (e.g., understanding, courtesy, mentoring) on the job. The Position Analysis Questionnaire (PAQ; McCormick, Jeanneret, & Mecham, 1972) includes items assessing interpersonal activities on the job and the extent to which employees may encounter frustrating situations, strained personal contacts, interpersonal conflict, and non-job-required social contact (e.g., socializing and small talk). Wilk and Moynihan (2005) used the interpersonal interaction items of the PAQ (along with some new items) to assess how important managers considered the interpersonal parts of their employees' jobs and found that this rating uniquely predicted employee emotional exhaustion. In addition, the aforementioned O*NET on-line database, which is based on job analysis evidence, has been used to operationalize the emotional and interpersonal requirements of jobs (e.g., Diefendorff et al., 2006; Glomb, Kammeyer-Mueller, & Rotundo, 2004). Overall, the evidence suggests that job analysis has utility for identifying the emotional labor requirements of jobs.

## Recruitment and Selection

Recruitment is the process of attracting qualified applicants (Barber, 1998), and selection is a set of procedures aiding the decision of whether to hire or exclude applicants from further consideration for a position (Gatewood, Feild, & Barrick, 2011). Several authors have argued for the importance of selecting employees based on their potential ability to meet emotional job demands (Arvey et al., 1998; Grandey & Brauburger, 2002; Morris & Feldman, 1997), and many studies have provided examples of organizations that claim to recruit for emotional competencies. For example, McDonald's managers are urged to hire counter employees who have a sense of humor and are sincere, enthusiastic, and confident (Rafaeli & Sutton, 1987), and Hochschild (1983) described how recruiters observed informal interactions among potential flight attendants to assess their ability to engage in animated, spontaneous conversations. A selection system for call center representatives involved assessments of personality, communication skills, and to a lesser extent, technical skills (e.g., computer skills; Callaghan & Thompson, 2002). As one manager stated: ". . . we recruit attitude. You can tell by talking to someone during an interview whether they smile, whether their eyes smile" (Callaghan & Thompson, 2002, p. 240); further examination revealed that "attitude" was analogous to communication skills, operationalized by vocal qualities such as tone, pitch, warmth, and energy.

Another way in which emotional aspects of job performance may be considered in selection systems is by taking the degree of person–job fit into account. Building on the work of Arvey et al. (1998), who argued that it may be possible to achieve person–job fit on emotional aspects of work, Greguras and Diefendorff (2009) recently demonstrated that the perceived fit between a job's emotional demands and an employee's emotional abilities is distinct from a variety of other fit perceptions (including the more general demands–abilities fit) and that it incrementally predicted a variety of outcomes, including job satisfaction, performance, and burnout. Also, Bono and Vey (2007) examined congruence between personality and emotional demands in an experimental setting, finding more support for the value of demands–personality congruence effects for extraversion than neuroticism.

As previously noted, organizations must rely on job analysis evidence to understand the emotional demands of the work and link these demands to corresponding traits. Given the vast array of possible emotional demands, the potential list of traits is quite long. But assuming that such an analysis identifies "service with a smile" as a central component of the job, a variety of personal attributes in the extant industrial/organizational psychology literature that have been linked to emotional displays and emotional labor may be used to identify qualified applicants. Examples include personality traits (e.g., Big Five, dispositional affectivity, emotional expressivity, self-monitoring; Gosserand & Diefendorff, 2005; Diefendorff, Croyle, & Gosserand, 2005) and emotional intelligence (Joseph & Newman, 2010). The main idea behind incorporating measures of emotional experience or expressivity into selection for emotional labor jobs is that individuals who tend to naturally feel the emotions required by the job or are more skilled at managing their emotions will be able to more easily engage in emotional labor and, as a result, they will experience fewer negative outcomes (Hülsheger & Schewe, 2011).

Customer orientation is another promising individual difference construct that may be relevant to selection. Some authors (e.g., Hogan, Hogan, & Busch, 1984) have conceptualized customer orientation as an amalgamation of traits such as sociability, likeability, and social skills, which overlap with Big Five traits such as agreeableness and extraversion. Other researchers (e.g., Donavan, Brown, & Mowen, 2004; Saxe & Weitz, 1982) define the construct more generally as an individual difference in the value that employees place on delivering high quality service. Recent research suggests that employees with a strong customer orientation are more likely to have intrinsic motivation congruent with organizational goals for high quality service (Allen, Pugh, Grandey & Groth, 2010) and that organizations can realize financial gains when they select employees with a strong customer orientation (Grizzle et al., 2009).

It is beyond the scope of this chapter to explore in depth the myriad individual differences that one could use to select for jobs with high emotional demands, and Dahling and Johnson (2013) provide an excellent discussion of individual differences relevant to emotional labor. However, our discussion highlights the following points. First, there is a great deal of evidence that organizations recruit and select individuals based on emotional competencies (see Thoits, 2004, for a discussion of the related notion of "emotional capital"). Second, there is a growing body of evidence that certain individual differences such as customer orientation are likely to predict the ability to successfully conform to display rules. Third, more research on emotional demands–abilities fit is needed to help determine the usefulness of this concept for predicting attitudinal and performance outcomes in a selection context. The fit perspective assumes that the match between emotional demands and abilities is the key determinant of success, such that differing levels of emotional "abilities" are best for different jobs Another possibility is that there are main effects for traits such as extraversion or customer orientation across all jobs requiring emotional labor (see Bono & Vey, 2007). Recall that the one job analysis specifically focused on emotional labor (Steinberg & Figart, 1999) found similar emotional demands for the very different jobs of police officers and nurses. If so, it may be that individual traits (or emotional capital; Thoits, 2004) generally predict performance across all jobs with some level of emotional demands.

## Training

Training can be defined as planned efforts by an organization to produce employee learning of knowledge, skills, abilities, and other characteristics (KSAOs) relevant to one's job (Noe, 2009). Interpersonal skills training – which may include emotional skills – is a staple in customer service jobs, and research suggests that many interpersonally-oriented behaviors require active practice and can be best learned through activities such as role playing and behavioral modeling (Taylor, Russ-Eft, & Chan, 2005). Further, there is an increased emphasis in the field on training emotional competencies specifically (Kunnanatt, 2004) based on the belief that individuals can learn to better manage interpersonal behaviors by managing their own and others' emotions more effectively.

In the emotional labor literature, much of the discussion of training in emotional labor contexts focuses on teaching emotion regulation strategies with an emphasis on *deep acting* (i.e., changing one's feelings regarding an interaction so that emotional expressions then naturally fall in line with expectations) over *surface acting* (i.e., changing one's expression only, such as pasting on a smile; Grandey, 2000; Hochschild, 1983). This emphasis may be based on the well-documented links of surface acting with a variety of negative outcomes (e.g., burnout, emotional exhaustion, low job satisfaction, poor customer evaluations) and the less documented, though often endorsed, view that deep acting provides a variety of benefits (Hülsheger & Schewe, 2011). Evidence does indicate that employees can be trained to influence their emotions through deep acting. Richard (2006) developed a training program focused on teaching employees to change their felt emotions to correspond with those desired by the organizations through reappraisal; and the experimental intervention produced an increase in high pleasure, low arousal emotions and a decrease in feelings of inauthenticity and depersonalization. Similar results were found by Totterdell and Parkinson (1999), and Hochschild's (1983) original work documented the value placed on deep acting in training by Delta Airlines.

There are many examples of training programs, however, that focus simply on changing emotional expressions rather than felt emotions. For example, Leidner (1993, p. 109) describes a training program for insurance agents focused on proper delivery of a joke to be included in every life insurance sales presentation. The training manual states: "A slight chuckle should be started and built up to a crescendo as you deliver the punch line [. . .] continuously laughing with several 'Ha-Ha's'" (Leidner, 1993, p. 112). Although felt emotions also were part of the training (the importance of positive attitude and optimism was highly stressed), much of the focus was on the proper display of emotion in the sales interaction. Even more extreme examples include training focusing only on the smile itself. At Japan's Keihin Electric Express Railway, employees must use "smile scan" cameras daily prior to their shifts. Using technology originally developed to identify smiles in digital photography, workers smile for a camera, and their smile is scored. Computer feedback for sub-par smiles offers suggestions on how to improve the appearance of the smile (Demetriou, 2009).

Although the smile scan example is extreme, it highlights the very different approaches of training programs focused on changing feelings versus those focused only on changing expressed emotion. Two potential research questions flow from these differences. First, how do employees react to training programs designed to influence their displayed emotions? Second, does an emphasis on surface versus deep acting change those reactions? There has been little research on reactions to either type of emotional labor training. In an unpublished Master's thesis, Grabarek (2011) found respondents had similar positive reactions to being offered emotional labor training (i.e., deep acting) versus training focused on other job skills. [1] However, there is some evidence that employees do not always see the value in training deep acting: Hochschild (1983) reported that some flight attendants viewed it as a waste of time, although a majority did perceive some benefits. Callaghan and Thompson (2002) reported that call center management emphasized training for deep acting and the expression of genuine emotion, but the authors found little evidence of deep acting among employees. Given an emphasis on call quantity, more employees engaged in surface acting, and employees place the greatest importance on the competencies of patience, tolerance and stamina. While one could argue that training in deep acting is preferable, given the negative effects of surface acting (Hülsheger & Schewe, 2011), an equally plausible argument is that surface acting training is more job-related and thus less personally intrusive than deep acting (Hochschild,

1983). Exploring reactions to emotional labor (EL) training is an area ripe for further study.

## *Performance Management and Monitoring*

Performance management refers to activities such as setting performance objectives, monitoring performance relative to those objectives, giving feedback aimed at ensuring that future performance is aligned with objectives, and providing rewards/punishments so as to reinforce desirable behaviors and discourage undesirable behaviors (den Hartog, Boselie, & Paauwe, 2004). These systems, as a whole, serve as a means by which the organization can exert top-down control over an individual's work. Often emotional display rules are communicated implicitly through high performance expectations in service contexts (Zapf, 2002); however, in many cases the monitoring of emotional displays is quite explicit (e.g., Leidner, 1993). Technological advancements are further aiding managers in monitoring the emotional content of service interactions, as revealed in research on call centers (van Jaarsveld & Poster, 2013). In call centers, technology now allows for the close monitoring of technical performance and the recording of agent phone calls, which can be scored for emotional performance criteria such as "friendliness" (Winiecki & Wigman, 2007). Moving beyond a subjective evaluation of emotional performance such as "friendliness," Poster (2011) describes interaction analytics software that can listen to and analyze the conversations of employees and customers. This software includes an "emotion detection" feature that uses wave frequencies of the human voice and specific words in conversations (e.g., angry, frustrated) to detect emotional content (Poster, 2011, p. 16).

Though the above discussion highlights potential avenues for organizations to manage their employees' displays on the job, there is debate as to whether monitoring should be viewed as beneficial or not. Some authors have argued that performance monitoring provides a more accurate portrait of employee performance (Grant & Higgins, 1989); however, many opponents view monitoring as a threat to autonomy and intrinsic motivation in the workplace (Alder, 1998). To date, work aimed at clarifying the impact of emotional labor monitoring has produced mixed results. Holman, Chissick, and Totterdell (2002) found that monitoring to assess performance and monitoring for developmental purposes both showed positive associations with indicators of well being, whereas the perceived intensity of monitoring (i.e., the monitoring is pervasive and cannot be escaped) was negatively related to well being. Thus, the mere presence of structures intended to monitor employees does not appear to be inherently detrimental, and indeed may be desired by employees as one way to provide feedback on performance (Callaghan & Thompson,

2002). However, as monitoring becomes more intense employees may suffer psychologically (e.g., Holman et al., 2002).

Rewards and compensation are part of the performance management process and have been implicated in emotional labor since the initial work of Hochschild (1983) who stated that emotions are "sold for a wage" (p. 7). Diefendorff and Croyle (2008) found that the degree to which employees perceived organizational rewards for positive emotional displays predicted employee motivation and commitment to displaying organizationally-desired emotions to customers. Grandey (2007) also has argued that financial rewards for emotional performance buffers employees from the strain of emotional labor, and initial lab and field results appear to support this argument (Grandey, Chi & Diamond, under review). These results may seem to contradict Hochschild's arguments that the negative effects of emotional labor stem from the fact that emotions are compensated. Yet, surprisingly little research has examined whether paying people for emotional labor is detrimental, beneficial, or neither. This is clearly an important area for future research, as emotional labor has been shown to lead to financial gains for employees (e.g., tips; Chi, Grandey, Diamond, & Krimmel, 2011). Research on monitoring and compensating emotional labor should focus on potential mediators. That is, does financially rewarding emotional labor emphasize its value to the organization, leading to feelings of competence and self-efficacy? Does monitoring accomplish the same? If so, emotional labor could have a positive effect on employee confidence and thereby buffer employees from the negative effects of expressing emotions not felt (e.g., Pugh et al., 2011).

## THE INFORMAL ORGANIZATION

In this section, we briefly discuss how socialization and organizational climate affect the emotional labor process. We refer to these influences as "informal" to contrast them with the explicit, formal, top-down policies discussed in the prior section. Though we acknowledge that socialization tactics and facets of organizational climate can be explicitly planned and directed by top-down processes, they are considered separately from formal human resource systems because often they are considered to be emergent and bottom-up (e.g., norms for emotional expression that arise through informal peer socialization).

### *Socialization*

Socialization is the process by which newcomers transition from organizational outsiders to insiders through acquisition of the attitudes, behaviors, beliefs, skills, and knowledge needed to be a functioning member of the organization (Van Maanen & Schein, 1979). Socialization may be deliberate, strategic, and orchestrated by management; it also may be shaped by emergent, bottom-up processes grounded in informal norms, work group histories, and the particular characteristics of organizational members. Several classic studies emphasize the importance of socializing emotions. Cahill's (1999) ethnography of mortuary science students revealed that their socialization into the profession helped to neutralize the negative emotional implications of their work. A similar effect is found in Smith and Kleinman's (1989) examination of medical school students. Developing appropriately controlled affect and displays of affective neutrality was seen as an important indicator of socialization into the medical profession; though courses did not address affective displays explicitly and faculty members did not discuss them with students, such lessons were described as part of the "hidden curriculum" (p. 57).

In other settings, talk about appropriate emotions to feel and display is more explicit. Taylor (2010) describes how emotion rules for animal shelter workers emerge from conversations among the workers. In this setting, the socialization is emergent; it is not driven by management goals but by worker's own understanding of the emotions required for individual employee and organizational functioning. Through discussions of "war stories," newcomers learn that feeling anger (particularly towards irresponsible pet owners and euthanasia) is expected in a shelter environment: they learn "it is not only acceptable to become upset about euthanasia, but that it is a *requirement*" (Taylor, 2010, p. 91; emphasis in original). Similar norms are found in veterinary hospitals (Sanders, 2010, p. 256). In organizations where the emotional style of the service delivery is a crucial and distinctive attribute, display rules are socialized by management in a very explicit manner. Sutton's (1991) study of bill collectors provides a classic example. From the moment the bill collectors he studied were hired, they were socialized to express urgency and slight irritation when on the phone with debtors. Norms for emotional displays were both explicitly trained in the classroom, reinforced by experienced collectors who coached newcomers, and socialized by observing coworkers. Disney provides a similar example with the goal of positive emotional displays (Van Maanen & Kunda, 1989). These examples show both top-down, strategic processes (Sutton, 1991) and bottom-up, informal ones (Taylor, 2010). Ultimately, both can result in effective socialization, leading to shared norms and value among employees, which serve as the building blocks for organizational climate, discussed below.

## Organizational Climate and Culture

At the organizational level of analysis, the main framework for examining organizational service performance is exemplified in the body of literature on service climate (e.g., Dietz, Pugh, & Wiley, 2004; Schneider & Bowen, 1985). Despite the considerable attention given to emotions in service encounters, this literature rarely mentions emotions explicitly; however, the importance of proper emotional displays may be inferred in these studies, which typically focus on the links between employee attitudes and customer satisfaction. Climate, as a general construct, refers to shared perceptions of what employees perceive is important in their organization (Schneider & Bowen, 1985). Culture is a highly related but more abstract construct, focused on values and meaning underlying climate (Kuenzi & Schminke, 2009). Most contemporary climate research adopts a strategic approach, that is, a climate for some particular element of the workplace (Kuenzi & Schminke, 2009). Thus, service climate is defined as "employee perceptions of the practices, procedures, and behaviors that get rewarded, supported, and expected with regard to customer service" (Schneider, White, & Paul, 1998, p. 151). When excellent service is an important theme in an organization, a positive service climate exists, and customers report receiving higher quality service (Dietz et al., 2004). A broad conclusion from the service climate literature is that positive service climates are created by organizations that utilize management and human resource practices (e.g., recruitment, selection, training, socialization, and performance monitoring; Rogg et al., 2001) that stress customer service quality and facilitate the delivery of service.

Clearly, a missing link in the research literature is work that fully integrates service climate with emotional labor. A few recent studies have moved in that direction. In the first study to explicitly integrate service climate and emotional displays, Lam, Huang, and Janssen (2010) found that service climate was positively associated with the display of positive emotion, and further, a positive service climate appears to buffer employees from the negative effects of both supervisor and employee emotional exhaustion. Grandey, Foo, Groth, and Goodwin (2012) also found that climate (in this case, a climate for authenticity among coworkers) buffers against the strain of emotional labor with patients. Drach-Zahavy (2010) found that when delivering good service (which included elements of emotional labor) in an organization with a positive service climate, there were positive effects on employee well-being, whereas delivering good service in a negative service climate had negative effects on well-being. Thus, it seems that climate has the potential to impact the emotional labor process at various points, as main and moderated effects. Future research could help clarify what specific elements of climate are responsible for creating such effects and whether climate impacts other aspects of the emotional labor process.

## Summary

In sum, in describing informal organizational influences on emotional labor, we have made the points that (a) socialization teaches newcomers the appropriate norms for felt and displayed emotions, (b) organizations develop a climate for service based on their perceptions of what management rewards, supports, and expects, and (c) although emotion is largely absent from the service climate literature, it is clear that when employees are learning norms for customer service, prescriptions for felt and displayed emotions are likely included. An obvious suggestion is that these literatures merit greater integration; a practical barrier to actually doing this research is that most service climate studies originate from data collected for large-scale organizational survey efforts, and typically measures of felt or displayed emotion are not part of this work. Yet, data to accomplish such a study may already exist, and we offer a specific suggestion for a study that could be (but to our knowledge has not been) done. As noted above (and see van Jaarslveld & Poster, 2013), service agent phone calls frequently are recorded and expressed emotion in the vocal tones and words of employees can be coded. If emotions can be conceptualized at the unit level, then across organizational units (e.g., different call centers of one organization), one should see (a) within-unit similarity in expressed emotions and (b) between-unit variance in expressed emotions (cf., Chan, 1998). These indicators could then be linked to employee assessments of service climate, and customer ratings of satisfaction or service quality. Similar approaches could be taken using other metrics commonly used to evaluate service at the unit level such as secret shopper reports or customer satisfaction data, provided these data assess elements that plausibly capture emotions (e.g., employee friendliness).

## CONCLUSIONS

In this chapter we have discussed organization-level influences on emotional labor: display rules or norms for expressed emotion; practices of job analysis, recruitment, selection, training, performance monitoring, and rewards, all of which facilitate and encourage adherence to display rules; and informal employee socialization and climate which help to communicate and perpetuate shared beliefs for what constitutes appropriate service behaviors. Although these processes were discussed somewhat in isolation, we expect that they interrelate and probably combine in bundles of practices aimed at producing particular employee emotional displays (e.g., Combs, Liu, Hall, & Ketchen, 2006). For example, high involvement human resource (HIHR) systems (including selective hiring, investment in initial training, job design allowing for individual discretion and learning, and ongoing investments in employees) have been linked to quit rates, sales, and customer satisfaction (Batt, 2002; Batt & Colvin, 2011). These practices are important in service organizations, argues Batt (2002), because they lead to the development of firm-specific human capital (e.g., product knowledge, knowledge of customer demands and preferences, and knowledge of the organization's internal systems).

It is interesting that Batt's work focused on how firm-specific capital facilitates the technical and cognitive aspects of service delivery (e.g., product knowledge), but does not mention emotional capital, which also drives customer satisfaction (Pugh, 2001). Thoits (2004) describes the construct of emotional capital as the knowledge of emotional culture, skill at managing one's own and others' emotions, and the ability to take on social emotions such as shame, guilt, embarrassment, and pride (p. 371). Thus, a fruitful next step in this area of research may be to apply these ideas toward the development of HIHR systems that develop emotion-based firm-specific capital. The literature on organizational service climate may also provide a basis for understanding how foundation issues (contextual issues that sustain work behavior, such as training and investments of resources) and service climate work together as a system to drive employee service behaviors and customer satisfaction (Schneider, White & Paul, 1998).

We have raised issues in this chapter that suggest we have much to learn about how organizational practices affect emotional labor, and as such, it may be useful to test some of the basic assumptions underlying the idea that emotional labor-related HR practices form a coherent system. The following questions come to mind:

- Do job analyses reveal unique emotional demands across jobs, such that selection and training must be tailored to unique job demands?
- Should training in emotional labor focus on deep acting, surface acting, or something else?
- Do financial incentives for emotional labor buffer its negative effects, or is pay for emotions a source of strain?
- Do unit-level, aggregated measures of organizational displayed emotion explain variance in organizational outcomes such as customer satisfaction, in a manner similar to what has been found in the service climate literature?

We are particularly intrigued by the training and financial incentives questions, as we suspect that both could influence feelings of autonomy (c.f. Grandy, Fisk, & Steiner, 2005), intrinsic motivation (Gosserand & Diefendorff, 2005) and the self concept (Pugh et al., 2011), but the question of how they affect these variables is not entirely clear.

In conclusion, the questions we raise here walk the line between organizational- and individual-level phenomena. HRM policies may originate at the organization level but they affect individuals. As such, investigating these issues requires a multilevel focus on emotional labor processes with individuals nested within organizations or other higher level structures (e.g., teams, units, stores, departments). For instance, unit-level or store-level data on the HRM policies and practices (e.g., availability of emotional labor training) could be obtained from supervisors and used to predict person-level emotional labor constructs (e.g., emotional display rule perceptions, emotion regulation) or moderate the links among emotional labor constructs (e.g., the strength of the display rule and emotion regulation relationship). Further complicating matters is the fact that the level of analysis, for much of what is predicted to occur in emotional labor, is at the event-level and involves interactions between employees and customers. This idea suggests the possibility of developing 3-level models (event-level interactions nested within persons and persons nested within stores/units) with data coming from multiple sources (employees, customers, managers). Although collecting such data presents challenges, it may yield great benefits in trying to understand the links of macro-level organizational policies, practices, and norms with employee emotional labor processes and customer satisfaction.

## ENDNOTES

1 Note, however, that this was a laboratory study using vignettes; one would suspect that in a field setting with actual employees, training emotional labor may have personal consequences. Further, Grabarek's study examined only training for deep acting; might a comparison with surface acting training have produced different results?

## REFERENCES

Alder, G.S. (1998). Ethical issues in electronic performance monitoring: A consideration of deontological and teleological perspectives. *Journal of Business Ethics*, 17(7), 729–743.

Allen, J.A., Pugh, S. D., Grandey, A., & Groth, M. (2010). Following display rules in good or bad faith?: Customer orientation as a moderator of the display rule–emotional labor relationship. *Human Performance*, 23, 101–115.

Arvey, R. D., Renz, G. L., & Watson, T. W. (1998). Emotionality and job performance: Implications for personnel selection. In G. R. Ferris (Ed.), *Research in personnel and human resources management (vol. 16)* (pp. 103–147). Greenwich, CT: JAI Press Inc.

Ashforth, B. E., & Humphrey, R. H. (1993). Emotional labor in service roles: The influence of identity. *Academy of Management Review, 18(1)*, 88–115.

Barber, A. E. (1998). *Recruiting employees: Individual and organization perspectives.* Thousand Oaks, CA: Sage Publications.

Basch, J., & Fisher, C. D. (2000). Affective events–emotions matrix: A classification of work events and associated emotions. In N. M. Ashkanasy, C. E. Hartel, & W. J. Zerbe (Eds.), *Emotions in the workplace: Research, theory, and practice* (pp. 36–48). Westport, CT: Quorum Books/Greenwood Publishing Group.

Batt, R. (2002). Managing customer services: Human resource practices, turnover, and sales growth. *Academy of Management Journal, 45(3)*, 587–597.

Batt, R., & Colvin, A. J. S. (2011). An employment systems approach to turnover: Human Resources practices, quits, dismissals. *Academy of Management Journal, 54(4)*, 695–717.

Becker, W. J., & Cropanzano, R. (under review). Taking emotional labor research to the next level: Display rules and emotional labor in work teams.

Bono, J. E., & Vey, M. A. (2005). Toward understanding emotional management at work: A quantitative review of emotional labor research. In C. E. Hartel, W. J. Zerbe, & N. M. Ashkanasy (Eds.), *Emotions in organizational behavior* (pp. 213–233). Mahwah, NJ: Lawrence Erlbaum Associates.

Bono, J. E., & Vey, M. A. (2007). Personality and emotional performance: Extraversion, neuroticism, and self-monitoring. *Journal of occupational health psychology, 12(2)*, 177–92. doi:10.1037/1076-8998.12.2.177

Bowen, D. E., & Schneider, B. (1988). Services marketing and management: Implications for organizational behavior. In B. M. Staw & L. L. Cummings (Eds.), *Research in organizational behavior* (Vol. 10, pp. 43–80). Greenwich, CT: JAI Press Ltd.

Cahill, S. E. (1999). Emotional capital and professional socialization: The case of mortuary science students (and me). *Social Psychology Quarterly, 62(2)*, 101–116.

Callaghan, G., & Thompson, P. (2002). "We recruit attitude": the selection and shaping of routine call centre labour. *Journal of Management Studies, 39(2)*, 233–254.

Chan, D. (1998). Functional relations among constructs in the same content domain at different levels of analysis: A typology of composition models. *Journal of Applied Psychology, 83(2)*, 234–246. doi:10.1037//0021-9010.83.2.234

Chi, N.W., Grandey, A. A., Diamond, J. A, & Krimmel, K. R. (2011). Want a tip? Service performance as a function of emotion regulation and extraversion. *Journal of Applied Psychology, 96(6)*, 1337–1346.

Combs, J., Liu, Y., Hall, A., & Ketchen, D. (2006). How much do high-performance work practices matter? A meta-analysis of their effects on organizational performance. *Personnel Psychology, 59(3)*, 501–528.

Costa, P. T., & McCrae, R. R. (1980). Influence of extraversion and neuroticism on subjective well-being: Happy and unhappy people. *Journal of Personality and Social Psychology, 38(4)*, 668–678.

Dahling, J., & Johnson, H.-A. (2013). Motivation, fit, confidence, and skills: how do individual differences influence emotional labor? In A. A. Grandey, J. M. Diefendorff, & D. Rupp (Eds.), *Emotional labor in the 21st century: Diverse perspectives on emotion regulation at work.* New York: Psychology Press/ Routledge.

Demetriou, D. (2009, July 6). *Workers have daily smile scans.* Retrieved November 11, 2011, from The Telegraph: http://www.telegraph.co.uk/news/world news/asia/japan/5757194/ Workers-have-daily-smile-scans.html

den Hartog, D. N., Boselie, P., & Paauwe, J. (2004). Performance management: A model and research agenda. *Applied Psychology: An International Review, 53(4)*, 556–569.

Diefendorff, J. M., & Croyle, M. H. (2008). Antecedents of emotional display rule commitment. *Human Performance, 21(3)*, 310–332.

Diefendorff, J. M., Croyle, M. H., & Gosserand, R. H. (2005). The dimensionality and antecedents of emotional labor strategies. *Journal of Vocational Behavior, 66(2)*, 339–359.

Diefendorff, J. M., Erickson, R. J., Grandey, A. A., & Dahling, J. J. (2011). Emotional display rules as work unit norms: A multilevel analysis of emotional labor among nurses. *Journal of Occupational Health Psychology, 16(2)*, 170–186.

Diefendorff, J. M., & Gosserand, R. H. (2003). Understanding the emotional labor process: A control theory perspective. *Journal of Organizational Behavior, 24(8)*, 945–959. doi:10.1002/job.230

Diefendorff, J. M., & Richard, E. M. (2003). Antecedents and consequences of emotional display rule perceptions. *Journal of Applied Psychology, 88*, 284–294.

Diefendorff, J. M., Richard, E. M., & Croyle, M. H. (2006). Are emotional display rules formal job requirements? Examination of employee and supervisor perceptions. *Journal of Occupational and Organizational Psychology, 79(2)*, 273–298.

Dietz, J., Pugh, S. D., & Wiley, J. W. (2004). Service climate effects on customer attitudes: An examination of boundary conditions. *Academy of Management Journal, 47*(1), 81–92.

Donavan, D. T., Brown, T. J., & Mowen, J. C. (2004). Internal benefits of service-worker customer orientation: Job satisfaction, commitment, and organizational citizenship behaviors. *Journal of Marketing, 68(1)*, 128–146.

Drach-Zahavy, A. (2010). How does service workers' behavior affect their health? Service climate as a moderator in the service behavior-health relationships. *Journal of Occupational Health Psychology, 15*(2), 105–119.

Erickson, R. J., & Ritter, C. (2001). Emotional labor, burnout, and inauthenticity: Does gender matter? *Social Psychology Quarterly, 64(2)*, 146. doi:10.2307/ 3090130

Fine, S. A., & Wiley, W. W. (1971). An introduction to functional job analysis: A scaling of selected tasks from the social welfare field. *Methods for Manpower*

*Analysis, No. 4.*, Kalamazoo, MI: The W. E. Upjohn Institute for Employment Research.

Gatewood, R. D., Feild, H. S., & Barrick, M. (2011). *Human resource selection (7th ed.)*. Mason, OH: South-Western.

Glomb, T. M., Kammeyer-Mueller, J. D., & Rotundo, M. (2004). Emotional labor demands and compensating wage differentials. *Journal of Applied Psychology, 89(4)*, 700–714.

Gosserand, R. H., & Diefendorff, J. M. (2005). Emotional display rules and emotional labor: The moderating role of commitment. *Journal of Applied Psychology, 90*, 1256–1264.

Grabarek, P. E. (2011). *Understanding "smile school": Emotional labor training occurrence and consequences*. Unpublished master's thesis; Pennsylvania State University.

Grandey, A. A. (2000). Emotion regulation in the workplace: A new way to conceptualize emotional labor. *Journal of Occupational Health Psychology, 5(1)*, 95–110.

Grandey, A. A. (2007). *Show me the money! Integrating financial rewards into the study of emotional labor*. Academy of Management Annual Meetings. Philadelphia, PA.

Grandey, A., & Brauburger, A. (2002). The emotion regulation behind the customer service smile. In R. Lord, R. Klimoski, & R. Kanfer (Eds.), *Emotions in the workplace: Understanding the structure and role of emotions in organizational behavior* (pp. 260–294). San Francisco: Jossey-Bass.

Grandey, A., Chi, N-W, & Diamond, J. (under review). Service with a $mile: Do Financial Rewards Enhance or Reduce the Satisfaction from Emotional Labor?

Grandey, A. A., Diefendorff, J. M., & Rupp, D. (2013). Emotional labor: Overview of definitions, theories, evidence. In A. A. Grandey, J. M. Diefendorff, & D. Rupp (Eds.), *Emotional labor in the 21st century: Diverse perspectives on emotion regulation at work.*

Grandey, A. A., Fisk, G. M., & Steiner, D. D. (2005). Must "service with a smile" be stressful? The moderating role of personal control for American and French employees. *Journal of Applied Psychology, 90(5)*, 893–904.

Grandey, A. A., Foo, S. C., Groth, M., & Goodwin, R. E. (2012). Free to be you and me: A climate of authenticity alleviates burnout from emotional labor. *Journal of Occupational Health Psychology*. doi:10.1037/a0025102

Grant, R., & Higgins, C. (1989). Monitoring service workers via computer: The effect on employees, productivity, and service. *National Productivity Review, 8*, 101–112.

Greguras, G. J., & Diefendorff, J. M. (2009). Different fits satisfy different needs: Linking Person–environment fit to employee commitment and performance using self-determination theory. *Journal of Applied Psychology, 94(2)*, 465–477.

Grizzle, J. W., Zablah, A. R., Brown, T. J., Mowen, J. C., & Lee, J. M. (2009). Employee customer orientation in context: How the environment moderates the influence of customer orientation on performance outcomes. *Journal of Applied Psychology, 94(5)*, 1227–1242.

Heskett, J. L., Sasser, W. E., & Schlesinger, L. A. (1997). *The service profit chain.* New York: The Free Press.

Hochschild, A. R. (1983). *The managed heart: Commercialization of human feeling.* Berkeley, CA: University of California Press.

Hogan, J., Hogan, R., & Busch, C. M. (1984). How to measure service orientation. *Journal of Applied Psychology, 69(1),* 167–173.

Holman, D., Chissick, C., & Totterdell, P. (2002). The effects of performance monitoring on emotional labor and well-being in call centers. *Motivation and Emotion, 26(1),* 57–81.

Hülsheger, U. R., & Schewe, A. F. (2011). On the costs and benefits of emotional labor: A meta-analysis of three decades of research. *Journal of Occupational Health Psychology, 16(3),* 361–399.

Joseph, D. L., & Newman, D. A. (2010). Emotional intelligence: An integrative meta-analysis and cascading model. *Journal of Applied Psychology, 95(1),* 54–78.

Kuenzi, M., & Schminke, M. (2009). A fragmented literature? A review, critique, and proposed research agenda of the work climate literature. *Journal of Management, 35,* 634–717.

Kunnanatt, J. T. (2004). Emotional intelligence: The new science of interpersonal effectiveness. *Human Resource Development Quarterly, 15(4),* 489–495.

Lam, C. K., Huang, X., & Janssen, O. (2010). Contextualizing emotional exhaustion and positive emotional display: The signaling effects of supervisors' emotional exhaustion and service climate. *Journal of Applied Psychology, 95(2),* 368–376.

Leidner, R. (1993). *Fast food fast talk: service work and the routinization of everyday life.* Berkeley: University of California Press.

McCormick, E. J., Jeanneret, P. R., & Mecham, R. C. (1972). A study of job characteristics and job dimensions based on the position analysis questionnaire (PAQ). *Journal of Applied Psychology, 56,* 347–368.

Memorial Medical Center. (2008). *Standards of Behavior.* Retrieved June 30, 2011, from Memorial Medical Center: http://www.memorialmedicalcenter.org/jobs/standards.html

Morris, J. A., & Feldman, D. C. (1997). Managing emotions in the workplace. *Journal of Managerial Issues, 9,* 257–274.

Mumby, D. K., & Putnam, L. L. (1992). The politics of emotion: A feminist reading of bounded rationality. *Academy of Management Review, 17*(3), 465–486.

National Center for O*NET Development. (2011). *O*NET OnLine.* Retrieved July 2, 2011, from O*NET OnLine: http://www.onetonline.org

Noe, R. A. (2009). *Employee training and development (5th ed.).* Boston: Irwin.

Poster, W. R. (2011). Emotion detectors, answering machines, and e-unions: multi-surveillances in the global interactive service industry. *American Behavioral Scientist, 55*(7), 868–901. doi:10.1177/0002764211407833

Prien, E. P., Goodstein, L. D., Goodstein, J., & Gamble, J. L. (2009). *A practical guide to job analysis.* San Francisco: John Wiley & Sons, Inc.

Pugh, S. D. (2001). Service with a smile: Emotional contagion on the service encounter. *Academy of Management Journal, 44,* 1018–1027.

Pugh, S. D., Groth, M., & Hennig-Thurau, T. (2011). Willing and able to fake emotions: a closer examination of the link between emotional dissonance and employee well-being. *Journal of Applied Psychology, 96*(2), 377–90. doi:10.1037/a0021395

Rafaeli, A. (1989). When clerks meet customers: A test of variables related to emotional expressions on the job. *Journal of Applied Psychology, 74*(3), 385–393. doi:10.1037/0021-9010.74.3.385

Rafaeli, A., & Sutton, R. I. (1987). Expression of emotion as part of the work role. *Academy of Management Review, 12(1)*, 23–37.

Rafaeli, A., & Sutton, R I. (1989). The expression of emotion in organizational life. In L. L. Cummings & B. M. Staw (Eds.), *Research in organizational behavior, 11*(1–42), 1–42. Greenwich, CT: JAI Press.

Richard, E. M. (2006). *Applying appraisal theories of emotion to the concept of emotional labor.* Unpublished doctoral dissertation, Baton Rouge, LA.

Rogg, K. L., Schmidt, D. B., Shull, C., & Schmitt, N. (2001). Human resource practices, organizational climate, and customer satisfaction. *Journal of Management, 27(4)*, 431–449.

Sackett, P.R., & Laczo. R.M. (2003). Job and work analysis. In W.C. Borman, D.R. Ilgen, & R.J. Klimoski (Eds.), Handbook of psychology: Industrial and organizational psychology (Vol. 12, pp. 21–37). New York: Wiley.

Sanders, C. R. (2010). Working out back: The veterinary technician and "dirty work". *Journal of Contemporary Ethnography, 39(3)*, 243–272.

Saxe, R., & Weitz, B. A. (1982). The SOCO scale: A measure of the customer orientation of salespeople. *Journal of Marketing Research, 19(3)*, 343–351.

Schneider, B., & Bowen, D. E. (1985). Employee and customer perceptions of service in banks: Replication and extension. *Journal of Applied Psychology, 70*(3), 423–433. doi:10.1037/0021-9010.70.3.423

Schneider, B., White, S. S., & Paul, M. C. (1998). Linking service climate and customer perceptions of service quality: Test of a causal model. *Journal of Applied Psychology, 83*(2), 150–163.

Smith, J. R., Dorsey, K. D., & Mosley, A. L. (2009). Licensed funeral directors: An empirical analysis of the dimensions and consequences of emotional labor. *International Management Review, 5*(2), 31–44.

Smith, A. C., & Kleinman, S. (1989). Managing emotions in medical school: Students' contacts with the living and the dead. *Social Psychology Quarterly, 52(1)*, 56–69.

Steinberg, R. J., & Figart, D. M. (1999). Emotional demands at work: A job content analysis. *The ANNALS of the American Academy of Political and Social Science, 561*(1), 177–191. Storey, J. (1995). Human resource management: still marching on, or marching out? In J. Storey (Ed.), *Human resource management: A critical text* (pp. 3–32). London: Routledge.

Sutton, R. I. (1991). Maintaining norms about expressed emotions: The case of bill collectors. *Administrative Science Quarterly, 36(2)*, 245–268.

Taylor, N. (2010). Animal shelter emotion management: A case of in situ hegemonic resistance? *Sociology, 44(1)*, 85–101.

Taylor, P. J., Russ-Eft, D. F., & Chan, D. W. (2005). A meta-analytic review of behavior modeling training. *Journal of Applied Psychology, 90(4)*, 692–709.

Thoits, P. A. (2004). Emotion norms, emotion work and social order. In S. R.

Manstead, N. Frijda, & A. Fischer (Eds.), *Feelings and emotions: The Amsterdam symposium* (pp. 359–378). Cambridge: Cambridge University Press.

Totterdell, P., & Parkinson, B. (1999). Use and effectiveness of self-regulation strategies for improving mood in a group of trainee teachers. *Journal of Occupational Health Psychology, 4(3)*, 219–232.

Tracy, S. (2005). Locking up emotion: moving beyond dissonance for understanding emotion labor discomfort. *Communication Monographs, 72*(3), 261–283. doi:10.1080/03637750500206474

van Jaarsveld, D., & Poster, W. (2013). Call centers: emotional labor over the phone. In A. A. Grandey, J. M. Diefendorff, & D. Rupp (Eds.), *Emotional labor in the 21st century: Diverse perspectives on emotion regulation at work.* New York.

Van Maanen, John, & Kunda, G. (1989). Real Feelings: Emotional Expression and Organizational Culture. In B. M. Staw & L. L. Cummings (Eds.), *Research in organizational behavior, 11*, 43–103. Greenwich, CT: JAI Press.

Van Maanen, J, & Schein, E. H. (1979). Toward a theory of organizational socialization. In B. M. Staw (Ed.), *Research in organizational behavior, 1*(1), 209–264. Greenwich, CT: JAI Press.

Wharton, A. S. (2009). The sociology of emotional labor. *Annual Review of Sociology, 35*(1), 147–165. Annual Reviews. doi:10.1146/annurev-soc-070308-115944

Wilk, S. L., & Moynihan, L. M. (2005). Display rule "regulators": The relationship between supervisors and worker emotional exhaustion. *Journal of Applied Psychology, 90(5)*, 917–927.

Winiecki, D., & Wigman, B. (2007). Making and maintaining the subject in call center work. *New Technology, Work and Employment, 22*(2), 118–131.

Zapf, D. (2002). Emotion work and psychological well-being: A review of the literature and some conceptual considerations. *Human Resource Management Review, 12(2)*, 237–268.

# Social and Cultural Influencers

Gender Effects on Emotional
Labor at Work and at Home

KATHRYN J. LIVELY

Three decades have passed since sociologist Arlie Russell Hochschild changed the way emotions are studied. Instead of focusing on the physiological components of emotion, she shifted our attention to the social rules – the feeling rules that tell individuals what to feel and how to express those feelings. To capture the process as it occurs in private life, Hochschild coined the term emotion work; to capture the process in public life – especially when done in exchange for a wage – she coined the term emotional labor.[1]

Since Hochschild's original arguments, several scholars have examined the emotion work individuals do in their personal relationships (e.g., Staske, 1996; Schrock, et al., 2009). Some of these studies focused on emotion work that occurs at home and involves intimates (e.g., DeVault, 1991; Lois, 2009), while others centered on emotion work that occurs in public settings and involves strangers (e.g., Schrock, et al., 2009). Others, however, focused their attention almost entirely on workers' emotional labor sold for a wage (e.g., Sutton, 1991), while others chose to blur the distinction between emotion work and emotional labor by documenting emotion work in the workplace or other formal organizations (e.g., Harlow, 2003; Lois, 2003; Wingfield, 2010). Others, still, documented individuals' emotion management in backstage areas for the purposes of performing emotional labor in front stage areas (Lively, 2000; Smith, 2008).

Throughout most of these studies, one trend is increasingly clear: emotion rules differ for women and men. Men and women are held to a different standard of emotion work/labor across contexts. To date, most explanations of this difference draw on either the cultural or the structural perspective on emotion. The cultural perspective suggests that emotion norms are a result of deeply held cultural understandings about women and men – with women being viewed as more emotional, caring, and nurturing than men, and men being more affectively neutral and stoic than women. The structural perspective suggests that individuals of lower status are held to a higher degree of emotion work (or labor) than their higher status counterparts. Given that women are routinely subordinate to men in the areas of home and at work, the structural effects and the cultural meanings associated with sex are often conflated, making it difficult to distinguish between them (but see Lively & Powell, 2006).²

In this chapter I discuss how the emotional culture in the U.S. – a culture which in part helps to reify the current social structural relationship between women and men – has shaped women's and men's emotion management at home, as well as their emotion management and emotional labor at work. I do so by bridging theoretical insights from status expectations states theory (Ridgeway, 2001) and affect control theory (Heise, 2007) and empirical research within the sociology of emotion. I conclude by discussing how this same emotional culture has shaped the type of research emotion scholars have produced regarding this topic, despite recent changes in the cultural expectations of young women and men (Gerson, 2010; Jayson, 2011), as well as women's changing structural position *vis-à-vis* men's position (Rosin, 2011).

## U.S. EMOTIONAL CULTURE

The U.S. has a highly gendered emotion culture (see Simon & Nath, 2004 for a more detailed discussion). According to this emotion culture, men and women expect to – and are expected to – engage in and benefit from emotion work and emotional labor to varying degrees. These differential expectations are based on different beliefs about men's and women's emotions and these shared cultural beliefs shape the types of emotion work/emotional labor that men and women are likely to perform. In particular, women are believed to be more caring and nurturing than are men, whereas men are believed to be more stoic and task oriented (Hochschild, 1983; Pierce, 1995; also see Heilman & Okimoto, 2007). These differential expectations of emotions that are "appropriate for" or "easily accessible for" men and women shape the types of emotional regulation that men and women are subject to. Additionally, women tend to get less credit for their caretaking and nurturing, which is a necessary but often undervalued part of social life, because it is "part of their nature" (Heilman & Okimoto, 2007). When men display similar emotions, however, they tend to be more highly valued and are more likely to be rewarded both socially and monetarily. Similarly, men's displays of stoicism and bravery are often overlooked (Lois, 2003), whereas the same emotions in women tend to be stigmatized or looked down upon (also see Milkie, Simon & Powell, 1997).

According to U.S. cultural norms, there are also gendered norms of emotional expression. Thoits (1991), for example, found that college student women, when faced with a stressful situation, are more likely to express their feelings and cope with their emotions by seeking social support than their male counterparts (also see Simon & Nath, 2004). Indeed, in a number of experimental studies, scholars have noted that females are more expressive than males in response to a variety of experimental stimuli (e.g., Kring & Gordon, 1998). Further, both males and females tend to judge and subsequently label females as more emotional and emotionally expressive than males (e.g., Robinson & Johnson, 1997). And in terms of emotion management *strategies*, Lively (2008) found that men and women may use "gender appropriate" emotional segues, or emotional transitions, when managing or regulating their emotions (also see Lively & Heise, 2004).[3]

According to Simon and Nath's (2004) extensive review of gender and emotions research, developmental scholars suggest that males are socialized to conceal their feelings at an early age, whereas women are socialized to express their emotions more freely (e.g., Brody, 1985). Notably, these arguments mirror those made by Hochschild (1979), when she suggested that U.S. women – particularly middle class white women – are socialized to be more in tune with their own and others' emotions and to trade emotions and emotion work in exchange for financial security and support. Although the bulk of research on gender and emotion is based upon U.S. and European samples, emotions scholars expect gender differences in emotional norms to be less pronounced in egalitarian countries and more pronounced in countries with more pronounced gender inequality (Brody, 1985; also see Smith, Umino & Matsuno, 1998).

As evidenced by the scholarship cited above, there are several gender differences within U.S. emotional culture that affect men and women in everyday life. What is less clear, however, is the how. *How* do cultural norms regarding emotion actually come to impinge upon men and women in their homes and in the workplace? In the following sections I will suggest one possible mechanism through which emotion culture, writ large, comes to affect men's and women's everyday emotional lives, including their performance of emotion work/labor across the domains of work and family. I do so by introducing two social psychological theories coming from sociology, both of which consider not only individual perception and behavior, but also culture and social structure. I will then illustrate how these theories are relevant, if only implicitly so, to recent empirical research on emotion work at home and emotional labor at work.

# EXPECTATION STATES THEORY: THE ROLE OF STATUS BELIEFS

One of the enduring observations of human life is that when people come together to accomplish a task, or shared goal, whether it is raising a child or putting together an airtight jury case, a social hierarchy soon emerges among the participants in which some have more social esteem and influence in the situation than others (Bales, 1950; Lonner, 1980; Ridgeway, 2006). To date, sociological explanations of such phenomena turn to expectation states theory, which, currently, is the most systematic and empirically well-documented theory of status processes in groups available (Berger, et al., 1974, 1977; Correll & Ridgeway, 2003; Wagner & Berger, 2002). As Ridgeway noted in her recent review of expectation states theory and emotion, "although expectation states theory is a theory of status, not emotion, it provides a framework in relation to which emotion in hierarchies can be articulated to understand how status affects emotion and emotion shapes status in interpersonal contexts" (2006, p. 347).

Simply put, expectation states theory is based on the concept of status beliefs. According to Ridgeway (2001), status beliefs are "widely held cultural beliefs that link greater social significance and general competence, as well as specific positive and negative skills, with one category of social distinction compared to another." Applied to studies of gender differences in emotion, women are often attributed competence of "matters of the heart," based on widely held cultural beliefs about gender and emotion. Expectation states theory posits that status beliefs arise from repeated interactions among group members of different social groups, in which members of one group are observed to have some sort of structural advantage over members of another group (Ridgeway, 2001). That is, they are perceived to have advantages in influencing members of other groups, due to possessing greater resources. Applied to differences in emotion, men are able to demand the positive emotions of women and to get by with performing less emotion work or emotional labor, because of their structural position relative to women. Ridgeway & Bourg (2004) note that if such perceived differences are observed across multiple interactions, in multiple contexts, they may become ingrained as a status belief. When that happens, as with the notion that women are more emotional than men, individuals tend to continue to reify them in future interactions.

According to expectation states theory, status beliefs can eventually give rise to a hierarchy in which dominant members come to have power, authority, and influence over subordinate groups. In the case of emotion work and emotional labor, this means that the higher group can demand more emotion work/emotional labor from the subordinate group and, at the same time, withhold emotion work/emotional labor from subordinates. As Ridgeway (2001) and others are careful to stress, the construction and reification of status beliefs typically appear consensual, if not cooperative. In other words, both the perceived higher and lower status groups take part in their formation, as well as their propagation (also see Lively, 2000).

Gender status beliefs attribute greater competence and social status to men than to women, just as they attribute greater emotional range and better skill at care-taking and nurturing to women than men (Ridgeway, 2001). Moreover, expectation states theory posits that status beliefs about gender (that is, gender stereotypes) are prescriptive in nature, meaning they represent what is, and what should be. Because both men and women have internalized and cooperatively enact these beliefs, women too often act in ways that 1) undermine their own power and status vis-à-vis men, and 2) leave them increasingly vulnerable to emotional burnout and psychological stress (Hochschild, 1983, 1989; Wharton, 1993).

It is important to note that expectation states theory views individuals not only as men/women but also as an aggregate whole of all identities that bestow them status in the eyes of others. The theory holds that while people are sex-categorized in almost every situation, they are also categorized according to other markers as well (e.g., race, education, or sexual orientation) (Ridgeway & Bourg, 2004). A key tenet of the theory is that it includes traditional demographic differences as important contributors to status beliefs and also important aspects of an individual's identity such as education, title, and occupational or family role. Depending on which status characteristics are salient at a given time, gender and such other identities will *combine* to influence the ultimate performance expectations held by the individual and observers. In summary, an individual's behavioral and status differences are determined not only by his/her gender, but they are also a function of the aggregate expectation of all identities relevant to a given task (Ridgeway, 2001).[4]

One of the long-standing questions surrounding expectation states theory research is the relatively marked inattention to where status beliefs actually originate. Offering one possible explanation, Ridgeway (2006) posited that the culturally shared expectations that individuals hold about self and others may stem from culturally shared fundamental dimensions of affective meaning attached to personal attributes. Drawing on insights from affect control theory (Heise, 2008), Ridgeway proposed that the status beliefs *may* depend largely on how good or bad someone is perceived to be, how powerful or impotent they are perceived to be, and how active or inactive they are perceived to be. Generally speaking, before any individual interaction occurs, men are affectively viewed as not quite as nice or active as women, but considerably more powerful. Thus individuals create interactions (or, to use Heise's terminology, "events") to confirm these beliefs.

## AFFECT CONTROL THEORY

Much like expectation states theory, affect control theory was not developed as a theory of emotion. Instead, the main objective of the theory, which combined insights from psycholinguistics (Osgood, 1962), empirical studies of impression formation (Heise, 1969, 1970) and a cybernetic model of perception (Powers, 1973), was to explain behavior – both the routine and the unexpected – within the context of social interactions. According to Robinson, Smith-Lovin, and Wiescup (2006), affect control became part of the new sociology of emotion for three reasons: 1) the theory assumes that cognitive understandings of social interaction around us cannot be separated from our affective reactions to them; 2) the core affect control principle is that people act to maintain the affective meanings that are evoked by a definition of the situation – thus making the control of *affect* the key feature underlying social life; and 3) the affect control model was elaborated soon after its development to conceptualize emotions as signals about self-identity meanings within a situation and how well those meanings are aligned with stable, fundamental self conceptions.[5]

According to affect control theory, individuals create events that confirm their fundamental sentiments. As noted above, one of the ways that status beliefs may come into play is *vis-à-vis* the affective meanings we have around social identities, behaviors, emotions, attributes, etc. (Ridgeway, 2006). Affect control theory posits that all elements of social events (i.e., social actors, behaviors, objects, emotions, attributes, and settings) can be classified in terms of three dimensions of affective meaning (Heise, 2008): Evaluation or "how good or bad someone or something is;" Potency or "how strong or weak someone or something is;" and Activation or "how active or inactive someone or something is."

Evaluation–Potency–Activation (EPA) dictionaries have been collected from numerous sources ranging from college students at a large Midwestern university to Jamband music fans (Hunt, 2008). These dictionaries represent a given culture or subculture's affective sentiments regarding how good or bad (E), powerful or weak (P), or active or inactive (A) any given identity, behavior, setting, attribute, or emotion is perceived within the surveyed culture or sub-culture.[6] Individual EPA values, which make up aggregated EPA profiles, are measured on a scale from –4 to +4, ranging from extremely bad, impotent, and quiescent to extremely good, powerful, and active. The mean is then calculated and reported. Based on the cross-cultural work of Osgood and associates, affect control theory has assumed that these fundamental sentiments are shared within and across cultures. Recent studies, however, have shown there are some situationally specific differences at the cultural level (Smith, 2002; also see Smith, Matsuno & Umino, 1994) and also differences at the sub-cultural level (Smith-Lovin & Douglass, 1992).[7]

The underlying assumptions of affect control theory have been implemented as a computer simulation program, *Interact*. *Interact* uses impression formation equations, based on a cybernetic model of human behavior that assumes individuals are motivated to minimize distance between their transient and fundamental identities, which allow researchers to mathematically predict not only individuals' emotions, but also their most likely next step to bring their situated identity (or their transient sentiments) back in line with their fundamental identity (or their fundamental sentiments; MacKinnon & Heise, 2010).[8] When transient sentiments fail to confirm fundamental sentiments regarding some aspect of a social interaction, individuals are expected to take restorative action, either behaviorally or cognitively.[9]

In summary, individuals create events that confirm their fundamental sentiments (measured in terms of Evaluation–Potency–Activation [EPA] values) about themselves, about others, about behaviors, and about settings. Simply put, individuals tend to engage in behaviors that confirm their fundamental sentiments regarding their identities, to experience and express emotions that are consistent with those identities, and to do so in complementary settings and with other actors who have consistent and/or complementary role identities.

Likely actions create post-event impressions that match fundamental sentiments. An action that deflects impressions away from these sentiments seems unlikely (Heise, 2008). Any action deflects impressions away from sentiments to some degree, but the deflection is small in the case of likely actions and large in the case of unlikely actions (Heise, 2008). For example, consider the following event: "Mother Kisses Child." According to affect control theory, you have a nice (Evaluation), powerful (Potency), and active (Activation) actor doing a nice, powerful, and active behavior to a much nicer, much less powerful, and more active object. This action creates impressions of mother and baby that are probably very close to culturally shared sentiments about mothers and babies, thus this action seems likely, even to the point of being something you expect of mothers. Theoretically speaking, this event creates no deflection (or sense of unlikelihood) either mathematically or affectively. However, now consider the following: "Mother Kicks Child." Here, you have a nice, powerful, and active actor doing a very bad, powerful, and active behavior to a much nicer, much less powerful, and more active object. This event, unlike the event "Mother Kisses Child," causes significant deflection (or sense of unlikelihood) both mathematically and affectively because it creates impressions that are probably very far from culturally shared sentiments about mothers and babies.[10]

According to the theory, the next action of the mother who kicked her child (to reconfirm her "Mother" identity) will have to be very, very nice (referring to Evaluation), less powerful (referring to Potency), and similarly active (referring to Activation), or else she will have to reframe her identity, her behavior, or the identity of her child. So, for example, if she were to reframe her actions as "Playing With," or if she were to reframe her child's identity as that of a "Demon" or a "Delinquent," or she were to reframe herself as an "Alcoholic," the event would create less deflection. Attributes can also be added as a tool for reframing. If individuals were to see a "Mother Kick a Child", they might label her as an "Abusive Mother" or a "Psychotic Mother" or label the child as "Evil" in order to minimize feelings of deflection caused by the event. A "Mother who Kicks a Child" may also label herself as an "Overwrought Mother" to the same purpose.

Affect control theory's model of identity confirmation is consistent with literature on harassment and undermining. Maas, Cadiny, Guarnieri and Grasselli (2003), for example, found that highly identified males (i.e., men who see themselves as very masculine or 'male-like'), following conditions of *threat* were more likely to sexually harass female interaction partners than those men who 1) were not highly identified males or 2) had not perceived a threat. According to affect control theory, highly identified males, following a threat condition, would feel compelled to engage in a somewhat negative, powerful, and somewhat active act (i.e., sending pornographic photographs to a female coworker) in order to confirm their identity as highly identified males. Notably, the act of sexual assault, while also negative, powerful, and active, would be too negative, too powerful, and too active an event to confirm the identity of highly identified male and would risk causing him to either self-identify or to be identified as a "Lout," a "Bully" or even as a "Rapist."

Similarly, Magley, Hulan, Fitzgerald and DeNardo's (1999) work on sexual harassment suggests that many women fail to report having been a victim of such treatment because to do so changes their identity of "Woman" or "Coworker" to that of "Victim." Interestingly, affect control theory's sentiment formation equations (Heise, 2008) capture society's tendency to blame the victim. When a woman is abused (or raped), one of the ways in which people make sense of that (or attempt to minimize deflection or the accompanying feeling of unlikelihood) is to ask: What kind of woman is likely to be abused or raped? Additionally, women who labeled the behavior as harassment were more likely to feel badly about it. Again, one of the questions that *Interact*'s impression formation equations allow scholars to model is what are the emotions that a woman who has been abused is likely to feel? Simply put, women who are harassed are expected to (and do) experience more distressing emotions than those who perceive that they have been merely flirted with or flattered (Magley, et al., 1999).

Notably, many of the social roles that actors occupy are gendered, and these gendered meanings are evident in differential Evaluation–Potency–Activation scores. For instance, based on the data collected from male college students in 2002–2004, the EPA values for "Mother" and "Father" (see Table 10.1) suggest that as a culture, we expect mothers to be similarly nice, fairly less powerful, and fairly more active than fathers. In terms of their behavior, especially their behaviors towards children, fathers are expected to cuddle, massage, caress, hug, forgive, smile at, sympathize with, embrace, listen to, counsel, and protect a child, whereas mothers are expected to cuddle, massage, embrace, hug, forgive, listen to, sympathize with, smile at, caress, make up with, wink at, console, soothe, counsel, hold, compromise with, dine with, reward, protect, reassure, and mother.[11] Note that not only does the order of the expected behaviors differ for fathers and mothers, but mothers have a much *longer* list of expected behaviors, including behaviors such as make up with, and compromise with, which reflect their lower power compared to that of fathers.

Just as social roles are gendered in the family, they are also gendered in the work place. For example: the EPA values for "Waitress" and "Waiter" suggest that we, as a society, expect waitresses to be more pleasant and more active than waiters, meaning not only do we expect them to work faster, if not harder, but also to be friendlier while they do it. Waitresses who fail to live up to these expectations may create deflection and cause them to be labeled negatively, thus causing them to lose tips when engaging in behaviors and displays that would be considered normal for a waiter. Notably, Hall (1993) suggests that the *work* of "waitressing" versus "waiting" is also gendered; in other words, the label linked to the *type of service* as well as to the person providing it. According to her analyses of 55 restaurants, "waitressing" was typical in restaurants that she described as low prestige (where servers, regardless of their sex, were expected to seat customers, serve coffee, make desserts, be affectively engaged, etc.), whereas "waiting" was typical in high prestige restaurants (where servers, regardless of their sex, were expected to instruct customers on wine and entrees and to literally wait with their hands behind their backs until the customer needed assistance). In this study, waitresses (be they male or female) are expected to be nicer and more active than waiters, which is consistent with the EPA values cited above.[12]

## THE EMPIRICAL EVIDENCE

When applied directly to emotion work/labor, actors who are nicer, less powerful, and slightly more active are more likely to experience more pleasant, less powerful, and more active emotions and engage in nicer, less powerful, and more active emotional displays as a means to confirm their views of themselves as well as the views of others. At home, this means that mothers (and wives) are normatively more affectively engaged, less powerful, and more active than the men in their lives (Hochschild, 1989; DeVault, 1991). Conversely, fathers can "get away with" being emotionally stoic disciplinarians who simply do less (or are less active) in terms of childrearing and other forms of emotional and domestic work (Coltrane, 1998; Hochschild, 1983; Lively, et al., 2010).

In the workplace, as suggested earlier, the story is somewhat more complicated. When women are employed in historically female-dominated occupations, such as nursing, teaching, caretaking, etc., it is relatively easy for them to satisfy the cultural expectations of being 1) female and 2) a member of a "caring occupation." Similarly, when men are in historically male-dominated professions or occupations, their twin obligations (of being male and being professional, simultaneously) are also easily met. When employed in historically male jobs or professions, however, women are automatically viewed as less pleasant, significantly less powerful, and less active, because the culturally shared fundamental sentiments regarding professional jobs are more consistent with the fundamental sentiments associated with men or being male. Indeed, Koenig et al's (2011) meta-analysis suggests that not only do men fit cultural constructions of leadership better than women do, they also have better access to leader roles and face fewer challenges in their enactment of those roles. When women act in ways that are consistent with professional/leadership roles, they (and those around them) experience deflection and may end up overcompensating with other gender-appropriate behaviors (Pierce, 1995), limiting themselves to androgynous – and, thus, relatively impotent – behaviors (Eagly and Karau, 2002), or adopting negative labels from themselves and others (Heise, 2007; also see Thoits, 1985).[13]

## *Gendered emotion work at home.*

Although there has been less empirical attention to the emotion work performed by individuals in private life than there has been to the emotional labor performed in public life (Hochschild, 1983), scholarship on both types of emotion management support the theoretical predictions made above. Most of the studies that document emotion work in families focus on individuals' attempts to manage their emotions and the emotional investments that are made in others, especially children.[14] DeVault (1991), for example, documents care work as a type of emotion work. Care work is typically carried out by women and includes such activities as gift giving, food preparation, tradition maintenance, relationship work, and remembering family birthdays, anniversaries, etc.[15]

Closely related, some scholars have studied the emotional costs that come when facing perceived inequities in the household division of labor. In her ethnography of dual earner families, Hochschild (1989) documented the emotion work spouses do when their gender ideology does not correspond to their domestic situation. For example, a feminist woman may find herself doing more than her fair share or a traditional male may find himself being asked to do more around the house than his father did. In order to manage their negative emotions, one or both parties must reframe their situations as "fair," creating what Hochschild (1989) termed "family myths."

Given wives' structurally subordinate positions within the marriage, greater financial need, and fear of divorce, they were more likely to construct myths that reaffirmed the status quo, while simultaneously managing their feelings of anger, disappointment, frustration, sadness, etc. Husbands, who also suffer emotionally from perceived inequity in the home even when they themselves are benefiting also participate in family myths. However, given their dominant structural position, plus men's greater belief that they can easily remarry, their participation in these myths tend to rest on behaviors (such as working longer hours or merely removing themselves from the situation) as opposed to the emotional gymnastics performed by their wives (Hochschild, 1983).

Other studies of emotion work in the home highlight the emotional nature of paid domestic labor. Hondagneau-Sotelo's (2001) study of

Latina domestic workers, for example, reveals that female domestic workers are often expected to engage in true "labors of love," many of which undermine their ability to ask for raises, bonuses, or other rights due more traditional employees. At the same time, the women who employ them are expected to manage the relationship between the worker and the family, which can, and often does, require emotional labor. Not surprisingly, one of the most notable features of these types of studies is the marked absence of men.[16] Again, the cultural expectations that we have about what constitutes women's work, that are upheld in large part by our affective assessment of how good or bad someone is, how powerful and impotent they are, and how active and quiet they are drives our expectations for behavior, which includes who does what – and who *feels* what – around the house and for the family.

## *Gendered emotional labor at work.*

The gendered pattern of emotion work/labor that occurs at home is reproduced in the workplace as well. Nowhere is this more apparent than in qualitative studies that compare women and men in similar, or even the same, organizations (Martin, 1999; Lois, 2003; Pierce, 1995). As these studies reveal, women expect (and are expected) to be more emotionally engaged, whereas their male counterparts expect (and are expected) to be less affectively involved. In particular, female police officers (Martin, 1999) and rescue workers (Lois, 2003) tend to assume the more emotionally draining responsibility of dealing with distraught, frightened, or angry victims and families, whereas their male counterparts are more likely to do the "real" work of policing, detecting, and rescuing. Similarly, in Pierce's study of male and female paralegals, women are expected to take on the emotionally-laden roles of the mothering paralegal, the cheerleader, and what Pierce refers to as the "perfect wife," roles that require not only managing their own emotions, but also calming down, building up, and caring for their disproportionately male attorneys. The male paralegals, however, were often exempt from this type of emotional labor, although they were expected to play the less emotionally involved roles of political "yes men," which required stoicism and "strategic friendliness."

In my own research on paralegals (Lively, 2000, 2001, and 2002), both male and female paralegals routinely used "the marriage metaphor" to describe their relationship with their attorneys; notably, however, the way in which this metaphor played out differed was highly gendered. As a 42-year-old female paralegal explained of her relationship with her male attorney: "It's just like we're married. I make his coffee, I pick up his dry cleaning, and when his dog needs to go to the vet, I do that too." Contrast that description to one provided by a 48-year-old male paralegal, speaking of his female attorney: "It's just like we're married. When she's wrong, I tell her she's wrong." These comments, as well as many others, illustrate how male and female paralegals and their female and male attorneys recreate cultural stereotypes about marriage and the relative status of women and men in the workplace. These stereotypes not only shape individuals' experience of work, but also their emotional experiences and expressions.

Notably, sex differences are not just limited to front line service occupations, but also can be found among professional jobs as well. The EPA values for "Attorney", for example, irrespective of sex are 0.66, 1.60, 0.94, suggesting that culturally attorneys are viewed as being slightly good, fairly powerful, and somewhat active.[17] However, when we add sex-based attributes – male or female – the affective meanings change (see Table 10.1): we expect female attorneys to be slightly nicer than, significantly less powerful than, and less active than their male counterparts. When a female attorney acts in ways that are deemed too powerful they may inadvertently lower their evaluation, causing deflection. This mechanism serves as the basis of the double bind that many female litigators face when attempting to be both female and professional at the same time (Pierce, 1995; also see Eagly & Karau, 2002). The differences between male versus female EPA profiles in historically male-/female-dominated fields have important implications for the behaviors that women and men engage in, as well as their emotional experiences (Lively & Heise, 2004) and expression (Lively & Powell, 2006).[18]

Further, in comparison to the Evaluation–Potency–Activation profiles for women employed in stereotypically female occupations such as waitressing or nursing, where females are viewed as fundamentally more pleasant, more powerful, and more active than their male counterparts, women in historically male-dominated professional roles tend to be viewed as being slightly less pleasant, significantly less powerful, and fairly less active when compared to similarly employed men. Just by virtue of being female and our cultural understandings of what it means to be a professional, women in professional occupations are viewed as less pleasant, less powerful, and less active than their male counterparts. Thus, in order for women to be seen as pleasant, as powerful, or as active as men, they must engage in some sort of self regulation, some of which may be behavior, but some of which is undoubtedly emotional. In fact, there have been numerous qualitative studies demonstrating that women in professional jobs must engage in an additional layer of self-regulation (or "emotional management") beyond the labor for the job itself (Bellas, 1999; Pierce, 1995).[19]

In a series of experimental studies, Heilman and Okimoto (2007) attempted to understand why it is that women are often disliked and interpersonally derogated, in addition to being overlooked, discriminated against, and under rewarded, when succeeding in historically male jobs (Heilman, 1995, 2001). Essentially, they tested the hypothesis that "women's success in a male domain arises from the perceived violation of communality prescriptions" (p. 82) and that evidence of communality – that is, exhibiting nurturing and socially sensitive attributes that demonstrate concern for others, such as being kind, sympathetic and understanding – will prevent the social disapproval and social penalties otherwise directed at a woman when she is successful in a male job.[20] They found that stereotypically female behavior – that is, behavior that corresponds with both our status expectations and our fundamental sentiments regarding women – only ameliorated the social sanctions if the information was "clearly indicative" of communal attributes, could be "unambiguously" attributed to the female manager, and could be conveyed by role information (i.e., motherhood status) or behavior. Although Heilman and Okimoto's focus is not on emotion work/emotional labor per se, their definition of communality is suggestive of the stereotypical emotion work/emotional labor required not only of mothers, but also middle class service workers.

Interestingly, men in historically female-dominated occupations (such as teaching or nursing) do not face the same challenges as women. In other words, men in these occupations are often granted special dispensation on the basis of their gender. Whereas earlier scholars documented men's rise to the top of these professions, using such terminology as "the glass elevator" (Williams, 1992), later scholars have suggested that men tend to create their own niches within female occupations, niches that include behaviors that occur in historically male-dominated settings, or grant them access to powerful interaction partners – all of which, according to an affect control theory perspective, allows them to confirm their fundamental sentiments about themselves as men. For example, male nurses tend to specialize in areas of medicine that require more brute strength or are sufficiently technical such that they have more contact with physicians than family members, thus freeing them of the more emotionally challenging aspects of the job (also see Lois, 2003).

## PUTTING IT ALL TOGETHER

Men and women do different types of emotional management in both work and family contexts. Generally speaking, women take on more emotionally expressive duties involving children, intimate partners, extended family members, colleagues, and customers, etc., than their male counterparts. Men on the other hand, are more likely to stay affectively neutral, rational, professional, and businesslike, etc., in their interactions with others, even those with whom they are on intimate terms. Although this idea is not new, to date there have been few systematic attempts to explain either how or why this happens. Why is it that others expect women to do more and also qualitatively different emotion work/labor than men? Why is it that the emotion work/emotional labor that women do is more likely to be viewed as more time-consuming, more strenuous, more degrading, *less* valuable, and more likely to result in feelings of inauthenticity or burnout (Erickson and Ritter, 2001)? Why is it that both men and women believe this is the way things are, and the way they should be (Ridgeway, 2006)?

Drawing on insights from core sociological theories within social psychology, this chapter provides one possible pathway through which cultural understandings about the social roles that women and men occupy and, indeed, about women and men more generally, influence everyday life. As a culture, we share fundamental sentiments about social roles, behaviors, settings, attributes, and emotions (Heise, 2008). These are the basic elements of all social interactions and, for the most part, we expect them to be consistent – i.e., we expect very good, slightly powerful, and fairly active social actors (e.g., women) to engage in very good, slightly powerful, and somewhat active behaviors (e.g., nurture, tease, care, etc.). Moreover, we expect them to do these things in very good, slightly powerful, and somewhat active settings (e.g., a home or a boutique), and while exhibiting very good, slightly powerful, and somewhat active attributes (e.g., friendly) or emotions (e.g., happy).[21]

These sentiments, which are culturally shared but may differ within certain subgroups of the population and most certainly differ across cultures, come to form the basis of our expectations states, *vis-à-vis* our status beliefs (Ridgeway, 2001). These status beliefs, many of which are built up through social interaction over time, get attached to gender, to social roles (many of which are gendered), to settings, as well as to attributes, which themselves get attached to social roles, interactively changing the meaning of that role.

Although status expectations theory was originally developed to explain status processes in small groups, many of which are task-oriented, one could argue that much of the behavior that occurs in work settings and in homes is also, loosely defined, task-related. Moreover, despite the dissimilarities that may or may not exist between small groups and the longer-term relationships that comprise work and family life, some of the same mechanisms that govern interaction in small groups seem to operate at the level of family and workplace (Heilman & Okimoto, 2007; Lively & Powell, 2006; Lively, et al., 2010).

Indeed, some scholars have suggested that family settings are ideal, though surprisingly underutilized, settings for groups research, especially when dealing with questions related to emotion (Steelman & Powell, 1996; see also Lively, Powell, Geist, & Steelman, 2008; Lively, et al., 2010). Others, however, have lauded the workplace as the ideal setting in which to test insights garnered from more traditional forms of groups research, calling for a more serious and systematic consideration of social psychological theory by those studying emotion in the workplace (Clay-Warner, 2006; Lively, 2008; but see Correll, Bernard & Paik, 2007).

Despite the utility of expectations states theory and the ease with which scholars can document the effects of status beliefs in small groups and, albeit less formally, and to a lesser degree, in workplace and family settings, the question remains: where do the status beliefs come from? How do they relate to emotion work/labor? And, perhaps even more importantly, to what degree are they subject to change? In this chapter, I have drawn on insights from affect control theory, arguing that the status beliefs that we, as a society, hold and reify in terms of our daily interactions come from our affective understandings of how good or bad someone is, how powerful or impotent someone is, and how active and inactive someone is. As the theory predicts, and numerous empirical studies support, social actors who see themselves in terms of a good, powerful, and active identity are expected to engage in good, powerful, and active ways and to experience and express good, powerful, and active emotions. Because affective sentiments are largely shared within a given culture, individuals who see themselves in terms of a good, powerful, active identity are affectively motivated to meet these behavioral and emotional expectations.

Affective sentiments impact men and women differently in a number of ways. First, the Evaluation–Potency–Activation profiles for the identities "Woman" or "Female" (discussed above) are significantly more pleasant, significantly less powerful, and slightly less active than the corresponding identities of "Man" or "Male." Second, some social roles are gendered, meaning that the role itself is gendered (such as "Mother" or "Waitress") regardless of the person who actually performs the work associated with that role; in this sense, men can "mother" just as easily as a woman, although it is not as common an occurrence (also see Heilman & Okimoto, 2007). Third, domains or settings that have been deemed historically as female or feminine tend to be more pleasant, less powerful, and more active (i.e., a "Home" versus a "Boutique" versus a "Hardware Store"). When in those settings, actors are expected to act in ways that confirm the fundamental definition of the situation. So, not only are nice, passive, and active actors expected to be in those settings, all actors are expected to behave in nicer, less powerful, and more active ways, including experiencing and expressing corresponding emotions. Finally, when gender is used as an attribute, it changes the affective meaning that society has of social roles. A female attorney, for example, is viewed more negatively than a male attorney because the Evaluation–Potency–Activation profiles of "Female" and "Attorney" are less consistent than the Evaluation–Potency–Activation profiles of "Male" and "Attorney." All of these considerations are important not only for the emotional experiences of men and women, but also for the emotional expectations that are placed on them by themselves and others.

One of the reasons a female attorney may be required to engage in an additional layer of emotional labor is because she may be viewing herself (and thus acting in ways appropriate to that vision) as an attorney, whereas her interaction partners, be it paralegals, secretaries, other attorneys, judges, clients, or witnesses, may be viewing her (and acting towards her) as if she were a female attorney, a woman, a female, or, in some cases, even a girl. Indeed, one of the biggest sources of frustration between Latina domestics and their, mostly white U.S. born, employers is the former's unwillingness to see themselves as domestic workers. This nearly unilateral reluctance stems in part from the stigma associated with "dirty" work and the fact that most of the immigrant domestic workers had previously held social roles with higher status, and thus different EPA values, such as college student, attorney, physician's assistant, etc., in their countries of origin. Further, many employers, the majority of whom were female, were reluctant to see themselves as employers or to acknowledge their domestic workers as anything other than "help." Whenever individuals enter into interactions with different definitions of themselves or others, social disruptions, misunderstandings, and hurt feelings are likely to ensue. When this happens, the lower status person, often, but not always female, is required to engage in emotional labor not only to manage her own anger, but also to put her interaction partner at ease (again, Harlow's (2003) and Wingfield's (2010) analyses of emotional regulation among black professionals).

Because cultures and, subsequently, affective sentiments and status beliefs are slow to change, much of the literature on emotion work/ emotional labor has continued to focus on events in which we know gender differences are most likely to occur – that is, husbands and wives in the home (especially following the birth of a child), the service industry, or women working in male-dominated fields or males working in female-dominated fields. Less attention has been paid to events that may be less influenced by tradition or power and, therefore, gender. When scholars focus on the extremes or differences, they tend to find them (Thorne, 1993). Indeed, in Thorne's seminal ethnography on school children, she admitted her natural gravitation towards the extremes (e.g., the popular kids) led her to report many gender differences. However, when she forced her attention to the less popular children, the differences

TABLE 10.1   Changes in Evaluation-Potency-Activation (EPA)
Profiles for Gendered Roles

|                  | 1978 (North Carolina) E, P, A | 2002–4 (Indiana) E, P, A |
|------------------|-------------------------------|--------------------------|
| Man              | 1.08, 1.07, 0.56              | 0.82, 1.56, 0.86         |
| Woman            | 2.34, 0.44, 1.12              | 1.27, –0.24, 0.34        |
| Father           | 1.77, 2.14, –0.68             | 2.46, 2.54, 0.76         |
| Mother           | 2.52, 1.50. –0.13             | 2.48, 1.96, 1.15         |
| Waiter           | 0.77, –0.33, 0.22             | 1.08, –0.45, 0.75        |
| Waitress         | 1.06, –0.39, 0.81             | 1.46, 0.25, 1.63         |
| Male Attorney    | 0.66, 1.56, .37               | 0.60, 1.86. 1.25         |
| Female Attorney  | 1.47, 0.76, 1.04              | 0.75, 0.25, 0.47         |

Note: Scores ranged from –4 to +4 and were obtained via the online program *Interact*, to represent Evaluation (E) = good or bad; Potency (P) = powerful or weak; or Active (A) = active or inactive.

were less clear. Moreover, when focusing solely on classroom/school yard interactions, where many teachers used sex as an organizing principle, gender differences were prevalent and easily seen. However, when watching children play in neighborhoods and parks, away from adults, the gender differences were less apparent.

Despite the enduring status beliefs (i.e., stereotypes) we have regarding women and men and roles that have been historically gendered (e.g., mother v. father or waitress v. waiter) affective sentiments are changing, as evidenced in Table 10.1. For instance, the EPA profiles for the pairs "Man" and "Woman," "Mother" and "Father," "Waiter and Waitress," each became more similar between the years 1978 and 2002–4 in terms of evaluation (i.e., pleasantness), yet more disparate in terms of potency (power).

Moreover, the identities of "Man" and "Woman" flip on the activation dimension, suggesting that women, over the last 25 years, are now seen as less active compared to men, even though stereotypically female roles, such as "Waitress" and "Wife" are still viewed as somewhat more active than their male counterparts. Because power and activation are such important components in emotional experience, expression, and management (Kemper, 1978; Lively & Powell, 2006), as is evaluation, these changes may have interesting, and important, implications for women's and men's emotion work/labor at both home and work.

# CONCLUSION

In this chapter, I have suggested that a cultured affective meaning regarding social roles, behaviors, emotions, and attributes (including attributes regarding gender), comes to form the foundation of our status beliefs, which, in turn, becomes status expectations. Research on status expectations has shown time and again, both in context-free and context-dependent situations, that the expectations we – and others – carry into an interaction affect not only our status, but also our behaviors and our emotions. They also affect our emotional behavior, including the expectation, the likelihood, and the quality of our emotional work/labor.

In undoubtedly the most lucid discussion of affect control theory ever written, David Heise (2008) argues that cultural sentiments – which, as I argue, form the basis of our status beliefs, which in turn become expectations states that shape emotional labor – come not only from our personal experience with particular types of social actors or from being in certain types of environments, but from our broader cultural experience with them. So, for example, even though we may have no personal experiences with vampires, our cultural sentiments regarding them in the 1970s were, nonetheless, extremely negative, very powerful, and somewhat inactive. In the late 1980s, one could argue after the publication of Anne Rice's widely popular vampire novels, the cultural sentiment around vampires changed: although still negative, vampires were viewed as considerably less powerful, yet more active. Given the recent popularization and, indeed, sexualization, of vampires, via Stephanie Meyer's *Twilight* series (2005) and the HBO series, "True Blood," I would imagine a further shift in sentiments regarding vampires over the next decade or so.

So what do vampires have to do with gender and the ways in which it affects men and women's emotional work/labor in the home and at work? Simply put, our cultural sentiments are shaped by interactions, personal experience, cultural representations, popular culture, economic realities, and structural conditions. As noted in Table 10.1, "Men" and "Women" were more similar in terms of perceived potency (also conceptualized as powerful) in 1978 than they were in 2002–4. Although this may seem counterintuitive, keep in mind that during the 1970s, "'women's lib' was on everyone's lips" (Evans, 1997, p. 287). In the 1980s, however, although women remained in favor of women's rights, they became less favorable in terms of the labels "women's lib" and "feminism" (McCabe, 2005).

At the same time, recent statistics reveal that for the first time in history, more women than men are in college, in graduate schools, in professional schools, and in management. These trends suggest that in the very near future, women may have the potential to outrank their male romantic partners and also to out-earn them (Rosin, 2011). Moreover, emotional labor skills – skills in which women have traditionally been socialized to excel since childhood – are no longer stigmatized, but are being touted by best-selling business authors as necessary for both corporate and managerial success (Godin, 2010; Goleman, 1997). And, given the changing nature of the U.S. and other post-industrial societies, socioeconomically disadvantaged men face the steepest job losses, whereas lower class women continue to seek and to find employment in service jobs that require emotional attentiveness, emotional labor, etc. Indeed, according to Rosin (2011), by 2020, women will out-earn their male partners in approximately 75% of couples.

Sea changes are occurring at home as well (Jayson, 2011). According to a survey of 5,000 single U.S. adults, men are expressing attitudes that have been historically associated with women (i.e., greater interest in love, marriage, and having kids) whereas women are expressing attitudes that have been historically associated with men (i.e., a desire for more independence and the idea that "hooking up" and romantic one-night stands are not necessarily just meaningless encounters).[22] These findings are consistent with Gerson's (2010) recent analyses of young men and women, who appear to want more flexible marriages for themselves and for their partners and who seemingly subscribe to less traditional notions of gender.

If our affective sentiments and our status beliefs and expectations regarding gender are changing, then we can expect that the types of emotion work/labor performed at work and home, by men and women, are also subject to change. If the demographic predictions hold true, then these changes may happen more quickly in the next thirty years than they did in the last thirty years. In order for scholars to keep up with these coming changes, we will have to develop new, increasingly agile methodologies. We will need to collect more data in more diverse situations, and do so more frequently over longer periods of time.

## ENDNOTES

1 Notably, Hochschild (1983) introduced a third term, emotion management, which she used interchangeably with emotion work but later scholars tended to use as an umbrella term that included both emotional labor and emotion management (Lively, 2000). Grandey (2000) introduced the term emotional regulation in an attempt to gain greater conceptual clarity. Although widely adopted among psychologists and other organizational scholars, "emotional regulation" has been relatively underutilized among sociologists (see Grandey, Diefendorff & Rupp, 2013 for a more detailed discussion of these theoretical and conceptual nuances).

2 Sociologists treat gender and sex as conceptually distinct. Sex refers to the

biological and, indeed, chromosomal differences between males and females. Gender, on the other hand, refers to a set of cultural practices that women and men "do" in order to present themselves as masculine or feminine (West and Zimmerman, 1987) or, in the case of transsexuals, as male or female (Schrock, et al., 2009).

3 Shortest-path analysis – a methodology that seeks out high-level correlations among concepts that is most often used in conjunction with network analysis – reveals that men may have an easier time transitioning through anger or pride when trying to get from distress to tranquility (or vice versa), whereas women may have an easier time transitioning from negative to positive emotions by first invoking joy, fear, or both (Lively, 2008).

4 Small group experiments have frequently shown that in the absence of task-related information, individuals with higher diffuse status characteristics tend to emerge as leaders, and that the contributions from individuals with lower status characteristics tend to be ignored, refuted, or co-opted by higher status others. Further, in mixed-sex task groups, men tend to emerge as the instru-mental or task leaders, whereas women are more likely to emerge as the social leaders and to exhibit for socio-emotional support and other "helping" behaviors (Ridgeway & Johnson, 1990).

5 Affect control theory, thus, is a variant of symbolic interaction, positing that social actors respond to a symbolically represented world and strive to maintain the meanings that are associated with the elements of that world (see MacKinnon, 1994 for a detailed discussion of the two theories). However, unlike the overly cognitive symbolic interactionist paradigm, affect control theory puts affect front and center, positing that the dynamics of affective processing underlie both routine role-taking behavior and creative, negotiated responses to non-routine situations.

6 Individuals are asked to rate identities, behaviors, settings, attributes, and emo-tion out of context. So, for example, although individuals may see their own fathers as very bad, very weak, and inactive, their rating of the cultural identity "father," may be more positive, more powerful, and more active. Affective sentiments that are culturally shared come from broader understandings in addition to personal experience.

7 Sub-cultural differences in EPA values tend to be limited to identities, behaviors, settings and attributes closely associated with the subculture. For example, drug users have different EPA values for marijuana use than individuals who have never used drugs (Heise, 2008).

8 Transient sentiments are the sentiments that arise within situated action. Again, we tend to think of fathers as good, powerful, and relatively active. However, if a father were to throttle an infant, a transient sentiment regarding that particular father would occur that does not correspond easily with our fundamental sentiment regarding fathers and how they should interact with infants.

9 To learn more about *Interact*, EPA Dictionaries, or the Affect Control Theory research community, go to http://www.indiana.edu/~socpsy/ACT/index.htm

10 The definition of deflection is literally the "unlikelihood" that an event will occur: it is the mathematical distance between what would confirm the event

and what actually happened. Because most individuals prefer cognitive consistency, it is often experienced as surprise, stress, or another form of dissonance.

11  These predictions were derived from *Interact*, the computer simulation tool mentioned above; extracted June 19, 2011. Expected behaviors, which are listed in order of most likely to least likely, are those that cause a deflection of 1 or less, meaning that they are highly likely and also confirm both the actor and the object's fundamental identities.

12  In support of the claim that the work role itself is gendered, Hall (1993) cites a male manager at the low prestige "Sandwich Shop" referring to his wait staff (both women and men) as waitresses, and female servers at the high prestige "Elegant Noveau" referring to themselves as waiters.

13  Qualitative studies of professionals, or paraprofessionals, suggest that women are more likely to inquire about and exhibit concern regarding the personal lives of support staff, refraining from making requests – or demands – for assistance that may be common from males in similar roles, and to manage the anger of higher status others than their male counterparts (Hochschild, 1983; Lively, 2000; Pierce, 1995).

14  In her ethnography of homeschooling, Lois (2010) uses the term emotional labor to describe the efforts of homeschooling mothers, who often find themselves managing their own emotions so to better elicit the desired state from their sometimes unruly "students." Here it is a "work role," but performed at home and with family, showing the fuzzy boundaries illustrated in Chapter 1 (Grandey, et al., 2013).

15  Men do partake in the more pleasant duties associated with childcare. Indeed, ethnographic studies reveal that men's involvement with kids tend to be more centered around weekend activities, events, and father–son/father–daughter excursions than around the routine day to day care giving, or mothering, provided by women (Hochschild, 1989).

16  Lois' (2009, 2010) analysis of homeschooling provides a similar story; although both parents may prefer homeschooling, the supervision of such a task, if not the implementation, almost always falls to the mother, even if homeschooling was not her first choice.

17  The EPA profile for Attorney is not the average of the EPA profiles for Male Attorney and Female Attorney. Instead, it has its own value. That value changes when it becomes associated with either gender *vis-à-vis* the impression formation models used by *Interact*. These EPA values were taken from the EPA Dictionary collected at Indiana University in 2002–4.

18  Sex differences have been found in EPA values, especially for identities, behaviors, emotions, and settings that relate specifically to men and women. For example, females tend to view the identity "woman" as slightly nicer, more powerful, and more active than males do. Gender differences in EPA values also tend to be more pronounced in more traditional societies (Smith, Umino & Matsuno, 1998).

19  See Harlow (2003) and Wingfield (2010) for similar discussions of the emotional lives of African-American professionals working in predominantly white settings.

20  According to Heilman and Okimoto (2007) it is not necessary for women to

actually behave counter-normatively – that is, engage in agentic behavior that demonstrates dominance, competitive, and achievement orientation. Indeed, "the mere knowledge that a woman has been successful in a male domain produces inferences that she has engaged in stereotype-violating behavior resulting in social penalties" (Heilman & Okimoto, 2007, p. 82).

21 Evaluation–Potency–Activation values associated with home are considerably more pleasant, less powerful, and less active than those associated with most workplace settings. Thus, all actors (male or female) are expected to experience and exhibit more pleasant, less powerful, and less active emotions at a home than they would at a work setting,

22 The survey, one of the largest of its kind focusing on single men and women, was conducted by biological anthropologist, Helen Fisher, who helped develop the survey with social historian Stephanie Coontz and Justin Garcia, a doctoral fellow with the Institute for Evolutionary Studies at Binghamton (N.Y.) University.

# REFERENCES

Bales, R. F. (1950). *Interaction process analysis*. Cambridge, MA: Addison-Wesley.

Bellas, M. L. (1999). Emotional labor in academia: The case of professors. *The ANNALS of the American Academy of Political and Social Science*, 561(1): 96–110

Berger J., Conner. T. L., & Fisek, M. H. (1974). *Expectations states theory: A theoretical research program*. Cambridge, MA: Winthrop.

Berger, J., Fisek, H. M., Norman, R. Z., & Zelditch Jr. M. (1977). *Status characteristics and social interaction: An expectation status approach*. New York: Elseveier Scientific.

Brody, L. R. (1985). Gender differences in emotional development: A review of theories and research. *Gender and Personality: Current Perspectives on Theory and Research*, 14–61.

Clay-Warner, J. (2006). Procedural justice and legitimacy: Predicting negative emotional reactions to work place injustice. *Advances in Group Processes*, (23), 207–227.

Coltrane, S. (1998). *Gender and families*. Newbury Park, CA: Pine Forge Press.

Correll, S. J., Bernard, S., & Paik, I. (2007). Getting a job: Is there a motherhood penalty? *American Journal of Sociology*, (112), 1297–1338.

Correll, S. J., & Ridgeway, C. L. (2003). Expectation states theory. In J. Delamater (Ed.), *Handbook of Social Psychology* (pp. 29–52). New York: Kluwer/Plenum.

DeVault, M. (1991). *Feeding the family: The social organization of caring as gendered work*. Chicago: University of Chicago Press.

Eagly, A. H., & Karau, S. J. (2002). Role congruity theory of prejudice toward female leaders. *Psychological Review, 109*(3), 573–598.

Erickson, R. J. & Ritter, C. (2001). Emotional labor, burnout, and inauthenticity: Does gender matter? *Social Psychology Quarterly* 64(2): 146–163.

Evans, S. M. (1997). *Born for liberty: A history of women in America*. New York: Free Press.

Gerson, K. (2010). *The unfinished revolution: How a new generation is reshaping family, work, and gender in America*. Oxford: Oxford University Press.

Goleman, D. (1997). *Emotional intelligence: Why it can matter more than IQ*. New York: Bantam Books.

Godin, S. (2010). *Linchpin: Are you indispensible?* New York: Penguin.

Grandey, A. A. (2000). Emotion regulation in the workplace: A new way to conceptualize emotional labor. *Journal of Occupational Health Psychology, 5,* 59–100.

Grandey, A. A., Diefendorff, J. M., & Rupp, D. E. (2013). Emotional labor: Overview of definitions, theories, and evidence. In A. A. Grandey, J. M. Diefendorff & D. E. Rupp (Eds.), *Emotional labor in the 21st century: Diverse perspectives on emotion regulation at work*. New York, NY: Psychology Press/Routledge.

Hall, E. J. (1993). Waitering/waitressing: Engendering the work of table servers. *Gender and Society, 7*(3), 329–346.

Harlow, R. (2003). 'Race doesn't matter, but . . .': The effect of race on professors' experiences of emotion management in the undergraduate classroom. *Social Psychology Quarterly, (66),* 348–363.

Heilman, M. E. (1995). Sex stereotypes and their effects in the workplace: What we know and what we don't know. *Journal of Social Behavior and Personality, 10,* 3–26.

Heilman, M. E. (2001). Description and prescription: How gender stereotypes prevent women's ascent up the organizational ladder. *Journal of Social Issues, 57,* 657–674.

Heilman, M. E., & Okimoto, T. G. (2007). Why are women penalized for success at male tasks?: The implied communality deficit. *Journal of Applied Psychology, 92*(1), 81–92.

Heise, D. R. (1969). Affective dynamics in simple sentences. *Journal of Personality and Social Psychology,* (11), 204–213.

Heise, D. R. (1970). Potency dynamics in simple sentences. *Journal of Personality and Social Psychology,* (16), 48–54.

Heise, D. R. (2008). *Expressive order: Confirming sentiments in social actions*. New York: Springer.

Hondagneu-Sotelo, P. (2001). *Doméstica: Immigrant workers cleaning and caring in the shadows of affluence*. Berkeley: University of California Press.

Hochschild, A. R. (1983). *The managed heart: Commercialization of human feeling*. Berkeley: University of California Press.

Hochschild, A. R. (1989 [2003]). *The second shift: Working parents and the revolution at home*. New York: Penguin.

Hochschild, A. R. (1979). Emotion work, feeling rules, and social structure. *American Journal of Sociology,* (85), 551–575.

Hunt, P. M. (2008). From festies to tour rats: Examining the relationship between jamband subculture involvement and role meanings. *Social Psychology Quarterly, 4*(71), 356–378.

Jayson, S. (2011). Men, women flip the script in gender expectation. *USA Today,*

Retrieved from http://yourlife.usatoday.com/sex-relationships/dating/ story/2011/02/Men-women-flip-the-script-in-gender-expectation/43219110/1

Kemper, T. D. (1978). *A social interactional theory of emotions.* New York, NY: Wiley.

Koenig, A. M., Eagly, A. H., Mitchell, A. A., & Ristikari, T. (2011). Are leader stereotypes masculine? A meta-analysis of three research paradigms. *Psychological Bulletin,* 137, 616–642.

Kring, A. M., & Gordon, A. H. (1998). Sex differences in emotion: Expression, experience and physiology. *Journal of Personality and Social Psychology,* (74) 686–703.

Lively, K. J. (2000). Reciprocal emotion management: Working together to maintain stratification in private law firms. *Work and Occupations,* (27), 32–63.

Lively, K. J. (2001). Occupational claims to professionalism: The case of para-legals. *Symbolic Interaction,* 24: 343–66.

Lively , K. J. (2002). Client contact and emotional labor: Upsetting the balance and evening the field. *Work and Occupations,* (29), 198–225.

Lively, K. J. (2008). Emotional segues and the management of emotion, by women and men. *Social Forces,* (87), 911–936.

Lively , K. J., & Heise, D. R. (2004). Sociological realms of emotional experience. *American Journal of Sociology,* (109), 1109–1136.

Lively, K. J., & Powell, B. (2006). Emotional expression at work and at home: Domain, status or individual characteristics? *Social Psychology Quarterly,* (69), 17–38.

Lively, K. J., Powell, B., Geist, C. & Steelman, L. C. (2008). Equity among inti-mates. In Hegtvedt, K. Clay-Warner, J. (Eds.) *Advances in Group Processes* (25), 87–116.

Lively, K. J., Steelman, L. C, & Powell, B. (2010). Equity, emotion, and the household division of labor. *Social Psychology Quarterly* (73), 358–379.

Lois, J. (2003). *Heroic efforts: The emotional culture of search and rescue volunteers.* New York: New York University Press.

Lois, J. (2009). Emotionally layered accounts: Homeschoolers' justifications for maternal deviance. *Deviant Behavior,* (30), 201–234.

Lois, J. (2010). The temporal emotion work of motherhood: Homeschoolers' strategies for managing time shortage. *Gender & Society,* (24), 421–426.

Lonner, W. J. (1980). The search for psychological universals. In H. Triandis & W. Lambert (Eds.), *Handbook of cross-cultural psychology* (pp. 143–204). Boston: Allyn and Bacon.

MacKinnon, N. J. (1994). *Symbolic interactionism as affect control theory.* Albany, NY: State University of New York Press.

Magley, V. J., Hulin, C. L., Fitzgerald, L. F., & DeNardo, M. (1999). Outcomes of self-labeling sexual harassment. *Journal of Applied Psychology,* 84(3), 390–402.

Martin, S. E. (1999). Police force or police service? Gender and emotional labor. *The ANNALS of the American Academy of Political and Social Science,* 561: 111–126

McCabe, J. (2005). What's in a label? The relationship between feminist self-identification and 'feminist' attitudes among U.S. women and men." *Gender & Society* 19 (4): 480–505.

Milkie, M. A., Simon, R.W., & Powell, B. (1997). Through the eyes of children: Youths' perceptions and evaluations of maternal and paternal roles. *Social Psychology Quarterly*, 60(3), 218–237.

Meyers, S. (2005). *Twilight*. New York: Little Brown and Company.

Osgood, C. E. (1962). Studies on the generality of affective meaning systems. *American Psychologist*, (17), 10–28.

Pierce, J. (1995). *Gender trials: Emotional lives in contemporary law firms*. Berkeley, CA: University of California Press.

Powers, William T. (1973). *Behavior: The control of perception*. Chicago: Aldine de Gruyter.

Ridgeway, C. L. (2006). Expectation states theory and emotion. In J. E. Stets & J. H. Turner (Eds.), *Handbook of the sociology of emotions* (pp. 347–367). New York: Springer.

Ridgeway, C. L., & Bourg, C. (2004). Gender as status. In A. H. Eagly, A. E. Beall & R.J. Sternberg (Eds.), *The psychology of gender* (pp. 217–241). New York: Guilford Press.

Ridgeway, C. L. (2006). Linking social structure and interpersonal behavior: A theoretical perspective on cultural schemas and social relations. *Social Psychology Quarterly*, (69), 5–16.

Ridgeway, C. L. (2001). Gender, status, and leadership. *Journal of Social Issues*, (57), 637–655.

Ridgeway, C., & Johnson, C. (1990). What is the relationship between socioemotional behavior and status in task groups? *American Journal of Sociology*, (95), 1189–1212.

Robinson, D. T., Smith-Lovin, L., & Wisecup, A. K. (2006). Affect control theory. In J. E. Stets & J. H. Turner (Eds.), *Handbook of the sociology of emotions* (pp. 179–202). New York: Springer Science Business Media.

Robinson, M. D., & Johnson, J. T. (1997). Is it emotion or is it stress? Gender stereotypes and the perception of subjective experience. *Sex Roles*, (36), 235–258.

Rosin, H. (2011). (July/August). The end of men. *The Atlantic Magazine*, Retrieved from http://www.theatlantic.com/magazine/archive/2010/07/the-end-of-men/8135/2

Schrock, D., Boyd, E. M., & Leaf, M. (2009). Emotion work in the public performances of male-to-female transsexuals. *Archives of Sexual Behavior*, (38), 702–712.

Simon, R. W., & Nath, L. K. (2004). Gender and emotion in the U.S.: Do men and women differ in self-reports of feelings and expressive behavior? *American Journal of Sociology*, (109), 1137–1176.

Smith, H. W. (2002). The dynamics of Japanese and American interpersonal events: Behavioral settings versus personality traits. *Journal of Mathematical Sociology*, 26: 71–92.

Smith, H. W., Matsuno, T. and Umino, M. (1994). How similar are impression-formation processes among Japanese and Americans? *Social Psychology Quarterly* (57), 124–139

Smith, H. W., Umino, M., & Matsuno, T. (1997). The formation of gender-differentiated sentiments in Japan. *Journal of Mathematical Sociology* (22), 373–95.

Smith, T. (2008). Passion work: The joint production of emotional labor in professional wrestling. *Social Psychology Quarterly*, (71), 157–176.

Smith-Lovin, L., & Douglass, W. (1992.) An affect control analysis of two religious subcultures. In V. Gecas & D. Franks (Eds.), *Social Perspectives on Emotions*, 1 (pp. 217–248). New York: JAI Press.

Staske, S. A. (1996). Talking feelings: The collaborative construction of emotion in talk between close relational partners. *Symbolic Interaction*, (19), 111–142.

Steelman, L. C., & Powell, B. (1996). The family devalued: The treatment of the family in small groups literature. *Advances in Group Processes*, (13), 213–238.

Sutton, R. (1991). Maintaining norms about expressed emotion: The case of bill collectors. *Administrative Science Quarterly*, (36), 245–268.

Thoits, P. A. (1991). Gender differences in coping with emotional distress. In J. Eckenrode (Ed.), *The social context of coping* (pp. 107–138). New York: Plenum.

Thoits, P. A. (1985). Self-labeling processes in mental illness: The role of emotional deviance. *American Journal of Sociology* 92, 2: 221–249.

Thorne, B. (1993). *Gender play: Girls and boys at school*. New Brunswick, N.J.: Rutgers University Press.

Wagner, D. G., & Berger, J. (2002). Expectation states theory: An evolving research program In J. Berger & M. Zelditch (Eds.), *New Directions in Contemporary Sociological Theory* (pp. 41–76). New York: Rowman and Littlefield.

West, C., & Zimmerman, D. H. (1987). Doing gender. *Gender and Society*, (1), 125–151.

Wharton, A. S. (1993). The affective consequences of service work. *Work and Occupations*, (20), 205–232.

Williams, C. L. (1992). The glass escalator: Hidden advantages for men in the "female" professions. *Social Problems, 39*(3), 253–267.

Wingfield, A. H. (2010). Are some emotions marked "whites only"? Racialized feeling rules in professional workplaces. *Social Problems, 2*(57), 251–268.

# A Cultural Perspective on Emotion Labor

BATJA MESQUITA • ELLEN DELVAUX

## EMOTION LABOR IS CULTURED

In her book *The Managed Heart*, the sociologist Arlie Hochschild described several guidelines that the airlines industry gave to their flight attendants: "The first recommended strategy is to focus on what the other person might be thinking and feeling: Imagine a reason that excuses his/her behavior" (1983, p. 113). If this fails, the next recommended strategy was "to fall back on the thought 'I can escape'" (p. 113). Finally, stewardesses were told that, failing all attempts to regulate the feeling itself, they could resort to more acceptable ways of expression: "chewing on ice" (p. 113), for example. The flight attendants were thus encouraged to perform emotion labor: As part of their job requirement, they were asked to accommodate their emotions to the customers' needs and expectations. And since the emotions to be felt and displayed in the job context were very different from the flight attendants' habitual feelings and expressions, this emotion management came at a cost: It was alienating and stressful.

Much of what we know about emotion labor comes from one specific cultural context. Hochschild's flight attendants were middle-class North American women who worked for a North American company. Moreover, the research on emotion labor that followed her groundbreaking work was also largely conducted in mainstream North American contexts (see for an exception Van Jaarsveld & Poster, 2013). But what if the flight attendants, or the airlines, had been Japanese or French, rather than North American? Would our understanding of emotion labor be different? This is the question we address in the current chapter.

The central tenet of our chapter is that emotion labor – and in fact all forms of emotion regulation – can only be fully understood in connection with its cultural context (Mesquita & Albert, 2007). This is true for cultural contexts that have to this point been neglected in research, but it is equally true for emotion labor in the North American contexts that have been the focus of most previous research. Emotion labor is 'cultured,' but it is hard to see how our own culture shapes the meaning and practice of emotion labor without contrasting it to other cultures.

## Cultural Differences in Everyday Emotion Regulation

We want to start this chapter off by comparing the emotion labor among North American flight attendants, reported in Arlie Hochschild's famous book *The Managed Heart*, to everyday emotion regulation practices as reported by Japanese respondents in a large qualitative interview study that we did several years ago (Mesquita et al., 2006). In our study we interviewed about 50 Japanese and 50 American respondents – both from student and community samples – about a situation in which they had been offended. Some, but not all, of the reported situations were job-related. Respondents were invited to narrate freely about these situations, but we also prompted them for different aspects of the situations and their emotions. We content-analyzed the interviews for emotions and emotion regulation, after which the coded text fragments were also submitted to a quantitative analysis.

The American and the Japanese narratives of their offense situations were very different. On the one hand, the great majority of American respondents in our study blamed the offender, reported that they had been aggressive towards the offender, and distanced themselves from him or her. Among American respondents there was thus clearly a tendency to claim one's right, to guard one's autonomy, and, if necessary, to do so by severing the relationship. Note that these emotional responses could not have been more different from the ways in which the flight attendants in Hochschild's monograph were expected to feel and respond at work. If we assume that the spontaneous reactions of the American flight attendants were like the ones described by our American sample in the interview study, there was a big gap between the emotions they naturally felt and the ones required to be felt and expressed by the airlines; bridging that gap would have required effort, and might have been stressful.

On the other hand, the self-reports by Japanese respondents in our study bore a striking resemblance to the strategies reported by the flight attendants in *The Managed Heart*. The most prevalently reported emotional responses were trying to justify the behavior of the offender by taking his/her perspective, taking responsibility for the situation, trying to restore the relationship or regain proximity to the offender, and deliberately doing nothing (letting the situation cool down). Japanese respondents coped with the offense in ways that served to maintain or re-establish a harmonious relationship with the offender, and their emotional responses were reminiscent of the strategies taught to the flight attendants in Hochschild's book.

Take, for example, the account of a 52-year-old Japanese man living in Tokyo, who was a member of the organizing committee for his high school reunion, and in charge of the invitation of alumni. At a board meeting, he was told by another board member that he had not done a good enough job calling the alumni, and he felt "offended and annoyed." Yet, when he elaborates on the incident during the interview, he engages in the first strategy suggested to Hochschild's flight attendants: trying to understand what the other person is feeling or thinking.

> She is the kind of person who is eager to do anything that is necessary for the organization. When I tried to call alumni, I often found out that they had already been contacted by this other person . . . She was worried about me, and she might have thought I was unreliable. She is a very strong person. Perhaps I am not that strong; I tend to worry that my phone calls will come at an inconvenient time, so I find it really hard to decide when to call these alumni up . . . She must have thought that she'd rather make those phone calls herself than asking me to do it.

While our respondent tries to muster understanding, as more than half of our Japanese respondents in our interviews did, the disagreement with the other board member remains. He is critical of her attempts to force unwilling alumni to attend the reunion: "I would have said that attending the alumni meeting is voluntary, but of course, if you leave it up to the alumni themselves to decide whether or not to come, attendance will be lower than when you make it mandatory." His solution is similar to the second strategy offered to the flight attendants: thinking you can escape. In his own words: "If the other board members wanted to make attendance compulsory, I would think about quitting."

Japanese ways of emotional coping, inside and outside of the work place, thus bear similarity to the strategies flight attendants were taught to use to avoid disruptive interactions with their customers. They are geared towards relational harmony. Yet, does this mean that Japanese perform emotion labor? Does the emotion regulation in which our

Japanese respondents are engaged compromise their authentic emotions? We would say not.

In this chapter we propose that emotional regulation at work may be alienating and stressful only to the extent that it contrasts with everyday regulation strategies. We will argue that this is primarily the case in North American cultural contexts, where emotions are felt to be expressions of individuality, and their regulation is a function of social expectations or norms, is not very well practiced and, moreover, is perceived to be curtailing this individuality. In many other cultures, accommodation of one's feelings and expressions to social norms is part and parcel of everyday life: It is very well rehearsed, and thus automatic[1], and it is itself a defining aspect of the mature self – a self that is necessarily enmeshed in social relationships.

In the remainder of the chapter, we first explain our conception of culture, explaining the notion of cultural models. We then discuss the evidence for cultural differences in emotion rules and emotion regulation that can be understood from variations in cultural models. Subsequently, we discuss the possibility that emotion labor is only detrimental to the individual's wellbeing to the extent that it deviates from everyday emotion regulation in a given culture. We conclude the chapter by giving some recommendations for future research.

## Cultural Models: The Example of North American vs. East Asian Cultural Models

The central tenet of this chapter is that emotion regulation – emotional labor included – is always contextualized by the cultural models of self and relating. These cultural models are at the same time forms of knowledge and practices (Bruner, 1990; D'Andrade & Strauss, 1992; Markus & Kitayama, 2003). They are models of the social reality in that culture, as well as models of the normative. Cultural models constitute the backdrop of emotion regulation because they define the feeling rules as well as the preferred and habitual regulation strategy.

Although there are many different cultural models, most of the relevant research has compared East Asian (or Asian American) and North American cultural contexts. For this reason, we discuss the prevalent cultural models in these contexts in some detail. These models have been referred to as independent and interdependent models respectively. Independent models include value orientations that can be referred to as individualistic, and interdependent models include collectivist value orientations (e.g., Hofstede, 1980). However, cultural models cannot be equated to value orientations; rather, they are clusters of meanings as well as practices at the individual and interpersonal level, but also at the level of societal structure and organization.

Middle-class American models of self and relating are an example of independent cultural models. According to these models, the individual should be independent and free from others, as well as stand out among them (Kim & Markus, 1999; Rothbaum, Pott, Azuma, Miyake, & Weisz, 2000; Triandis, 1995). Consequently, it is very important that individuals think of themselves as possessing the positive characteristics that enable them to be autonomous and self-reliant; hence, there is an emphasis on self-esteem and happiness (Heine, Lehman, Markus, & Kitayama, 1999; Hochschild, 1995). Close relationships are not necessarily less valued than in cultures with interdependent models of self and relating (e.g., Japan), but the meaning and dynamics of relationships in American contexts strongly reflect independence concerns (Rothbaum et al., 2000). Continued engagement in relationships is based on trust – not a guarantee – that the relational partner will remain committed to oneself. Relationships are evaluated for the extent to which they meet one's personal needs, and conflicts are viewed as inevitable due to the frequent expression and negotiation of those needs. An individual is not expected to just accept the constraints imposed by others, but rather close relationships ought to afford independence and support personal initiative. Furthermore, mutual approval – enhancing each other's self-esteem – is an important quality of friendship in American cultural models (Kitayama & Markus, 2000), and relationships in general are expected to contribute to one's pursuit of personal achievement and happiness (Rothbaum et al., 2000; Triandis, 1994).

In contrast, according to the prevalent model in Japanese cultural contexts, individuals experience themselves as interdependent – that is, in relation to others, belonging to social groups, or significantly and reciprocally enmeshed in families, communities, or work groups (Kanagawa, Cross, & Markus, 2001; Kondo, 1990; Markus & Kitayama, 1991). The dominant goals for the self are to be like others, and to enhance the fit between what one is doing and what is expected (Heine et al., 2001; Kim & Markus, 1999; Lebra, 1992, 1994; Oishi & Diener, 2003). Self-improvement is a persistently salient concern, as it is accepted as necessary for meeting relational expectations (Karasawa, 2001; Lewis, 1995; Mesquita & Markus, 2004). In order to self-improve, individuals need to be aware of their shortcomings. Hence, they tend to focus on information about their own failures or mistakes, rather than accomplishments: Many events give rise to drops in self-esteem (Kitayama, Matsumoto, Markus, & Norasakkunkit, 1997). Close relationships ought to consist of mutual sympathy between self-critical individuals (Kitayama & Markus, 2000), and these relationships are based on the assurance that all relationship partners will meet role-based obligations and remain loyal to significant social in-groups (Rothbaum et al., 2000). The degree to which relationships meet one's personal needs is de-emphasized, and conflict is avoided in favor of conciliatory behaviors meant to preserve relational harmony.

This contrast between American and Japanese cultures illustrates that people in different socio-cultural contexts live different realities – or systems of practices and meanings – that we call cultural models of self and relating. Individuals' attempts to regulate their feelings never occur in a social vacuum, but rather must be situated in these cultural models. While the American and Japanese cultural models are certainly not unique, they represent different extremes of the cultural continuum. Moreover, much of the literature that we discuss can be understood by reference to those models. At the few places in the chapter where we present data from cultural contexts other than the North American and the East Asian, we will attempt to provide the information relevant to the pertinent cultural models.

## *Heterogeneity in Models*

A focus on cultural models of self and relating does not mean that people in a given context are homogeneous clones of one another (Markus et al., 1997). No two individuals in a culture will engage a given model in exactly the same way. An individual's particular representations of a model are specific to his or her learning history within that culture and level of engagement with specific cultural meanings and practices. Furthermore, a cultural framework does not negate individual differences in biologically-based temperament that individuals bring to their encounter with the socio-cultural world. What is critical, though, is that the world – the meanings, practices and institutions that are prevalent in a particular culture – still powerfully reflects dominant cultural models (Shweder, 1991, 1999). Thus, even if individuals have not fully internalized the cultural models, those models are still reflected in the daily routines and organizational structures in which the individuals engage, the reward structures that are in place, and the expectations of others.

## CULTURAL DIFFERENCES IN EMOTION RULES AND REGULATION STRATEGIES

Feelings rules and strategies of emotion regulation vary across cultural contexts, in ways that can be understood from the prevalent cultural models of self and relating in different cultures (Mesquita & Albert, 2007).

## Cultural Differences in Emotion Rules

Cultural differences in the desirable types of emotions, i.e., the feeling rules, have been suggested by different cross-cultural studies. For instance, Eid and Diener (2001) found in survey research that cultural differences in the *normative emotions – i.e. emotions that are considered desirable and appropriate* – accounted for differences in the frequency and intensity of emotions. We may thus assume that normative emotions act as feeling rules, and give direction to regulatory efforts. Respondents in the study by Eid and Diener were students from two independent (United States and Australia) and two interdependent cultural contexts (China and Taiwan) who answered questions about the desirability, frequency, and intensity of four positive (i.e., joy, affection, pride and contentment) and four negative (i.e., anger, fear, sadness and guilt) emotions. The largest cross-national differences were found for pride (for the positive emotions), and guilt (for the negative emotions). Pride, an emotion that may be thought to mark individual success, was considered most appropriate and desirable in the independent cultures, neutral in Taiwan (a country that has both independent and interdependent cultural influences), and undesirable and inappropriate in China. Guilt, an emotion acknowledging individual shortcomings and thus relevant to the continuous monitoring and adjustment central to an interdependent cultural model, was considered less undesirable and inappropriate in China than in the other three countries. Reported mean frequencies and intensities of emotions were positively related to the desirability and appropriateness of specific emotions, though the relationship between normative and actual emotions was more consistent for the positive than the negative emotions. That is, generally people seem to find it easier to stick to rules for positive than for negative emotions.

Evidence for differences in feeling rules also comes from research yielding cultural differences in *ideal emotions,* that is, the emotions that people would like to have ideally. In this research, ideal emotions predicted up to 28% of the variation in actual emotions, depending on the octant of the affective circumplex. When asked about their ideal emotions, East Asians indicated low arousal positive emotions (LAP) such as calm and content, whereas North Americans reported high arousal positive emotions (HAP), such as excited and energetic (Tsai, Knutson & Fung, 2006). That there are differences in ideal affect was, moreover, corroborated by survey data about leisure activities, music preferences, and drug use: The most prevalent activities in North American contexts – active vacations, upbeat music and stimulants – were likely to elicit HAP emotions, whereas the most prevalent activities in East Asian cultures – relaxing vacations, slow music, and narcotics – were more likely to bring out LAP emotions.

For instance, when asked about their ideal holidays, European Americans preferred places where they could explore and do exciting things, whereas Hong Kong Chinese preferred places where they could relax (Tsai, 2007).

Subsequent research tied the differences in feeling rules to the respective cultural models. Across a number of studies (Tsai, Miao, Seppala, Fung, & Yeung, 2007), participants preferred having HAP emotions when their task was to assert their personal needs, and change others' behaviors to meet those needs: This type of task is central to independent cultural models. In contrast, participants preferred having LAP emotions when they had to suppress their own needs in order to meet others' expectations, a task that is central to interdependent cultural models. In one study, comparing European American, Asian American and Hong Kong Chinese respondents, the cultural differences in preference for either HAP or LAP emotions were mediated by influence goals and adjustment goals, respectively. Thus, a preference for HAP emotions was associated with influence goals, and a preference for LAP emotions was linked to adjustment goals. The experimental research confirms that HAP emotions may be pursued in North American cultural contexts *because* they afford influencing, whereas LAP emotions may be the goal in East Asian cultural contexts *because* they allow for better adjustment.

Not only feeling rules, but also display rules can be understood from the cultural models. In a questionnaire study on display rules, Safdar and colleagues (2009) asked students from the US, Canada and Japan to report on the regulation of each of seven emotions (i.e., happiness, surprise, fear, sadness, anger, disgust, contempt) they deemed appropriate in one of two settings (public vs. private) with regard to close, distant, or in-between others. Students completed the Display Rule Assessment Inventory (Matsumoto, Yoo, Hirayama, & Petrova, 2005), in which they chose between seven behavioral options, among others amplifying, de-amplifying, neutralizing and masking the emotional experience. Consistent with interdependent models that foster accommodation to others rather than influence and control, Japanese reported more display rules against the expression of 'powerful' emotions, such as anger, and against positive emotions, such as happiness and surprise, than did North American respondents. Moreover, in the Japanese context, the display rules for powerful emotions varied according to interaction partner. Therefore, as could be expected on the basis of the Japanese cultural model, emotional regulation depended on the specific relational needs of that interaction.

## Feeling Rules at Work

Feeling rules at work appear to differ across cultures as well. In many interdependent contexts, it is of foremost importance to cultivate and maintain the relationships with co-workers and customers. In that sense, work is seen as an extension of private life. Employees in interdependent cultural contexts will adjust their emotions to the needs and expectations of others at work, just as they do at home. There are many examples of this relational work ideology in interdependent cultural contexts. For instance, *chaebol* is the ideal state of work relations in South-Korea; it is the imperative of treating one's colleagues as family members, which would entail expressing positive emotions. *Simpatía*, which translates to being in harmony, showing empathy and respect, and avoiding conflict with colleagues, is valued in Hispanic cultures (Sanchez-Burks & Lee, 2007); simpatía involves both the expression of positive emotions and the avoidance of conflict emotions.

The emphasis on personal relationships is in contrast with the task focus promoted in the North American cultural context (Sanchez-Burks, Nisbett, & Ybarra, 2000), where work and out-of-work time are strictly separated. In the North American context, managing one's emotions to please others, or even taking time to foster one's relationship, may seem to distract from the task goals one is actually pursuing. The contrast between cultural ideologies about work is nicely illustrated by an American expatriate manager who describes his experiences in China:

> To plunge right into business is considered impolite, rude, so you sit through countless hours of showing one another's pictures of families, talking about your background. On the whole, Asians truly enjoy that and I think for them it creates a bond with an otherwise completely foreign person – this person looks different, and this person talks different.
>
> (Jassawalla, Truglia & Garvey, 2004, p. 843)

In independent cultural contexts, especially the North American, the task should take precedence over the relationship, and certainly does not coincide with it. Against this backdrop, the perception of emotion regulation as *effortful* may thus be more pronounced.

Display rules at work also vary across different *independent* cultural contexts. One study compared display rules at work in France, Israel, Singapore and the US (Grandey, Rafaeli, Ravid, Wirtz & Steiner, 2010). Respondents were college students enrolled in management or industrial classes who had recently had paid employment: about two-thirds of the respondents worked in service jobs and one-third had supervisory experience. Respondents were asked what "they should do if they were interacting with [a customer/a co-worker/their supervisor] and feel [anger/happiness]." The expression of anger to any work target was considered more acceptable in both France and in Israel as compared to the US and Singapore; the expression of happiness, on the other hand, was highly valued in the US, and least in France, with the other two countries falling in between. The higher endorsement of happiness by US respondents is not surprising given that companies socialize their employees to provide "service with a smile," but also given the value placed on happiness as a marker of success and independence in American culture (Hochschild, 1995). Differences in the endorsement of these emotions appear to reflect variations in cultural values or goals. For instance, happiness can be seen as a marker of mastery, whereas anger is a response to violations of autonomy (Mesquita, Marinetti, & Delvaux, 2012; Rozin, Lowery, Imada & Haidt, 1999). In fact, mastery is an important value in the US, where the endorsement of happiness displays was higher, and both autonomy and egalitarianism are important value domains in France, where anger displays were condoned more.

## Cultural Differences in Regulation Strategies

Not only the feeling rules, but also the most prevalent *regulation strategies* appear to differ across cultures. Most psychological research has focused on two regulation strategies, re-appraisal and suppression (e.g., Gross & John, 2003; Gross & Thompson, 2007). *Re-appraisal* refers to adopting a different perspective of the situation, thereby changing not only the appraisal, but also the feeling itself. The number one regulation strategy suggested to Hochschild's flight attendants – trying to understand what happens from the point of view of the customer – is an example of re-appraisal. Re-appraisal is a regulatory strategy that takes place before the emotion is consciously experienced, and actually changes the emotion itself. Re-appraisal is thus a form of deep acting. On the other hand, *suppression* targets the responses of emotion. The strategy suggested to the flight attendants as a last resort, "chewing on ice," was an example of suppression, as it would help these women to conceal their distress or annoyance. Suppression is a regulatory strategy used to modify the behavioral responses after the fact. Since it does not address the emotion itself, but only its outward expression, it may be considered a form of surface acting (Hochschild, 1983).

Cross-cultural research yields a number of cultural differences in regulation strategies. First, it submits that participants in independent cultural contexts have a strong preference for re-appraisal (deep acting) over suppression (surface acting) as regulation strategy, whereas the preference for re-appraisal over suppression is much weaker, and in some cases even absent, among participants in interdependent cultures (e.g., Matsumoto et al., 2008; Novin, Banjeree, Dadhkah, & Rieffe, 2009; Soto, Perez, Kim, Lee & Minnick, 2011). These culturally different preferences for regulation strategies can be understood from the respective cultural models. In independent cultures, surface acting may be tantamount to hiding one's inner feelings, and may thus be seen as a loss of identity and, in that sense, less preferable than deep acting. In interdependent cultures, on the other hand, deep acting and surface acting may both be seen as potentially viable strategies to achieve the relational goal of harmony, and as such be equally valued. Consistently, research has also yielded different relationships between deep acting and surface acting for independent and interdependent cultural contexts respectively: re-appraisal and suppression are negatively correlated in independent, and positively correlated in interdependent cultures. Again, in interdependent cultural contexts, one may use the two regulatory strategies in combination, whereas these strategies may be thought to have opposite outcomes in independent cultural contexts. We discuss some of the evidence in more detail.

In survey research, for instance, Matsumoto and colleagues (2008) investigated the relationship between cultural values and the use of certain emotion regulation strategies. Respondents from 23 different countries completed an emotion regulation questionnaire measuring whether they habitually suppress or re-appraise their emotions. In interdependent cultures, adoption of suppression and re-appraisal were positively related, meaning that a person who regulates her emotions in those cultures will use both strategies equally. On the other hand, the use of suppression and re-appraisal strategies were negatively related for respondents from contexts with independent cultural models, implying that the people using re-appraisal and those using suppression as their main regulatory strategy were not the same.

Similarly, Novin and colleagues (2009) compared the regulatory strategies of Dutch and Iranian 10- and 11-year-olds; Dutch children live in predominantly independent cultural contexts, whereas Iranian cultures are brought up in a context that can be characterized as interdependent. Iranian children reported more suppression than their Dutch counterparts. For instance, 96% of the Iranian children reported having concealed sadness at least once, against only 82% of the Dutch children. Thus, the relative prevalence of suppression was higher in the interdependent than the independent context of study. Moreover, Iranian and Dutch children provided different reasons for suppression: Iranian children referred to prosocial motives – i.e., being concerned with others, for instance "I don't want him to feel bad" – as the main reason to hide their emotions, whereas Dutch children referred to self-protective motives – i.e., avoiding negative outcomes for the self, for instance "Otherwise I'll get punished" (Novin et al., 2009).

## *Summary*

In sum, both feeling rules and regulation strategies vary across cultures, in ways that can be understood from the cultural models. These differences in the general emotion regulation practices may have consequences for the understanding of emotion labor across cultures. Notably, when feeling rules differ across cultures, these differences may be manifested in the work place as well. Thus, the display of happiness at work may be normative only in cultures where happiness marks the success and independence of an individual, or alternatively in cultures where it marks the smoothness of relationships. The implication is that when multinationals set the same display rules in different cultures, these may not have the same meaning cross-culturally; across cultures, display rules may therefore have a different effect on the employees. Multi-nationals may require all their sales managers to smile, but this could be much more natural to employees in a culture in which happiness is a normative emotion than in one in which it is not. Cultural differences in regulatory strategies may be similarly relevant to emotion labor, in ways that will be discussed in the next section.

## CULTURAL DIFFERENCES IN THE COSTS OF EMOTION LABOR

One of the key reasons to study emotion labor is that it is thought to be stressful to the employee (cf. Grandey, Diefendorff, & Rupp, 2013). There is in fact ample evidence that emotion labor may be stressful in North American samples (Hülsheger & Schewe, 2011). Evidence for the deleterious effects of emotion labor is limited to North American samples. For instance, a recent cross-national survey study (Allen, Diefendorff & Ma, 2012) yielded higher costs from emotion regulation in the workplace for American than Chinese service workers. Emotion labor, and particularly surface acting, was personally more costly in terms of job burnout (i.e., exhaustion and depersonalization) to the American than to the Chinese group of employees. Deep acting, on the other hand, was unrelated to job burnout in American employees, but it was *negatively* associated for Chinese employees. The latter suggests that emotion regulation in the Chinese sample could even lead to a higher level of psychological well-being, presumably because it was tantamount to successfully managing the cultural task of social adjustment or harmony.

In the extant literature, three different but related mechanisms have been supposed to underlie the harmful effects of emotion labor to the employee: 1) displaying different emotions than one actually feels causes dissonance, which is stress-provoking; 2) emotion regulation is effortful, and thus taxing in the long run, and 3) emotion regulation, particularly surface acting, appears phony and is reacted to negatively by others (Hülsheger & Schewe, 2011). In fact, cross-cultural evidence with respect to each of these mechanisms suggests that emotion labor is less stressful and less costly for people in interdependent than independent cultures.

## Cultural Differences in Emotion-display Dissonance

The first mechanism proposed is that of emotive or emotional dissonance (Hochschild, 1983); that is, emotion labor may be stressful to the extent that the emotions expressed are discrepant from the emotions felt. The idea is rooted in an independent cultural model that considers feelings, emotions, and preferences as defining features of individuality (Markus & Kitayama, 2003). According to this model, what distinguishes Mary from Anne is that she is timid, that she is angry at her parents, and that she likes the outside. Requiring Anne to act in an outgoing way, to be excited to see her parents, or to spend a lot of time inside would go against Anne's very nature, and it would thus compromise her individuality. According to this cultural model, emotions are located within the individual. Consistently, when inferring emotions from facial expressions, an isolated face suffices for respondents from Western cultural contexts (Masuda et al., 2008). By Western definition, emotions are tied to the individual person; accommodation of these emotions to social requirements is seen to compromise their core; or even, to be a violation of the individual's authenticity. Not so in many non-Western cultures.

In these non-Western cultural contexts, emotions are considered to take place between people (Uchida, Townsend, Markus, & Bergsieker, 2009). For instance, Japanese respondents inferred more emotions in Olympic athletes when these athletes were portrayed together with other people than when they appeared in pictures by themselves, or when the athletes mentioned relationships in their self-descriptions than when they described themselves without reference to other people; the findings were reversed for American respondents (Uchida et al., 2009). Similarly, Japanese, unlike American respondents inferred an individual's emotions not just from his own facial expressions, but also from the facial expressions of the surrounding people (Masuda et al., 2008). When a target person looked happy, but the people surrounding him looked angry, Japanese respondents rated him as less happy than when the people surrounding the target person looked happy as well. In many non-Western cultural contexts, notably Japan, the prevalent idea is thus that emotional expression (and emotion itself) is always the outcome of accommodations to other people's needs and expectations. Whereas the adjustment of one's emotions to the needs and expectations of others may be burdensome for people in Western cultures, because it is perceived to violate their independence (cf. Morling, Kitayama, & Miyamoto, 2002), it may come as "natural" to people in interdependent cultures. If anything, performing emotion regulation would be considered a sign of maturity in interdependent contexts, not inauthentic.

That a discrepancy between feelings or preferences on the one hand and expressions on the other is less disturbing in interdependent, notably Japanese cultural contexts, than in independent cultural contexts is also consistent with research about cognitive dissonance (e.g., Kitayama, Snibbe, Markus, & Suzuki, 2004). In this research, people from Japanese contexts did not feel any dissonance over behavior that was inconsistent with their own preferences. It is possible, then, that "emotion-display dissonance" (see Grandey, et al., 2013) simply does not exist in inter-dependent cultural contexts. A recent study among North American employees with service jobs shows that the value for emotional authenticity varies at the individual level and moderates whether surface acting is, in fact, distressing (Pugh, Groth & Hennig-Thurau, 2011). Surface acting meant lower levels of job satisfaction and higher levels of emotional exhaustion for employees who valued emotional authenticity. However, the negative effects of surface acting were attenuated for employees who did not value authenticity. We submit that these individual level findings can be generalized to the cultural level; employees from interdependent cultures are less likely to value authentic emotional expressions and thus less likely to see the negative effects from surface acting.

A related way to explain the cultural differences is that, in interdependent cultural contexts, the very act of adjusting to the social environment is part of one's identity. Emotional labor may only be harmful or stressful to employees to the extent it is felt as self-betrayal, or felt inauthenticity at work (Erickson & Wharton, 1997). When one's personal purposes and those of the job coincide, i.e., when emotion labor fits the individual's salient and valued personal and social identities, those negative consequences may be cancelled (cf. Ashforth & Humphrey, 1993). This is the type of explanation given by Grandey and her colleagues (2005) to account for the finding that surface acting meant low job satisfaction in American, but not in French employees. In the US, suppressing one's personal emotional expression for organizational goals is to lose one's identity; French employees supposedly believe that their emotional regulation at work is self-chosen, rather than imposed, and thus are less likely to experience it as costly to the self.

## Cultural Differences in the Effort of Emotion Regulation

The second mechanism for why emotion regulation – particularly surface acting – is thought to be distressing to employees is the expended effort from regulating oneself. There is extensive research on the costs and benefits of different regulation strategies, in particular re-appraisal and suppression; concepts that are comparable to those of deep acting and surface action in the emotion labor literature (see Hülsheger & Schewe, 2011). Most of the research on emotion regulation has focused exclusively on respondents from independent cultural contexts (Gross & Levenson, 1997; Gross & John, 2003; Richards & Gross, 2000). In this research, there is ample evidence that suppression – surface acting – comes at a cost in North American, independent cultural contexts. In most of the pertinent experimental research, participants were assigned to one of three conditions, in which they were (a) asked to suppress their emotional expression, (b) asked to re-appraise the situation (in particular, to take distance from it), or in the control condition (c), not asked to do anything. Though suppression effectively reduced the expression of the (undesired) emotions (compared to the control condition), it (a) failed to change the emotional experience, (b) was associated with an increase in physiological arousal, and (c) used up cognitive resources. For example, suppression was found to reduce memory for an emotional event; re-appraisal had some decrement compared to the control condition but not as much as suppression (Richards & Gross, 2000).

However, in interdependent cultures the emotion regulation may not require as much effort – and thus there should be fewer signs of stress and performance costs compared to the Western respondents. Support for this idea was obtained in a study by Mauss and Butler (2010). They measured cardiovascular responses known to be associated with threat and challenge in participants who had just been provoked by an experimenter making nasty comments, while also performing a cognitively demanding task. Participants were women from either independent European American or interdependent Asian American contexts. To the extent that Asian American respondents endorsed emotional control as a value, the women reported feeling less angry, were coded as expressing less anger, and had a challenge pattern of cardiovascular responding. Therefore, Asian American women who valued emotional control were efficacious in applying it. On the other hand, European American women valuing emotional control successfully managed their angry *behavior*, but not their angry feelings. Moreover, the cardiovascular pattern observed in the latter group was typical of a threat response, suggesting that the task demands exceeded these women's coping potential. The results are consistent with the idea that Asian American contexts support and encourage suppression, and thus offer good opportunity for practice to those who value it, and that mainstream North American contexts do not. Such opportunities for practice may thus translate into less effortful emotion regulation.[2]

Finally, cross-cultural survey research yields converging results, showing that suppression (or surface acting) is more costly in independent than in interdependent cultural contexts, although this research is not work-specific. In one study (Soto et al., 2011), European American and Hong Kong Chinese participants reported on their habitual emotion regulation strategies as well as their psychological functioning. Habitual suppression in European Americans was related to both depressive symptoms and low levels of life satisfaction. In contrast, suppression was unrelated to psychological well-being in the Hong Kong Chinese group. Yet another study that focused only on anger regulation among European and Asian American students yielded similar conclusions (Cheung & Park, 2010). In this study, the positive relationship between suppression and depressive symptoms, found in a European American student sample, was attenuated in the Asian American student sample. In sum, whereas emotional suppression appears to be costly in European American contexts, it is not as taxing in a number of Asian and Asian American cultural contexts. As suggested before, the difference may be a result of levels of practice, in addition to the identity and value differences that make the dissonance of surface acting less distressing.

## *Cultural Differences in the Social Reaction to Emotion Regulation*

Lastly, emotion regulation, especially surface acting, is thought to be distressing due to the social costs and negative reactions to inauthentic displays from others (Hülsheger & Schewe, 2010). Again, this assumption is based on Western culture norms and research. When experimental research manipulating suppression has been applied to dyads in the US (Butler, et al., 2003), people judged their partners as less responsive and more hostile and withdrawn when these partners were instructed to suppress their emotions than when they were not instructed to regulate their emotions. Thus, when people tried to suppress their emotions in these experiments, this impaired their social interaction with their (American) partner. This is consistent with holding a value for authenticity in this independent cultural context.

More recent, culturally comparative research has suggested that emotion suppression may not be viewed negatively by people from interdependent cultural contexts. In one study using a paradigm similar to the one described above, women from one independent (European American) and one interdependent (Asian American) cultural context watched a movie, and discussed it afterwards (Butler, Lee & Gross, 2007). One third of the dyads consisted of two European American women, one third were Asian American women, and one third of the dyads was mixed. In the experimental condition, one of the partners was asked to suppress her emotions during the discussion phase. Both European and Asian Americans who were instructed to suppress their emotions were perceived by their partners to be less responsive and more hostile and withdrawn than European and Asian Americans in the control condition, but the difference between the conditions was significantly smaller for Asian American women (Butler, et al., 2007). Interestingly, the negative perceptions of suppressing partners were also moderated by the cultural values of the suppressors. This may suggest that Asian American who strongly endorse bi-cultural values are more practiced suppressors, whose social functioning will be less hampered by suppression. Such research on the social costs of suppression has clear implications for cross-cultural work interactions and the need for future research to consider the cultural context of both parties in the interaction.

## CONCLUSIONS

The flight attendants cited in Hochschild's book *The Managed Heart* described how they strategically managed their emotions in order to cajole their customers, and keep the peace in the cabin. This was perceived as an effortful task, even alienating. Emotion labor researchers since have confirmed the negative effects of display rule requirements on employee well-being. But what if the flight attendants had been Japanese or French? Would the task of emotion labor have been equally daunting? Would they have experienced the same negative consequences? We submit that the answer is that culture matters.

Based on cross-cultural studies on emotion regulation, we propose that emotion labor may be cultured in a number of different ways. First, feeling rules at work will be informed in large part by the larger cultural context. Multinationals importing feeling rules from other cultural contexts may thus ran up against a brick wall: It will be hard to impose a feeling rule that is not shared by the larger cultural context. Similarly, when enforced, imported feeling rules may have higher personal costs when they are inconsistent with one's self-definition (Syed, Ali, & Winstanley, 2005), which is culturally informed.

Furthermore, emotion regulation strategies may be particularly costly when they are not well practiced, or also at odds with the cultural models of self and relatedness. In contrast, regulation strategies that are culturally afforded may be well practiced and, therefore, without effort. Long-term negative consequences for employees may not be produced by particular emotion regulation strategies themselves, but rather by the fact that they are at odds with their (culturally defined) identity, thus impacting their own sense of self and how others respond to them.

In sum, the focus on a single type of cultural context by definition obscures the role of cultural context. Culturally comparative research will be needed to reveal different practices of emotion labor, but also the different consequences of certain forms of emotion regulation for the individual's well-being.

Understanding culture is all the more important with an increasingly diverse work force, and a growing global market. First, managing diversity itself may be a source of emotion labor, which so far has not been a topic of study. Research is needed on the emotion regulation required to work in culturally diverse teams. What is the emotion labor involved when different employees assume different feeling rules? How do employees try to adjust to social norms and expectations with which they are not even familiar? How do migrant workers learn about the normative emotions of the majority culture?

Second, culturally comparative research may reveal just how much emotion regulation in companies is dictated by the cultural contexts in which it takes place. It could reveal very different regulatory endpoints and strategies. Moreover, it may find that the conditions under which emotion regulation is personally costly differ strongly across cultures. As such, cross-cultural research on emotion labor may show the limits to exporting emotion norms to foreign cultural contexts, as multinationals often try to do.

To fully understand emotion labor, the specific cultural contexts in which it takes place will need to be considered. Research is needed that maps cultural diversity in the condoned emotion strategies, the feeling rules, and the reasons for regulation. We expect that emotion labor is costly to the individual to the extent that the company or organization imposes different endpoints, strategies and reasons than are customary in the daily cultural practice. Insight into emotion labor thus requires that it be culturally contextualized.

## ENDNOTES

1   This view is consistent with that of Ashforth & Humphrey (1993; see Grandey, Diefendorff & Rupp, 2013) who argued that emotional labor can become automatic and thus effortless.

2   Incidentally, in North American research referred to before (Pugh, et al., 2011), the negative effects of emotion labor for employees were buffered by self-efficacy for regulation: the relationship of surface acting with job satisfaction and emotional exhaustion was weaker for high efficacy as compared to low efficacy employees, suggesting that emotion labor, even within a US sample, was less deleterious for those who were good at it.

# REFERENCES

Allen, J. A., Diefendorff, J. M., & Ma, Y. (2012). *Differences in emotional labor across cultures: China vs. the United States.* Unpublished manuscript.

Ashforth, B. E., & Humphrey, R. H. (1993). Emotional labor in service roles: The influence of identity. *The Academy of Management Review, 18*(1), pp. 88–115.

Bruner, J. (1990). *Acts of meaning.* Cambridge, MA: Harvard University Press.

Butler, E. A., Egloff, B., Wilhelm, F. H., Smith, N. C., Erickson, E. A., & Gross, J. J. (2003). The social consequences of expressive suppression. *Emotion, 3,* 48–67.

Butler, E. A., Lee, T. L., Gross, J. J. (2007). Emotion regulation and culture: Are the social consequences of emotion suppression culture-specific? *Emotion 7*(1), 30–48.

Cheung, R. Y. M., & Park, I. J. K. (2010). Anger suppression, interdependent self-construal, and depression among Asian American and European American college students. *Cultural Diversity & Ethnic Minority, 16*(4), 517–525.

D'Andrade, R. G., & Strauss, C. (1992). *Human motives and cultural models.* Cambridge, UK: Cambridge University Press.

Eid, M., & Diener, E. (2001). Norms for experiencing emotions in different cultures: Inter- and intranational differences. *Journal of Personality and Social Psychology, 81,* 869–885.

Erickson, R. J., & Wharton, A. S. (1997). Inauthenticity and depression. *Work and Occupations, 24,* 188–213.

Grandey, A. A., Diefendorff, J. M., & Rupp, D. E. (2013). Emotional labor: Overview of definitions, theories, and evidence. In A. A. Grandey, J. M. Diefendorff & D. E. Rupp (Eds.), *Emotional labor in the 21st century: Diverse perspectives on emotion regulation at work.* New York, NY: Psychology Press/Routledge.

Grandey, A. A., Fisk, G. M., & Steiner, D. D. (2005). Must "service with a smile" be stressful? The moderating role of personal control for American and French employees. *Journal of Applied Psychology, 90,* 893–904.

Grandey, A., Rafaeli, A., Ravid, S., Wirtz, J., & Steiner, D. D. (2010). Emotion display rules at work in the global service economy: The special case of the customer. *Journal of Service Management, 21*(3), 388–412.

Gross, J. J., & John, O. P. (2003). Individual differences in two emotion regulation processes: Implications for affect, relationships, and well-being. *Journal of Personality and Social Psychology, 85,* 348–362.

Gross, J. J., & Levenson, R. W. (1997). Hiding feelings: The acute effects of inhibiting negative and positive emotion. *Journal of Abnormal Psychology, 106,* 95–103.

Gross, J. J., & Thompson, R. A. (2007). Emotion regulation: Conceptual foundations. In J.J. Gross (Ed.), *Handbook of emotion regulation* (pp. 3–24). New York, NY: Guilford Press.

Heine, S. J., Kitayama, S., Lehman, D. R., Takata, T., Ide, E., Leung, K., et al. (2001). Divergent consequences of success and failure in Japan and North America: An investigation of self-improving motivations and malleable selves. *Journal of Personality and Social Psychology, 81*(4), 599–615.

Heine, S. J., Lehman, D. R., Markus, H. R., & Kitayama, S. (1999). Is there a universal need for positive self-regard. *Psychological Review, 106*(4), 766–794.

Hochschild, A. R. (1983). *The managed heart: Commercialization of human feeling.* Berkeley: University of California Press.

Hochschild, J. L. (1995). What is the American dream? In J. L. Hochschild (Ed.), *Facing up to the American dream: Race, class and the soul of the nation* (pp. 15–38). Princeton: Princeton University Press.

Hofstede, G. (1980). *Culture's consequences.* Beverly Hills, CA: Sage.

Hülsheger, U. R., & Schewe, A. F. (2011). On the costs and benefits of emotional labor: A meta-analysis of three decades of research. *Journal of Occupational Health Psychology, 16*(3), 361–389.

Jassawalla, A., Truglia, C., & Garvey, J. (2004). Cross-cultural conflict and expatriate management adjustment: An exploratory study. *Management Decision, 42*(7), 837–849.

Kanagawa, C., Cross, S. E., & Markus, H. R. (2001). "Who am I?" The cultural psychology of the conceptual self. *Personality and Social Psychology Bulletin, 27*(1), 90–103.

Karasawa, M. (2001). Nihonnjinnni okeru jitano ninnshiki: Jikohihan baiasuto tasyakouyou baiasu [A Japanese mode of self-making: Self-criticism and other enhancement]. *Japanese Journal of Psychology, 72*(4), 198–209.

Kim, H., & Markus, H. R. (1999). Deviance or uniqueness, harmony or conformity? A cultural analysis. *Journal of Personality and Social Psychology, 77*(4), 785–800.

Kitayama, S., & Markus, H. R. (2000). The pursuit of happiness and the realization of sympathy: Cultural patterns of self, social relations, and well-being. In E. Diener & E. Suh (Eds.), *Subjective well-being across cultures* (pp. 113–161). Cambridge, MA: MIT Press.

Kitayama, S., Matsumoto, D., Markus, H. R., & Norasakkunkit, V. (1997). Individual and collective processes in the construction of the self: Self-enhancement in the US and self-criticism in Japan. *Journal of Personality and Social Psychology, 72*(6), 1245–1267.

Kitayama, S., Snibbe, A. C., Markus, H. R., & Suzuki, T. (2004). Is there any "free" choice?: Self and dissonance in two cultures. *Psychological Science, 15,* 527–533.

Kondo, D. (1990). *Crafting selves: Power, gender, and discourses of identity in a Japanese workplace.* Chicago: University of Chicago Press.

Lebra, T. S. (1992). Self in Japanese culture. In N. E. Rosenbergeer (Ed.), *Japanese sense of self.* New York: Oxford University Press.

Lebra, T. S. (1994). Mother and child in Japanese socialization: A Japan–US comparison. In P. M. Greenfield, & R. R. Cocking (Eds.), *Cross-cultural roots of minority child development* (pp. 259–274). Hillsdale: Erlbaum.

Lewis, C. C. (1995). The roots of discipline: Community and commitment. In *Educating hearts and minds: Reflections on Japanese preschool and elementary education* (pp. 101–123). Cambridge, UK: Cambridge University Press.

Markus, H. R., & Kitayama, S. (1991). Culture and the self: Implications for cognition, emotion, and motivation. *Psychological Review, 98,* 224–253.

Markus, H. R., & Kitayama, S. (2003). Models of agency: Sociocultural diversity in the construction of action. In J. J. Berman & V. Murphy-Berman (Eds.), *Cross-cultural differences in perspectives on the self* (Vol. 49, pp. 18–74). Lincoln, NE: University of Nebraska Press.

Markus, H. R., Mullally, P. R., & Kitayama, S. (1997). Selfways: Diversity in modes of cultural participation. In U. Neisser, & D. A. Jopling (Eds.), *The conceptual self in context: Culture, experience, self-understanding* (pp. 13–61). Cambridge, UK: Cambridge University Press.

Masuda, T., Ellsworth, P. C., Mesquita, B., Leu, J., Tanida, K., & van de Veerdonk, E. (2008). Placing the face in context: Cultural differences in the perception of facial emotion. *Journal of Personality and Social Psychology, 94*(3), 365–381.

Matsumoto, D., Yoo, S. H., Hirayama, S., & Petrova, G. (2005). Development and validation of a measure of display rule knowledge: The display rule assessment inventory. *Emotion, 5,* 23–40.

Matsumoto, D., Yoo, S. H., Nakagawa, S., Anguas-Wong, A. M., Arriola, M., Bauer, L. M., et al. (2008). Culture, emotion regulation, and adjustment. *Journal of Personality and Social Psychology, 94*(6), 925–937.

Mauss, I. B., & Butler, E. A. (2010). Cultural context moderates the relationship between emotion control values and cardiovascular challenge versus threat responses. *Biological Psychology, 84,* 521–530.

Mesquita, B., & Albert, D. (2007). The cultural regulation of emotions. In J. J. Gross (Ed.), *The handbook of emotion regulation* (pp. 486–503). New York: Guilford Press.

Mesquita, B., Karasawa, M., Haire, A., Izumi, S., Hayashi, A., Idzelis, M., et al. (2006). *What do I feel: The role of cultural models in emotion representation.* Unpublished manuscript.

Mesquita, B., Marinetti, C., & Delvaux, E. (2012). The social psychology of emotions. In S. Fiske & N. Macrae (Eds.), *Sage handbook of social cognition* (pp. 297–317). Thousand Oaks, CA: Sage.

Mesquita, B., & Markus, H. R. (2004). Culture and emotion: Models of agency as sources of cultural variation in emotion. In N. H. Frijda, A. S. R. Manstead, & A. H. Fischer (Eds.), *Feelings and emotions: The Amsterdam symposium* (pp. 341–358). Cambridge, MA: Cambridge University Press.

Morling, B., Kitayama, S., & Miyamoto, Y. (2002). Cultural practices emphasize influence in the United States and adjustment in Japan. *Personality and Social Psychology Bulletin, 28,* 311–323.

Novin, S., Banjeree, R., Dadhkah, A., & Rieffe, C. (2009). Self-reported use of display use in the Netherlands and Iran: Evidence for sociocultural influence. *Social Development, 18*(2), 397–411.

Oishi, S., & Diener, E. (2003). Goals, culture, and subjective well-being. *Personality and Social Psychology Bulletin, 29*(8), 939–949.

Pugh, S. D., Groth, M., & Hennig-Thurau (2011). Willing and able to fake emotions: A closer examination of the link between emotional dissonance and employee well-being. *Journal of Applied Psychology, 96*(2), 377–390.

Richards, J. M., & Gross, J. J. (2000). Emotion regulation and memory: The cognitive costs of keeping one's cool. *Journal of Personality and Social Psychology, 79,* 410–424.

Rothbaum, F., Pott, M., Azuma, H., Miyake, K., & Weisz, J. (2000). The development of close relationships in Japan and the United States: Paths of symbiotic harmony and generative tension. *Child Development, 71*(5), 1121–1142.

Rozin, P., Lowery, L., Imada, S., & Haidt, J. (1999). The moral emotion triad hypothesis: A mapping between three moral emotions (contempt, anger, disgust) and three moral ethics (community, autonomy, divinity). *Journal of Personality and Social Psychology, 76*, 574–586.

Safdar, S., Friedlmeier, W., Matsumoto, D., Yoo, S. H., Kwantes, C. T., Kakai, H., Yoo, S. H. (2009). Variations of emotional display rules within and across cultures: A comparison between Canada, USA, and Japan. *Canadian Journal of Behavioural Science/Revue Canadienne des Sciences du Comportement, 41*, 1–10.

Sanchez-Burks, J. , & Lee, F. (2007). Culture and workways. In S. Kitayama & D. Cohen (Eds.), *Handbook of Cultural Psychology* (Vol 1, pp. 346–369). New York: Guilford Press.

Sanchez-Burks, J., Nisbett, R., & Ybarra, O. (2000). Cultural styles, relational schemas and prejudice against outgroups. *Journal of Personality and Social Psychology, 79*(2), 174–189.

Shweder, R. A. (1991). *Thinking through cultures.* Cambridge, MA: Harvard University Press.

Shweder, R. A. (1999). Why cultural psychology? *Ethos, 27*(1), 62–73.

Soto, J. A., Perez, C. R., Kim, Y.-H., Lee, E. A., & Minnick, M. R. (2011). Is expressive suppression always associated with poorer psychological functioning? A cross-cultural comparison between European Americans and Hong Kong Chinese. *Emotion, 11*, 1450–1455.

Syed, J., Ali, F., & Winstanley, D. (2005). In pursuit of modesty: Contextual emotional labour and the dilemma for working women in Islamic societies. *International Journal of Work Organization, 1*(2), 150–167.

Triandis, H. C. (1994). *Culture and social behavior.* New York: McGraw-Hill.

Triandis, H. C. (1995). *Individualism and collectivism.* Boulder, CO: Westview Press.

Tsai, J. (2007). Ideal affect: Cultural causes and behavioral consequences. *Perspectives on Psychological Science, 2*, 242–259.

Tsai, J. L., Knutson, B., & Fung, H. H. (2006). Cultural variation in affect valuation. *Journal of Personality and Social Psychology, 90*, 288–307.

Tsai, J.L., Miao, F.F., Seppala, E., Fung, H.H., & Yeung, D.Y. (2007). Influence and adjustment goals: Sources of cultural differences in ideal affect. *Journal of Personality and Social Psychology, 92*, 1102–1117.

Uchida, Y., Townsend, S. S. M., Markus, H. R., & Bergsieker, H. B. (2009). Emotions as within or between people? Cultural variation in lay theories of emotion expression and inference. *Personality & Social Psychology Bulletin, 35*(11), 1427–1439.

Van Jaarsveld, D., & Poster, W. (2013). Call centers: Emotional labor over the phone. In A. A. Grandey, J. M. Diefendorff & D. E. Rupp (Eds.), *Emotional labor in the 21st century: Diverse perspectives on emotion regulation at work.* New York, NY: Psychology Press/Routledge.

# PART V

# Multi-Disciplinary Perspectives: Reflections and Projections

# 12

# Reflections and Projections from Pioneers in Emotions Research

## INTRODUCTION

As is evidenced by the citations in our introductory chapter and other chapters in this book, there are several scholars whose work on emotions has been central to the field of emotional labor. In addition to Arlie Hochschild (see Foreword), we invited five essays from "emotion pioneers" in the fields of organizational behavior (Ashforth & Humphrey; Ashkanasy & Daus; Rafaeli), psychology (Gross), and sociology (Wharton). We asked them for their reflections on the state of emotional labor research and their projections regarding exciting future directions. We are grateful for the contributions of these authors; we believe that they set the stage for the multi-disciplinary study of emotional labor in the 21st century.

The Editors (Alicia, Jim, and Deb)

# EMOTIONAL LABOR: LOOKING
# BACK NEARLY 20 YEARS

BLAKE E. ASHFORTH • RONALD H. HUMPHREY

It's pretty safe to describe any publication that has been cited 2,685 times (according to the Web of Science as of November 9, 2011) as generative and inspirational, and Arlie Hochschild's (1983) brilliant book – along with the riveting qualitative research and theorizing of Anat Rafaeli and Bob Sutton – certainly was for us. Given that our own modest extension of this pioneering work on emotional labor was published nearly 20 years ago (Ashforth & Humphrey, 1993), this seems like an opportune moment to take stock of three topics that we regarded as important but not very evident in the emotional labor literature at that time.

## *Acting May Support Rather than Contradict One's Self-Conception*

Following Hochschild's (1983) strong concerns regarding the pernicious effects of surface acting and deep acting on the individual, much subsequent research on emotional labor in organizations has focused on dysfunctional outcomes such as burnout and job (dis)satisfaction. However, we suspected that individuals who identify with their service role – who define themselves at least in part through the help they provide for others – would view surface and deep acting as helpful ways to meet their service obligations if they were not currently feeling the emotions they were expected to express. When one identifies with one's role, one sees enacting that role as expressing one's identity, as being true to oneself. However, there are often obstacles to role enactment. In the case of meeting display rules, perhaps a person is tired or preoccupied, or doesn't really connect with the client, or doesn't feel an emotion as strongly as the display rules require, and so on. For newcomers in particular, the service role identity may be *aspirational* in the sense that newcomers want to be, say, an exemplary salesperson or coach, but do not spontaneously feel or cannot project the appropriate emotion. For them, surface and deep acting may enable them to "fake it until they make it."

To be sure, even if one identifies with the service role, surface and deep acting may be nonetheless taxing and take a long term toll, just as physical labor may be taxing for a gardener or plumber and take a long term toll. However, because one is "faking in good faith" (Rafaeli & Sutton, 1987, p. 32; i.e., one is acting on behalf of display rules one endorses), there is little threat to one's authenticity, to one's sense of self. As a consultant put it:

if acting means kind of emphasizing points and being energetic if the
situation desires it or putting on some sort of a show to make a point or
something like that, then I would say I do a lot [of] acting . . . You need to.
But you do it because you believe in it.

(Ashforth & Tomiuk, 2000, p. 191)

Accordingly, we're very encouraged by the spate of research on variables
that predict the motivation and ability to engage in emotional labor
and that moderate the negative impact of emotional labor on the
individual and his or her work adjustment. The list includes: (1) individual
differences variables such as emotional adaptability, extraversion, self-
monitoring, and emotional intelligence (see Dahling & Johnson, 2013,
Chapter 3); (2) situational variables such as autonomy, interactional justice, supportive leadership, and occupational differences; and (3) person–
situation "fit" variables such as customer orientation, commitment to
display rules, job involvement, and organizational identification (e.g.,
Allen, Pugh, Grandey, & Groth, 2010; Bono & Vey, 2007; Brotheridge &
Grandey, 2002; Grandey, Fisk, & Steiner, 2005; Rupp & Spencer, 2006;
Schaubroeck & Jones, 2000). We particularly encourage research that
takes an *interactionist* perspective, examining how combinations of all
three types of variables facilitate not only the enactment of valued role
identities but perhaps even psychological health (e.g., exploring how
emotional labor may foster a sense of community; e.g., Shuler & Sypher,
2000).

## Natural and Genuine Emotional Labor

One of the biggest changes that has occurred since our 1993 article has
been the recognition of natural and genuine emotional labor. Hochschild
(1983), of course, described two major forms of emotional labor: surface
acting and deep acting. She also emphasized the prevalence of "emotive
dissonance" (p. 90) between the emotions that employees feel and those
they are required to display, whereas Rafaeli and Sutton (1987) argued
that there could instead be "emotional harmony" (p. 32). Building on this,
we argued that there is a third form of emotional labor: natural and
genuine expression of expected emotion. We reasoned that service agents
could spontaneously and naturally feel emotions that comply with display
rules:

a service agent may naturally feel what he or she is expected to express
without having to work up the emotion in the sense discussed by
Hochschild. A nurse who feels sympathy at the sight of an injured child has
no need to 'act'.

(Ashforth & Humphrey, 1993, p. 94).

Further, in line with our earlier discussion, we argued that employees who identify with their service role are more likely to spontaneously experience the expected emotions.

Although it seemed reasonable that people could spontaneously experience and express emotions that comply with display rules, research continued to focus on surface and deep acting until breakthrough studies by Glomb and Tews (2004) and Diefendorff, Croyle, and Gosserand (2005). Glomb and Tews surveyed five samples across various industries. They found that employees do report spontaneously expressing positive and negative emotions at work, and that these genuine emotional expressions are empirically distinct from other forms of emotional labor. Moreover, the expression of genuine emotions was consistent with occupational differences in display rules. Also, the expression of genuine positive emotions was negatively related to emotional dissonance, whereas faking the expression of positive emotions was positively related to dissonance and emotional exhaustion.

Diefendorff et al. (2005) examined employees who worked in a variety of "people work" (p. 344) occupations. Their confirmatory factor analysis supported the hypothesis that the expression of naturally felt emotions is a third form of emotional labor, empirically distinct from surface acting and deep acting. Moreover, they found that the three types of emotional labor correlated differently with dispositional and situational factors (e.g., surface acting was positively related to neuroticism and self-monitoring and negatively related to extraversion, conscientiousness, and agreeableness, whereas the expression of naturally felt emotions was positively related to extraversion and agreeableness). The authors concluded that the expression of naturally felt emotions may actually be quite common in organizations and that researchers should give considerably greater attention to this form of emotional labor.

In the wake of these two ground-breaking articles, other researchers have taken up the call to explore the benefits of genuine and natural emotional expression. For example, Hennig-Thurau, Groth, Paul, and Gremler (2006) found that customers respond more favorably to genuine emotional displays as long as they comply with display rules (see Groth, Hennig-Thurau, & Wang, 2013, Chapter 6). And Dahling and Perez (2010) found that older and more mature service workers were more likely to express naturally felt emotions. Such studies suggest that genuine and natural emotional labor is an effective form of emotional labor that deserves more research attention.

## *Emotional Labor: Not Just for Service Workers*

Another big change that has occurred since 1993 concerns extending the emotional labor concept beyond service workers. We argued that emotional labor occurs not just in service jobs but in a wide variety of roles: "Given that roles are essentially bundles of social expectations and that emotions are inevitably experienced in the performance of roles, it is difficult to imagine an organizational role to which display rules would *not* apply at various points" (Ashforth & Humphrey, 1993, pp. 109–110). Indeed, our original submission to *Academy of Management Review* did not focus on service workers in particular. However, the reviewers encouraged us to make this our focus, perhaps because: (1) research was overwhelmingly centered on service roles (and many of our examples came from this work); (2) display rules are often an explicit occupational requirement of such roles; and (3) service workers are the face of the organization, and thus their emotional labor is very consequential for the organization (as well as the workers).

Until recently, almost all research on emotional labor continued to focus on service workers. But there are important exceptions. For instance, Brotheridge and Grandey (2002) were the first to compare the frequency with which managers and service workers use emotional labor. They found that managers performed emotional labor at rates equivalent to that of sales and customer service workers, clearly demonstrating the prevalence of emotional labor in roles beyond frontline service. Diefendorff, Richard, and Croyle (2006) found that diverse display rules (e.g., "acting friendly to others," "suppressing annoyance that I feel at work," p. 283) were thought of as formal job requirements by most employees (and their supervisors) from various service and non-service occupations.

Leaders in particular may have high rates of performing emotional labor. Studies have shown that leaders' emotions are contagious to followers (e.g., Bono & Ilies, 2006). Humphrey and his colleagues have argued that leaders may use emotional labor and emotional regulation strategies to take control of their own emotional reactions and displays and thus to influence the emotional contagion process (e.g., Ashkanasy & Humphrey, 2011; Humphrey, Pollack, & Hawver, 2008). Leaders, like any other workers, are often exposed to workplace stressors, unforeseen events, and other emotionally challenging episodes. To control their emotional expressions, leaders may use deep acting and other emotional regulation tactics. These tactics may help the leaders feel better themselves while also allowing them to portray the appropriate emotions to boost their followers' mood and morale. However, as with other workers, leaders who use surface acting may actually feel worse because of emotional dissonance. Although many leadership models have posited that leaders express emotions as a way of influencing followers (see Côté, Van Kleef, & Sy, 2013, Chapter 4), the leadership literature has generally not considered the psychological effects that expressing emotions tends to have on leaders. Accordingly, the leadership literature can benefit from incorporating research from the emotional labor literature on the effects of engaging in emotional labor. The emotional labor performed by leaders may differ in important ways from that performed by service workers. Humphrey et al. (2008) compared the emotional labor performed by leaders with that performed by three types of service workers (customer service, caring professions, social control agents) and developed 15 propositions concerning how leaders use emotional labor. Other researchers have also begun to explore how leaders use emotional labor tactics (e.g., Gardner, Fischer, & Hunt, 2009). These recent theoretical articles suggest that how leaders use emotional labor is an area with a high potential for future research.

In closing, a hallmark of great theories is that every answer begs richer questions. By that measure, we have little doubt that Hochschild's (1983) provocative work on emotional labor will continue to be as generative and inspirational for scholarship – and management practice – in the years ahead as it has been since its early days.

# REFERENCES

Allen, J. A., Pugh, S. D., Grandey, A. A., & Groth, M. (2010). Following display rules in good or bad faith? Customer orientation as a moderator of the display rule–emotional labor relationship. *Human Performance, 23*, 101–115.

Ashforth, B. E., & Humphrey, R. H. (1993). Emotional labor in service roles: The influence of identity. *Academy of Management Review, 18*, 88–115.

Ashforth, B. E., & Tomiuk, M. A. (2000). Emotional labour and authenticity: Views from service agents. In S. Fineman (Ed.), *Emotion in organizations* (2ⁿᵈ ed., pp. 184–203). London: Sage.

Ashkanasy, N. M., & Humphrey, R. H. (2011). A multi-level view of leadership and emotions: Leading with emotional labor. In A. Bryman, D. Collinson, K. Grint, B. Jackson, & M. Uhl-Bien (Eds.), *Sage handbook of leadership* (pp. 365–379). London: Sage.

Bono, J. E. & Ilies, R. (2006). Charisma, positive emotions and mood contagion. *Leadership Quarterly, 17*, 317–334.

Bono, J. E., & Vey, M. A. (2007). Personality and emotional performance: Extraversion, neuroticism, and self-monitoring. *Journal of Occupational Health Psychology, 12*, 177–192.

Brotheridge, C. M., & Grandey, A. A. (2002). Emotional labor and burnout: Comparing two perspectives of "people work." *Journal of Vocational Behavior, 60*, 17–39.

Côté, S., Van Kleef, G. A., & Sy, T. (2013). The social effects of emotion regulation in organizations. In A. A. Grandey, J. M. Diefendorff, & D. E. Rupp (Eds.), *Emotional labor in the 21st Century: Diverse perspectives on emotion regulation at work*. New York: Psychology Press/Routledge.

Dahling, J. J., & Johnson, H. (2013). Motivation, fit, confidence, and skills: How do individual differences influence emotional labor? In A. A. Grandey, J. M. Diefendorff, & D. E. Rupp (Eds.), *Emotional labor in the 21st Century: Diverse perspectives on emotion regulation at work*. New York: Psychology Press/Routledge.

Dahling, J. J., & Perez, L. A. (2010). Older worker, different actor? Linking age and emotional labor strategies. *Personality and Individual Differences, 48*, 574–578.

Diefendorff, J. M., Croyle, M. H., & Gosserand, R. H. (2005). The dimensionality and antecedents of emotional labor strategies. *Journal of Vocational Behavior, 66*, 339–357.

Diefendorff, J. M., Richard, E. M., & Croyle, M. H. (2006). Are emotional display rules formal job requirements? Examination of employee and supervisor perceptions. *Journal of Occupational and Organizational Psychology, 79*, 273–298.

Gardner, W. L., Fischer, D., & Hunt, J. G. (2009). Emotional labor and leadership: A threat to authenticity? *Leadership Quarterly, 20*, 466–482.

Glomb, T. M., & Tews, M. J. (2004). Emotional labor: A conceptualization and scale development. *Journal of Vocational Behavior, 64*, 1–23.

Grandey, A. A., Fisk, G. M., & Steiner, D. D. (2005). Must "service with a smile" be stressful? The moderating role of personal control for American and French employees. *Journal of Applied Psychology, 90*, 893–904.

Groth, M., Hennig-Thurau, T., & Wang, K. (2013). The customer experience of emotional labor. In A. A. Grandey, J. M. Diefendorff, & D. E. Rupp (Eds.), *Emotional labor in the 21st Century: Diverse perspectives on emotion regulation at work*. New York: Psychology Press/Routledge.

Hennig-Thurau, T., Groth, M., Paul, M., & Gremler, D. D. (2006). Are all smiles created equal? How emotional contagion and emotional labor affect service relationships. *Journal of Marketing, 70*(3), 58–73.

Hochschild, A. R. (1983). *The managed heart: Commercialization of human feeling*. Berkeley, CA: University of California Press.

Humphrey, R. H., Pollack, J. M., & Hawver, T. (2008). Leading with emotional labor. *Journal of Managerial Psychology, 23*, 151–168.

Rafaeli, A., & Sutton, R. I. (1987). Expression of emotion as part of the work role. *Academy of Management Review, 12*, 23–37.

Rupp, D. E., & Spencer, S. (2006). When customers lash out: The effects of customer interactional injustice on emotional labor and the mediating role of discrete emotions. *Journal of Applied Psychology, 91*, 971–978.

Schaubroeck, J., & Jones, J. R. (2000). Antecedents of workplace emotional labor dimensions and moderators of their effects on physical symptoms. *Journal of Organizational Behavior, 21*, 163–183.

Shuler, S., & Sypher, B. D. (2000). Seeking emotional labor: When managing the heart enhances the work experience. *Management Communication Quarterly, 14*, 50–89.


# EMOTIONAL LABOR ACROSS FIVE LEVELS OF ANALYSIS: PAST, PRESENT, FUTURE

NEAL M. ASHKANASY • CATHERINE S. DAUS

It is now ten years since we (Ashkanasy & Daus, 2002; Ashkanasy, Härtel, & Daus, 2002) commented on where we felt the research on emotions in the workplace was positioned, and where we saw it heading. Little were we to know then that we were on the cusp of the "affective revolution" (Barsade, Brief, & Spataro, 2003, p. 3), and what an explosion of scholarly interest regarding emotions in work settings would ensue. In this commentary, we refer to this work and address how emotional labor research has progressed over the past ten years.


## What We Once Reckoned We Knew About Emotional Labor

In Ashkanasy et al. (2002, p. 328), we wrote of the "emergence of a true field of research on the organizational domain called *emotions in the workplace,* one worthy of study in its own right (like organizational attitudes or leadership)." We are excited to see that our crystal ball-gazing has been validated: the sub-discipline of emotion is now recognized within organizational psychology/behavior (evidenced by chapters on mood/emotions in leading organizational behavior (OB) textbooks; e.g., Robbins & Judge, 2010). Ten years ago, scholars needed to make a case for studying emotion in work contexts . . . no more! The field has evolved so we no longer must argue that emotions are part and parcel, indeed, *core,* to experiencing life in organizations. We have arrived!

Specifically regarding emotional labor, we suggested in our earlier writings that most of what we knew at the time regarding emotional labor was still based on Hochschild's (1983) work. As Grandey and her colleagues point out so eloquently in Chapter 1 (2013), it is clear now that the state of empirical work has moved well beyond Hochschild, including identification of different perspectives on emotional labor and understanding of the intersection of emotional labor and emotional regulation. We (Ashkanasy et al., 2002) also suggested that emotional labor was undergoing somewhat of an existential crisis. It is therefore good to see that research in this field is starting to clarify the issues we identified although, as Grandey and her colleagues point out, there is still ongoing debate regarding construct specification and definitions (2013, Table 1.1).

In particular, the past decade of emotional labor research has substantially clarified much conceptual confusion, even going beyond the core construct itself, clarifying important, key constructs within the emotional labor domain. Clearly, much of the conceptual work that has occurred in the past decade has resulted in a more fine-grained conceptual specification of emotional labor, as witnessed in the chapters in this volume.

In our review (Ashkanasy & Daus, 2002), we covered a body of research that, up to that time, had demonstrated the endemic effects that emotional labor can have for both employees enacting it and organizations requiring it. We knew that emotional labor had both positive and negative effects, depending on what criterion was chosen (e.g., employee well-being, see Erikson & Stacey, 2013; or bottom-line performance, see Groth, Hennig-Thurau, & Wang, 2013), and who the lens was focused on (e.g., employee or organization). The chapters in this volume confirm that emotional labor has wide-reaching effects for employees, their respective organizations, as well as the targets of emotional labor (often the customer, but also other employees and managers in the employee's environs (Niven, Totterdell, Holman, & Cameron, 2012) and even the employee's family (Lively, 2013).

## What We Argued Was Needed and How the Chapters in this Volume Have Met This

In Ashkanasy et al. (2002), we suggested that the future of emotional labor hinged upon researchers coming to some agreement regarding definitional aspects and terminology. In this respect, Grandey and colleagues (2012) present a masterful case for delineating both the history of the construct, as well as the present state of affairs regarding agreement. Moreover, the chapters in this volume serve to reinforce that for the most part, researchers are much clearer and focused regarding what emotional labor is, and what it is not. We note that, while we see much convergence, there is also room for (a need for) more integration across broad fields of emotional labor researchers. In particular, we would like to see greater cross-fertilization across the sociological and psychological disciplines. We applaud the editors of this book in their efforts to encourage such a cross-disciplinary focus, through both their choices of contributing authors, as well as stimulating conversations between researchers. Such cross-fertilization is crucial, and continues as researchers intentionally become aware of research outside their typical "domain." We acknowledge, also, the inclusion of a marketing scholar (Hennig-Thurau) and are excited to see some reference to marketing theory (e.g., "lifetime value"). We suggest that there are other important literatures (e.g., "customer delight" in marketing, Oliver, Rust, & Varki, 1997; *Six Sigma* quality, Noone,

Namasivayam, & Tomlinson, 2010) that might help the field move beyond merely achieving customer satisfaction and delivery beyond what is expected in customer interactions (see Groth, et al., 2013).

## *Advances in the State of Emotional Labor Research*

Research on emotions in organizations has notably advanced to reflect understanding that emotion is inherently a multi-level phenomenon. As Ashkanasy's (2003) proposed five levels of analysis introduced, a multi-level perspective is now embraced. Indeed, the overall structure of this volume underscores the importance of considering different lenses of viewing emotional labor via distinct levels of analyses. We see all levels reflected: Level 1, within-person (Beal & Trougakos, 2013), Level 2, between-person (Dahling & Johnson, 2013), Level 3, dyadic (Côté, van Kleef, & Sy, 2013), Level 4, group-level (Lively, 2013; Niven et al., 2013), and Level 5, culture and climate (Mesquita & Delvaux, 2013; Pugh, Diefendorff, & Moran, 2013). We applaud the editors for their careful choices of researchers who addressed each of these levels of influence. Collectively, the chapters reflect the advanced level of emotional labor research by: a) identifying such levels regarding their value in understanding the emotional labor process; and b) demonstrating the multi-level impact emotional labor might have which reflects conclusions from Ashkanasy and Humphrey's (2011) recent review of emotions in organizational behavior.

We are also extremely gratified to see such an emphasis on the importance of context in exploration of emotional labor. Most recently, we wrote about the importance of context in examining and thinking about emotional intelligence's influence and predictive ability (Jordan, Dasborough, Daus, & Ashkanasy, 2010). Relatedly, emotional labor processes do not occur in a vacuum; as such, it is critical to understand exactly when emotional labor is predicted to have larger effects. As mentioned above regarding levels, several in this book highlight context: Beal and Trougakos (2013 micro events); Pugh, Diefendorff and Moran (2013; organizational norms and processes) and Mesquita and Delvaux (2013; cross-culture). Other chapters underscore the importance of the gendered norms regarding emotional labor (Lively, 2013) as well as the unique context of emotional labor in call centers, where there are no visual cues to actors' emotion states (van Jaarsveld & Poster, 2013). The discussion of emotional labor in caregiver occupations by Erickson and Stacey (2013) helps in particular to position emotional labor as a critical component of human interaction and mutual understanding. As such, these chapters help us to answer a critical question: *When does emotional labor matter, and for whom?*

We also acknowledge research in this volume giving appropriate attention to *targets* of emotional labor. Based on the latest research in this field (Groth et al., 2013), the customer (target of emotional labor) is seen to exert reciprocal, iterative forces on the emotional labor processes. We find in this volume that scholars are truly grasping the dynamic nature of emotional labor, and the role that the targets play in the overall process. Future research needs to find a way to capture such dynamism, and in particular the role of emotions and emotional labor in organizational change. Possibly the model of organizational culture dynamics and change proposed by Hatch (2011) might provide a lead in this respect.

We need also to mention the exciting unique methodological advances represented in the chapters in this volume, and especially the unique ways of assessing emotional labor. For example, related to our above point regarding cross-fertilization of disciplines, Lively (2013) shares how the Expectation States Theory analysis approach can be used to ascertain core dimensions of emotional labor. We feel that such examinations need to be undertaken on a broader scale to help determine the true impact of emotional labor. Beal and Trougakos (2013) also present an inventive new method to study emotional labor based on within-persons analysis of affective episodes that they have used successfully to study a wide range of workplace variables including job satisfaction, performance, and stress. The study by Beal, Trougakos, Dalal, and Weiss (2011) of emotional regulation and stress in restaurant wait staff looks especially intriguing. We encourage, and are encouraged by, such a vast array of analytical techniques to help advance understanding of the emotional labor process.

## What Lies Ahead?

To conclude, we identify three areas that we feel are still empirical gaps that represent opportunities for emotional labor researchers. First, as Grandey and her colleagues (2013) argue, emotional labor processes come into play across the gamut of occupations. As such, we feel that an examination of emotional labor processes of jobs that would not classify as endemically high emotional labor jobs might provide fruitful opportunities for research. As seen in Table 1.2, the extent that different jobs are characterized by display rules and requirements for emotional labor is quite variable. Thus, one challenge for emotional labor researchers may be to examine these processes in occupations that are not, at first blush, high on emotional labor demands (e.g., accountants, engineers, IT designers). Joseph and Newman's (2010) meta-analysis of emotional intelligence (in the post-hoc analyses), illustrates an attempt to categorize such jobs into high and low emotional labor requirements and examine the interactions with emotional intelligence. We hope such results pave the way for researchers to examine emotional labor processes in "atypical" sorts of occupations. Related, we have argued elsewhere (Ashkanasy & Daus, 2005; Daus & Ashkanasy, 2005), and continue to believe that the nexus of emotional intelligence and emotional labor needs more attention. Emotional intelligence dimensions of perception, assimilation, understanding, and regulation have clear application to emotional labor (Dahling & Johnson, 2013; Newman, Joseph, & MacCann, 2010), and intuitively, emotional intelligence provides a natural linkage between the emotional labor and concomitant outcomes.

Second, we feel that the organizational communication literature provides an untapped domain of development regarding emotional labor processes. With the exception of Miller, Considine, and Garner's (2007) study of emotional narratives, we know of no research that has yet focused on the role of communication in conveying display rule norms.

Last, we come full circle regarding our earlier (Ashkanasy et al., 2002) musings on emotions in organization and contend that emotional labor research should consider literature from diversity-related and cross-cultural studies. How would collectivistic versus individualistic societies differ regarding emotional labor norms and outcomes? How might marginalized individuals (e.g., women, minority groups) feel more (or less) compelled to try to fit emotional labor norms? Clearly there is scope for further compelling research to address such questions.

# REFERENCES

Ashkanasy, N. M. (2003). Emotions in organizations: A multilevel perspective. In F. Dansereau and F. J. Yammarino (Eds.), *Research in multi-level issues* (Vol. 2, pp. 9–54). Oxford, UK: Elsevier/JAI Press.

Ashkanasy, N. M., & Daus, S. D. (2002). Emotion in the workplace: the new challenge for managers. *Academy of Management Executive, 16*(1), 76–86.

Ashkanasy, N. M., & Daus, C. S. (2005). Rumors of the death of emotional intelligence in organizational behavior are vastly exaggerated. *Journal of Organizational Behavior, 26*, 441–452.

Ashkanasy, N. M., Härtel, C. E. J, & Daus, C. S. (2002). Diversity and emotion: The new frontiers in organizational behavior research. *Journal of Management, 28*, 307–338.

Ashkanasy, N. M., & Humphrey, R. H. (2011). Current research on emotion in organizations. *Emotion Review, 3*, 214–224.

Barsade, S. G., Brief, A. P., & Spataro, S. E. (2003). The affective revolution in organizational behavior: The emergence of a paradigm. In J. Greenberg (Ed.), *Organizational behavior: The state of the science* (pp. 3–52). Mahwah, NJ: Lawrence Erlbaum and Associates.

Beal, D.J., & Trougakos, J.P. (2013). Episodic intrapersonal emotion regulation: Or, dealing with life as it happens. In Grandey, A. A, Diefendorff, J. M. & Rupp,

D.E. (Eds.), *Emotional labor in the 21st century: Diverse perspectives on emotion regulation at work*. New York, NY: Psychology Press/Routledge.

Beal, D. J., Trougakos, J. P., Dalal, R. S., & Weiss, H. M. (2011). Emotion regulation, stress, and fatigue in restaurant wait staff. Manuscript in preparation.

Côté, S., Van Kleef, G.A., & Sy, T. (2013). The social effects of emotion regulation in organizations. In Grandey, A. A, Diefendorff, J. M. & Rupp, D.E. (Eds.), *Emotional labor in the 21st century: Diverse perspectives on emotion regulation at work*. New York, NY: Psychology Press/Routledge.

Dahling J.J. & Johnson, H. (2013). Motivation, fit, confidence, and skills: How do individual differences influence emotional labor? In Grandey, A. A, Diefendorff, J. M. & Rupp, D.E. (Eds.) *Emotional labor in the 21st century: Diverse perspectives on emotion regulation at work*. New York, NY: Psychology Press/Routledge.

Daus, C. S., & Ashkanasy, N. M. (2005). The case for an ability-based model of emotional intelligence in organizational behavior. *Journal of Organizational Behavior, 26*, 453–466.

Erickson, R. & Stacey, C.L. (2012). Attending to mind and body: Engaging the complexity of emotion practice among caring professionals. In Grandey, A. A, Diefendorff, J. M. & Rupp, D.E. (Eds.), *Emotional labor in the 21st century: Diverse perspectives on emotion regulation at work*. New York, NY: Psychology Press/Routledge.

Grandey, A., Diefendorff, J., Rupp, D. E. (2013). Emotional labor: Overview of definitions, theories, and evidence. In A. Grandey, J. Diefendorff, & D.E. Rupp (Eds.), *Emotional labor in the 21st century: Diverse perspectives on emotion regulation at work*. New York, NY: Psychology Press/Routledge.

Groth, M., Hennig-Thurau, T., & Wang. K. (2013). The customer experience of emotional labor. In Grandey, A. A, Diefendorff, J. M. & Rupp, D.E. (Eds.), *Emotional labor in the 21st century: Diverse perspectives on emotion regulation at work*. New York, NY: Psychology Press/Routledge.

Hatch, M. J. (2011). Material and meaning in the dynamics of organizational culture and identity with implications for the leadership of organizational change. In N. M. Ashkanasy, C. E. P. Wilderom, & M. F. Peterson (Eds.), *The handbook of organizational culture and climate, second edition* (pp. pp. 341–358). Thousand Oaks, CA: Sage Publications.

Hochschild, A. R. (1983). *The managed heart: Commercialization of human feeling.* Berkeley, CA: University of California Press.

Jordan, P. J., Dasborough, M. T., Daus, C. S., & Ashkanasy, N. M. (2010). A call to context. *Industrial and Organizational Psychology: Perspectives on Science and Practice, 3*, 145–148.

Joseph, D. L. & Newman, D. A. (2010). Emotional intelligence: An integrative meta-analysis and cascading model. *Journal of Applied Psychology, 95(1)*, 54–78.

Lively, K.J. (2013). Social and cultural influencers: Gender effects on emotional labor at work and at home. In Grandey, A. A, Diefendorff, J. M. & Rupp, D.E. (Eds.), *Emotional labor in the 21st century: Diverse perspectives on emotion regulation at work*. New York, NY: Psychology Press/Routledge.

Mesquita, B. & Delvaux, E. (2013). A cultural perspective on emotion labor. In

Grandey, A. A, Diefendorff, J. M. & Rupp, D.E. (Eds.), *Emotional labor in the 21st century: Diverse perspectives on emotion regulation at work.* New York, NY: Psychology Press/Routledge.

Miller, K. I., Considine J., & Garner, J. (2007). "Let me tell you about my job." Exploring the terrain of emotion in the workplace. *Management Communication Quarterly, 20*, 231–260.

Newman, D. A., Joseph, D. L., & MacCann C. (2010). Emotional intelligence and job performance: The importance of emotion regulation and emotional labor context. *Industrial and Organizational Psychology: Perspectives on Science and Practice, 3*, 159–164.

Niven, K., Totterdell, P., Holman, D., & Cameron, D. (2013). Emotional labor at the unit-level. In Grandey, A. A, Diefendorff, J. M. & Rupp, D.E. (Eds.), *Emotional labor in the 21st century: Diverse perspectives on emotion regulation at work.* New York, NY: Psychology Press/Routledge.

Noone B. M., Namasivayam K., & Tomlinson H. S. (2010). Examining the application of six sigma in the service exchange. *Managing Service Quality, 20*, 273–293.

Oliver, R. L., Rust, R. T., & Varki, S. (1997). Customer delight: Foundations, findings, and managerial insight. *Journal of Retailing, 73*, 311–336.

Pugh, S.D., Diefendorff, J.M. & Moran, C.M. (2013). Emotional labor: Organization-level influences, strategies, and outcomes. In Grandey, A. A, Diefendorff, J. M. & Rupp, D.E. (Eds.), *Emotional labor in the 21st century: Diverse perspectives on emotion regulation at work.* New York, NY: Psychology Press/Routledge.

Robbins, S. P., & Judge, T. (2010). *Organizational behavior, 14ᵗʰ edition.* Englewood Cliffs, NJ: Prentice-Hall.

van Jaarsveld, D. & Poster, W. (2013). Call centers: Emotional labor over the phone. In Grandey, A. A, Diefendorff, J. M. & Rupp, D.E. (Eds.), *Emotional labor in the 21st century: Diverse perspectives on emotion regulation at work.* New York, NY: Psychology Press/Routledge.

# CONCEPTUALIZING EMOTIONAL LABOR: AN EMOTION REGULATION PERSPECTIVE

JAMES J. GROSS

Hochschild (1983) defined emotional labor as "the management of feeling to create a publicly observable facial and bodily display" (p. 7). This definition – and Hoschild's many other seminal contributions – prepared the ground for a wide range of compelling theoretical and empirical developments on this topic in sociology, psychology, and management. Many of these developments are ably reviewed in the present volume, and the vitality of this field of enquiry is well demonstrated by Grandey, Diefendorff, and Rupp's (2012) graphical depiction of the exponential growth of research on emotional labor.

In considering future directions for this field, I find it useful to take an emotion regulation perspective. This is because I see emotional labor as one (important) form of emotion regulation, namely emotion regulation that occurs in a work context. From this perspective, I believe that lessons learned in the broader field of emotion regulation may shed light on the processes that are implicated in emotional labor, and suggest future research directions. At the same time, I believe that the many important insights gained by work on emotional labor have much to offer researchers in the field of emotion regulation.

## An Emotion Regulation Perspective

Emotions can be conceptualized as multi-faceted, embodied phenomena that involve loosely-coupled changes in the domains of *subjective experience, behavior,* and *peripheral physiology* (Mauss, Levenson, McCarter, Wilhelm & Gross, 2005). These coordinated changes can be (and often are) very useful to us in achieving our goals. However, emotions are not always useful: when emotions are of the wrong type or intensity in a given situation, we may try to influence an emotion's trajectory.

The umbrella term given to all such attempts is *emotion regulation.* Somewhat more formally, emotion regulation can be defined as "the activation of a goal to modify the emotion-generative process" (Gross, Sheppes, & Urry, 2011; p. 767). Emotion regulation may take many forms, and one framework for analyzing emotion regulation is the process model of emotion regulation (Gross, 1998). This framework takes as its starting point the idea that emotions unfold in situations that are attended to and evaluated in particular ways. Emotion regulatory acts are, from this perspective, seen as having their primary impact on different stages of the emotion generative process (Gross, 1998). Figure 12.1 provides a sketch of this model, highlighting five points in the emotion–generative process at which individuals can regulate their emotions.

On this scheme, *situation selection* refers to efforts to influence the situation one will encounter, with a view to increasing (or decreasing) the likelihood that certain emotions will arise. *Situation modification* refers to attempting to change the external features of a situation in a way that will alter one's emotional responses. *Attentional deployment* refers to directing attention in a way that the emotion–response trajectory is altered. *Cognitive change* refers to altering a situation's meaning in a way that influences the emotions that situation will produce. Finally, *response modulation* refers to trying to change one or more of the experiential, behavioral, or physiological components of an emotional response.

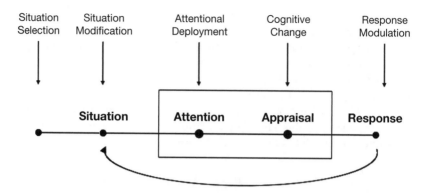

**Figure 12.1** A process model of emotion regulation that highlights five families of emotion regulation strategies (from Gross & Thompson, 2007).

## *How an Emotion Regulation Perspective Might Contribute to the Study of Emotional Labor*

From an emotion regulation perspective, emotional labor is emotion regulation that takes place in a work context. One benefit of adopting this perspective is that it permits scholars interested in emotional labor to benefit from the many insights that have been gleaned from research on emotion regulation in the past two decades (Gross, 2007). Because it is not possible to review this large body of research here, I instead draw out three insights that may be useful.

One key finding from studies of emotion regulation is that different forms of emotion regulation have different affective, cognitive, and social consequences. For example, expressive suppression (a form of response modulation which involves an attempt to inhibit ongoing emotion-expressive behavior) has little impact on negative emotion experience, magnifies physiological responding, increases feelings of inauthenticity, decreases subsequent memory, and has negative social consequences. By contrast, reappraisal (a form of cognitive change that involves attempts to influence emotion by altering the meaning of a situation) leads to lower levels of negative emotion experience, smaller brain responses in regions associated with emotion generation, and few if any cognitive or social costs (Gross, 2002). This finding suggests that all forms of emotional labor are not created alike. One important direction for future research will be probing the specific psychological and neurobiological processes that are engaged in different contexts while assessing a full range of affective, cognitive, and social outcomes.

A second – and related – finding from research on emotion regulation is that it is generally unhelpful to categorize particular forms of emotion regulation as "always good" or "always bad." What is good or bad for an individual depends upon the individual's immediate and longer-term goals. Interestingly, what is good or bad may also depend upon the cultural context. For example, many of the adverse effects of expressive suppression seem to be absent in Asian cultural contexts (Butler, Lee, & Gross, 2007), which Mesquita and Delvaux discuss in the current volume (2013). This finding suggests that even after it is clear what emotion regulation processes are activated by those engaging in emotional labor, it still remains to be determined whether such processes are helpful, harmful, or neutral to the individuals concerned.

A third key finding from studies of emotion regulation is that people have a wide range of emotion regulation goals, and these vary by context. Common sense holds that people want to increase positive emotions and decrease negative emotions. However, researchers have found that there are situations in which individuals try to increase negative emotions and decrease positive emotions (Tamir, Chiu, & Gross, 2007). One such example is when a sports team tries to get "mad as hell" to rally for the second half. Another example is when a negotiator tries to cultivate feelings of anger in order to negotiate more successfully, as discussed in this book (Côté, Van Kleef, & Sy, 2013). These findings suggest that emotional labor might not just consist of hedonically congruent forms of emotion regulation, but also in non-hedonic forms as well, and one important direction for future research will be broadening the focus to capture the full range of emotion–regulatory activities.

## How Work on Emotional Labor Might Contribute to the Study of Emotion Regulation

My emphasis thus far has been on the ways scholars interested in emotional labor might benefit from an integration of this field of enquiry with the larger field of emotion regulation. However, I believe that a more complete integration of these two fields would substantially benefit researchers in emotion regulation as well.

One valuable feature of work on emotional labor is its interdisciplinary nature. Methods and perspectives from sociology, psychology, and management science are knit together, providing a much richer understanding of the complex forces at work in emotional labor than would be the case if the field were dominated by a single field (see Grandey et al., 2013). Emotion regulation researchers also would benefit from such cross-disciplinary cross-pollination, and this represents one important future direction for the field.

A second valuable feature of work on emotional labor is its sensitivity to historical and cultural context. Hochschild opened her influential 1983 book by comparing a 19th century English child laboring in a wallpaper factory to a 20th century American adult working as a flight attendant. Since this time, scholars interested in emotional labor have been acutely sensitive to time and place in their analyses of how cultural practices and institutions give rise to calls for different types of emotional labor. This suggests the value of such contextual awareness in other types of research on emotion regulation. This type of contextual awareness may take many different forms, such as focusing on the unique contexts of call centers (van Jaarsveld & Poster, 2013), and caring work (Erickson & Stacey, 2012). For example, Sheppes and Gross (2011) have shown that in some contexts (those characterized by relatively low levels of emotion), reappraisal is as effective as distraction. In other contexts, however (those characterized by high levels of emotion), reappraisal seems to be less effective in diminishing negative emotion than distraction.

A third – and related – feature of research on emotional labor is the attention paid to the work context. Most adults spend a large percentage of their waking hours in work contexts, and a growing number of people are engaged in service sector jobs. These jobs usually involve working with colleagues (see Niven, Totterdell, Holman & Cameron, 2013) as well as clients (see Groth, Hennig-Thurau, & Wang, 2013), often in a hierarchical work environment. Given the power of social interactions and social hierarchy to elicit emotions, it is inevitable that emotions – and their regulation – figure prominently in many of our lives. One thing that emotion regulation researchers stand to gain from these insights is a greater appreciation of context-specific patterns of emotion regulation.

## Concluding Comment

I have argued that emotional labor is emotion regulation that takes place in a particular context, namely work. This conception of emotional labor suggests that the two research communities – one concerned with emotional labor, and the other with emotion regulation – have much to gain from a more thorough integration. Important steps in this direction already have been made by Grandey (2000), Côté (2005), and others. The present volume represents another valuable step towards this integration. I look forward with anticipation to the natural merging of these two vibrant fields of enquiry as they take their rightful place at the center of the emerging field of affective science (Gross, 2010).

# REFERENCES

Butler, E.A., Lee, T.L., & Gross, J.J. (2007). Emotion regulation and culture: Are the social consequences of emotion suppression culture-specific? *Emotion*, 7, 30–48.

Côté, S., Van Kleef, G.A., & Sy, T. (2013). The social effects of emotion regulation in organizations. In Grandey, A. A, Diefendorff, J. M. & Rupp, D.E. (Eds.), *Emotional labor in the 21st century: Diverse perspectives on emotion regulation at work*. New York, NY: Psychology Press/Routledge.

Erickson, R. & Stacey, C.L. (2013). Attending to mind and body: Engaging the complexity of emotion practice among caring professionals. In Grandey, A. A, Diefendorff, J. M. & Rupp, D.E. (Eds.), *Emotional labor in the 21st century: Diverse perspectives on emotion regulation at work*. New York, NY: Psychology Press/Routledge.

Grandey, A., Diefendorff, J., Rupp, D. E. (2013). Bringing emotional labor into focus: A Review and integration of three research lenses. In A. Grandey, J. Diefendorff, & D.E. Rupp (Eds.), *Emotional labor in the 21st century: Diverse perspectives on emotion regulation at work*. New York, NY: Psychology Press/Routledge.

Gross, J.J. (1998). The emerging field of emotion regulation: An integrative review. *Review of General Psychology*, 2, 271–299.

Gross, J.J. (2002). Emotion regulation: Affective, cognitive, and social consequences. *Psychophysiology*, 39, 281–291

Gross, J.J. (2010). The future's so bright, I gotta wear shades. *Emotion Review*, 2, 212–216.

Gross, J.J. (Ed.) (2007). *Handbook of emotion regulation*. New York, NY: Guilford Press.

Gross, J.J., Sheppes, G., Urry, H.L. (2011). Emotion generation and emotion regulation: A distinction we should make (carefully). *Cognition and Emotion*, 25, 765–781

Gross, J.J., & Thompson, R.A. (2007). Emotion regulation: Conceptual foundations. In J.J. Gross (Ed.), *Handbook of emotion regulation* (pp. 3–24). New York, NY: Guilford Press.

Groth, M., Hennig-Thurau, T., & Wang. K. (2013). The customer experience of emotional labor. In Grandey, A. A, Diefendorff, J. M. & Rupp, D.E. (Eds.), *Emotional labor in the 21st century: Diverse perspectives on emotion regulation at work*. New York, NY: Psychology Press/Routledge.

Hochschild, A.R. (1983). *The managed heart: Commercialization of human feeling*. Berkeley, CA: University of California Press.

Mauss, I.B., Levenson, R.W., McCarter, L., Wilhelm, F.H., & Gross, J.J. (2005). The tie that binds? Coherence among emotion experience, behavior, and physiology. *Emotion*, 5, 175–190.

Mesquita, B. & Delvaux, E. (2013). A cultural perspective on emotion labor. In Grandey, A. A, Diefendorff, J. M. & Rupp, D.E. (Eds.), *Emotional labor in the 21st century: Diverse perspectives on emotion regulation at work*. New York, NY: Psychology Press/Routledge.

Niven, K., Totterdell, P., Holman, D., & Cameron, D. (2013). Emotional labor at the unit-level. In Grandey, A. A, Diefendorff, J. M. & Rupp, D.E. (Eds.), *Emotional labor in the 21st century: Diverse perspectives on emotion regulation at work.* New York, NY: Psychology Press/Routledge.

Sheppes, G., & Gross, J.J. (2011). Is timing everything? Temporal considerations in emotion regulation. *Personality and Social Psychology Review, 15,* 319–331.

Tamir, M., Chiu, C., & Gross, J.J. (2007). Business or pleasure? Utilitarian versus hedonic considerations in emotion regulation. *Emotion, 7,* 546–554.

van Jaarsveld, D. & Poster, W. (2013). Call centers: Emotional labor over the phone. In Grandey, A. A, Diefendorff, J. M. & Rupp, D.E. (Eds.), *Emotional labor in the 21st century: Diverse perspectives on emotion regulation at work.* New York, NY: Psychology Press/Routledge.

# REFLECTING ON EMOTIONAL LABOR AS A SOCIAL MEME

ANAT RAFAELI

I was on a business trip to Ukraine while writing this essay. Walking around the frozen city (the temperature was minus 10 throughout my visit) and the empty stores (Ukraine's economy is in disastrous shape, haunted by corruption and by a history of Russian invasions), I saw little of the "classic" emotional labor: waiters and store clerks occasionally smiled, and border guards and police officers tended to be harsh and nasty – just like Bob Sutton and I had described in our original thought pieces on emotional labor (Rafaeli and Sutton, 1987; 1989). But these behaviors were more the exception than the norm. The general impression I had was emotional neutrality; people keeping to themselves, and sharing little of their emotions with others.

The introduction to this volume (Grandey, Diefendorff, & Rupp, 2013) would suggest that occupational requirements for specific emotion displays do not prevail in Ukraine: indeed the idea of people acting out certain emotions because of occupational and organizational require-ments seems really distant from the everyday Ukrainian experience. Contemplating this gap between everyday experiences in California (where I started my work on emotional labor), Israel (where I live and did a great deal of my empirical research), other places I visited and Ukraine have made me think: Why is emotional labor prevalent in some places more than others? In what other places would I have a similar experience (of little or no emotional labor)? Why??

I am not sure I can fully account for the seeming lack of emotional labor in various places, but I do believe I have a partial answer that can ele-vate our thinking and future research on emotional labor. My (beginning of an) answer is that emotional labor is a pattern of social behavior that is a member of the family of "social memes." The idea of social memes was defined by Dawkins (1976) as social behaviors that behave like "social genes" – they spread from person to person within a culture, and act as carriers of cultural ideas, symbols or practices. Memes have been suggested to be transmitted from one human mind to another through writing, speech, gestures, rituals or other imitable phenomena (Blackmore, 1999), exactly the dynamics that typify emotional labor. And memes are argued to evolve over time to fit the social environment, just like genes evolve to fit the biological environment (Dawkins, 1976).

We (Bob Sutton and I) started working on the idea of emotional labor (amazingly this was 25 years ago! Am I really that old? Feels like yesterday), because I noticed what I can now say was the manifestation of this meme in the USA (or as some people may say – in California). The story that we used to tell in describing how we started is that I (being a newcomer to the USA from Israel) mentioned to Bob that I was amazed that everywhere I went people smiled at me. "Come on Anat, it's not because they like you," Bob said (he was always very kind and empathetic to me . . . see Sutton & Rafaeli, 1990), ". . . they are paid to smile." I responded with, "So why does the OB or management literature not describe or discuss this anywhere?" Fortuitously, we had both read Arlie Hochschild's book *The Managed Heart* (1983), and connected this conversation to the sociological analysis that Hochschild presented (and it is tempting at this point to say "the rest, as they say, is history"). The idea that "people smile because they have to, not because they want to" was born (Rafaeli & Sutton, 1987, p. 23).

It is satisfying to see the rich evolution of research since our original ideas in this volume. We learn that there is "episodic intrapersonal emotion labor," which is how Beal and Trougakos (2013) label the way that people deal with everyday emotional demands; we also now know that individual differences such as motivation, self-confidence, and skills influence emotional labor (Dahling & Johnson, 2013), and that there is dyadic intra- and inter-personal regulation of emotion (Côté, Van Kleef & Sy, 2013). Groth, Henning-Thurau and Wang (2013) expand the emotional labor equation by bringing in target persons, which connects well to the meme idea, by suggesting that employee emotional labor symbolizes or indicates for customers the quality of the service they have received. Note that this suggestion is meaningful only where quality of service is an important value; so the role of the emotional labor meme appears to be an element of modern, Westernized economies. Aha! That's why it is lacking in Ukraine's economy!

Niven, Totterdell, Holman and Cameron (2013) and Pugh, Diefendorff, Moran (2013) further support the "emotional labor as meme" idea by suggesting that social units, i.e., collectives, groups or organizations, define emotional labor rules and expectations. In meme language, the social evolution of memes governs which rules or expectations will evolve in different social units.

Social evolution of memes, like biological evolution of genes, means adaptation of the meme to unique environmental constraints or demands, and this is evident in several chapters in the book. Van Jaarsveld and Poster (2013) depict the evolution of emotional labor for interactions conducted over the phone rather than face-to-face, and Erickson and Stacey (2012) discuss adaptations to emotional labor that are required due to expectations for "care," such as in the fields of health care and education. Similarly, Lively (2013) identifies adaptations to fit socially evolved societal gender roles, and Mesquita and Delvaux (2013) articulate emotion labor adaptations to the cultural uniqueness of Japan and the USA.

Considering the concept of emotional labor as a meme helps explain why emotional labor has not yet evolved in Ukraine (and maybe to Eastern Europe as a whole? To other non-Westernized economies?). It also helps sharpen our thinking about emotional labor. In fact, perhaps a more accurate term would be "emotion labor" or "labor on emotion". The labor regards displays of emotion but can rely on cognitions and behaviors as well as emotions. Susan Blackmore defines memes as habits, skills, stories, or any other kind of information that is copied from person to person, with variation and selection. When people write about emotional labor they actually refer to multiple small behaviors: emotion displays, verbal expressions and non-verbal gestures. Blackmore (1999) defined these types of individual behaviors as memes, and would label this adaptive complex of behaviors as "meme complexes."

As social animals, people can recognize and relate to the memes or meme complexes that they know. Other memes baffle them. This is why we feel people in other cultures or countries behave strangely: they exercise a different set of memes. Over the years, I have found this discomfort with foreign memes to be a barrier to productive academic conversations: My findings on emotional labor in Israel were well received in the USA and in different parts of the Western or "developed" world: People clearly understood what I was talking about. But my attempts to describe or discuss emotional labor in poorer places, such as Romania or Ukraine, encountered a numb and irresponsive audience. People appear to be thinking (and perhaps feeling), "What the hell is she talking about?" The concept – the meme or meme-complex – is alien to them. It does not seem to belong in these countries, and thus does not reverberate with these audiences.

As I try to make sense of Ukraine and also cogitate on ideas for this essay, it occurs to me that "emotional labor" is a luxury meme that only affluent places can afford, which sort of makes sense – people who worry about food are less likely to worry about emotion displays. When basic needs are at stake people worry about survival. This is a mere extension of the observation that emotional labor is a meme of societies where quality of service is a critical factor.

Considering emotional labor as a meme places it in the broader context of academic discourse on social behavior, and can stimulate our thinking about the construct and about future research. For example, a meme perspective suggests that emotional labor belongs with other globalization phenomena as per Thomas Friedman's idea of *The World is Flat*, a part of broader ideologies that moved from the USA or North America to other parts of the world along with the customer service ideology (Raz & Rafaeli, 2007; Grandey, Rafaeli, Ravid, Wirtz & Steiner, 2010). Emotional labor, therefore, does not belong only with research on emotion; rather, it is an artifact of certain economic values and perhaps even a symbol or an indicator of financial well-being of a community or an organization. In terms of research, this implies that emotional labor should be examined as a dependent variable of other factors instead of solely as an independent variable, e.g., in what social contexts or communities will we see what forms or magnitudes of emotional labor? What dynamics of social evolution connect specific social contexts or communities to specific forms of emotional labor? And what are the psychological foundations of the social evolution dynamics? Are they based on emotions? On thoughts and cognitions? Perhaps both? (cf. Rafaeli & Vilnai-Yavetz, 2004)

Another angle that the meme perspective raises is that emotional labor may not result from an intentional policy or be imposed by organizational or hierarchical forces. Rather, as per institutional theory (Dimaggio & Powell, 1983), as emotional labor becomes a quality of the culture or the social environment, the normative adaption of emotional labor emerges through mimicking and promotes legitimacy (Suchman, 1995). My recent research on the influence of customer anger displays on service employees shows that people tend to spontaneously enact emotional labor when confronted with the anger of other people, and invest cognitive resources in processing it rather than in performing tasks for which they could be rewarded (Rafaeli, Erez, Derfler, Efrat-Treister & Ravid, in press). I love this finding, because it shows that emotional labor can occur without external demands and that it has more powerful effects than economic and financial incentives. But of course! Emotional labor is the result of social evolution of the meme, and we know that evolution is more powerful than any organizational force!

The meme perspective also raises questions about what forms or aspects of emotional labor should be studied. The popular focus on surface acting and deep acting, for example, may not be the most important distinction to be studied. Looking through the meme lens, the question to be asked is what forms of emotional labor are retained and spread among social communities. Retention and spreading mean more sustainability of some forms of emotional labor and a phasing out of others. So looking at emotional labor as a meme moves us forward: It integrates research on emotional labor with a wide array of organizational research and identifies emotional labor as one of the social genes of organizational behavior.

# REFERENCES

Beal, D.J., & Trougakos, J.P. (2013). Episodic intrapersonal emotion regulation: Or, dealing with life as it happens. In Grandey, A. A, Diefendorff, J. M. & Rupp, D.E. (Eds.), *Emotional labor in the 21st century: Diverse perspectives on emotion regulation at work*. New York, NY: Psychology Press/Routledge.

Blackmore, Susan J. (1999). *The meme machine*. Oxford: Oxford University Press

Côté, S., Van Kleef, G.A., & Sy, T. (2013). The social effects of emotion regulation in organizations. In Grandey, A. A, Diefendorff, J. M. & Rupp, D.E. (Eds.), *Emotional labor in the 21st century: Diverse perspectives on emotion regulation at work*. New York, NY: Psychology Press/Routledge.

Dahling J.J. & Johnson, H. (2013). Motivation, fit, confidence, and skills: How do individual differences influence emotional labor? In Grandey, A. A, Diefendorff, J. M. & Rupp, D.E. (Eds.), *Emotional labor in the 21st century: Diverse perspectives on emotion regulation at work*. New York, NY: Psychology Press/Routledge.

Dawkins, Richard (1976). *The selfish gene*. New York City: Oxford University Press.

Dimaggio, P. J., & Powell, W. W. (1983). The iron cage revisited: Institutional isomorphism and collective rationality in organizational fields. *American Sociological Review, 48*, 147–160.

Erickson, R. & Stacey, C.L. (2012). Attending to mind and body: Engaging the complexity of emotion practice among caring professionals. In Grandey, A. A, Diefendorff, J. M. & Rupp, D.E. (Eds.), *Emotional labor in the 21st century: Diverse perspectives on emotion regulation at work*. New York, NY: Psychology Press/Routledge.

Grandey, A., Diefendorff, J., & Rupp, D. E. (2013). Bringing emotional labor into focus: A Review and integration of three research lenses. In A. A. Grandey, J. M. Diefendorff & D. E. Rupp (Eds.), *Emotional labor in the 21st century: Diverse perspectives on emotion regulation at work*. New York, NY: Psychology Press/Routledge.

Grandey, A., Rafaeli, A., Ravid, S., Wirtz, J., & Steiner, D. (2010). Emotional display rules: The special case of customer service providers. *Journal of Service Management, 21*(3), 388–412.

Groth, M., Hennig-Thurau, T., & Wang. K. (2013). The customer experience of emotional labor. In Grandey, A. A, Diefendorff, J. M. & Rupp, D.E. (Eds.), *Emotional labor in the 21st century: Diverse perspectives on emotion regulation at work*. New York, NY: Psychology Press/Routledge.

Hochschild, A. (1983). *The managed heart: Commercialization of human feeling.* Los Angeles: University of California Press.

Lively, K.J. (2013). Social and cultural influencers: Gender effects on emotional labor at work and at home. In Grandey, A. A, Diefendorff, J. M. & Rupp, D.E. (Eds.), *Emotional labor in the 21st century: Diverse perspectives on emotion regulation at work.* New York, NY: Psychology Press/Routledge.

Mesquita, B. & Delvaux, E. (2013). A cultural perspective on emotion labor. In Grandey, A. A, Diefendorff, J. M. & Rupp, D.E. (Eds.), *Emotional labor in the 21st century: Diverse perspectives on emotion regulation at work.* New York, NY: Psychology Press/Routledge.

Niven, K., Totterdell, P., Holman, D., & Cameron, D. (2013). Emotional labor at the unit-level. In Grandey, A. A, Diefendorff, J. M. & Rupp, D.E. (Eds.), *Emotional labor in the 21st century: Diverse perspectives on emotion regulation at work.* New York, NY: Psychology Press/Routledge.

Pugh, S.D., Diefendorff, J.M. & Moran, C.M. (2013). Emotional labor: Organization-level influences, strategies, and outcomes. In Grandey, A. A, Diefendorff, J. M. & Rupp, D.E. (Eds.), *Emotional labor in the 21st century: Diverse perspectives on emotion regulation at work.* New York, NY: Psychology Press/Routledge.

Rafaeli, A., & Sutton, R. I. (1987). The expression of emotion as part of the work role. *Academy of Management Review, 12*(1), 23–37.

Rafaeli, A., & Sutton, R. I. (1989). The expression of emotion in organizational life. In L. L. Cummings & B. M. Staw (Eds.), *Research in Organizational Behavior* (Vol. 11, pp. 1–42). Greenwich, CT: JAI Press.

Rafaeli, A., Erez, A., Derfler, R., Efrat-Treister, D., & Ravid, S. (in press). When customers exhibit verbal aggression employees pay cognitive costs. *Journal of Applied Psychology.*

Rafaeli, A., & Vilnai-Yavetz, I. (2004). Emotion as a Connection of Physical Artifacts and Organizations. *Organization Science, 15*(6), 671–686.

Raz, A., & Rafaeli, A. (2007). Emotion Management in a Cross-Cultural Perspective: "Smile Training" in Japanese and North American Service Organizations. In N. Ashkanasy, W. Zerbe & C. E. J. Hartel (Eds.), *Research on Emotion in Organization* (Vol. 3, pp. 199–201).

Suchman, M. C. (1995). Managing legitimacy: Strategic and institutional approaches. *Academy of Management Review, 20*(3), 571–610.

Sutton, R. I., & Rafaeli, A. (1990). How we untangled the relationship between store sales and displayed emotion: A tale of bickering and optimism. In P. J. Frost & R. Staeblin (Eds.), *Doing exemplary research* (pp. 115–128). London: Sage.

van Jaarsveld, D. & Poster, W. (2013). Call centers: Emotional labor over the phone. In Grandey, A. A, Diefendorff, J. M. & Rupp, D.E. (Eds.), *Emotional labor in the 21st century: Diverse perspectives on emotion regulation at work.* New York, NY: Psychology Press/Routledge.

# BACK TO THE FUTURE

## AMY S. WHARTON

In his classic 1973 book, *The Coming of Post-Industrial Society*, sociologist Daniel Bell aimed to capture the transformative changes taking place in the U.S. economy. He juxtaposed the "post-industrial era" against the two fundamental societal shifts preceding it – the agricultural era, which Bell described as "a game against nature" and the industrial era, characterized as a "game against fabricated nature" (Bell 1973, 116). Bell (1973) argued that society was in the process of shifting once again, this time to a post-industrial era in which a "game between persons" best depicted the forces at play in economic life. Bell's effort to pin down what was salient about the emerging service economy was prophetic in many respects, but perhaps most important was his recognition of the centrality of social interaction to the forces fueling the economy.

Ten years later, in *The Managed Heart*, Arlie Hochschild (1983) picked up where Bell left off by offering a way to make sense of service jobs and the distinctive elements of work in a service economy. In particular, she brilliantly described the emergence and implications of "commodified" social relations and the central role of emotion in that process. Now, after thirty years, the seeds planted by Hochschild have given rise to hundreds of studies on the concept of emotional labor and the role of emotion at work more generally.

Asked to make recommendations for future research directions, one response is to identify what new topics require examination. In contrast, when I reflect on what is important in the area of emotional labor, my advice is for researchers to not lose sight of two core themes that motivated this research in the first place, but have become somewhat less central over time. The first theme takes us back to Bell's (1973) and Hochschild's (1983) attempts to identify the distinctive features of service jobs, while the second relates to the centrality of social interaction and relationality in this effort.

Grandey, Diefendorff, and Rupp's (2013) history of the construct of emotional labor suggests that, over the past few decades, emotional labor research has fundamentally shifted its focus. This shift has meant that the particular aspects of emotional labor foregrounded by researchers have changed. Of the three approaches to emotional labor described in Chapter 1, the "occupational approach" emerged first, as researchers began to apply Hochschild's ideas about emotional labor to a variety of service jobs. Following Hochschild, many of these early studies were qualitative case studies, well-suited to portraying workers' experiences on the job and their interactions with customers. Paules' (1991) study of waitresses, Leidner's (1993) research on fast food workers and insurance salespeople, and Pierce's (1995) analysis of lawyers and paralegals are sociological classics in this area. Over time, as Grandey and colleagues' Chapter 1 framework usefully illustrates, the center of gravity in emotional labor research moved inward, away from the broader work setting or job to focus on the individual worker who performs emotional labor – what Niven and colleagues (2013) call "the agent." In the 1990s, this focus involved attention to "emotional displays," while a move to "intrapsychic processes" characterizes the most recent work. The "emotional display" literature attends to issues of occupational and organizational context through its emphasis on the role expectations that govern workers' behavior. Studies of intrapsychic processes examine individual responses to emotional labor demands. As all of the chapters in this volume demonstrate, each iteration of emotional labor research has added value to our knowledge of this construct. Most impressive have been the gains in our understanding of the mechanics of emotional labor – how it is performed, though what mechanisms, under what conditions, and with what consequences for the self.

As the "occupational requirements" framework has been slowly eclipsed by other approaches, however, something has been lost as well as gained. This loss is two-fold. The first loss concerns the relative lack of attention to the interactive dynamics involved in emotional labor. Although emotional labor is fundamentally relational, the customer or recipient has become a less central player in our research. Second, and more important, the study of emotional labor has become somewhat disconnected from the jobs, workplaces, and organizational settings that help define its particular characteristics and expression.

After reading these chapters, I have learned that these views are not mine alone. In fact, several contributors urge emotional labor researchers to turn their attention outward – to the unit-level (Niven et al., 2013), the customer (Groth, Hennig-Thurau, & Wang, 2013; van Jaarsveld & Poster, 2013), the occupational sector (Erickson & Stacey, 2013), the organization (Pugh, Diefendorff, & Moran, 2013), or societal-level culture (Lively, 2013; Mesquita & Delvaux, 2013). Although I do not have the space to take up all of their arguments, I will point to a couple of fruitful pathways for further research. I focus on these pathways not only because of their contributions to our understanding of emotional labor, but also for their ability to help us address key issues in the 21$^{st}$ century workplace.

Consider that of the thirty occupations projected to grow the most between 2008 and 2018, all but a handful involve emotional labor by most any definition (Lacey & Wright 2009). Roughly 20 per cent of these fast-growing jobs are in health care, including registered nurses, health aides, and physicians. Others are in education (e.g., childcare workers, elementary and postsecondary school teachers, and teaching assistants), or involve work in customer sales or service (e.g., receptionists, customer service representatives, and retail sales workers) or other frontline service jobs (e.g., fast food servers, waiters and waitresses). As much as ever, work is "a game between persons." Yet, the emotional labor requirements of jobs such as these are nuanced and complex. These complexities derive from the jobs' interactional requirements, but also from other characteristics of the work, including those of the workers who typically fill these jobs.

These issues are well-illustrated in Part III of this volume. Customer service work is an archetypal emotional labor job and the call center represents such work in its most routinized form. As Groth and colleagues (2013) remind us, however, we know more about the effects of emotional labor on workers who perform than on the intended recipient. By directing attention to customers' reactions, this chapter underscores the fact that emotional labor is performed to influence the emotional states (and behavior) of others. This theme is even more central to van Jaarsveld and Poster's (2013) discussion of call centers. These authors shift the focus away from the call center worker to the dynamics of the interaction with the customer. Even in such a highly routinized environment, these interactions can be highly variable, with different effects on both workers and customers. Perhaps the most notable feature of the call center, however, is the fact that communication in these settings is technologically mediated. In the version of the "game between persons" that characterizes the 21ˢᵗ century workplace, this is an aspect of workplace interaction that should not be overlooked by students of emotional labor. Although much attention has been devoted to social media and its effects on society at large, its implications for interactive service work remain less explored.

One of the most important developments in emotional labor research since Hochschild is the emphasis on caregiving as a type of emotional labor (and emotion management). Erickson and Stacey (2013) trace the connections between carework – a concept emerging out of feminist philosophy and studies of women's work – and the emotional labor literature. They invoke the idea of the "service context" as a way to call attention to the differences between human service and frontline service jobs, as well as to highlight the difference between occupational sectors organized according to emotion norms emphasizing care vs. those sectors organized around norms of commerce.

These authors argue that attention to service context is crucial for understanding workers' involvement in emotional labor. Although analytically distinct, however, Erickson and Stacey note that the particular contexts of caring and commerce are increasingly intertwined (and often in conflict) in contemporary care sector workplaces, such as hospitals and schools. Moreover, they suggest that it is this dynamic of competing or conflicting contextual forces that creates the unique challenges facing workers who perform emotional labor in these settings. With jobs in health and education representing roughly 40 per cent of those expected to increase the most over the next decade, Erickson and Stacey's attempt to capture the distinctiveness of these occupational groups is highly relevant.

As several chapters observe, the workplace is a site of emotion management as well as emotional labor. The care vs. commerce distinction thus has implications beyond health and education, and it can be extended from the occupational level to organizations more generally (see Pugh, et al., 2013). For example, the growing literature on compassion at work explores how workers and organizations respond to others' pain and suffering, as well as the effects of compassion on recipients, other workers, and the organization itself (Kanov et al., 2004; Lilius et al., 2008). The study of compassion at work is closely linked to caregiving, as well as to several other areas of organizational research, including studies of pro-social behavior, work–life, and research on positive organizational practices, policies, and culture. This research is not confined to care sector organizations, but encompasses organizations firmly anchored on the commerce end of the continuum. For example, work-life research seeks to facilitate organizations' ability to respond to employees' work–life needs in ways that reflect the intrinsic value of work–life integration, not simply its contributions to the bottom line (Blair-Loy, Wharton, & Goodstein 2011; Pitt-Catsouphes & Googins 2005). To extend Erickson and Stacey (2013), these studies aim to understand and promote carework *in the context* of commerce.

Although all of the chapters raise many issues for exploration, my aim here has been to show the continuing significance of the "occupational requirements" approach to emotional labor and reveal some of the possibilities and directions for this line of work. Greater attention to context – in all its specificity and across all of its dimensions – would enhance our ability to understand the varieties of emotional labor, their expression, and consequences. What is also at stake in this effort – as both Bell (1973) and Hochschild (1983) demonstrated so profoundly – is the continuing need for research that captures the dynamics and dilemmas facing workers, employers, and society as each confronts the 21st century workplace. Emotional labor research has never been more relevant to and ready for this challenge.

## REFERENCES

Bell, D. (1973). *The coming of post-industrial society: A venture in social forecasting.* New York: Basic Books.

Blair-Loy, M., Wharton, A.S., and Goodstein, J. (2011). Exploring the relationship between mission statements and work–life practices in organizations. *Organization Studies, 32,* 427–450.

Erickson, R. & Stacey, C.L. (2013). Attending to mind and body: Engaging the complexity of emotion practice among caring professionals. In Grandey, A. A, Diefendorff, J. M. & Rupp, D.E. (Eds.), *Emotional labor in the 21st century: Diverse perspectives on emotion regulation at work.* New York, NY: Psychology Press/Routledge.

Grandey, A., Diefendorff, J., & Rupp, D. E. (2013). Bringing emotional labor into focus: A Review and integration of three research lenses In A. A. Grandey, J. M. Diefendorff & D. E. Rupp (Eds.), *Emotional labor in the 21st century: Diverse perspectives on emotion regulation at work.* New York, NY: Psychology Press/Routledge.

Groth, M., Hennig-Thurau, T., & Wang. K. (2013). The customer experience of emotional labor. In Grandey, A. A, Diefendorff, J. M. & Rupp, D.E. (Eds.), *Emotional labor in the 21st century: Diverse perspectives on emotion regulation at work.* New York, NY: Psychology Press/Routledge.

Hochschild, A. R. (1983). *The managed heart: Commercialization of human feeling.* Berkeley: University of California Press.

Kanov, J.M., Matlis, S., Worline, M.C., Dutton, J.E., Frost, P.J.and Lilius, J.M. (2004). Compassion in organizational life. *American Behavioral Scientist, 47,* 808–827.

Lacey, A.T. and Wright, B. (2009). Occupational projections to 2018. *Monthly Labor Review* (Nov.), 82–123.

Leidner, R. (1993). *Fast food, fast talk: Service work and the routinization of everyday life.* Berkeley: University of California Press.

Lilius, J.M., Worline, M.C., Maitlis, S., Kanov, J.M., Dutton, J.E. and Frost, P.J. (2008). The contours and consequences of compassion at work. *Journal of Organizational Behavior 29,* 192–218.

Lively, K.J. (2013). Social and cultural influencers: Gender effects on emotional labor at work and at home. In Grandey, A. A, Diefendorff, J. M. & Rupp, D.E. (Eds.), *Emotional labor in the 21st century: Diverse perspectives on emotion regulation at work.* New York, NY: Psychology Press/Routledge.

Mesquita, B. & Delvaux, E. (2013). A cultural perspective on emotion labor. In Grandey, A. A, Diefendorff, J. M. & Rupp, D.E. (Eds.), *Emotional labor in the 21st century: Diverse perspectives on emotion regulation at work.* New York, NY: Psychology Press/Routledge.

Niven, K., Totterdell, P., Holman, D., & Cameron, D. (2013). Emotional labor at the unit-level. In Grandey, A. A, Diefendorff, J. M. & Rupp, D.E. (Eds.), *Emotional labor in the 21st century: Diverse perspectives on emotion regulation at work.* New York, NY: Psychology Press/Routledge.

Paules, G. F. (1991). *Dishing it out: Power and resistance among waitresses in a New Jersey restaurant.* Philadelphia: Temple University Press.

Pierce, J. (1995). *Gender trials: Emotional lives in contemporary law firms.* Berkeley: University of California Press.

Pitt-Catsouphes, M. and Googins, B. (2005). Recasting the work–family agenda as a corporate social responsibility. In E.E. Kossek & S.J. Lambert (Eds.),

*Work and integration: Organizational, cultural, and individual perspectives* (pp. 469–490). Mahwah, NJ: Lawrence Erlbaum Associates.

Pugh, S.D., Diefendorff, J.M. & Moran, C.M. (2013). Emotional labor: Organization-level influences, strategies, and outcomes. In Grandey, A. A, Diefendorff, J. M. & Rupp, D.E. (Eds.), *Emotional labor in the 21st century: Diverse perspectives on emotion regulation at work*. New York, NY: Psychology Press/Routledge.

van Jaarsveld, D. & Poster, W. (2013). Call centers: Emotional labor over the phone. In Grandey, A. A, Diefendorff, J. M. & Rupp, D.E. (Eds.), *Emotional labor in the 21st century: Diverse perspectives on emotion regulation at work*. New York, NY: Psychology Press/Routledge.

# Author Index

Aarts, H. 47, 111, 114
Abel, E. K. 178
Abrams, R. A. 33
Ackerman, J. M. 115
Ackerman, P. L. 48
Aik, V. C. 134
Aiken, L. H. 136
Albert, D. 252, 256
Alcover, D. M. 106
Alder, G. S. 209
Alderson, M. 182
Ali, F. 267
Allen, J. A. 60, 61, 141, 206, 262, 277
Ambady, N. 134, 141, 163
Anderson, C. 91
Andersson, L. M. 135
Anguas-Wong, A. M. 260, 261
Archer, M. 187
Arnould, E. J. 138
Arriola, M. 260, 261
Arvey, R. D. 11, 204, 205
Ashforth, B. E. 4, 5, 6, 11, 17, 21, 62, 63, 105, 131, 135, 176, 181, 184, 185, 200, 202, 203, 264, 268n1, 275, 276, 277, 279
Ashkanasy, N. M. 4, 20, 21, 94, 275, 279, 282, 283, 284, 286
Atkins, C. P. 164
Austin, E. J. 60, 69
Austin, J. T. 48, 49
Axtell, C. M. 141
Azuma, H. 255

Bain, P. 154, 155

Baird, B. M. 65
Baker, W. 105, 109, 116, 118
Bakker, A. B. 60, 67, 116, 136, 183, 184
Baldamus, W. 43
Bales, R. F. 226
Bandura, A. 59, 66, 67, 68, 163
Banjeree, R. 260, 261
Barger, P. 12, 89, 103, 130, 133
Bargh, J. A. 47, 115, 133
Barndollar, K. 47
Barnes, C. M. 46
Bar-On, R. 69
Barrick, M. R. 142, 205
Barros, E. 33, 34, 42, 43
Barry, B. 67
Barsade, S. G. 4, 95, 104, 132, 282
Bartel, C. A. 106, 109, 214
Basch, J. 204
Batt, R. 167, 168
Bauer, L. M. 260, 261
Baumeister, R. 16, 44, 48, 83, 114
Beal, D. J. 8, 10, 11, 12, 13, 33, 34, 38, 42, 43, 44, 45, 46, 57, 64, 66, 73, 103, 137, 158, 284, 285, 295
Beatty, S. E. 143
Beaupré, M. 82
Bechtoldt, M. 155, 163
Becker, W. J. 203
Beckman, C. 13
Beersma, B. 13, 87, 94, 95, 163
Belenky, M. 178
Bell, D. 300, 303
Bell, S. J. 137

Bellas, M. L. 235
Belt, V. 164
Bem, S. L. 164
Bennett, C. 143
Berger, C. 105, 106
Berger, J. 226
Bergsieker, H. B. 263
Bernard, S. 238
Bernieri, F. J. 142
Berry, L. L. 127, 142
Bettenhausen, K. 94, 137
Bhappu, A. D. 143
Blackmore, S. 296
Blair-Loy, M. 303
Blairy, S. 133
Blau, P. 155
Boler, M. 176, 182, 186
Bolton, S. 9, 18, 175, 176, 177, 178,
  181, 182, 185, 186, 187, 188
Bone, D. 185
Bono, J. 13, 14, 18, 46, 58, 59, 60, 64,
  65, 72, 79, 93, 94, 183, 205, 206,
  277, 279
Boselie, P. 209
Bourdieu, P. 177, 179, 187, 188, 190,
  191
Bourg, C. 227
Bowen, D. E. 92, 136, 203, 204, 212
Bowen, J. 138, 139
Bower, G. H. 132
Boyd, C. 9, 18
Boyd, E. M. 223, 243n2
Boyle, G. J. 68
Boyle, M. V. 71
Brackett, M. A. 141
Bradley, B. P. 82
Bradley, C. 111
Brady, M. K. 141
Brandes, P. 165
Bratslavsky, E. 114
Brauburger, A. 205
Braver, T. S. 33
Brett, J. 91
Brief, A. P. 4, 92, 282
Briner, R. 93
Brody, L. R. 225
Bromley, S. 164
Brotheridge, C. 8, 10, 14, 16, 60, 64,
  128, 135, 136, 180, 191n1, 277,
  279
Brown, D. J. 93

Brown, K. G. 47
Brown, S. 136, 140, 141
Brown, T. J. 141, 206
Bruner, J. 254
Bryk, A. S. 117
Budig, M. 189
Bunge, S. A. 47, 48
Busch, C. M. 206
Buss, A. H. 59, 68
Buswell, B. N. 83, 95
Butler, E. A. 38, 44, 265, 266, 267,
  291
Byington, E. 107
Byrne, C. J. 60, 62, 63
Byrne, Z. S. 137

Cacioppo, J. T. 82, 85, 86, 132
Cahill, S. E. 211
Callaghan, G. 154, 205, 208, 209
Cameron, D. 12, 184, 283, 284, 292,
  295, 301
Cancian, F. M. 178, 181
Caprara, G. V. 68, 72
Cargile, A. C. 164
Caruso, D. R. 69
Carver, C. S. 34, 37, 47, 49, 58, 59, 60,
  62, 104
Carver, V. H. 86
Castelfranchi, C. 38
Cena, F. 158
Ceschi, G. 134
Chan, D. 117, 207, 213
Chartrand, T. L. 47, 132, 133
Chen, S. 92
Cherry, B. 143
Cheung, F. Y. 60, 69, 70
Cheung, R. Y. M. 266
Chi, N.-W. 13, 16, 60, 69, 72, 131,
  210
Chin, W. W. 38
Chissick, C. 135, 156, 209, 210
Chiu, C. 291
Chowdhury, S. 133
Chun, W. Y. 34, 49
Cialdini, R. B. 141
Ciarocco, N. J. 16
Clark, M. A. 105
Clark, M. S. 86
Clarke, S. P. 136
Clay-Warner, J. 238
Clinchy, B. 178

Clore, G. L. 114, 133
Coleman, J. E. 143
Coltrane, S. 232
Colvin, A. J. S. 214
Combs, J. 214
Congdon, R. 117
Conklin, L. 141
Connelly, C. E. 159
Connelly, S. 94
Conner, T. L. 226
Considine, J. 286
Conway, M. A. 33
Cooper, J. T. 48, 49
Cordes, C. L. 190
Correll, S. J. 226, 238
Corrigall, E. A. 184
Cosker, D. 95
Côté, S. 10, 11, 12, 13, 16, 18, 20, 31,
    34, 44, 58, 59, 63, 79, 81, 82, 83,
    84, 86, 87, 88, 91, 92, 93, 94, 95,
    101, 102, 104, 108, 109, 114, 115,
    280, 284, 291, 292, 295
Cotton, J. L. 136
Critchley, H. D. 44
Cronin, J. J. Jr 141
Cropanzano, R. 38, 136, 137, 203
Crosby, F. 164
Cross, R. 105, 109, 116, 118
Cross, S. E. 255
Croyle, M. H. 4, 10, 11, 15, 58, 60, 61,
    62, 65, 102, 128, 182, 202, 205,
    206, 210, 278, 279
Csikszentmihalyi, M. 43
Custers, R. 47

Dadhkah, A. 260, 261
Dahling, J. J. 8, 13, 14, 60, 62, 63, 64,
    72, 73, 106, 107, 116, 162, 163,
    183, 202, 203, 206, 277, 278, 284,
    286, 295
Dalal, R. S. 46, 285
Damen, F. 13, 87, 94
D'Andrade, R. G. 254
Daniels, A. K. 178
Das, D. 165
Dasborough, M. T. 284
Daus, C. S. 4, 15, 17, 21, 275, 282,
    283, 284, 286
Davies, C. 185
Davis, J. M. 142
Davis, M. H. 141

Dawkins, R. 295
D'Cruz, P. 165
Deci, E. L. 43, 114
De Dreu, C. K. W. 85, 86, 87, 88, 91
Deery, S. 160
de Grip, A. 157
Deibler L. S. 138
Delvaux, E. 260, 284, 291, 296, 301
Demaree, H. 45
Demerouti, E. 116, 136, 184, 208
DeNardo, M. 231
den Hartog, D. N. 209
De Pater, I. E. 163
Derfler, R. 297
Deshmukh, S. G. 127
Deshon, R. P. 47
DeVault, M. 223, 232, 233
Dharwadkar, R. 165
Diamond, H. 118
Diamond, J. 13, 16, 60, 69, 72, 131,
    139, 210
Dickter, D. N. 160, 164
Diefendorff, J. M. 4, 8, 10, 11, 13, 14,
    15, 16, 17, 20, 34, 37, 57, 58, 59,
    60, 61, 62, 64, 65, 72, 79, 81, 102,
    104, 106, 107, 116, 128, 129,
    144n1, 155, 156, 181, 182, 183,
    186, 191n1, 201, 202, 203, 205,
    206, 210, 215, 242n1, 244n14,
    262, 264, 268n1, 278, 279, 283,
    284, 285, 288, 291, 294, 295, 300,
    301, 303
Diener, E. 255, 257
Dietz, J. 136, 212
Di Giunta, L. 68, 72
Dijksterhuis, A. 111, 115
Dik, G. 111, 115
Dimaggio, P. J. 297
Dimberg, U. 82
Dodson, L. 177, 178
Dolan, R. J. 44
Donavan, D. T. 141, 206
Dore, T. C. P. 60, 69
Dorsey, K. D. 202
Dossani, R. 165
Dougherty, T. W. 190
Douglass, W. 229
Dovidio, J. F. 164
Drach-Zahavy, A. 12, 13, 212
Dustin, S. L. 142
Dutson, E. 114

Dutton, J. E. 303

Eagly, A. H. 232, 233, 235
Easterbrook, J. A. 41
Eckel, C. C. 130
Edwards, J. R. 37
Efrat-Treister, D. 297
Egloff, B. 38, 44, 266
Ehrenreich, B. 178
Eid, M. 257
Eisenberg, N. 68, 72, 102
Ekman, P. 45, 82, 84, 130, 156, 181
Elfenbein, H. A. 81, 82, 134, 141, 163
Ellsworth, P. C. 263
Elmehed, K. 82
England, P. 178, 189
Enz, C. 12, 130
Epitropaki, O. 118
Erez, A. 137, 297
Erickson, E. A. 38, 44, 266
Erickson, R. J. 8, 9, 10, 13, 14, 20, 60, 64, 73, 106, 107, 116, 129, 135, 181, 182, 183, 188, 191n1, 201, 202, 203, 237, 264, 283, 284, 292, 296, 301, 302, 303
Evans, A. M. 142
Evans, S. M. 241

Fabes, R. A. 102
Fagerhaugh, S. 181
Feild, H. S. 205
Feldman, D. C. 6, 7, 13, 14, 15, 128, 179, 180, 183, 186, 189, 190, 205
Felps, W. 107
Fenstermaker Berk, S. 178
Fernie, S. 154
Ferris, G. R. 60, 64, 69
Festinger, L. 13, 16
Figart, D. M. 204, 207
Fine, S. A. 204
Finkel, E. J. 111, 116
Finkenauer, C. 110, 112, 115
Fischer, D. 60, 69, 280
Fisek, M. H. 226
Fishbach, A. 34, 49
Fisher, C. D. 204
Fisk, G. 12, 14, 45, 84, 86, 89, 131, 159, 215, 264, 277
Fiske, S. T. 92
Fitness, J. 93
Fitzgerald, L. F. 231

Fitzsimons, G. M. 111, 116
Fizzell, C. 136
Folbre, N. 189
Foldes, H. J. 18, 46, 93
Fombrun, C. 118
Foo, M. D. 134, 142
Foo, S. C. 212
Ford, W. S. Z. 130
Forgas, J. P. 133
Förster, J. 49
Fox, K. E. 117
Fragale, A. R. 87
Francis, L. E. 105, 106
Frank, M. G. 45, 130, 134
Frenkel, S. J. 135, 154, 155, 166, 168
Frese, M. 60, 70
Friedlmeier, W. 258
Friedman, R. 34, 49, 91
Friesen, W. V. 45, 84, 134, 156
Frijda, N. H. 33, 38, 41, 50, 82
Frone, M. 9
Frost, A. C. 158, 168
Frost, P. J. 105, 110, 116, 303
Fugate, M. 105
Fung, H. H. 257, 258

Gaddis, B. 94
Gaertner, S. L. 164
Gagné, M. 43
Galinsky, A. D. 88
Gallo, I. S. 17
Gamble, J. L. 204
Gardner, W. L. 60, 69, 280
Garner, J. 286
Garvey, J. 259
Gatewood, R. D. 205
Geddes, D. 15, 184
Geiger-Oneto, S. 38
Geist, C. 238
George, J. M. 93, 94, 105, 109, 115, 137
Gerson, K. 224, 242
Gianino, A. 105
Giardini, A. 60, 70
Gilbert, D. T. 40
Gillis, J. S. 142
Giluk, T. L. 142
Glenn, E. N. 175, 189
Glomb, T. A. 8, 9, 20
Glomb, T. M. 85, 86, 93, 94, 179, 189, 205, 278

Goates, N. 91
Godin, S. 190, 242
Goffman, E. 9, 10, 104
Goldberg, L. 8, 156, 160, 166
Goldberger, N. 178
Goldman, B. M. 131
Goldstein, N. J. 115
Goleman, D. 242
Gollwitzer, P. M. 17, 47
Gonzalez, R. 41
Goodstein, J. 204, 303
Goodstein, L. D. 204
Goodwin, R. E. 135, 166, 212
Googins, B. 303
Gordon, A. H. 225
Gosserand, R. H. 8, 11, 15, 17, 34, 37,
    58, 59, 60, 61, 62, 64, 65, 72, 102,
    104, 156, 181, 182, 201, 202, 206,
    215, 278
Grabarek, P. E. 208, 215n1
Grahe, J. E. 142
Grandey, A. 6, 7, 8, 9, 10, 12, 13, 14,
    15, 16, 17, 32, 45, 57, 60, 61, 64,
    69, 72, 79, 81, 84, 86, 89, 102,
    103, 106, 107, 116, 128, 129, 130,
    131, 133, 135, 137, 139, 141,
    144n1, 155, 156, 160, 162, 163,
    164, 166, 168, 182, 183, 184, 202,
    203, 205, 206, 207, 210, 212, 215,
    242n1, 244n14, 259, 262, 264,
    268n1, 277, 279, 282, 283, 285,
    288, 291, 292, 294, 297, 300, 301
Grant, R. 209
Gray, J. R. 47
Green, S. G. 45, 64, 137, 158
Greenis, J. L. 47
Greguras, G. J. 8, 20, 186, 205
Gremler, D. D. 127, 130, 131, 132,
    133, 278
Grizzle, J. W. 206
Gross, J. 4, 13, 14, 15, 21, 32, 34, 37,
    38, 41, 42, 43, 44, 45, 47, 48, 80,
    81, 83, 84, 260, 265, 266, 267,
    275, 289, 290, 291, 292
Groth, M. 11, 12, 14, 16, 58, 60, 61,
    67, 84, 86, 89, 130, 131, 132, 133,
    134, 135, 139, 140, 141, 143, 166,
    206, 210, 212, 215, 264, 268n2,
    277, 278, 283, 284, 285, 292, 295,
    301, 302
Grove, W. C. J. 129, 183

Grumet, M. 185
Gurstelle, W. 158
Gutek, B. A. 143
Guthrie, I. K. 102
Gwinner, K. P. 127

Haidt, J. 80, 82, 87, 260
Hall, A. 214
Hall, E. J. 232, 244n12
Hall, J. A. 141
Hall, P. A. 168
Hallett, T. 10
Hanges, P. J. 136
Hareli, S. 31, 44, 109, 112, 115
Harker, L. 83
Harlow, R. 73, 224, 239, 244n19
Harris, L. C. 161
Härtel, C. E. J. 4, 71, 282, 283, 286
Harter, J. K. 136
Hartmann, H. 178
Harvey Wingfield, A. 177
Harvie, P. 136
Hatch, M. J. 285
Hatfield, E. 85, 86, 132
Hawver, T. 279, 280
Hayes, T. L. 136
Headley, T. 114
Heatherton, T. F. 83
Heilman, M. E. 225, 235, 236, 237,
    238, 244n20
Heine, S. J. 255
Heise, D. R. 224, 225, 228, 229,
    230, 231, 233, 235, 237, 241,
    243n7
Hennig-Thurau, T. 11, 12, 14, 16, 58,
    60, 67, 81, 84, 86, 89, 127, 130,
    131, 132, 133, 134, 135, 139, 140,
    210, 215, 264, 268n2, 278, 283,
    284, 285, 292, 295, 301, 302
Hershcovis, M. S. 115
Heskett, J. L. 135, 136, 137, 199
Hess, U. 82, 133
Heuven, E. 60, 67, 183
Hideg, I. 64, 92, 158
Hietanen, J. K. 130, 134
Higgins, C. 209
Higgins, E. 49
Hill, T. D. 111
Himmelweit, S. 184, 189, 190
Hirayama, S. 258
Hobfoll, S. E. 165

Hochschild, A. R. 3, 4, 5, 7, 8, 9, 13,
14, 15, 17, 18, 20, 32, 37, 43, 57,
80, 81, 83, 84, 101, 102, 106, 118,
127, 128, 135, 144n1, 153, 154,
164, 176, 178, 179, 181, 185,
186, 188, 189, 190, 191, 200,
201, 202, 204, 205, 207, 208, 210,
223, 225, 227, 232, 233, 242n1,
244n13, n15, 251, 253, 255, 260,
263, 275, 276, 277, 280, 282, 288,
291, 295, 300, 302, 303
Hochwarter, W. A. 60, 71
Hofstede, G. 167, 254
Hogan, J. 206
Hogan, R. 206
Holman, D. 12, 13, 15, 17, 70, 102,
103, 104, 105, 106, 111, 112, 113,
114, 117, 118, 135, 156, 162, 164,
166, 167, 168, 184, 209, 210, 283,
284, 292, 295, 301
Holman, E. A. 39
Holtgrewe, U. 167, 168
Holz, M. 166, 191n1
Homan, A. C. 87, 94, 95
Homburg, C. 136
Hondagneu-Sotelo, P. 233
Houlihan, M. 168
Howes, J. C. 137
Hsu, A. C. F. 71
Huang, X. 212
Huang, Y.-M. 11, 12, 89, 130, 132
Huisman, N. 60, 67
Hulin, C. L. 86, 93, 94, 231
Hülsheger, U. R. 14, 15, 16, 128, 135,
201, 206, 207, 208, 262, 265, 266
Humphrey, R. H. 4, 5, 6, 11, 17, 21,
62, 131, 135, 176, 181, 184, 185,
200, 202, 203, 264, 268n1, 275,
276, 277, 279, 280, 284
Humphrey, S. E. 4
Hunt, J. G. 60, 69, 280
Hunt, P. M. 229
Hüppe, M. 161
Hurst, C. 16, 46, 60, 69
Huynh, T. 182

Ide, E. 255
Ilies, R. 94, 279
Imada, S. 260
Inglehart, M. 41
Isic, A. 155, 166

Iverson, R. 160
Izard, C. E. 41

Jackson, C. E. 181
Jackson, C. L. 8, 10, 11, 13, 44, 67
Jaggar, A. 185
James, N. 180, 181, 185, 186
Jansen, K. J. 12, 45, 84, 86, 89, 131
Janssen, O. 212
Jassawalla, A. 259
Jayson, S. 224, 242
Jeanneret, P. R. 204
Jex, S. 187
John, O. P. 34, 38, 47, 59, 68, 69, 260,
265
Johnson, C. 243n4
Johnson, D. E. 137
Johnson, H. 13, 58, 60, 69, 70, 72, 73,
162, 163, 206, 277, 284, 286, 295
Johnson, J. T. 225
Johnson, R. 137
Johnston, L. 95
Jones, J. R. 8, 10, 20, 60, 65, 73, 135,
182, 277
Jones, T. O. 136
Jordan, C. L. 60, 65
Jordan, P. J. 284
Joseph, D. L. 58, 60, 69, 70, 71, 206,
285, 286
Judge, T. A. 16, 46, 60, 67, 69, 282
Juslin, P. N. 82

Kacelnik, A. 130
Kacmar, C. J. 60, 71
Kahn, W. A. 111
Kakai, H. 258
Kammeyer-Mueller, J. D. 8, 9, 179,
189, 205
Kanagawa, C. 255
Kanfer, R. 48
Kanov, J. M. 303
Kappas, A. 95
Karasawa, M. 255
Karau, S. 116, 233, 235
Keil, A. 17
Kelly, J. R. 104
Keltner, D. 80, 82, 83, 85, 87, 92, 95,
105
Kemper, T. D. 240
Kenney, M. 165
Kent, R. L. 164

Kern, J. 9
Kernis, M. H. 131
Ketchen, D. 214
Kiffin-Petersen, S. A. 60, 65
Kim, H. 60, 65, 82, 255
Kim, Y.-H. 260, 266
Kinman, G. 159, 166, 167
Kipnis, D. 104
Kitayama, S. 254, 255, 256, 263, 264
Klee, A. 130
Klein, H. J. 48, 49
Klein, K. J. 32
Kleinman, S. 8, 202, 211
Knopoff, K. 13
Knutson, B. 83, 257
Kobasa, S. C. 163
Koenig, A. M. 232
Kondo, D. 255
Kopelman, S. 90, 91
Korczynski, M. 154, 155, 168
Kozlowski, S. W. J. 32
Kramer, R. M. 86
Kraus, M. 92
Kreiner, G. E. 105
Krimmel, K. 13, 16, 60, 69, 72, 131, 210
Kring, A. M. 225
Kruglanski, A. W. 34, 49, 80, 88
Krumhuber, E. 95
Kruml, S. 15, 184
Kuenzi, M. 212
Kulik, J. A. 136
Kunda, G. 13, 200, 203, 204, 211
Kunnanatt, J. T. 207
Kupfer, A. 68, 72
Kurby, C. A. 33
Kwantes, C. T. 258
Kwek, M. H. 142
Kwon, H. 168

Lacey, A. T. 301
Laczo, R. M. 204
LaFrance, M. 40
Lam, C. K. 212
Lam, S. K. 136, 140
Larsen, R. J. 37
Latham, G. P. 43
Law, K. S. 69
Lazarus, R. S. 38, 39, 40
Leaf, M. 223, 243n2
Lebra, T. S. 255

Lee, E. A. 260, 266
Lee, F. 259
Lee, J. 143
Lee, J. M. 206
Lee, R. T. 16, 60, 64, 128, 136, 191n1
Lee, T. L. 266, 267, 291
Lee, T.-W. 44
Lee-Chai, A. 47
LeFevre, J. 43
Lehman, D. R. 255
Leidner, R. 7, 9, 127, 201, 208, 209, 301
Leiter, M. P. 136
LePine, J. A. 137
Leu, J. 263
Leung, K. 255
Levenson, R. W. 40, 41, 80, 81, 83, 84, 265, 289
Lévesque, M. 82
Lewis, B. P. 141
Lewis, C. C. 255
Lewis, K. M. 93, 94
Lewis, P. 186
Liao, H. 137, 161, 163
Liao-Troth, M. A. 143
Liberman, N. 49
Licata, J. W. 141
Lilius, J. M. 303
Lippi-Green, R. 164
Lisco, C. C. 91
Little, B. R. 64
Little, L. M. 167
Liu, F. 117
Liu, Y. 60, 64, 69, 71, 214
Lively, K. J. 5, 8, 9, 73, 105, 109, 164, 177, 191, 224, 225, 227, 232, 234, 235, 237, 238, 240, 242n1, 243n3, 244n13, 283, 284, 285, 296, 301
Lockard, J. S. 13
Locke, E. A. 43
Locke, K. 105
Lois, J. 223, 224, 225, 234, 236, 244n14, n16
Longen, J. 157
Lonner, W. J. 226
Lopez, S. H. 177, 182, 185, 186, 188, 190
Lord, R. G. 93
Losch, M. E. 82
Loveman, G. W. 135
Lowery, L. 260

Lucas, R. E. 65
Luce, C. 141
Luminet, O. 110, 112, 115
Luo, X. 136

Ma, Y. 262
MacCann, C. 286
MacDermid, S. M. 33, 34, 42, 43
MacKinnon, N. J. 229, 243n5
MacLeod, C. 82
Macrae, C. N. 95
Magee, J. C. 88
Magley, V. J. 231
Maitlis, S. 117
Manstead, A. S. R. 85, 86, 87, 88, 91, 95
Marinetti, C. 260
Mark, A. 185
Markus, H. R. 254, 255, 256, 263, 264
Marsh, A. A. 134
Marshall, D. 95
Marshall, J. N. 155
Martin, J. 13
Martin, L. L. 42, 86
Martin, S. E. 234
Martinez-Inigo, D. 15, 17, 106
Maslach, C. 181
Masuda, T. 263
Mathews, A. 82
Mathieu, J. E. 136
Matlis, S. 303
Matsumoto, D. 255, 258, 260, 261
Matsuno, T. 225, 229, 244n18
Matthews, G. 68
Mattila, A. 12, 45, 84, 86, 89, 130, 131, 143
Mauss, I. B. 40, 47, 48, 265, 289
May, T. 155
Mayer, J. D. 69, 141, 162
Mayer, M. 143
McCabe, J. 241
McCance, A. S. 60, 71, 141, 160
McCarter, L. 41, 289
McClure, E. B. 142
McCormick, E. J. 204
McCrae, R. R. 59, 68, 69
McCulloch, K. C. 17
McInnerney, J. 187
Meanwell, E. 10
Mecham, R. C. 204
Medvec, V. H. 90

Melwani, S. 95
Menguc, B. 137
Mertini, H. 166
Mesquita, B. 82, 252, 255, 256, 260, 263, 284, 291, 296, 301
Metcalf, D. 154
Meyers, J. 40
Miao, F. F. 258
Miceli, M. 38
Miles, G. 133
Miles, L. 95
Milkie, M. A. 225
Miller, K. I. 286
Mineka, S. 82
Minnick, M. R. 260, 266
Mirchandani, K. 165
Misra, J. 178
Mitchell, A. A 232
Mitchell, T. R. 107
Miyake, K. 255
Miyamoto, Y. 263
Moberly, N. J. 50
Mogg, K. 82
Monahan, K. 105, 106
Moran, C. M. 13, 284, 295, 301, 303
Morgan, L. 10, 20, 44
Morgeson, F. P. 4
Morling, B. 263
Morris, J. A. 6, 7, 13, 14, 15, 128, 179, 180, 183, 186, 189, 190, 205
Morris, M. W. 85, 105
Morton, D. M. 60, 62, 63
Moskowitz, D. S. 58, 59, 63
Mosley, A. L. 202
Moss, S. E. 164
Mowen, J. C. 141, 206
Moynihan, L. M. 60, 67, 157, 163, 202, 204
Mulholland, K. 161
Mullally, P. R. 256
Mumby, D. K. 201
Mumford, M. D. 94
Munz, D. C. 15, 17
Muraven, M. 44, 48, 114, 184
Muros, J. P. 18, 46, 93
Murphy, S. T. 41

Nahrgang, J. D. 4
Nakagawa, S. 260, 261
Namasivayam K. 284
Nath, L. K. 224, 225

Nelson, D. L. 167
Nelson, M. K. 178
Neuberg, S. L. 141
Newcombe, M. 94
Newman, D. A. 58, 60, 69, 70, 71,
    206, 285, 286
Nisbett, R. 259
Niven, K. 12, 104, 105, 111, 112, 113,
    114, 115, 117, 184, 283, 284, 292,
    295, 301
Nocera, C. C. 47
Noe, R. A. 207
Nohara, H. 168
Nolen-Hoeksema, S. 41
Noone B. M. 283
Norasakkunkit, V. 255
Norman, R. Z. 226
Noronha, E. 165
Novin, S. 260, 261
Nowicki, S. Jr 163
Nowotny, H. 189

O'Donovan, K. M. 60, 69
Öhman, A. 82
Oishi, S. 255
Okimoto, T. G. 225, 235, 236, 237,
    238, 244n20
Olekalns, M. 91
Oliver, R. L. 127, 142, 283
Opengart, R. 69
Organ, D. W. 137
Osgood, C. E. 228, 229
O'Sullivan, M. 134

Paauwe, J. 209
Paik, I. 238
Parasuraman, A. 127, 142
Park, I. J. K. 266
Parker, A. 105, 109, 116, 118
Parker, P. A. 136
Parker, S. K. 141
Parkinson, B. 104, 117, 208
Pataki, S. P. 86
Paul, M. 131, 132, 133, 212, 214, 278
Paules, G. F. 300
Payne, J. 182
Pearson, C. M. 135
Perez, C. R. 260, 266
Perez, L. A. 64, 73, 278
Perrewé, P. L. 60, 64, 69, 71
Petrova, G. 258

Petty, R. E. 82
Philippot, P. 110, 112, 115
Phillips, D. 185
Pierce, J. L. 105, 225, 233, 234, 235,
    244n13, 301
Pitt-Catsouphes, M. 303
Pleydell-Pearce, C. W. 33
Pollack, J. M. 279, 280
Poster, W. 13, 158, 165, 209, 213, 252,
    284, 292, 296, 301, 302
Pott, M. 255
Powell, B. 5, 8, 9, 224, 225, 232, 235,
    237, 238, 240
Powell, W. W. 297
Powers, W. T. 228
Prati, L. M. 60, 64, 69
Price, L. 138
Prien, E. P. 204
Prus, R. 187
Pu, J. 45
Pugh, D. 14
Pugh, S. 12, 13, 16, 58, 60, 61, 67,
    89, 103, 116, 130, 132, 133, 135,
    136, 141, 206, 210, 212, 214, 215,
    264, 268n2, 277, 284, 295, 301,
    303
Pugliesi, K. 37, 114, 136, 184
Putnam, L. L. 201

Quade, M. 167

Radin, M. J. 178
Rafaeli, A. 5, 6, 10, 11, 12, 13, 15, 16,
    21, 31, 44, 79, 89, 105, 108, 109,
    112, 115, 128, 141, 162, 168, 181,
    183, 184, 200, 202, 203, 205, 259,
    275, 276, 277, 294, 295, 297
Randolph, K. L. 60, 62
Rapson, R. L. 85, 86, 132
Raudenbush, S. W. 117
Ravid, S. 168, 259, 297
Raz, A. 297
Reay, D. 189
Reich, T. C. 115
Reiser, M. 102
Renz, G. L. 11, 204, 205
Revelle, Q. R. 142
Reynolds, J. R. 33
Reynolds, K. E. 143
Reynolds, K. L. 161
Rich, B. L. 67

Richard, E. M. 4, 8, 10, 15, 16, 34, 60, 65, 72, 128, 202, 205, 207, 279
Richard, H. M. 191n1
Richards, J. M. 38, 44, 47, 265
Richardson, R. 155, 164
Ridgeway, C. 189, 226, 227, 228, 237, 243n4
Rieffe, C. 260, 261
Rimé, B. 110, 112, 115
Ristikari, T. 232
Ritter, C. 10, 13, 20, 181, 188, 191n1, 201, 237
Robbins, S. P. 282
Robinson, D. T. 228
Robinson, J. 45
Robinson, M. D. 225
Robinson, S. 105, 110, 116
Rochat, S. 8, 16, 20, 102, 191n1
Rockstroh, B. 17
Rogg, K. L. 212
Rohrmann, S. 163
Rosengren, S. 130, 133
Rosette, A. S. 91
Rosin, H. 224, 241, 242
Rosin, P. L. 95
Rothbaum, F. 255
Rotundo, M. 8, 9, 179, 189, 205
Rozin, P. 260
Rubin, R. S. 15, 17
Rupp, D. E. 9, 12, 17, 57, 60, 71, 79, 81, 129, 136, 137, 141, 144n1, 155, 160, 162, 242n1, 244n14, 262, 264, 268n1, 277, 283, 285, 288, 291, 294, 300
Russ-Eft, D. F. 207
Rust, R. T. 127, 283
Ryan, A. M. 137
Ryan, K. 137
Ryan, R. M. 114

Saavedra, R. 13, 82, 86, 87, 93, 94, 106, 109, 115
Sackett, P. R. 204
Safdar, S. 258
Saklofske, D. H. 68
Salmela, M. 131
Salovey, P. 69, 141, 162
Salvaggio, A. N. 136
Sanchez-Burks, J. 259
Sanders, C. R. 211
Sasser, W. E. J. 135, 136, 137, 199

Saxe, L. 164
Saxe, R. 206
Schachter, S. 41
Scharlemann, J. P. W. 130
Schaubroeck, J. 8, 10, 20, 60, 65, 73, 135, 182, 277
Schaufeli, W. B. 60, 67, 116
Scheier, M. F. 34, 37, 47, 49, 58, 59, 60, 62, 104
Schein, E. H. 211
Scherer, K. R. 39, 40, 82, 134
Schewe, A. F. 14, 15, 16, 128, 135, 201, 206, 207, 208, 262, 265, 266
Schlesinger, L. A. 135, 136, 137, 199
Schmeichel, B. J. 45
Schmidt, D. B. 212
Schmidt, F. L. 136
Schmidt, S. M. 104
Schmidt-Atzert, L. 161
Schminke, M. 212
Schmit, M. J. 137
Schmitt, N. 212
Schmitte, B. 166
Schneider, B. 92, 136, 203, 204, 212, 214
Schoenewolf, G. 132
Schrock, D. 223, 243n2
Schwarz, N. 114, 133
Scott, B. A. 46, 67
Seery, B. L. 184
Seery, M. D. 39
Seiden, V. 90
Seifert, C. 166
Seiter, J. S. 114
Seppala, E. 258
Seth, N. 127
Shaffer, J. A. 142
Shah, J. Y. 34, 49
Shapiro, J. R. 115
Shaw, J. C. 67
Sheppes, G. 289, 292
Shi, J. 137, 161, 163
Shire, K. 154, 155, 168
Shuler, S. 277
Shull, C. 212
Shweder, R. A. 256
Sideman, L. 12, 45, 84, 86, 89, 131
Sieben, I. 157
Silver, R. C. 39
Simon, R. W. 224, 225
Simons, G. 117

Sin, H. P. 160, 164
Sinaceur, M. 88, 91
Singer, J. 41
Singh, J. 137
Skarlicki, D. P. 161
Sleeth-Keppler, D. 34, 49
Sliter, M. 187
Sloan, M. 4, 8, 188
Sloane, D. M. 136
Sluyter, D. 141
Smith, A. 141
Smith, A. C. 202, 211
Smith, D. B. 136
Smith, H. W. 225, 229, 244n18
Smith, J. R. 202
Smith, N. C. 38, 44, 266
Smith, P. 186
Smith, R. T. 111
Smith, T. 224
Smith-Lovin, L. 228, 229
Snibbe, A. C. 264
Söderlund, M. 130, 133
Solomon, M. R. 139
Song, L. J. 69
Sonnemans, J. 41, 50
Sonntag, K. 60, 71, 141, 160
Sorensen, O. 157
Soskice, D. 168Soutar, G. N. 60, 65
Soto, J. A. 260, 266
Spataro, S. E. 4, 282
Spector, P. E. 58, 60, 69, 70, 73
Speer, N. K. 33
Spencer, S. 9, 12, 17, 60, 71, 141, 160, 162, 277
Stacey, C. L. 9, 106, 135, 177, 178, 182, 186, 189, 283, 284, 292, 296, 301, 302, 303
Stanton, J. 155
Staske, S. A. 223
Staw, B. M. 58
Steca, P. 68, 72
Steelman, L. C. 232, 237, 238
Steinberg, R. J. 204, 207
Steiner, D. D. 14, 168, 215, 259, 264, 277, 297
Stenross, B. 8
Stepper, S. 86
Stewart, G. L. 142
Stillwell, A. M. 83
Stone, D. 178
Storey, J. 203

Strack, F. 86
Strauss, A. 181
Strauss, C. 254
Stride, C. B. 115, 117
Suchman, M. C. 297
Suczek, B. 181
Sundie, J. M. 38
Surakka, V. 130, 134
Surprenant, C. F. 139
Sutton, R. I. 5, 6, 10, 11, 12, 13, 15, 16, 58, 63, 79, 89, 105, 108, 128, 141, 156, 162, 181, 183, 184, 200, 202, 203, 205, 211, 223, 276, 277, 294, 295
Suzuki, T. 264
Swallow, K. M. 33
Swartz, D. 188
Swider, B. W. 142
Sy, T. 11, 12, 13, 18, 82, 86, 87, 93, 94, 101, 104, 109, 114, 115, 280, 284, 291, 295
Syed, J. 58, 60, 62, 63, 185, 267
Sypher, B. D. 277

Takata, T. 255
Tam, M. 154, 168
Tamir, M. 291
Tan, H. H. 134, 142
Tang, C. S. 60, 69, 70
Tanghe, J. 109, 116
Tangney, J. P. 39
Tanida, K. 263
Tardino, V. M. S. 15, 17
Tarule, J. 178
Tata, P. 82
Taylor, N. 211
Taylor, P. 154, 155, 207
Terkel, S. 3
Tesser, A. 42
Tett, R. P. 117
Tews, M. J. 20, 85, 278
Theodosius, C. 13, 177, 178, 182, 185, 186, 187, 188
Thoits, P. A. 4, 7, 8, 105, 107, 184, 206, 207, 214, 225, 233
Thompson, L. 86, 90, 91
Thompson, M. 182
Thompson, P. 154, 205, 208, 209
Thompson, R. A. 260, 290
Thorne, B. 239
Thunberg, M. 82

Tice, D. M. 114
Tichy, N. M. 118
Tidd, K. L. 13
Tiedens, L. Z. 87, 88, 91
Tolich, M. B. 7, 9
Tomiuk, M. A. 63, 277
Tomlinson H. S. 284
Torre, I. 158
Toth, P. 137
Totterdell, P. 12, 15, 17, 70, 93, 102,
    103, 104, 105, 106, 111, 112, 113,
    114, 115, 117, 118, 135, 156, 162,
    164, 166, 167, 184, 208, 209, 210,
    283, 284, 292, 295, 301
Townsend, S. S. M. 263
Tracy, S. 201
Tramontano, C. 68, 72
Treynor, W. 41
Triandis, H. C. 255
Tronick, E. Z. 105
Tronto, J. C. 178
Trötschel, R. 47
Trougakos, J. P. 8, 10, 11, 12, 13, 33,
    44, 45, 46, 57, 64, 66, 73, 103,
    137, 158, 284, 285, 295
Truglia, C. 259
Tsai, J. L. 257, 258
Tsai, W.-C. 11, 12, 89, 130, 132
Tschan, F. 8, 16, 20, 102, 191n1
Turel, O. 159
Turner, J. H. 187
Tushman, M. L. 118
Tuttle, J. M. 136
Tversky, B. 33
Twigg, J. 178

Uchida, Y. 263
Umino, M. 225, 229, 244n18
Urry, H. L. 289

Vahey, D. C. 136
Valley, K. L. 86
van Baaren, R. 132, 133
Van der Flier 109, 116
van de Veerdonk, E. 263
van Dick, R. 161, 163
van Jaarsveld, D. 13, 158, 161, 168,
    209, 213, 252, 284, 292, 296, 301,
    302
Van Kleef, G. A. 11, 12, 13, 18, 31, 80,
    82, 85, 86, 87, 88, 91, 92, 94, 95,

101, 102, 104, 114, 280, 284, 291,
    295
van Knippenberg, B. 13, 87, 94
van Knippenberg, D. 13, 87, 93, 94,
    95
Van Maanen, J. 13, 200, 203, 204, 211
Van Rooy, D. L. 136, 137
Vargas,D. 136
Varki, S. 283
Vey, M. A. 13, 14, 58, 59, 60, 64, 65,
    72, 79, 183, 205, 206, 277
Vilnai-Yavetz, I. 297
Vinson, G. 18, 46, 93
Virkki, T. 189
Viswesvaran, C. 136, 137
Vogt, J. 159, 166
Vohs, K. D. 16
von Bernstorff, C. 161, 163
Vrat, P. 127

Wagner, D. G. 226
Walker, D. D. 158, 161
Wall, T. 118
Walsh, G. 16, 81, 84, 86, 89, 131, 134,
    139, 140
Walsh, J. 160
Wang, A. 117
Wang, K. 11, 12, 278, 283, 284, 285,
    292, 295, 301, 302
Wang, M. 137, 161, 163
Ward, A. 167
Ward, J. C. 38
Warner, R. M. 141
Watkins, E. R. 31, 50
Watson, W. W. 11, 204, 205
Webster, J. 164
Wecking, C. 159
Wegge, J. 159, 161, 163
Weiss, E. 155
Weiss, H. M. 33, 34, 38, 42, 43, 45,
    46, 64, 92, 137, 158, 285
Weisz, J. 255
Weitz, B. A. 206
West, C. 243n2
Wharton, A. S. 4, 5, 6, 7, 8, 9, 10, 18,
    21, 73, 191n1, 201, 264, 275, 303
White, J. 134
White, S. S. 212, 214
Whitman, D. S. 136, 137
Wiener, C. 181
Wigman, B. 209

Wiley, J. W. 136, 212
Wiley, W. W. 204
Wilhelm, F. H. 38, 41, 44, 266, 289
Wilk, S. L. 60, 67, 157, 163, 202, 204
Wilkinson, I. 104
Williams, C. L. 236
Williams, K. 116
Williams, L. E. 47
Williams, M. 105
Wilson, R. K. 130
Wilson, T. D. 40
Wingfield, A. H. 223, 239, 244n19
Winiecki, D. 290
Winstanley, D. 267
Wirtz, J. 168, 259, 297
Wisecup, A. K. 228
Wisse, B. 109, 116
Wolfe, J. D. 10
Wolford, K. 187
Wong, C. S. 69
Woodward, V. M. 185
Woodzicka, J. A. 40

Woolf, E. F. 16, 46, 60, 69
Worline, M. C. 303
Wright, B. 301

Yang, J. 15, 16
Ybarra, O. 259
Yeung, D. Y. 258
Yoo, S. H. 258, 260, 261

Zablah, A. R. 206
Zacks, J. M. 33
Zajac, D. M. 136
Zajonc, R. B. 41, 187
Zapf, D. 8, 16, 20, 102, 155, 166, 176, 181, 191n1, 209
Zech, E. 110, 112, 115
Zeithaml, V. A. 127, 142
Zelditch, M. Jr 226
Zerbe, W. 6, 13, 14, 15
Zhan, Y. 137, 161, 163
Zimmerman, D. H. 243n2
Zincavage, R. M. 177, 178

# Subject Index

affect control theory 224, 228–32, 236, 238, 241, 243n5, n9
affect infusion 133, 135
affective delivery 11
affective events 35, 38, 40–4, 61, 71
affective forecasting 40, 43
affective reactions mechanisms 85–8
"affective revolution" 4, 282
affective states 37, 44, 102, 106
affectivity 65, 206; dispositional 206; negative (NA) 14, 142, 162–4, 183; positive 162, 183
agreeableness 58, 60, 95, 142, 206, 278
antecedent-focused strategies 38, 102
appraisal strategies 38–42; anticipatory 38, 39–40, 43; concurrent 38, 40–1
attentional deployment 42, 289–90
authenticity/inauthenticity 6, 11, 16, 45, 84, 86, 87, 89, 95, 131, 133, 140, 141–4, 180, 183, 201, 207, 211, 237, 263–4, 266, 276, 290
autonomy 186, 214, 252, 260, 277; individual 190; job 139, 219 see also self-determination

behavioral concordance model 58, 59, 63, 71
Big Five model 58, 60, 61, 67, 68, 206
burnout 15, 135, 136, 137, 181, 183, 190, 205, 207, 227, 237, 262, 276

call centers 67, 138, 153–69, 302; automation in 157–8; and

nationality 165–6; and race 164; sex differences in 164
caring labor 178, 302
caring professionals 7, 9, 20, 135, 175–91, 232, 284
chaebol 259
cognitive change 289–90
compassion 108, 303
component process model 39–40
contagion gains 12
control theory 34, 37, 49, 58, 59, 60–3, 71, 72, 104, 224
coping 13, 16, 40, 162, 164, 253, 265
cultural control 204
cultural models 254–
culture 5, 165, 167, 185, 229, 237–9, 241; Chinese 257–9, 262; East Asian 257–8, 291; and emotion regulation 252–4, 256–8, 260–2, 265–6, 291; emotional 18, 82, 188, 214, 224–6; and emotional labor 251–68; and gender 231; Japanese 252–6, 263, 264, 296; organizational 185, 200, 201, 203, 204, 212, 285, 303; and regulation strategies 260–2, 267; and relationships 254–6; US 224–6, 255–6, 257–60, 262–3, 296
customer characteristics 140–2, 144
customer–employee relationships 142–3
customer mistreatment 161–3
customer satisfaction 130–1, 135, 136, 137, 142, 155, 212–15, 284
customer service 34, 36, 45, 48, 60,

61, 80, 88, 89, 110, 111, 133, 138, 162, 302; research on 90–1
customization 138–9

deep acting 6, 13, 14–15, 37, 46, 62, 65, 69–70, 83–4, 90, 92, 93, 102, 107, 128, 131, 135, 143, 156, 160, 162, 163, 166, 167, 179–80, 183, 184, 191, 207, 208, 214, 260–1, 265, 276–9, 297
"Delta personality" 57
depletion 16, 45, 50, 115, 116, 137, 139, 165
Diagnostic Analysis of Nonverbal Accuracy Test (DANVA) 163
Disney 199
Display Rule Assessment Inventory 258
display rules 6, 8, 10–11, 17, 31, 35, 61–2, 65, 106, 128, 144n1, 156–60, 165, 166, 167, 179, 181, 183, 189, 191, 200, 213, 267, 276, 277–9, 286; and culture 258–9; differentiating 8; emotional 8, 14, 31–2, 201–3; integrative 8, 10; masking 8, 10; organizational 34, 128; unit-level 183
dissonance: cognitive 264; emotion–display 15–16, 263–4; emotion–rule 15–16, 17; emotional 6, 11, 14, 15–16, 67, 70, 71, 156, 159, 161, 162, 163, 166, 183, 262–3, 266, 277, 280
distraction strategies 42–3

EL jobs 6–10, 18, 154, 180, 206, 285
emotion amplification 84–5
emotion detection systems 158, 209
emotion expression 82, 93, 103, 118, 132, 165, 169, 182, 203, 208, 240, 263, 277–8
emotion management 3, 5, 6, 7, 9, 16, 18, 19, 67, 118, 128, 158, 168, 176–7, 179, 181, 201, 236, 240, 242n1, 259, 302, 303; in health care 182–9
emotion practice 176, 177, 182, 186–7, 190–1
emotion recognition 134–5, 140, 163
emotion regulation 13, 14, 17, 31–51, 65, 67, 69, 73, 79–96, 118–19,

128–9, 131–2, 135, 143–4, 158, 163, 165, 200, 202, 207, 239
289–92, 295; automatic 47–8; and culture 252–4, 256–8; definition of 102; direction of 84–5, 86–7, 89, 90, 92, 94, 111; and discrete emotions 85, 86, 87; and EL 18–20, 282, 290–2; episodic 32–5, 50, 103, 108–9; form of 83–4, 86; humor as 106; interpersonal 32, 69, 104–11, 113–17; in organizations 79–96, 106; research on 16, 80, 83, 128, 292; social effects of 80, 85–8; strategies of 17, 37–48, 80–1, 86–7, 90, 107, 111, 117, 135, 138, 140, 143–4, 202, 207, 254, 256–62, 264–7, 279, 290; targets of 20, 102–4, 107–115; temporal structure of 32–3, 51; unit-level 101, 103–4, 106–9, 112, 115–19; in wrestling 111 *see also* emotional labor
emotion rules *see* display rules; feeling rules
emotion suppression 84–5, 159, 161, 203, 260–1, 265, 291
emotion work 6, 9, 18, 19, 20, 67, 167, 182, 185–6, 189, 202, 223–7, 232–4, 236–40, 242
emotional capital 189, 191, 206, 207, 214
emotional contagion 12, 70, 86, 92, 102, 114, 116, 132–3, 135, 136, 140, 279; conscious 132–3; primitive 12, 132–3
emotional culture 188, 214, and gender 225–6; in US 224–6
emotional deviance 6, 11
emotional displays 5–6, 8–14, 17, 20, 31, 34, 57, 61–3, 79, 81, 86, 89, 91, 105, 131, 134–5, 140–1, 144, 166, 201–3, 208, 210, 213, 277–8, 297, 301
emotional duration 50
emotional enhancement 184
emotional exhaustion 67, 70, 115, 135, 136, 156–7, 160, 163, 166–7, 184, 205, 207, 212, 264, 268n2, 278
emotional expressivity 162, 206
emotional harmony 6, 11, 13, 15, 277

emotional intelligence 58, 60, 69–71, 93, 134, 141, 162, 163, 206, 277, 284–6; models of 69
emotional labor (EL) 3–21, 37, 50, 57–73, 81, 102–7, 116, 118, 131, 141, 159–60, 162, 168–9, 200, 276–80, 282–6, 288–92, 294–8, 300–3; agents of 81–2, 86–7, 89–90, 92, 102–10, 112–16, 118, 128, 301; in call centers 153–69; and carework 175–91; and congruence 58, 59; and culture 251–68; consequences of 166–8; customer experience of 127–44; and customer outcomes 128–9, 138, 142–4; definition of 5, 11, 14, 18, 20, 102, 106, 144n1, 153, 185, 188, 200, 223–4, 242n1, 283, 288; dramaturgical model of 43; emotional display pathway of 128–35; and emotion regulation 18–20, 282, 290–2; as emotional displays 5–6, 8–13, 17; employee well-being pathway of 135; gender/sex differences in 164, 179, 185, 188–9, 224–42, 296; and individual differences 58–63, 66, 71, 73; as intrapsychic processes 5–7, 13–17, 57; literature on 4, 59–60, 64, 178, 191n2, 201, 239, 265, 280; and motivation 58, 60–3, 206, 210, 215; as occupational requirements 5–10, 17 and organizational practices 199–215; perspectives on 5–18; and political skill 71; and race 164; research on 4–5, 20–1, 32, 57, 71, 73, 101, 113, 116–17, 128, 155, 160–1, 167, 182, 200, 202, 209, 275, 278, 280, 282–5, 292, 300, 303; targets of 20, 102–4, 107–16, 285, 295; third parties in 110–12, 115, 116 *see also* emotion regulation
emotional quality 50
Emotion Regulation of Others and Self (EROS) scale 117
emotional self-regulation 16, 18, 61, 65, 68, 71, 104–9, 111, 114–15, 117, 157, 235
empathy 8, 116, 132, 259
employee health 10
employee sabotage 163
employee strain 9, 14
encore gains 12
enhanced interaction technologies 158–60
environmental disturbances 17, 61
Evaluation–Potency–Activation (EPA) 229–32, 235, 239, 240, 243n9, 244n17, n18, 245n21
exhaustion 116, 262; emotional 67, 70, 115, 135, 136, 156–7, 160, 163, 166–7, 184, 205, 207, 212, 264, 268n2, 278
expectations states theory 224, 226–8, 237–8, 241, 285
expression-focused strategies 43–6; suppression 44; faking 44–5
expressions, modifying 6
extra-role behaviors 137, 139
extraversion 58, 60, 65, 69, 72, 142, 206, 207, 277, 278

facial displays 82
facial feedback 12, 16, 132
fairness/unfairness 9, 38, 160–2, 178, 233 *see also* justice
faking 11, 44–6, 141, 159, 161, 276
feeling rules 6, 8, 10, 257–62
feelings, management of 6, 17, 19, 102
feminism 178, 233, 241, 302
Framework for Unit-Level Emotional Labor (FUEL) 101, 112–13
free trait theory 64
friendliness 16, 34, 79, 89, 127, 130, 131, 156, 199, 209, 213, 231, 234, 237, 279
Functional Job Analysis 204

gender stereotypes 227
goal conflicts 63
goal contagion 111, 114
goals 17, 33–7, 43, 44, 47–9, 72, 82, 180; conflicting 49; display 44, 49; hierarchy of 49, 62, 63; organizational 14, 18, 61–2, 102, 206, 264

high arousal positive (HAP) emotions 257–8
high involvement human resource (HIHR) systems 214

human resource management (HRM)
129, 168, 200, 201, 203–210, 215
ideal emotions 257
identity 187, 227, 229–31, 238,
244n18, 264; cultural 243n6, 267;
employee 201; loss of 261, 264;
national 165–7; organizational
135; professional 176; racial
164; role 276; self- 228; sense of
191
identity conformation 230
immediate gains 12
implicit theories of leaders' emotions
(ITLEs) 93–4
impression management 104
incivility 71, 187
independent cultural contexts 254–5,
257–61, 263–6
inferential processes mechanisms
87–8, 102
institutional theory 297
*Interact* program 229, 231, 243n9,
244n11
interdependent cultural contexts
254–5, 257–61, 263–6
interpersonal influence 104
interpersonal interactions 21, 72, 92,
127, 204
interviews 6, 18

job analysis 204–5
job design 214
job performance 10, 69, 70, 103, 134,
135, 136, 166, 205, 285
job satisfaction 10, 15, 45, 67, 70,
103, 135, 137, 159, 166, 205, 207,
264, 268n2, 276, 285
jobs and gender 8, 10
justice/injustice 160–1, 179, 277 *see
also* fairness/unfairness

leadership 83, 105, 115, 280; research
on 92–5, 280; theories of 93
low arousal positive (LAP) emotions
257–8

marketing 5, 20, 127, 135, 140, 142,
144, 154, 283
meme complexes 296
mimicry 86, 132–4

motivation 15, 58–63, 72, 92, 114,
141, 161–2, 164, 166, 185, 206,
210, 215, 277, 295; epistemic 80,
88, 94; intrinsic 43, 184, 201, 206,
209, 215 *see also* motives
motives 6, 9, 92, 261 *see also*
motivation

national identity centrality 165–6
national identity management 165
negotiations 80, 81, 87–8, 95, 105;
distributive 86, 87; research on 88,
90–2; strategies in 90
networks 112, 115; social 117–18
neuroticism 58, 60, 65, 142, 206,
278
norms 93, 106, 127–8, 190, 200, 202,
203, 213, 286, 302; cultural 169;
emotional 7, 79, 106–7, 116, 175,
177, 225; feeling 6, 8; gendered
225, 284; organizational 10–11,
102–3, 105, 114, 190, 200, 203;
professional 9; of reciprocity 137,
186; shared 106–7; social 9, 11,
254; unit-level 106–7, 109

organizational behavior 4, 5, 20, 128,
275, 282, 284, 298
organizational citizenship behaviors
(OCB) 137
organizational climate 200, 201,
210–13
organizational culture 185, 200, 201,
203, 204, 212, 285

performance episodes 33–6, 42
performance management 200, 201,
203, 209–10
performance monitoring 155–7, 161,
165, 209, 212, 213
person–job fit 11, 205, 277
perspective-taking 71, 115, 132, 141,
160
Positional Analysis Questionnaire
(PAQ) 204
power 5, 80, 88; differentials in 8, 9,
186, 191, 238, 240
principle controls 34
proactive personality 62
productivity 137, 177
pro-social behavior

psychology 4, 5, 7, 14, 20, 67, 87, 101, 105, 130, 182, 206, 275, 282, 283, 288, 291; social 133, 226, 237, 238

racism 164
rationality 185
reappraisal 39, 41–2, 260–1, 264–5, 290; cognitive 38
recruitment 201, 203, 205–6, 212
regulatory resources 16, 48, 50, 64, 159, 165
religiosity 60, 62
response-focused regulation 102
response modulation 289–90
rewards 203, 209, 210, 213; financial 18, 210
role expectations 10–12, 137, 200, 202, 203, 301
rumination 42, 50

selection (of personnel) 200, 201, 203, 205, 212, 214
self-blame 39, 42
self-determination 114 *see also* autonomy
self-efficacy 58, 59, 60, 66–8, 163, 210; varieties of 76
self-monitoring 60, 65, 206, 277, 278
self-regulatory outsourcing 111, 116
service delivery 11, 34, 127, 128, 131, 135, 138–41, 143–4, 159, 168, 211, 214
service economy 5, 300
service typologies 138–9
sexual assault 230–1
sexual harassment 231
*simpatia* 258
situation modification 289–90
situation selection 38, 289–90
smiles 3, 95, 127, 130, 131, 133, 134, 155, 205; Duchenne 45, 84, 134; non-Duchenne 84

social behaviors 16, 295, 297
social cognitive theory 59, 66–7, 71
social feedback 12
social functional perspectives 81–2, 85
social memes 295–8
social sharing of emotions 110, 112, 113, 115
socialization 8, 107, 203, 204, 210–11, 212, 213, 225
sociology 4, 5, 7, 20, 101, 105, 224, 226, 228, 237, 275, 283, 288, 291, 300
spirituality 60
Stanislavski system 37
status beliefs 226–8, 238, 241
status shields 10, 164
strain 116; job 9
stress 63, 79, 135, 137, 279, 285; cardiovascular 65; psychological 227
surface acting 6, 13, 14–16, 37, 43, 46, 67, 70, 83–4, 90, 92, 93, 102, 107, 128, 131, 134–5, 136, 156, 162, 164, 166–7, 179–80, 183, 184, 207, 214, 215n1, 260–1, 264, 265, 266, 268n2, 276, 277, 278, 297

training 105, 154, 157, 165, 200, 201, 203, 207–9, 212, 214, 215
trait theory 59, 68–9, 71, 83
trust building 105
turnover 94, 135, 136, 166

vampires 241

well-being 12–13, 16, 42, 70, 103, 129, 135, 136, 144, 166, 190, 191, 202, 209, 211, 267, 268; financial 13, 297
Women's Lib 241